Publisher: Military History Group, London, United Kingdom.

E-Mail: milhisgroup@gmail.com

Print: Lulu Press, Inc., Lulu Press, Inc. 627 Davis Drive Suite 300 Morrisville, NC 27560, USA. Massachusetts, US; Wisconsin, US; Ontario, Canada; Île-de-France, France; Wielkopolska, Poland; Cambridgeshire, United Kingdom; Victoria, Australia.

Hardcover: ISBN 978-1-915453-06-8

Table of Contents

CHAPTER I

Introduction

1

Read First

To publish an authentic representation of the included German documents in this edited volume, this translation remains as close to the original text as possible. This presents unique challenges which have led to specific editorial decisions that are explained in this introduction.

The first challenge is undeniably the German language itself. Composite words and phrases in "military German" from the 1930s and 1940s can often not be translated word-for-word into English. Doing so would come at the price of losing information, nuance and accuracy, while at the same time reducing the legibility of the text. The translation of historical documents is not an exact discipline, as such we cannot rule out misleading or unclear phrases in this translation. Therefore, it is possible that the English translation leaves some room for interpretation that is not given in the original document. Equally, certain sentences might present the reader with awkward phrases, which is a by-product of the attempt to remain close to the original meaning of the German text. To clarify certain passages, aspects or terminology for the reader, we provided footnotes when needed. Following is a short overview of important aspects that need to be considered when reading and using the original and translated texts. The translation uses the U.S. American spelling of English words.

Considering the structure of the presented documents, a certain standard had to be set to present a unified, rather than disjointed collection. Throughout this volume, we aimed to retain some of the original formatting, yet the editorial focus lay on legibility. One of the main editorial changes was that, to present a clearer layout, we did not follow the original page count as this would have resulted in empty or near empty pages throughout the book. Instead, the text has been reformatted to follow a more conventional structure, page by page. Specific editorial choices are described on the cover page of each document. Similarly, in some cases the placement of figures was also changed.

This book is best read from cover to cover but you should also be able to just pick one document at a time. To facilitate this, footnotes of particular importance are repeated between documents instead of limiting them to the first appearance. Footnotes that refer to the Glossary list the English translation first, followed by the German original and its abbreviation, where applicable, in "(...)" and "[...]" respectively.

The documents themselves were sorted into thematic sections. The first part incorporates key documents pertaining to the tasks, training and envisioned employment of Ju 87 dive-bombers, with the two following parts focusing on experience reports and special Ju 87 equipment respectively. On the Junkers Ju 87 itself, we have made the decision to label it as "Ju 87" instead of the more common "Ju-87". The latter style is often seen nowadays and was most likely influenced by the U.S. American nomenclature that used a "-" for all models e.g., P-47, B-25 or B-17. Yet the unhyphenated version "Ju 87" was the German standard of the time for this and other planes, although in rare cases deviations can be found. We have largely avoided using the word "Stuka" as this was a generic abbreviation of the German word "Sturzkampfbomber", meaning dive-bomber. When reading through the original documents collected in this volume, it will also become obvious that this abbreviation was rarely used. The irony of using this term for our book title is not lost on us. For the Junkers "Jumo" engines, the spelling differed within the originals more often, jumping between an all capitalized "JUMO" and "Jumo". In our translation, we have opted to use "Jumo". The word is an abbreviation of the company's name Junkers Motorenwerke. In the original documents various abbreviations and shortcuts were used for weapons and other terminology, e.g., "St.G." for "Sturzkampfgeschwader" or "BK" for "Bordkanone". These were written inconsistently, yet we have attempted to use a standardized format throughout the book.

Another challenge was the question of how to translate the German organizational terminology of "Geschwader", "Gruppe" and "Staffel" into English. First, approximate equivalents of the United States Army Air Force (USAAF) and Royal Air Force (RAF) followed a different standard. To make matters even more complicated, the US War Department TM 30-506 English-German Military Dictionary from May 1944 also differed from both the USAAF and RAF standard. As such we have opted to retain the German formation names. More information on this can also be found in the Chapter The Sturzkampfgeschwader and in the Glossary under unit type (Kampfflieger, Jagdflieger, Schlachtflieger, Sturzkampfflieger).

Concerning speed and altitude figures, our text uses the metric system of the original. However, footnotes have been added on relevant pages giving a close approximation in feet or miles per hour for altitude and speed. Feet were rounded to the nearest hundred. Footnotes with conversions are quoted only once per page for each figure.

Except for Luftwaffe Druckvorschrift L.Dv. 20/2 and L.Dv. 366, the original writing was in "Latin text" and not in Fraktur. Germany switched from Fraktur to a regular Latin alphabet in 1940/41, going so far as to ban the former. Naturally, this process took some time to be completed.

3

To allow for a convenient separation between original visuals and those added by us, captions of images found in the original documents use "Figure", while our own additions are labelled "Illustration". Similarly, for original document photographs we use "Picture", whereas for photographs that we added we use "Photo" as a label.

The original documents contain few footnotes, but these were kept and are situated above our added footnotes. To differentiate between the original and our footnotes, we have preserved the original formatting and numbering of the former, which was a superscript number followed by a closing parenthesis, e.g., [1]).

Finally, we must address the illustrations included in this book. It was our aim to recreate these visuals as close to the original as possible. For the numbering of the figures, we used the original numbers of each document. If there is a deviation for a particular document this is discussed in the preamble of the specific document. Certain inaccuracies in the thickness of the lines and various other dimensions of the symbols might occur.

Acknowledgements

Throughout our work on this project, various individuals have provided constructive insights and criticism that have helped us in making this publication. At this point, we would like to thank them, most especially: Roman Töppel for feedback and assisting in the creation of this book through sources and his photographic collection. We would also like to thank Calum E. Douglas, John Rider Renshaw Jordan and Phillipp for their help and feedback on the engine, weaponry and bombing sections of this book. We would also like to thank Jens Wehner and Marcus Faulkner for their help.

A big thank you to Al Murray, Amiral Crapaud, Bo Time, Drachinifel, Greg from Greg's Airplanes and Automobiles, James Holland, ManyMilesAway, Matthew Moss from The Armorer's Bench/Historical Firearms, Mike Burns from Bloke on the Range, MikeGoesBoom, Nicholas "The Chieftain" Moran, Oxy, the Real Time History Team, Victoria Taylor and Wolfpack345 for their fantastic support in sharing our project with their communities. Andrew Gianelli, Andy Zhao, Calum E. Douglas, Justin Pyke, John Rider Renshaw Jordan and Miles Stratton for reviewing the drafts, providing feedback and for their continuous support. We are very grateful to the staff of the Bundesarchiv in Freiburg and the Royal Air Force Museum London for dealing with our various requests and supporting our research. Equally, we would like to thank Archiv Hafner and deutscheluftwaffe.de for their help with this project and Samuel W. Wolfe for his

3.7 cm ammunition visuals. For continuous support throughout the years of our YouTube Channels we would like to thank Andrew Gianelli, Chris V., Fred B., Jack Ray, Joe Kudrna, Stefan Jovanovich, Bo Time Gaming, Drachinifel, MagzTV, Navaronegun and vonKickass. An additional thank you for all those who have helped spread the word about this project.

We would also like to extend a special thanks to our Patreon, YouTube Members, PayPal and Subscribestar supporters, as well as our Discord crews and wider community for supporting our continuous endeavors. Without them, this project would never have seen the light of day.

Producers

Special thanks go to the following Producers, who made this publication possible:

Hamish Scotford [UK], Jørn Erik Mella [NO], Mark Geldof [CA],

Jordan Stuart [US], David Gast [DE], Keith Skelhorne [UK],

Alex Pocklington [UK], Erand Pelinku [US], Lance Everett [US],

Jack Ray [US], Gavin M. Waddell [US], Dallas Hayes [US],

Michael Latina [US], Michael Emborg [DK], Daryl J. Lloyd [AU],

Bob Lehner [US], Ben Price [US], Joshua Lapple [US],

Andrew James Kleeves [US], John Peters [US], Michael Lambert [US],

John Wayne Kettner [CA], Stephen Kunz [CH], Josh Warne [CA],

Andreas Schuster [ES].

(In order of pledges)

Production of the Ju 87

Why talk about Production?

Compared to its post-war prominence, the Ju 87 was numerically of limited significance throughout the war in terms of its overall numbers built and serving on the frontline during the Second World War. As can be seen in Illustration 1[1], as a specialized aircraft it ranks low in terms of production numbers, compared to other prominent Luftwaffe aircraft of the time. Equally, the Luftwaffe's initial Ju 87 force number of around 350 aircraft during the invasion of Poland was largely kept stable throughout the early campaigns. Starting in 1943, the Ju 87 was being phased out in favor of new Fw 190 fighter-bombers, with production stopping in mid-1944.

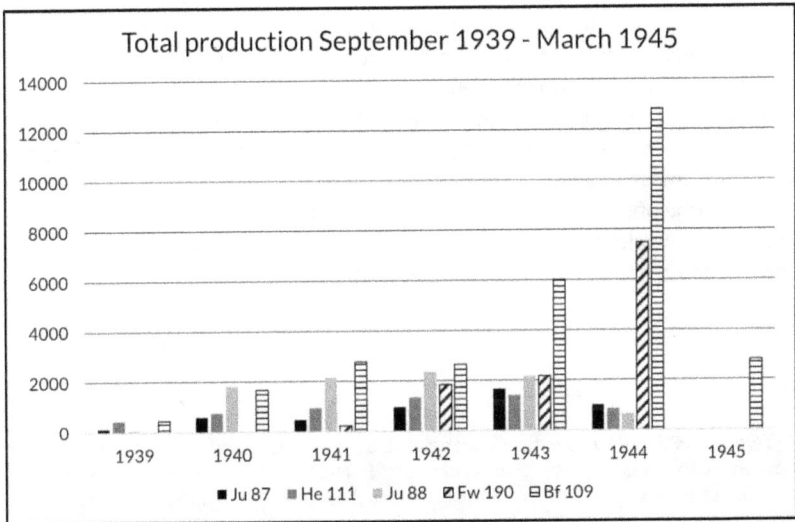

Illustration 1: Production of selected planes between September 1939 to March 1945.

Considering the relatively low production figure and contrasting it to the aircraft's popular fame, it appears pertinent to discuss the production history of this aircraft. There are two additional reasons for this. First, although bearing the

---

[1] Note that the Ju 88 was also converted into a night-fighter. These production figures are not included in the graph: "Ju 88 (Bomber)" refers to the Ju 88 that were built as bombers.

7

Junkers name, the plane was not built or developed beyond the initial variants by the Junkers company. Second, its production history, rather than technical development, is still relatively unexplored in many of the key works on the Ju 87.[2]

The Junkers Company

In the early 1930s, most aircraft manufacturers in Germany were small companies, often centralizing their production within one city. For Junkers, this was Dessau.[3] The company expanded with increased state funding after 1933 and, with the forced nationalization of industry by the National Socialist government, Hugo Junkers was forced to cede control. Unlike some of his colleagues like Ernst Heinkel and Willy Messerschmitt, he was also forced into retirement, instructed to leave Dessau, and prohibited from further contact with his erstwhile employees.[4] As a conservative nationalist, Hugo Junkers welcomed rearmament but his past meddling in politics, his industrial influence and the fact that he headed the largest aircraft company in Germany were reasons enough for the new government to prevent him from playing a further role in German aviation.[5] As with all other companies, on the surface an illusion of private ownership was maintained.[6] Junkers Motorenwerke merged with its sister company, Junkers Flugzeug- und Motorenwerke AG, and grew rapidly to become one of the most important elements of Germany's aviation industry. It also produced one of the mainstay German aero-engines of the time, the Jumo 211.[7] This engine would also see usage in the Ju 87.[8] Towards the end of the war, Junkers also produced the Jumo 004 jet engine.

---

[2] Two works that deal specifically with the Ju 87 production and the company history of the contractor *Weser Flugzeugbau GmbH* are F.-Herbert Wenz, *Flughafen Tempelhof - Chronik des Berliner Werkes der "Weser" Flugzeugbau GmbH - Bremen*, Stedinger Verlag, Lemwerder, 2000, and Hartmut Pophanken, *Gründung und Ausbau der "Weser"-Flugzeugbau Gmbh 1933 bis 1939*, H. M. Hauschild GmbH, Bremen, Germany, 2000.

[3] Dessau is still home to the Technikmuseum Hugo Junkers, a museum dedicated to the history of the company.

[4] Technikmuseum Hugo Junkers Dessau, *Lebenslauf - Hugo Junkers*, 4 February 2019, available at: https://technikmuseum-dessau.org/lebenslauf/#page-content (last accessed 06.08.2021).

[5] Adam Tooze, *The Wages of Destruction, The Making & Breaking of the Nazi Economy*, Penguin Books, London, UK, 2007, p. 126-127.

[6] Edward L. Homze, *Arming the Luftwaffe - The Reich Air Ministry and the German Aircraft Industry, 1919-39*, University of Nebraska Press, Lincoln, Nebraska, USA, 1976, p. 73.

[7] Junkers Aircraft and Motor Works.

[8] More information on the Jumo 211 can be found in the *Engine Data Sheets*.

8

In only three years, Germany's air industry grew from just over 3 000 workers in 1933 to 124 000 in 1936.[9] Junkers was at the heart of this expansion, becoming one of the most prolific employers, operating a production triangle in the Magdeburg-Dessau-Leipzig area, and kickstarting rapid urbanization. As with all aircraft companies at this time, this rapid expansion also coincided with a growing trend in fostering a nationalist-socialist ideology and ideals within each firm.[10] Throughout these years, production output rose considerably, although limited industrial capacity and the domestic worker pool was unable to meet production demands. As Adam Tooze notes, this problem was universal in Germany at the time with the labor pool stretched thin as "breakneck rearmament in the 1930s coincided with the reintroduction of conscription".[11]

The Junkers company entered the competition for a new dive-bomber in 1934. Competing against proposals by Arado, Blohm & Voß and Heinkel, the Junkers design was chosen as the Luftwaffe's future dive-bomber. An early order of Ju 87 A-1, to be delivered between 1936 and 1938, would set in motion the production of this dive-bomber. Junkers, already struggling to meet the production orders for other planes on order, would only build a portion of these and handed off production to Weser Flugzeugbau GmbH (WFG).[12]

Ju 87 War Production at Weser Flugzeugbau GmbH

Being one of the biggest German aviation companies of the war, it is perhaps surprising that relatively few Ju 87s were built by Junkers itself. With the exception of a shared production run of the early Ju 87 A, Weser Flugzeugbau GmbH[13] (WFG) took over all Ju 87 production. WFG, founded in 1934, was itself a subsidiary of the Deutsche Schiff- und Maschinenbau AG (DESCHIMAG[14]).

---

[9] Edward L. Homze, *Arming the Luftwaffe – The Reich Air Ministry and the German Aircraft Industry, 1919-39*, University of Nebraska Press, Lincoln, Nebraska, USA, 1976, p. 73.
[10] Daniel Uziel, *Arming the Luftwaffe – The German Aviation Industry in World War II*, McFarland & Company, Jefferson, NC, USA, 1967, p. 23.
[11] Adam Tooze, *The Wages of Destruction, The Making & Breaking of the Nazi Economy*, Penguin Books, London, UK, 2007, p. 361.
[12] Eddie J. Creek, *Junkers Ju 87 – From Dive-Bomber to Tank-Buster 1935-1945*, Classic Publication, Hersham, UK, 2012, p. 23-42. See also Heinz J. Nowarra, *Die Deutsche Luftrüstung 1933-1945*, Part 3, Bernard & Graefe Verlag, Koblenz, Germany, 1993, p. 75.
[13] Often also colloquially known as "Weser-Flug" or simply "Weser".
[14] DESCHIMAG was a cooperation of German shipyards building civilian ships since 1926, followed by destroyers, U-Boats and the uncompleted *Admiral Hipper*-class cruisers

Merging the struggling Rohrbach Metall-Flugzeugbau GmbH into its company, Weser began constructing license-built aircraft or parts for Junkers, Dornier, Heinkel and Focke-Wulf.[15] In this capacity, it became not just a producer but would, with the commencement of series production of the B-variant, have de-facto complete control over the Ju 87 design, consolidating all development and production of this aircraft until 1944.[16] With around 350 workers in 1934, the company would rapidly expand to 8 000 by 1937 and 12 000 workers in 1939. It peaked with 29 000 in 1944, a number that reduced to 25 000 by the end of the war.[17]

In 1936, WFG had the first 70 Ju 87 A on order.[18] It would go on to build these and all subsequent Ju 87 models at Lemwerder near Bremen and from 1940 onwards at a new production facility situated within the halls of the Berlin Tempelhof airport.[19] This site was chosen as it was both able to house a larger assembly area, had housing attached to it for workers, and was assumed to be more difficult to strike by Allied bombers. This assumption must naturally be considered within the context of the time it was made, that being the late 1930s. Preliminary preparations for the move to Berlin started in 1939 and most of the higher management and planning offices moved by the end of the year. Initially limited to refitting existing aircraft models, Ju 87 production would also move to Berlin in 1941 with the first models being completed in June.[20] Bremen had by this point experienced multiple RAF bombings and the attack on the 4th of July 1941 destroyed a significant number of tools, parts and even the prototypes for the new D-variant.[21] The vulnerability of this plant was once again underlined a

Seydlitz and Lützow for the Kriegsmarine. Its name can be translated to "German Ship and Engine Construction Works".

[15] Hartmut Pophanken, *Gründung und Ausbau der "Weser"-Flugzeugbau Gmbh 1933 bis 1939*, H. M. Hauschild GmbH, Bremen, Germany, 2000, p. 41-44, 53, 56.

[16] Heinz J. Nowarra, *Die Deutsche Luftrüstung 1933-1945*, Part 4, Bernard & Graefe Verlag, Koblenz, Germany, 1993, p. 37.

[17] Hartmut Pophanken, *Gründung und Ausbau der "Weser"-Flugzeugbau Gmbh 1933 bis 1939*, H. M. Hauschild GmbH, Bremen, Germany, 2000, p. 74-75, 108.

[18] Hartmut Pophanken, *Gründung und Ausbau der "Weser"-Flugzeugbau Gmbh 1933 bis 1939*, H. M. Hauschild GmbH, Bremen, Germany, 2000, p. 56.

[19] WFG would also build Ju 88s and Fw 190s at their Berlin site, as well as a smaller number of planes from Blohm & Voss, Dornier, Junkers as well as Focke-Achgelis helicopters.

[20] F.-Herbert Wenz, *Flughafen Tempelhof – Chronik des Berliner Werkes der "Weser" Flugzeugbau GmbH – Bremen*, Stedinger Verlag, Lemwerder, Germany, 2000, p. 46-47.

[21] This attack appears to have been a low-level raid by 12 Blenheims of 105 Squadron RAF. Australian Wing Commander Hughie Edwards received the Victoria Cross for this attack. 4 Blenheims were lost. See Martin Middlebrook; Chris Everitt, *The Bomber*

year later in June and especially September 1942, when production was impacted by a successful bombing raid.[22]

Additional facilities were built to support production. This included workshops near Bunzlau (today Bolesławiec in Poland), and in the occupied regions of Czechoslovakia. A centralized plant was also set up between 1942 and 1944 in current-day Slovakia, with the aim to supply both the Luftwaffe and Slovakian Air Force with Ju 87s. Through this agreement, the Reichsluftfahrtministerium[23] (RLM) also hoped to first train Slovakian workers locally in Germany, thus covering part of the manpower requirements, before sending these back to produce Ju 87s in their home country.[24]

Foreign & Slave Workers

The intended use of Slovakian workers was in line with the general shift in strategy on overcoming the manpower shortages in the Luftwaffe's production. As the agreement with the Slovakian authorities started to become more concrete in late 1942, this appears to largely follow the 1941 requirements of the Luftwaffe in significantly increasing production. As Tooze notes, the drive to expand industrial capacity began towards the autumn of 1940 while "in June 1941 the Air Ministry proposed a doubling of output to 20 000 aircraft per year over the following three years", while in the summer of 1942, Milch demanded an increase of production by 150% to a monthly output of 3 000 aircraft.[25]

The Slovakian workers would not be the only source of foreign labor for Ju 87 production. Indeed, during the Second World War the Luftwaffe would consistently increase the ratio of foreign laborers compared to the German work force. While in 1939, the workforce included only 300 000 workers labeled as "foreigners and jews", this increased to over 2.5 million by 1941, made up of 1.2 million prisoners of war and 1.3 million "civilians". By 1944, this number

---

Command War Diaries - An Operational Reference Book, 1939-1945, Penguin Books, Harmondsworth, UK, 1985, p. 171.

[22] BArch, RL 3/17, *Stenographischer Bericht über die GL-Besprechung*, 1. December 1942. 251 aircraft attacked Bremen on the night of 4/5. September, losing 12 aircraft but inflicting heavy damage on the WFG plant. See also Martin Middlebrook; Chris Everitt, *The Bomber Command War Diaries - An Operational Reference Book, 1939-1945*, Penguin Books, Harmondsworth, UK, 1985, p. 306.

[23] See Glossary: *Reich's Ministry of Aviation (Reichsluftfahrtministerium)*.

[24] BArch, RL 3/17, *Stenographischer Bericht über die GL-Besprechung*, 1. December 1942; and BArch, RL 3/16, *Stenographischer Bericht über die GL-Besprechung*, 27. October 1942.

[25] Adam Tooze, *The Wages of Destruction, The Making & Breaking of the Nazi Economy*, Penguin Books, London, UK, 2007, p. 451.

increased to 7.9 million.[26] It is important here to note that the worker pool was split between German workers (male and female), as well as foreigners with a myriad of classifications between them, as German officials did not use the term "Zwangsarbeiter" or "forced laborer".[27] The complex nature of foreign labor classification in Germany can be see in Illustration 2.[28]

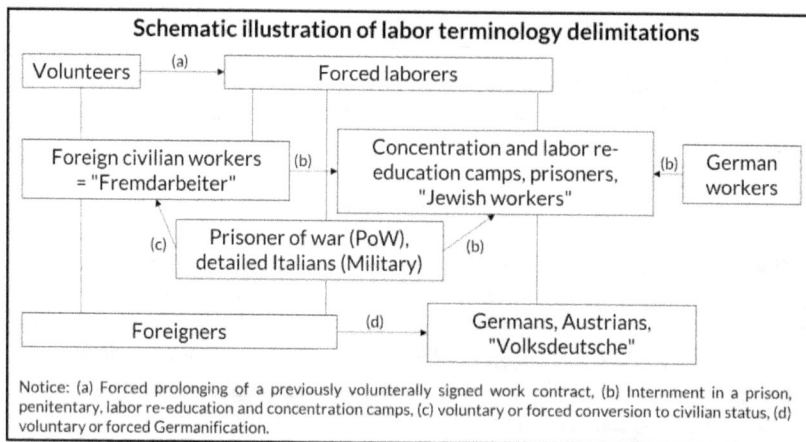

Schematic illustration of labor terminology delimitations

| Volunteers | (a) → | Forced laborers |

| Foreign civilian workers = "Fremdarbeiter" | (b) → | Concentration and labor re-education camps, prisoners, "Jewish workers" | (b) ← | German workers |

| (c) | Prisoner of war (PoW), detailed Italians (Military) | (b) |

| Foreigners | (d) → | Germans, Austrians, "Volksdeutsche" |

Notice: (a) Forced prolonging of a previously volunterally signed work contract, (b) Internment in a prison, penitentary, labor re-education and concentration camps, (c) voluntary or forced conversion to civilian status, (d) voluntary or forced Germanification.

Illustration 2: Schematic illustration of labor terminology delimitations.

Following the early campaigns of 1939 and 1940, the Luftwaffe started to draft foreigners into their work force. This early "recruitment" was partially covered by prisoners of war, as well as a foreign labor force from the newly occupied territories coming from "western" countries such as the Benelux states, France and Denmark. Early recruitment seems to have been the result of coercion, direct pressure or the promise of paid labor but this limited influx would not cover production needs.

---

[26] Adam Tooze, *The Wages of Destruction, The Making & Breaking of the Nazi Economy*, Penguin Books, London, UK, 2007, p. 358, 517.

[27] Mark Spoerer, *Die soziale Differenzierung der ausländischen Zivilarbeiter, Kriegsgefangenen und Häftlinge im Deutschen Reich*, in *Das Deutsche Reich und der Zweite Weltkrieg, Band 9/2 – Die deutsche Kriegsgesellschaft 1939 bis 1945, Ausbeutung, Deutungen, Ausgrenzung*, DVA, Stuttgart, Germany, 2005, p. 487.

[28] Based on illustration MGFA 04767-01, in Mark Spoerer, *Die soziale Differenzierung der ausländischen Zivilarbeiter, Kriegsgefangenen und Häftlinge im Deutschen Reich*, in *Das Deutsche Reich und der Zweite Weltkrieg, Band 9/2 – Die deutsche Kriegsgesellschaft 1939 bis 1945, Ausbeutung, Deutungen, Ausgrenzung*, DVA, Stuttgart, Germany, 2005, p. 487 (translation by the author).

The initial expansion of production capacity and substitution of German workers with foreign labor was comparatively limited at first. The tipping point appeared around the time of the invasion of the Soviet Union in June 1941, which coincided with Hitler's orders demanding the quadrupling of industrial output for the Luftwaffe.[29] Already understaffed prior to 1939, for the German air industry such a massive expansion was no longer possible with a reserved use of prisoners of war, and by a limited influx of foreign laborers. The ratio of Germans within the workforce had been decreasing steadily since 1939, as they were pulled out of factories and drafted into the armed forces. Thus, a critical gap in the industry's capacity worsened.[30]

Amongst the WFG workforce building the Ju 87 a significant number was made up of foreign labor. This is an aspect less explored in the existing literature on the Ju 87, with German researcher Franz-Herbert Wenz appearing as the main author to have written on this aspect in detail.[31] Drawing upon his research, this section will provide additional aspects concerning the use of foreign laborers and highlight their relevance in the production of the Ju 87.

Since early 1940, Eastern Europeans and especially Polish workers were increasingly moved by force to Germany to work, followed later by Soviet citizens.[32] Specifically at WFG, the majority of incoming laborers from January 1941 were of foreign origin.[33] By June 1942 the growth in foreign labor even prompted a projection that if current "recruitment" trends continued, the Weserwerke work force would be more than 80% foreigners.[34] Although this figure was not reached, it's a strong indication of the emerging trend. As Wenz highlights, foreigners already made up to 27% of the total work force in the

---

[29] Horst Boog, *Die deutsche Luftwaffenführung 1935-1945 – Führungsprobleme, Spitzengliederung & Generalstabsausbildung*, DVA, Stuttgart, Germany, 1982, p. 240. See also Adam Tooze, *The Wages of Destruction, The Making & Breaking of the Nazi Economy*, Penguin Books, London, UK, 2007, p. 517.

[30] Adam Tooze, *The Wages of Destruction, The Making & Breaking of the Nazi Economy*, Penguin Books, London, UK, 2007, p. 358.

[31] F.-Herbert Wenz, *Flughafen Tempelhof – Chronik des Berliner Werkes der "Weser" Flugzeugbau GmbH – Bremen*, Stedinger Verlag, Lemwerder, 2000.

[32] Tempelhofer Unfreiheit, *Zwangsarbeit bei Unternehmen auf dem Gelände des Flughafen Tempelhof: Weser Flugzeugbau*, available at https://www.tempelhofer-unfreiheit.de/de/zwangsarbeit-bei-unternehmen-auf-dem-gelaende-des-flughafen-tempelhof, (last accessed 06.09.2021).

[33] On the 2nd of January 1941, WFG confirms receiving 329 new laborers, of which 36 were Germans. An additional request for 2336 additional laborers appears to include only 540 Germans.

[34] BArch, RL 3/15, *Stenographischer Bericht über die GL-Besprechung*, 19. June 1942.

various WFG plants by mid-1942, amounting to 5 000 of 18 600 workers, although individual plants could go as high as 40%.[35]

Between 1942 and 1943, 2.8 million more foreign workers would be moved to Germany.[36] By now not only was it required to drastically increase production numbers, but many foreign laborers (mainly from "Western" European countries such as France) who operated under various "contracts" refused to extend them. Due to this, Junkers Motorenwerke itself lost 38% of its foreign laborers, a staggering drop considering the importance of the Jumo 211 for Germany's bomber and Ju 87 fleet.[37] One example would be French workers, who constituted among the largest share of foreigners at this time. When their "performance" worsened in early 1942, Carl Frydag[38] indicates that 80 French workers were already sent to "detention camps in the East", while Reichsluftzeugmeister[39] Erhard Milch demanded that the local SS-office should be brought in to "intervene", and that "those refusing to work should be put up against the wall and shot in front of everyone"[40].

These were merely early indications of the measures by which means an industry ever more pressed to increase production attempted to fulfill its quotas, although these severe measures were not new. Especially workers from Eastern Europe had already experienced such conditions.[41] While the overall ratio of foreign to German labor in Germany reached around 20% at its height, as Tooze notes, the Luftwaffe had ratios that "routinely exceeded 40 per cent. On

---

[35] F.-Herbert Wenz, *Flughafen Tempelhof – Chronik des Berliner Werkes der "Weser" Flugzeugbau GmbH – Bremen*, Stedinger Verlag, Lemwerder, Germany, 2000, p. 133, 135.

[36] Adam Tooze, *The Wages of Destruction - The Making & Breaking of the Nazi Economy*, Penguin Books, London, UK, 2007, p. 517.

[37] Daniel Uziel, *Arming the Luftwaffe – The German Aviation Industry in World War II*, McFarland & Company, Jefferson, NC, USA, 1967, p. 149.

[38] Carl Frydag, Director of Henschel Flugzeugwerke and Chairman of the Ernst Heinkel AG. Member of the Industrial Council since 1941. See Georg Hentschel, *Die Geheimen Konferenzen des Generalluftzeugmeisters, Ausgewählte und Kommentierte Dokumente zur Geschichte der Deutschen Luftrüstung und des Luftkrieges 1942-1944*, Bernard & Graefe Verlag, Koblenz, Germany, 1989, p. 235.

[39] The Reichsluftzeugmeister was a position in the RLM. This position oversaw the development, testing and procurement of aircraft and aircraft equipment, matters of suppy and industrial planning.

[40] Original Milch: "*Ich verlange, daß bei Arbeitsverweigerung die Leute sofort an die Wand gestellt und vor der Belegschaft erschossen werden*". See BArch, RL 3/13, *Stenographischer Bericht über die GL-Besprechung*, 5. May 1942.

[41] Hans Umbreit, *Die Auswirkungen des "totalen Krieges" auf die deutsche Besatzungsherrschaft*, in *Das Deutsche Reich und der Zweite Weltkrieg, Band 5/2 - Organisation und Mobilisierung des deutschen Machtbereichs: Kriegsverwaltung, Wirtschaft und personelle Ressourcen 1942-1945*, DVA, Stuttgart, Germany, 1999, p. 212.

14

individual production lines the percentage could be even higher".[42] By 1944 the air industry also accounted for 40% of total war production, outstripping that of the German Army and Navy.[43] Likewise, since the start of the war, prisoners of war had been pulled into production in increasing numbers.[44]

At WFG, the use of foreign laborers continuously increased. One study indicates that by the end of the war, at least half of the work force at WFG Berlin-Tempelhof was composed out of forced laborers.[45] Wenz indicates similar numbers, with the number of foreign laborers increasing to 50% by 1943, staying at this ratio until 1945 when it dropped again to 40%. The housing, provisions and personal rights of foreign laborers and especially Eastern Europeans were limited and further curtailed.[46] Laborers drafted from concentration camp were also used in the construction of subterranean production lines.[47] In this constellation, it would not be unusual to see resentment result in sabotage. The frequency of these can not be directly ascertained, nor whether sabotage was correctly identified as such, and how many acts happened unobserved. One WFG plant manager described sabotage as a seldom occurrence: "Sabotage at WFG was, due to energetic, immediate action a rare occurrence. These occurrences were snuffed out at their core through the instantaneous arrest of the relevant person and similar actions against such elements."[48] In this the company collaborated with security forces and used in-house policing by German workers. It is noteworthy that this statement, underlining the supposedly "effective anti-

---

[42] Adam Tooze, The Wages of Destruction - The Making & Breaking of the Nazi Economy, Penguin Books, London, UK, 2007, p. 517-518.

[43] Based on figures quoted by Uziel. Work force in July 1944: Luftwaffe 2,330,000, Heer 1,940,000 and Kriegsmarine 530,000 workers. Daniel Uziel, Arming the Luftwaffe - The German Aviation Industry in World War II, McFarland & Company, Jefferson, NC, USA, 1967, p. 2. See also Horst Boog, Die deutsche Luftwaffenführung 1935-1945 – Führungsprobleme, Spitzengliederung & Generalstabsausbildung, DVA, Stuttgart, Germany, 1982, p. 41.

[44] Hans Umbreit, Die Auswirkungen des "totalen Krieges" auf die deutsche Besatzungsherrschaft, in Das Deutsche Reich und der Zweite Weltkrieg, Band 5/2 - Organisation und Mobilisierung des deutschen Machtbereichs: Kriegsverwaltung, Wirtschaft und personelle Ressourcen 1942-1945, DVA, Stuttgart, Germany, 1999, p. 210.

[45] Bremische Bürgerschaft Landtag 11. Wahlperiode, Einsatz von Zwangsarbeitern während der nationalsozialistischen Herrschaft in Bremen, Drucksache 11/804, 16. December 1986, p. 6.

[46] F.-Herbert Wenz, Flughafen Tempelhof - Chronik des Berliner Werkes der "Weser" Flugzeugbau GmbH - Bremen, Stedinger Verlag, Lemwerder, Germany, 2000, p. 133, 135-140.

[47] Hartmut Pophanken, Gründung und Ausbau der "Weser"-Flugzeugbau GmbH 1933 bis 1939, H. M. Hauschild GmbH, Bremen, Germany, 2000, p. 109.

[48] Walter Pichon, 1955 in discussion with West-German Defense ministry, as quoted by Hartmut Pophanken, Gründung und Ausbau der "Weser"-Flugzeugbau GmbH 1933 bis 1939, H. M. Hauschild GmbH, Bremen, Germany, 2000, p. 109.

sabotage measures", was made post-war in 1955. Although Pophanken and Wenz both describe that WFG employed hard measures to combat sabotage, it is questionable how effective these measures were.[49]

The use of foreign labor in constructing Ju 87s was not just limited to the airframes at WFG. As one of the main German companies building aircraft and engines for the Luftwaffe, Junkers contributed their Jumo 211 engine to their erstwhile dive-bomber until the end of its production. Junkers, as an early recipient of foreign laborers, employed under various "contracts" just over 3 000 by September 1940, a figure that grew to 7 400 the following year. This was the equivalent of just under 10% of its entire work force. By the end of the war Junkers' workforce had risen to 147 000, of which 67 000 were foreign laborers, including concentration camp inmates and prisoners of war. These were distributed among a network of 96 production facilities scattered across Germany.[50]

It can thus be seen that foreign laborers made up a significant part of the WFG and Junkers labor forces and contributed significantly to the output of Ju 87 and Jumo 211 engines for the Luftwaffe. Without them, this output would have neither been attainable nor sustainable. Although certainly not as prolific in the popular discussions about the Second World War, the Luftwaffe, its equipment and its pilots, it should be remembered that if not for the indiscriminate foreign labor, the Luftwaffe would have been far less combat capable. Its aircraft, engines and ammunition production output depended on foreign labor. That legacy is as much part of the Luftwaffe's history as are the more convenient and popular themes.

Production Numbers

The production goals of the Ju 87 were raised in late 1942 from below 100 aircraft/month, to 150, with the final goal being 350 aircraft/month planned for 1944. The timing of this increase is noteworthy, as it also corresponds with the increasing obsolescence of the aircraft. Difficulties exist in pinpointing the exact number of built Ju 87s. One estimate indicates a total of 5 752 Ju 87s of all

---

[49] Hartmut Pophanken, *Gründung und Ausbau der "Weser"-Flugzeugbau GmbH 1933 bis 1939*, H. M. Hauschild GmbH, Bremen, 2000, p. 109. See also F.-Herbert Wenz, *Flughafen Tempelhof – Chronik des Berliner Werkes der "Weser" Flugzeugbau GmbH – Bremen*, Stedinger Verlag, Lemwerder, Germany, 2000, p. 139-140.
[50] Daniel Uziel, *Arming the Luftwaffe – The German Aviation Industry in World War II*, McFarland & Company, Jefferson, NC, USA, 1967, p. 2.

models.[51] A similar estimate indicates 3 720 completed in Bremen between 1937-1944 and 2 020 in Berlin from 1940-1944.[52] Difficulties in establishing an exact number exist also due to the various refits that were made within the factories to existing airframes. For example, various D-3 models were refitted into G-1s carrying the 3.7cm BK anti-tank cannon. Illustration 1 compares these production figures with other Luftwaffe aircraft of the time during the time of the Second World War.

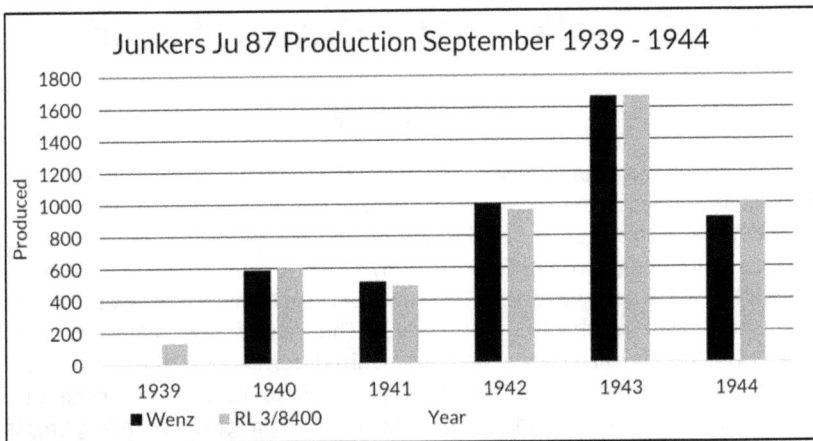

Junkers Ju 87 Production September 1939 - 1944

Illustration 3: Junkers Ju 87 production between September 1939 to October 1944.

The number of Ju 87 built during September 1939 to late 1944 sits at just under 5 000. For this period, Wenz shows a figure of 4 664 aircraft built, whereas another source indicates a wartime production of 4 865.[53] This breakdown is shown in Illustration 3.[54] The Ju 87 production that pre-dates the start of the war in September 1939 can be added on top of this. According to Wenz, this would be

---

[51] Eddie J. Creek, *Junkers Ju 87 – From Dive-Bomber to Tank-Buster 1935-1945*, Classic Publication, Hersham, UK, 2012, p. 327-330.

[52] Total by Pophanken: 5 740. This seems to include the number of Ju 87 A built by Junkers, although this is not specifically cited in his tables. The quoted breakdown summarizes Ju 87 planes completed in the centralized locations of Bremen Lemwerder and Berlin Tempelhof. Smaller facilities and assembly works contributed to this production by sending individual parts to these centralized works. See Hartmut Pophanken, *Gründung und Ausbau der "Weser"-Flugzeugbau GmbH 1933 bis 1939*, H. M. Hauschild GmbH, Bremen, Germany, 2000, p. 116.

[53] See F.-Herbert Wenz, *Flughafen Tempelhof – Chronik des Berliner Werkes der „Weser" Flugzeugbau GmbH – Bremen*, Stedinger Verlag, Lemwerder, Germany, 2000, p. 42-101; and BArch, *RL 3/8400 – Flugzeugproduktion*, n.d.

[54] BArch, RL 3/8400, *Flugzeugproduktion*, n.d.

17

551 aircraft for a total of 5 215 aircraft build by WFG alone.[55] Creek indicates 5 193 for WFG and adds another 559 built by Junkers for a total of 5 752, although he makes reference to another estimate of 5 930 aircraft, which is most likely inflated.[56] The deviation in numbers between are most likely linked to how the sources counted complete or incomplete assemblies of aircraft, as well as repaired or refitted aircraft.

STUKA! – The Ju 87 in Picture, Sound and Memory

The mental image of a diving Stuka remains perhaps as one of the most prominent images of the Second World War. It is this iconic picture that stands at the heart of this section. The Ju 87 is a popular representation of the early successful campaigns of the German Army[57] during the Second World War, a critical link in the early victories[58] that saw a German Army "easily" swat aside its opposition with mechanized formations. The reality was quite different. Although the German Army had mechanized formations, their numerical significance in 1939-1940 does not correspond to its popular image that continues to shape perceptions of it nowadays. This image is also in large parts constructed via the uncritical usage of propaganda footage in documentaries and books. The Ju 87 presents us with a similar picture. Although only one aspect of the Luftwaffe, and even though its operational numbers generally did not rise above 350 planes at a time, it retains a special place in the memory and depiction of the Second World War. Just like with the Army however, this image is one that

---

[55] F.-Herbert Wenz, *Flughafen Tempelhof – Chronik des Berliner Werkes der "Weser" Flugzeugbau GmbH – Bremen*, Stedinger Verlag, Lemwerder, Germany, 2000, p. 98-99.

[56] Eddie J. Creek, *Junkers Ju 87 – From Dive-Bomber to Tank-Buster 1935-1945*, Classic Publication, Hersham, UK, 2012, p. 330.

[57] The Heer (German Army) was, next to the Luftwaffe (German Air Force) and Kriegsmarine (German Navy), one of the three branches of the Wehrmacht. The German Army (Heer) is often confused with the Wehrmacht. The Wehrmacht however was the armed forces as a whole, composed out of the three branches of German Army, German Air Force and Germany Navy.

[58] Commonly referred to as "Blitzkrieg". In regulations the German military did not use "Blitzkrieg" and the word shows up very rarely in the pre-war literature and not always coherently. Meanwhile the word "Bewegungskrieg" literally "movement war" is used regularly, which is the opposite to "Stellungskrieg" meaning "static war(fare)" or better trench warfare. Tanks, aircraft and radios were to be used to achieve a "Bewegungskrieg", yet this was seen as a kind of "return" to older styles of warfare and not as some kind of "revolution".

was created, developed and carefully curated by German propaganda and later rose to lasting post-war prominence due to an often uncritical reception and reproduction in mass media, a process that is in parts still ongoing. It is for this reason that at least a cursory examination of German propaganda and its relevance to the Ju 87 is in order.

German propaganda, from posters, radio shows, books and the Wochenschau[59] providing weekly curated features from the front lines. Indeed, the Wochenschau was a highly effective tool. As Karl Prümm notes, "the superiority of the Kriegswochenschau over a feature film rests most likely upon the fact that it is able to eliminate the remaining distance to the viewer and to make us experience the moment"[60]. Indeed, it was considered by the German propaganda ministry as the "main" and most "decisive political tool"[61]. Using music, sound effects and carefully curated, often staged scenes and stock footage, the Wochenschau delivered "an impression of a highly mechanized war "[62]. Although every nation utilized propaganda during the conflict, Daniel Uziel highlights the singularity of the German Propagandakompanie (propaganda company usually abbreviated with "PK"). These special propaganda units[63] were the only unit integrated into an armed force during Second World War with the sole purpose of waging a total "psychological" war. Set up prior to 1939, it was a unit with a civilian origin in Goebbels propaganda ministry that first experimented with embedding civilian reporters into units during the military maneuvers of 1936-1937. After these, an agreement between the Ministry and the Wehrmacht

---

[59] The "Wochenschau" was the weekly German newsreel. Literally translated it means "Week(ly) Show/Act".

[60] Karl Prümm, *Klangbilder des Krieges - Zu den Propagandastrategien des Kompilationsfilmes*, in Rainer Rother and Judith Prokasky (eds.), *Die Kamera als Waffe - Propagandabilder des Zweiten Weltkrieges*, Richard Boorberg Verlag GmBH & Co KG, München, Germany, 2010, p. 121.

[61] Rainer Rother, *Die Kriegswochenschau - Entstehung einer Form*, in Rainer Rother and Judith Prokasky (eds.), *Die Kamera als Waffe - Propagandabilder des Zweiten Weltkrieges*, Richard Boorberg Verlag GmBH & Co KG, München, Germany, 2010, p. 40, 46.

[62] Karl Prümm, *Klangbilder des Krieges - Zu den Propagandastrategien des Kompilationsfilmes*, in Rainer Rother and Judith Prokasky (eds.), *Die Kamera als Waffe - Propagandabilder des Zweiten Weltkrieges*, Richard Boorberg Verlag GmBH & Co KG, München, Germany, 2010, p. 125.

[63] A Propagandakompanie in September 1939 had an authorized strength of about about 160 men.

integrated this unit formally into the body of the Wehrmacht prior to the invasion of Poland.[64]

In this constellation, the Ju 87 was featured prominently. In their features on the Poland campaign, German propaganda focused on the Ju 87. Next to becoming a stylized symbol of German technological "superiority", the Stuka pilot's reputation of "willingness for action, daredevils and cold-bloodedness" became woven into the pattern of propagated national socialist ideology.[65] With its distinctive look and overdramatized wail of its siren, it was a propagandistic asset. Yet closer inspection of German propaganda footage often reveals the absence of this noise-making device on the gear fairings of the pictured Ju 87, even as the memorable acoustic sound is overlaid for dramatic effect. The usage of this footage and accompanying audio continues to this day in many documentaries, showing the ongoing association between the siren sound and the Stuka. Placing a camera inside the cockpit during a dive or by silencing music to deliver the effect of the siren, the Ju 87 featured continuously on the Wochenschau as well as in feature movies like *Feldzug in Polen (Campaign in Poland)* released in 1940 and *Stukas*, released in 1941. In such productions, the Ju 87s and its pilots are continuously linked to technological and ideological superiority. *Stukas* serves as a clear example, as the full opening minute is dedicated to nothing but repeated attacks by Ju 87s destroying pinpoint (and mainly staged) targets. This is accompanied by sirens and music, followed by jubilant pilots (actors), celebrating their collective achievement which they judged to be as "snappy as a Reichsparteitag".[66]

Pushing for a "new zenith"[67] in aerial videography, the *Wochenschau* was filmed, cut and featured as a cinematic experience to attract viewership and

---

[64] Daniel Uziel, *Propaganda, Kriegsberichterstattung und die Wehrmacht – Stellenwert und Funktion der Propagandatruppen im NS-Staat*, in Rainer Rother and Judith Prokasky (eds.), *Die Kamera als Waffe – Propagandabilder des Zweiten Weltkrieges*, Richard Boorberg Verlag GmBH & Co KG, München, Germany, 2010, p. 13-15.

[65] Christian Kehrt, *Moderne Krieger – Die Technikerfahrungen deutscher Militärpiloten 1910-1945*, Ferdinand Schöningh, Paderborn, Germany, 2010, p. 232-233.

[66] The Reichsparteitag or Reich's Party Congress, was a recurring event between 1923 – 1938, which the Nazi party used for propaganda purposes. From 1933 onwards they occurred annually in Nuremberg and became more commonly known as the Nuremberg Rallies. Karl Ritter, *Stukas*, UFA, 1941, available at: https://archive.org/details/1941-Stukas (last accessed 02.01.2022).

[67] Klaus Kreimeier, *Sensomotorik – Das unbegriffene Erbe der Propagandakompanien*, in Rainer Rother and Judith Prokasky (eds.), *Die Kamera als Waffe – Propagandabilder des Zweiten Weltkrieges*, Richard Boorberg Verlag GmBH & Co KG, München, Germany, 2010, p. 310.

overtone its more blatant propagandistic nature by placing the viewer, past and present, into the shoes of the "privileged observer".[68] In this publication, various pictures created by PKs are also printed, something we decided to clearly label next to their associated picture credit.[69] Many of these photos appear almost innocent, depicting Ju 87s in various, seemingly normalized, and harmless settings. This normalization of the war is an ongoing trend within PK photography. The reader can interact with these pictures on their own accord, but we invite them to consider their origin and purpose.

Photo 1: A camera mounted on to the gear fairing of a Junkers Ju 87. While the pilot and ground crew appear to get ready for take-off, whether this mounting was used in flight is unclear. Original caption: North Africa, Tunisia. Junkers Ju 87 prepares for take-off with a camera mounted on the gear fairing under the wing, pilot in cockpit. Approximately 1942/1943. Credit: BArch, Bild 101I-421-2062-07, Fotograf(in): Jaworsky.

---

[68] Kreimeier argues that the PKs are an extreme example of the illustrative reconstruction of the privileged observer. See Klaus Kreimeier, *Sensomotorik - Das unbegriffene Erbe der Propagandakompanien*, in Rainer Rother and Judith Prokasky (eds.), *Die Kamera als Waffe - Propagandabilder des Zweiten Weltkrieges*, Richard Boorberg Verlag GmBH & Co KG, München, Germany, 2010.

[69] These pictures are from the Bundesarchiv Militärarchiv, the German Military Archive, and are credited with "BArch", followed by the picture identification number and photographer.

Considering the continued use of German propaganda footage from the Second World War, recordings and pictures in historical works, or documentaries, this should give impetus to pause and reflect upon their origin. Historians, amongst others, have continuously highlighted the difficult relationship between using German footage as an educational or visual aid in documentaries, considering that their curated nature and propagandistic content continue to, as Keilbach argues, "influence our perception of the Second World War"[70]. Indeed, in the words of Rother, the influence of such works had a "considerable impact of astonishingly longevity".[71] In other words, our image of the German armed forces is predominantly shaped by German war propaganda.

Of course, the question must be asked: If the majority of photo and film originate from the propaganda units, what can we use instead? The absence of viable alternatives ultimately preordains the inconvenient truth that documentaries (and to a degree historians) continue using and publishing the creations of the PK. Considering this, the question of what else can be used is legitimate. But considering the lack of clear alternatives, perhaps the question should rather be: how do we use it, how do we contextualize it, and how aware are we – when engaging with these products – of their origins and how they were intended to show us a particular image, rather than the grim reality found around the corner? While singular and innovative approaches continue to tackle this issue, how can this be done practically and consistently in mass media? This is a question that remains an ongoing topic for historians and media to debate, although only the former appears to be willing to do so. Whether such a discussion even appears convenient for a portion of those producing documentaries is questionable. As Edgar Lersch notes: "Can footage be contextualized, without it breaking the flow of the narrative? Within the context of the mass media, this is an unsolvable problem."[72] Of course, an obvious counter-point to this would be to ask why is it so problematic for documentaries to not break "the flow of the narrative"? As both authors are actively publishing

---

[70] Judith Keilbach, *Krieg recyceln – Zum Einsatz von PK-Aufnahmen in bundesdeutschen Fernsehdokumentationen*, in Rainer Rother and Judith Prokasky (eds.), *Die Kamera als Waffe – Propagandabilder des Zweiten Weltkrieges*, Richard Boorberg Verlag GmBH & Co KG, München, Germany, 2010, p. 297.

[71] Rainer Rother, *Die Kriegswochenschau – Entstehung einer Form*, in Rainer Rother and Judith Prokasky (eds.), *Die Kamera als Waffe – Propagandabilder des Zweiten Weltkrieges*, Richard Boorberg Verlag GmBH & Co KG, München, Germany, 2010, p. 39.

[72] Edgar Lersch, *Gegen das Diktat der Bilder? Die Fernsehserie Das Dritte Reich 1960/61*, in Rainer Rother and Judith Prokasky (eds.), *Die Kamera als Waffe – Propagandabilder des Zweiten Weltkrieges*, Richard Boorberg Verlag GmBH & Co KG, München, Germany, 2010, p. 293.

video essays on YouTube on the Second World War and other time eras, we would argue that the emergence of new formats outside the traditional media might provide the answer to this question.

PK images continue to influence our perception of the Second World War, influencing how we present and interact with this history in re-enactments, living history, museums, wargames, tabletop, simulations or videogames. The good news is that they are not omnipotent. The bad news is that they remain a powerful visual influence. This is and remains, as Klaus Kreimeier so clearly put it, "the unknown legacy of the Propagandakompanien".[73]

Beyond photos, sound and film reels provided straight out of the German propaganda machine, literary work on the Ju 87 were also published at the time. One of these will be discussed here as it has a particular connection to this book.

This book is *Stukas!* by Curt Strohmeyer.[74] Published in 1940 with a foreword by General der Flieger von Richthofen, it contains 50 war stories supposedly authored by soldiers, describing their "Erlebnisse" (experiences) "in their own words"[75]. Although perhaps loosely based on real events, these stories are likely little more than fiction. *Stukas!*, as well as a whole range of similar "war stories" were published for propagandistic gain, rather than symbolizing an honest attempt to relate the true experiences of these units. Within chapters such as *The Bravest, The Mission is Everything – and I am nothing!*, *We Hunted Them Where We Found Them* and *The Jersey Potato War*[76], the war is told as an adventure, a coming of age story with an hefty infusion of the death-worship and glamorization of the sacrificial young hero so common in Nationalist-Socialist propaganda.

It is at this point that a critical word about the cover of the book you hold in your own hands is needed. This was adapted from Strohmeyer's *Stukas!*. The reason for this is simple: it captures the popular image of the Ju 87 at its core. Many readers might rightly argue that a book should not be judged by its cover. Yet, as many publishers and authors might argue, it is certainly often bought at

---

[73] Klaus Kreimeier, *Sensomotorik – Das unbegriffene Erbe der Propagandakompanien*, in Rainer Rother and Judith Prokasky (eds.), *Die Kamera als Waffe – Propagandabilder des Zweiten Weltkrieges*, Richard Boorberg Verlag GmBH & Co KG, München, Germany, 2010, p. 312.

[74] Curt Strohmeyer, *Stukas! – Erlebnis eines Fliegerkorps*, Die Heimbücherei, Berlin, Germany, 1940.

[75] Curt Strohmeyer, *Stukas! – Erlebnis eines Fliegerkorps*, Die Heimbücherei, Berlin, Germany, 1940, p. 7.

[76] Translations from the German chapters in presented order: *Die Tapfersten; Der Auftrag ist alles – das Ich: nichts!; Wir jagten sie, wo wir sie trafen; Der Kartoffelkrieg von Jersey.*

least in part due to the cover, just like YouTube videos are often watched due to their thumbnails and titles. It would be disingenuous to argue that the cover of this book does not conjure up the very real nature of the Stuka dive-bomber but then not claim that it does not also tap into its more popular image that was predominantly shaped by German propaganda. This linkage is unavoidable, given the Ju 87's iconic look from any angle, except by not showing a plane at all or potentially its wreckage. As such, at least from the point of the author, we must readily admit that our choice of cover speaks volumes of not just the iconic image of the Stuka, but also its commercial legacy. Here, we orientated ourselves towards the "market", as our strategy tends to be "popular cover – factual content". Whether this cover has ultimately influenced the purchase of this book, is a question only the reader can answer.

Photo 2: Ju 87 B of Sturzkampfgeschwaders 2 "Immelmann" over Novgorod, Soviet Union, Summer 1941. Credit: NARA.

CHAPTER II

Doctrine, Training and Operational Thinking

The Sturzkampfgeschwader

At the onset of the war, the Luftwaffe fielded a large number of twin-engine bombers. These were relatively well suited to the short, continental campaigns Germany waged against its most immediate neighbors like Poland and France. With planes like the Do 17, He 111 and the upcoming Ju 88 making up the bulk of the bomber force, it is important to consider that the Ju 87 was also part of the bomber force. Although nowadays its specialization as a dive-bomber causes it to be considered as a separate instrument, the Ju 87 was tied to the bombers in the run-up to as well as throughout the Second World War until a major reform in 1943. This is not just represented in Luftwaffe doctrine and training, but also in the thinking and make-up of the command structures within the Luftwaffe.

Doctrine

Heavily curtailed by both the Versailles treaty and subsequent agreements, Germany was forbidden from developing competitive military aircraft models. Although limited air operations in Germany and abroad (for example in Sweden or the Soviet Union) continued, the restrictions effectively prevented the Reichswehr to field a conventional air force. Nevertheless, as the historian James Corum points out, the Reichswehr[77] under the tutelage of General Hans von Seeckt established the "organizational foundation and doctrine of a new air force"[78] even by the early 1920s. Though von Seeckt was forced to retire in 1926, the core of the future Luftwaffe's doctrine had already been developed. When Adolf Hitler became Chancellor in 1933, he and his government accelerated the process of establishing an air force. After the public unveiling of the Luftwaffe in 1935, General Walther Wever served as its Chief of Staff until his death in 1935. Wever himself focused on achieving air superiority and operational support for the army, with tight coordination between the Luftwaffe and the German Army along the latter's main offensive thrusts. In this constellation, the bomber was considered as the "decisive factor in aerial warfare"[79]. This has prompted historians to often consider Wever to be a strong proponent of strategic bombing, but closer inspection shows that neither he nor any other influential

---

[77] The Reichswehr (1919-1935) was the predecessor of the Wehrmacht (1935-1945). It was the unified armed forces of the Weimar Republic. The organizational main difference was that the Reichswehr had only two branches: the Army and the Navy, whereas the Wehrmacht also had the Air Force as a branch.

[78] James S. Corum, *The Luftwaffe – Creating the Operational Air War, 1918-1940*, University Press of Kansas, Lawrence, USA, 1997, p. 50.

[79] James S. Corum, *The Luftwaffe – Creating the Operational Air War, 1918-1940*, University Press of Kansas, Lawrence, USA, 1997, p. 138.

Luftwaffe General or Staff officer considered Germany ready to field such a force in 1936, or that this was even seen as a necessity. Doctrinally, the core of the Reichswehr thoughts on air war would later see partial reflection in the 1935 publication: *Luftwaffendruckvorschrift 16: Luftkriegsführung*[80] *(L.Dv. 16)*. With only a few revisions, *L.Dv. 16* established the operational air war (Operative Luftkrieg) of the Luftwaffe and remained its guiding principle.

Although not revolutionary[81], in the minds of German theorists, a Luftwaffe equipped with "a large number of medium bombers and dive-bombers would suffice for the operational air war, that being the independent fight against the enemy's air fleet and its capacity to wage war, as well as the support of land and sea operations"[82]. This placed it "between two extremes: Douhetism and total subordination to the Army"[83]. With this balance came ambiguity, as *L.Dv. 16* "subtly depicted the existing state of the Luftwaffe"[84]. Nevertheless, these guidelines and their practical repercussions, as well as the technological and developmental state of the Luftwaffe contributed to an innate connection between the dive-bomber and the conventional bomber within the Luftwaffe's doctrinal thought. The publication of *L.Dv. 16* also corresponds roughly to the restructuring of the dive-bomber force into the Inspectorate of Bombers[85].

The close conceptual connection between dive-bombers and bombers within the Luftwaffe can be gleamed from the document: *Aerial Tactics: The Dive-Bomber* included in this book. Published by the Inspectorate for Instruction and

---

[80] Translation: *Luftwaffe Regulation 16: The Conduct of the Aerial War.*
[81] Edward Homze considers *L.D.v 16* as a "conversative concept", while Corum argues it was a "synthesis of the views of General Wever, the air staff and existing doctrine" which "expressed no revolutionary new theories of air warfare". See Edward Homze, *Arming the Luftwaffe – The Reichs Air Ministry and the German Aircraft Industry, 1919-39*, University of Nebraska Press, Lincoln, USA, 1976, p. 132; and James S. Corum, *The Luftwaffe – Creating the Operational Air War, 1918-1940*, University Press of Kansas, Lawrence, USA, 1997, p. 144. See also BArch, RL 1/658, *L.Dv. 16 Luftkriegführung und Luftkriegführung als Nachdruck*, RLM, Berlin, Germany, 1935.
[82] Karl-Heinz Völker, *Die Deutsche Luftwaffe 1933-1939 – Aufbau, Führung und Rüstung der Luftwaffe sowie die Entwicklung der deutschen Luftkriegstheorie*, DVA, Stuttgart, Germany, 1967, p. 73 (translation by the author).
[83] Michel Forget, *Die Zusammenarbeit zwischen Luftwaffe und Heer bei den französischen und deutschen Luftstreitkräften im Zweiten Weltkrieg*, in Horst Boog (ed.), *Luftkriegführung im Zweiten Weltkrieg. Ein internationaler Vergleich*, E.S. Mittler & Sohn GmbH, Bonn, Germany, 1993, p. 490.
[84] Edward Homze, *Arming the Luftwaffe – The Reichs Air Ministry and the German Aircraft Industry, 1919-39*, University of Nebraska Press, Lincoln, USA, 1976, p. 132.
[85] See *Command Structures of the Luftwaffe* in this chapter.

Education[86], this document would have been used as instructional material in the Luftwaffe academies. It details the tasks of the dive-bomber units, as well as their organizational structure, tactical guidelines and the cooperation with other air formations, as well as the Army and Navy[87]. As part of the instructional curriculum, the document also highlights four additional pamphlets. Three of these were identified by us in archives and constitute the core of this edited volume. So far, we were unable to locate the remaining *Pamphlet on the Employment and Training of Dive-Bombers – 1937 Edition (Merkblatt über Einsatz und Ausbildung von Sturzkampffliegern – Ausgabe 1937)*. As such, the reader is presented with a near complete collection of documents that arguably stand at the center of the Luftwaffe curriculum on dive-bombers by 1939.

Considering the doctrinal and operational overlap of bomber and dive-bomber units, three aspects are noteworthy within the document. First, under *Tasks and Applications*, the original guidelines for dive-bomber targets are provided. As shown in this list, the main targets were static and largely mirrored those given to bomber units.[88] Only the additionally listed category includes moving targets such as trains, motorized columns, the enemy's navy and merchant shipping, as well as targets traversing a bottleneck. A direct usage on the frontlines, as a close air support asset, is not specifically mentioned. It appears likely that next to a conceptual linkage of bombers and dive-bombers, the Luftwaffe interpreted their experiences with Ju 87s in early Wehrmacht war games and maneuvers as providing further indication that their usage should be restricted to point targets or only in very specific circumstances against enemy ground formations on the actual battlefield. The 1937 Wehrmacht maneuver was the first time the dive-bomber units were in a large exercise.[89] The Luftwaffe sums up its experience with using dive-bombers during this maneuver with the following: "The usage of Stuka-formations against columns travelling on open streets promises little success; more successful are attacks on enemy movements, also from tank units in bottle necks and smaller villages; the destruction of streets and the collapse of buildings are especially lasting, as are the destruction of bridges in river crossings. The attack of Stuka-formations on tank units on the battlefield promises no success. The small number of bombs and the difficulty in hitting a

---

[86] Original: Inspektion des Erziehungs- und Bildungswesens der Luftwaffe (L. In. 10). For more information on the Inspectorates, see *Command Structures of the Luftwaffe* in this chapter.

[87] Specifically, the Heer (Army) and Kriegsmarine (Navy).

[88] L.In. 10, *Leitfaden für den Unterricht auf den Luftkriegsschulen – Lufttaktik*, p. 18-20.

[89] Karl-Heinz Völker, *die Deutsche Luftwaffe 1933-1939 – Aufbau, Führung und Rüstung der Luftwaffe sowie die Entwicklung der deutschen Luftkriegstheorie*, DVA, Stuttgart, Germany, 1967, p. 90.

small, very mobile target speak against such a usage."[90] Second, within the *Employment Guidelines*, the Stuka is directly mentioned as the "sniper among the bombers", to be used against those targets that can only be destroyed with a disproportionate use of ammunition and aircraft by conventional bombers. Additionally, the guidelines under *Cooperation* indicate only "Corresponding with the same section on the bombers[91]", indicating once more the close, intertwined operational use of both these units.

This line of thinking is also reflected in mass-printed instructional manuals that were distributed to service personnel, Luftwaffe academies and youth organizations.[92] How widely accepted the conceptualization of dive-bombers as part of, rather than separate from, a conventional bomber force was in Germany at the time, can also be glimpsed from important literary works of the time. One of these is the *Handbuch der neuzeitlichen Wehrwissenschaften*, an encyclopedia on contemporary military matters published between 1936 to 1939. The centrality of this publication is highlighted by the written pre-ambles of Reichsminister of War and Commander-in-Chief of the Wehrmacht Generalfeldmarschall Werner von Blomberg, Commander-in-Chief of the Germany Army Generaloberst Werner von Fritsch, Commander-in-Chief of the German Army Admiral Erich Raeder and the Reich's Air Minister and Commander-in-Chief of the Luftwaffe Hermann Göring throughout the different volumes. As with other documents of the time, within this encyclopedia, the listing considers the Sturzkampfbomber as only one aspect of the bomber force that additionally includes medium and heavy bombers[93].

Of course, it should be noted that doctrine and intended operational use often diverge with reality as soon as the contact with opposing forces is made.

Command structures of the Luftwaffe

How closely intertwined the dive-bomber and bomber units were, can also be seen by their representation at the higher command levels of the Reichsluftfahrtministerium (RLM – German Air Ministry). General Erhard Milch was nominated as both the state secretary (Staatssekretär) of the RLM and the

---

[90] BArch, RL 2-II/157, *Bd. 4 Bericht Wehrmachtsmanöver (Luftwaffe)*, 1937, p. 31.
[91] See Glossary: Bomber (Kampfflugzeug/ Kampfflieger).
[92] Fritz-Herbert Dierich, *Der Flieger – Dienstunterricht in der Fliegertruppe, Handbücher der Luftwaffe*, E.S. Mittler & Sohn, Berlin, Germany, 1940, p. 5.
[93] Hermann Franke, *Handbuch der neuzeitlichen Wehrwissenschaften – Dritter Band 2. Teil: Die Luftwaffe*, Walter de Gruyter & Co, Berlin, Germany, 1939, p. 108.

inspector general (Generalinspekteur) of the Luftwaffe[94]. This effectively made him the "Number 2" under General[95] Hermann Göring, who was the Reich's Minister of Aviation (Reichsminister der Luftfahrt) and Commander-in-Chief of the Air Force (Oberbefehlshaber der Luftwaffe)[96]. In the structure of the RLM, the Luftwaffen-Inspectorates were situated just below Milch's position and would number at the start of the war first 14, then 15 Inspectorates.[97] An inspector was a leading position usually occupied by a General or senior officer. He represented the specific branch assigned to him within the High Command of the Luftwaffe (Oberkommando der Luftwaffe [OKL]) and concerned himself with the operational readiness, training, tactics and the collection of experience reports of his assigned units. Although the inspectorate structure was revised multiple times, dive-bombers, together with bomber units were mainly represented by the Inspectorate for Bombers and Dive-Bombers[98]. It took until September 1943 for dive-bombers to be officially removed from their bomber cousins and be folded into a new inspectorate focusing on close air support. This

---

[94] After the suicide of Ernst Udet in November 1941, Erhard Milch became Generalluftzeugmeister which placed him, amongst others, at the head of the technical committees for the development of new aircraft, engines and equipment for the Luftwaffe. Organizationally, he was thus "his own boss" as his ongoing Generalinspekteur post was set just above his new Generalluftzeugmeister position.

[95] From 1938, Generalfeldmarschall.

[96] Translation: Reich's Minister of Aviation / Commander-in-Chief of the Air Force.

[97] For an overview of the changing horizontal and vertical operational dynamics, see Horst Boog, *Die deutsche Luftwaffenführung 1935-1945 – Führungsprobleme, Spitzengliederung, Generalstabsausbildung*, DVA, Stuttgart, Germany, 1982, p. 576-587.

[98] At first, the Inspectorate of Fighters and Dive-Bombers (Inspektion der Jagd- und Sturzkampfflieger) represented the dive-bomber units from 1934 onwards. The Inspectorate of Bombers (Inspektion der Kampfflieger) was expanded to include dive-bomber and reconnaissance units with the short-lived 1939 revision, before being renamed the Inspectorate of Bombers, Dive-Bombers and Reconnaissance (Inspektion der Kampf-, Sturzkampf- und Aufklärungsflieger). In 1940, reconnaissance was folded into its own inspectorate and the position became the Inspectorate of Bombers and Dive-Bombers (Inspektion der Kampf- und Sturzkampfflieger). With the September 1941 revision this again became known as the Inspectorate of Bombers (Inspektion der Kampfflieger), with the commanding officer known as the General der Kampfflieger, although the dive-bomber units were retained. It appears that a (semi-)independent Inspectorate of Dive-Bombers (Inspektion der Sturzkampfflieger) existed for a short period in mid-1943 before the last major restructuring occurred in September 1943. With this organizational change, the newly created General der Nahkampfflieger (renamed into General der Schlachtflieger one month later) consolidated all dive-bombers, fighter-bombers and anti-tank units of the Luftwaffe under his position. See Horst Boog, *Die deutsche Luftwaffenführung 1935-1945 – Führungsprobleme, Spitzengliederung*, Generalstabsausbildung, DVA, Stuttgart, Germany, 1982, p. 196, 250-272, 578-581.

long-lasting linkage between bombers and dive-bombers shows once again how closely intertwined these units were in the opinion of the Luftwaffe.

Operational structures

The Luftwaffe was a branch of the Wehrmacht, the German Armed Forces. It was broken-up into multiple Luftflotten[99]. Each Luftflotte commanded flying units, anti-aircraft units, transport and logistics and presided over territorial air structures such as airfields. The Luftflotten itself were commonly organized into Fliegerkorps and Fliegerdivisionen. Below this operational level the individual Geschwader would be stationed.[100]

There is some difficulty involved in trying to compare the organization and structure of the Luftwaffe's air units with that of the Allies, as each service established operationally comparable but slightly different force structures. Linguistically, this comparison is also not helped by the fact that the German Gruppe is of a different authorized strength compared to a USAAF or RAF Group, which themselves are distinct of each other even though the words are the same. Variance in terms of operational to authorized strength (Ist-Stärke vs Soll-Stärke[101]), special theater compositions, difference between bomber, dive-bomber, fighter and other units and any non-standard anomalies cannot be accounted for. Because of the inconsistencies involved in unit sizes, this book will continue to use German unit designations. For more information on this, see the Glossary: Dive-bomber squadron, group and wing (Sturzkampfstaffel, -gruppe, -geschwader).

Organizational Structure of a Sturzkampfgeschwader

A Geschwader was organized in the following manner:

Each Gruppe would be designated by a Roman numeral, while each Staffel had an Arabic number. Command units or the headquarters companies, would be designated with "Stab". This system allows quick identification what formation is meant, as II./St.G. 1 designates the 2nd Gruppe while 2/St.G. 1 designates the 2nd Staffel (of I./St.G.) of Sturzkampfgeschwader 1. A quick overview can be found in Illustration 4.

---

[99] Translation: Air Fleet.
[100] It should be noted that between 1939-1945 this structure changed continuously, with the individual Geschwader sometimes placed within different structures where regional or ad hoc units flattened or deepened this structure.
[101] German terms for operational and authorized strength numbers. Directly translated, "Ist-Stärke" stands for "is-strength", while "Soll-Stärke" would be "should-(be)-strength".

33

```
                    ┌─────────────────────────────┐
                    │   Sturzkampfgeschwader      │
                    │           Stab              │
                    └─────────────────────────────┘
          ┌────────────────┬──────────────┬────────────────┐
   ┌────────────┐   ┌────────────┐   ┌────────────┐
   │ I. Gruppe  │   │ II. Gruppe │   │ III. Gruppe│
   │   Stab     │   │   Stab     │   │   Stab     │
   │ 1. Staffel │   │ 4. Staffel │   │ 7. Staffel │
   │ 2. Staffel │   │ 5. Staffel │   │ 8. Staffel │
   │ 3. Staffel │   │ 6. Staffel │   │ 9. Staffel │
   └────────────┘   └────────────┘   └────────────┘
```

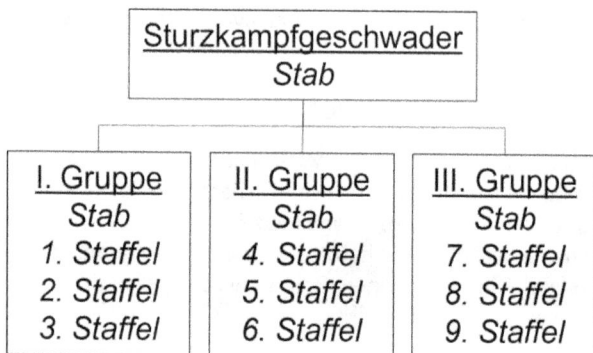

Illustration 4: Organizational structure of a Sturzkampfgeschwader.

Visualization of a Sturzkampfgeschwader

The breakdown found within *Aerial Tactics: The Dive-Bomber* gives a glimpse of the intended force structure of a Sturzkampfgeschwader. It indicates the authorized strength number of each Staffel, Gruppe and Geschwader in terms of crews, planes, mechanics and administrative personnel. This shows that each Staffel was intended to have 9 Ju 87s (excluding 3 in reserve), giving each Gruppe an authorized strength of 30 aircraft (including the Stab but excluding 9 reserves). Consequently, each Geschwader's authorized operational strength was 93 aircraft (including Geschwader Stab but excluding the reserves). These authorized numbers are also reflected in the Kriegsstärkenachweisungen[102] of the Luftwaffe on dive-bomber units[103]. Illustration 5 shows the size of an assembled Sturzkampfgeschwader based on the authorized figures found in *Aerial Tactics: The Dive-Bomber*. Under operational conditions and depending on requirements, this intended frontline strength could vary considerably with the actual operational numbers in the field. Throughout the Second World War, it was common that the Geschwader's Gruppen operated independently from each other. It was even possible to find Gruppen of the same Geschwader in different operational theaters. Likewise, individual Staffeln were sometimes "detached" and folded into various Luftwaffe formations if operational requirements demanded it, whereas Ergänzungsstaffeln[104] might be attached to a dive-bomber unit if needed.

---

[102] Basically a table of organization and equipment.
[103] BArch, RL 2-III/561, *Kriegsstärkenachweisung (Luftw.) Nr. 1185 – 1188 (L)*, November 1939, p. 85-96.
[104] This can be loosely translated as "replacement training squadron".

One interesting change occurred with the establishment of Panzerjägerstaffeln[105] (Pz) that operated Ju 87s armed with the 3.7cm BK anti-tank gun. These would be set up as additional Staffeln, usually designated 10.(Pz)/St.G.[106] and attached to whatever unit and operational area required anti-tank capability. This "tenth" Staffel, which could be an additional "fourth" Staffel in a Gruppe, included the suffix (Pz) which is the German abbreviation for Panzer, thus designating it as an anti-tank unit. After the disbandment of all Sturzkampfgeschwader and reorganization as Schlachtgeschwader, this special Staffel's number and suffix was also retained.

Various German Nachtschlachtgruppen (NSGr), which can be loosely translated to Night Attacker Gruppen, flew Ju 87s.[107] Operating as Gruppen, rather than within a Geschwader, they were attached to the various larger Luftwaffenkorps, -kommandos or -flotten. The size of these appears somewhat unorthodox, and it no longer tied to the original, authorized strengths of Sturzkampfgeschwader and Gruppen. For example, Nick Beale notes an average strength of around 30 aircraft for NSGr.9.[108]

Beyond these changes Germany's dive-bomber units never underwent a significant structural change which revised the number of operational Gruppen and Staffeln. By 1943, the first Sturzkampfgeschwader transitioned from the Ju 87 to the Fw 190. This change eventually led to the discontinuation of the Sturzkampfgeschwader, which were renamed into Schlachtgeschwader[109].

Transport, Reconnaissance and Courier Aircraft

In Illustration 5, planes in the transport and recon category have been visualized with the Ju 52 and Fi 156 (Storch) since these are perhaps the most well-known German aircraft used in this role. However, a wide range of other planes were also used by Sturzkampfgeschwader in these roles, including older, outdated or foreign models. As such, the Ju 52 and Fi 156 are representative only. Transport planes would be used to move spare parts, equipment, fuel, personnel and heavier loads. Ideally, the transport planes should also be able to load all personnel (excluding the Ju 87 crews) when evacuation or a quick relocation was required in a single trip.

---

[105] This can be loosely translated as "tank-hunter Staffel".
[106] After the reorganization of the Sturzkampfgeschwader into Schlachtgeschwader, this would change to 10.(Pz)/S.G.
[107] For more information, see *An Introduction on Night-Bombing with the Ju 87*.
[108] Nick Beale, *Ghost Bombers - The Moonlight War of NSG 9, Luftwaffe Night Attack Operations from Anzio to the Alps*, Classic Publications, Manchester, UK, 2001.
[109] See Glossary: Close air support unit (Schlachtflieger).

The reconnaissance aircraft were part of a special reconnaissance Staffel, known as the Aufklärungsstaffel (K)[110], supporting each Gruppe with reconnaissance information. Ideally, pilots would be given reconnaissance pictures or up-to-date information regarding the location and disposition of enemy forces or the stationary target just prior to their attack. These could, depending on target and range, also be acquired by other reconnaissance Staffeln. The Aufklärungsstaffel (F) (or FAG)[111] focused on operational reconnaissance, while the Aufklärungsstaffeln (H) (or NAG) operated on the tactical level. These were generally attached to mechanized units at the corps or divisional level. The Aufklärungsstaffel (K) was more independent, serving mainly the needs of the Stuka-Gruppe although there is little tangible information on how these units were used in practice. These planes could also be used for liaison or light transport duties.

The two-courier aircraft within the Stab/St.G. are indicated as being part of aircraft class A/B-1 and B-2[112]. Due to the very diverse, one might even say chaotic requisition model of the Luftwaffe, they have again been visualized here by generic plane models. As can for example be seen in the chapter on the Air-Sea Battle of Crete, planes like the Do 17 or Bf 110 could also be found flying these missions. The categories in themselves would be:

- class A 1: Aircraft for one person with an all-up weight[113] of up to 500 kg,
- class B 1: Aircraft for one to four people with an all-up weight of 1000 to 2500 kg,
- class B 2: Aircraft for one to eight people with an all-up weight of 2500 to 5000 kg.[114]

---

[110] See Glossary: Reconnaissance aircraft K (K-Aufklärungsflugzeug).
[111] See Glossary: Reconnaissance aircraft F (F-Aufklärungsflugzeug) [F.-]).
[112] See Glossary: Aircraft-class (Flugzeugklasse).
[113] Translated from "Fluggewicht". While we could not find a period-accurate description, this term is usually used in German manuals to designate the maximum gross weight of an aircraft (all-up weight/ AUW).
[114] Fritz-Herbert Dierich, *Der Flieger – Dienstunterricht in der Fliegertruppe*, Handbücher der Luftwaffe, E.S. Mittler & Sohn, Berlin, Germany, 1940, p. 63.

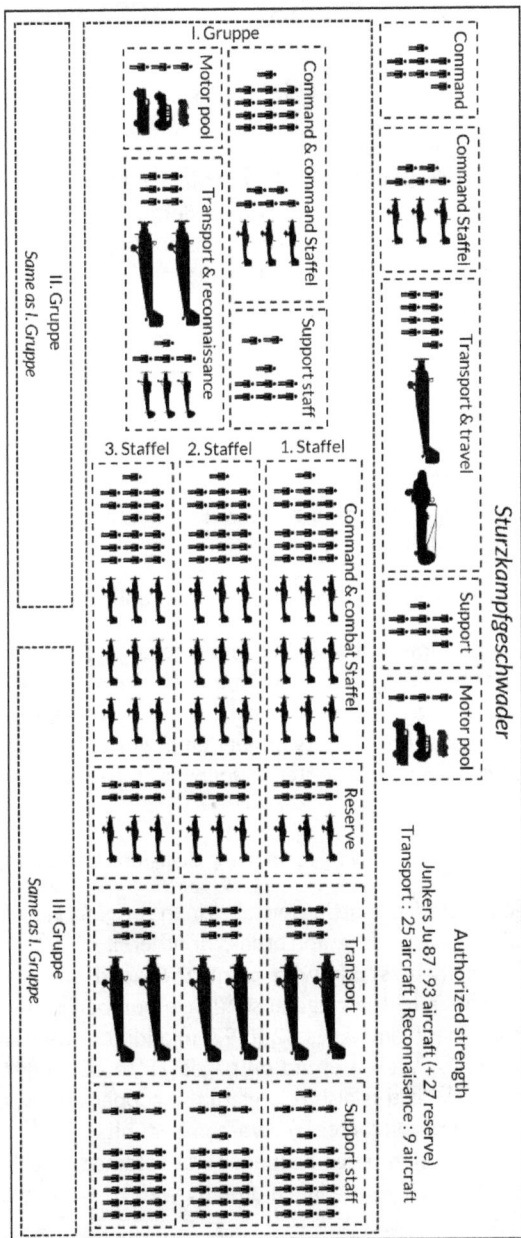

Illustration 5: Visualized structure of a Sturzkampfgeschwader.

Document: Aerial Tactics: The Dive-Bomber

This document can be found in the Russian Archives under TsAMO, F. 500 Op. 12452 D. 239: *Aerial Tactics: The Dive-Bomber*. Included are the relevant sections on the dive-bomber units of the Luftwaffe, detailing their purpose, function organizational structure and recommendations on cooperation with other aerial units and ground forces. This sets out the guidelines on how dive-bombers were to be used by the Luftwaffe and includes a reference to four additional documents that were considered complimentary to *Aerial Tactics* on dive-bomber operations. Three of these four additional documents can be found within this book.

Although no date is given, this document most likely is the Aerial Tactics publication from 1939. We assume this due to its referencing of late 1930s pamphlets, the information contained, as well as the fact that the 1943 version found in the German Military Archive is different.

Preliminary Notes / Source Situation, Actuality and Formatting

Throughout this volume, we aimed to retain some of the original formatting, yet the editorial focus lay on legibility. One of the main editorial changes was that, in order to present a clearer layout, we did not follow the original page count as this would have resulted in empty or near empty pages throughout the book. Instead, the text has been reformatted to follow a more conventional structure, page by page.

Please be aware of the following formatting decisions and changes:

- We corrected formatting mistakes in the original version (for example missing spaces, paragraph breaks or others).
- The document starts with point 156.) and ends with 185.) This corresponds to the original sequence number in *Aerial Tactics: The Dive-Bomber* from pages 82 to 97. In addition, we have added point 145.) through 154.) found on pages 75 to 80 from the section on Bombers[115] as this also relates to the cooperation with other aerial units and ground forces by dive-bomber units.
- The original numbered sequence was retained, but the beginning of each paragraph was aligned directly with the referenced number to

---

[115] See Glossary: Bomber (Kampfflieger).

make the best use of the available space. Overall, these changes allow us to transfer this document into a more legible layout that is consistent with the other documents found in this book. This also includes the deletion of unnecessary spacing between subs-sections.

- The organizational charts on the make-up of a dive-bomber squadron, group and wing were retained in the original format, with only minimal adjustments to the spacing to provide a coherent structure. This results in a long listing of crews and personal, which can be difficult to navigate. To provide a visual representation, we have added illustrations in the introduction of this chapter.

- Two important German words in the original were "Anmarsch" and "Anflug". Both can be translated into English with "approach", as is for example the case in *TM 30-506: German Military Dictionary*. Given the context, in German "Anmarsch" implies a longer distance, whereas "Anflug" suggests the final stretch to the target. This is similar to "final approach" in English which signifies the final flight distance of an aircraft during a landing. As such, we have translated "Anflug" with "approach". While a possible solution would be translating "Anmarsch" to "approach march", this might be confusing and not exactly fitting as "march" generally has a ground-based connotation. Equally, the text often used the word "marsch" to signify movement of a flight or formation. Due to this and the constant changes in context, a repeated use of the English word "march" might be the cause of some confusion. As such, we have translated the text in such a way that we avoid the use of "march" and maintain a distinction from approach by translating "Anmarsch" with "en-route" or "route [to the target]".

- As noted in the previous chapter, we have retained the German designations of Staffel, Gruppe and Geschwader.

Compendium for the Education at the Air-War Colleges

Proof-Nr..103

Secret!

Compendium for the Education at the Air-War Colleges.

Aerial Tactics

Edited and published

by the

Inspectorate of Instruction and Education of the Luftwaffe[116]

Command of the Air-War Colleges

This compendium includes .... pages, in words: ....

.... pages, excluding the table of content.

Printed in the Reich's Printing Office

---

[116] The Inspectorate of Instruction and Education (Inspektion des Erziehungs- und Bildungswesens der Luftwaffe [L.In. 10]) held the overall responsibly for the training and education of Luftwaffe personnel and specifically officer candidates. It remained in service until December 1944. See also Horst Boog, *Die deutsche Luftwaffenführung 1935-1945 – Führungsprobleme, Spitzengliederung, Generalstabsausbildung*, DVA, Stuttgart, Germany, 1982, p. 570.

[Following is Chapter B. detailing the dive-bomber.]

B. The Dive-Bomber;

based on[117] "Pamphlet for the Employment and Training of Dive-Bombers"[118] 1937 Edition and

"Pamphlet for the Employment of Bomber- and Dive-Bomber Units against Fast-Moving Ground Forces", Genst. 3. Abt. Nr. 4300/38 geh. from 22.9.1938[119] and

Pamphlet on "Attacking AA-Defenses with Bombers", Genst. 3. Abt. Nr. 3550/38 (III) from 19.8.1938.[120]

Reprint: "Guidelines for Dive-Bombing Training."[121]

1. Tasks and Applications.

156.) The dive-bomber's main task is to attack fixed enemy installations of military, wartime or critical importance[122], which have a small extension (single or point targets[123]).

Such targets are:

command buildings, hangars, fuel depots and ammunition stockpiles at airports,

headquarters and radio stations,

---

[117] The original German word was "nach". The literal translation would be "after".

[118] This document was not found during our research, which included amongst others a search within and contact with the German Military Archive, the Centre for Military History and Social Sciences of the Bundeswehr and the Bundeswehr Centre for Public Affairs.

[119] See *Pamphlet for the Employment of Bomber- and Dive-Bomber Units against Fast-Moving Ground Forces.*

[120] See *Pamphlet on Attacking AA-Defenses with Bombers.*

[121] See *L. Dv. 20/2: Luftwaffe Regulation 20/2 – Guidelines for Dive-Bombing Training.*

[122] The original German word was "lebenswichtiger Bedeutung". The literal translation would be "vital importance".

[123] See Glossary: Point target (Einzelziel, Punktziel).

bridges and infrastructure buildings,

ammunition depots,

electricity, water, gas and converter plants,

vital parts in factories and industrial plants.

157.) The dive-bomber's maneuverability and armament also enable it to attack live and moving targets, e.g.,

railroad trains, tanks and motorcades,

warships and merchant ships of all types,

troop concentrations and marching columns, especially when crossing choke points.

2. Table of Organization & Equipment.[124]

158.) In wartime, dive-bomber formations depend for maintenance and care on the airdrome operating companies[125] of the airports which they deploy to[126]. Equipment, tools, baggage and excess personnel, to the extent they cannot be accommodated in transport or courier aircraft, will be carried in motor vehicles detailed in the table of organization and equipment[127].

159.)   The Dive-Bomber Staffel[128] (Stz.Kpf.Staff[129])

(Table of organization and equipment Nr. 1187 (L))

1 Staffel commander

---

[124] The following section includes a breakdown of the authorized strength of a dive-bomber Staffel, Gruppe and Geschwader. Note that although the presentation format between these three units was broadly similar, there were a few differences and inconsistencies.

[125] See Glossary: Airdrome operation company (Flughafenbetriebskompanien).

[126] The original German word was "einfallen". The literal translation would be "falling in". Meant here is not the capturing of an enemy airfield by landing on it. Instead, it describes a relocation of a dive-bomber unit, which could be part of a sudden, unexpected or hasty transfer. Naturally, this might also include a relocation to a former enemy airfield.

[127] See Glossary: Table of organization and equipment (Kriegsstärkenachweisung).

[128] See Glossary: Dive-bomber squadron (Sturzkampfstaffel).

[129] "Stz.Kpf.Staff" is the abbreviation of "Sturzkampfstaffel", indicating "Dive-Bomber Staffel".

a) <u>Flying staffel</u>[130]

8 pilots

9 radio operators (gunner)

9 dive-bombers[131]

b) <u>Staffel H.Q.</u>[132]

1 company sergeant major[133]

1 accountant and pay non-commissioned officer (also mess sergeant[134])

1 clerk

2 pilots

2 radio operators (gunner)

2 flight engineer (gunner)

1 aircraft[135] master sergeant[136] and

12 aircraft mechanics

1 airman armorer master sergeant and

1 airman armorer

1 ordnance master sergeant und

---

[130] Indicating the frontline authorized strength, excluding reserves.

[131] The original German word was "Frontflugzeug". The literal translation would be "frontline aircraft". Implied here is the Ju 87, although this word could be used interchangeably across fighter, bomber or other units to indicate the main aircraft used.

[132] See Glossary: Staffel H.Q. (Staffeltrupp).

[133] See Glossary: Company sergeant major (Hauptfeldwebel).

[134] Translation based on TM 30-506. Since this was a post, it is not necessarily a given that the individual in question would be the rank of a Sergeant (Feldwebel).

[135] In the original text "Flzg." is the abbreviation of "Flugzeug", indicating "aircraft", while "Fl." is the abbreviation of "Flieger", indicating "airman". This distinction is most likely made to highlight the specialisation of each role, separating the aircraft mechanics with the more general role of weapon maintainers. Note that "Flieger" is also used by the Luftwaffe to denote the entry rank of a soldier (NCO) in the Luftwaffe. See the listing of ranks in the Glossary: Non-commissioned officer with sword knot (Portepeeunteroffizier).

[136] Meant here is the crew chief.

2 aircraft ordnance personnel

1 aircraft radio master sergeant

2 transport aircraft

c) Staffel reserve

3 pilots

3 radio operators (gunner)

3 dive-bombers[137]

Total authorized strength of a Dive-Bomber Staffel:

6 officers

46 NCOs and enlisted men

12 dive-bombers

2 transport aircraft

As additional roles[138] the following positions are to be filled

navigational officer

technical officer

armorer and ordnance officer

radio officer.

160.)   The Dive-Bomber Gruppe[139] (Stz.Kpf.Gr. [140])

The dive-bomber Gruppe consists of:

---

[137] The original German word was "Frontflugzeug". The literal translation would be "frontline aircraft". Implied here is the Ju 87, although this word could be used interchangeably across fighter, bomber or other units to indicate the main aircraft used.

[138] These roles constitute an additional task or position and are not necessarily linked to the individual rank of the each solider. In each respective role, the relevant officer would be in charge of navigational, technical, weapon or communication matters.

[139] See Glossary: Dive-bomber group (Sturzkampfgruppe).

[140] "Stz.Kpf.Gr" is the abbreviation of "Sturzkampfgruppe", indicating "Dive-Bomber Gruppe".

the Stab of a dive-bomber Gruppe and

3 dive-bomber Staffeln.

The Stab of a Dive-Bomber Gruppe (Stb.Stz.Kpf.Gr. [141])

(Table of organization and equipment Nr. 1186 (L))

a) Gruppen Stab

1 commander of the dive-bomber Gruppe

1 adjutant

1 Major at the Stab[142]

1 navigation and radio officer

1 technical officer

3 clerks

1 technical civil servant for weapons

4 quartermaster sergeants[143] (aircraft)

b) Gruppe administration

1 civil servant administrator

1 administrator master sergeant

c) Aircraft group[144]

5 pilots

---

[141] "Stb.Stz.Kpf.Gr" is the abbreviation of "Stab der Sturzkampfgruppe", indicating "Stab of the Dive-Bomber Gruppe".

[142] The original German word was "Major beim Stabe", the literal translation would be "Major at the staff".

[143] Translation based on *TM 30-506*. Since this was a post, it is not necessarily a given that the individual in question would be the rank of a Sergeant (Feldwebel). The literal translation of "Gerätverwalter" would be "equipment administrator".

[144] The original German word was "Flugzeuggruppe". The literal translation is "aircraft group", which in this case is applicable. Meant here is not the Gruppe as a whole, as this would include the attached Staffeln, but rather the group of men and aircraft within the Gruppe command.

3 observers (Lte.)[145]

8 radio operators (gunner)

2 aircraft flight engineers (gunner)

1 aircraft master sergeant[146] and

3 aircraft mechanic

1 ordnance master sergeant and

1 aircraft ordnance personnel[147]

1 aircraft radio master sergeant

3 dive-bombers[148] (as Stabs Kette[149])

3 reconnaissance aircraft (as Reconnaissance Kette [150] K)

2 transport aircraft

d) Motor pool.

3 drivers

1 heavy motorcycle with sidecar[151]

1 medium car

1 medium cross-country truck.

Total authorized strength of a Dive-Bomber Gruppe:

8 officers

---

[145] It is unclear what is meant by "Lte.".

[146] Meant here is the crew chief.

[147] Note that there appears to be no armorer in the line-up of the Gruppe command. This is most likely because this role could be covered by the ordnance personnel or because the command would be stationed on the same airfield as a Staffel and could thus rely on their armorers.

[148] Instead of "Frontflugzeuge" as with the previous entries, the original text used "Sturzkampfflugzeuge", which translate directly to dive-bombers.

[149] See Glossary: Leading flight (Führungskette).

[150] See Glossary: Reconnaissance aircraft K (K-Aufklärungsflugzeug).

[151] See Glossary: Motorcycle (Krad).

2 civil servants

33 NCOs and enlisted men

3 dive-bombers

3 reconnaissance aircraft

2 transport aircraft

2 vehicles

1 motorcycle with a sidecar

The role of motor pool officer is to be filled.

The Dive-Bomber Geschwader[152] (Stz.Kpf.Geschw. [153])

161.) The dive-bomber Gruppe consists of:

the Stab of a dive-bomber Geschwader and

3 dive-bomber Gruppen.

162.) The Stab of a Dive-Bomber Geschwaders (Stb.Stz.Kpf.Geschw.[154])

(Table of organization and equipment[155] Nr. 1185 (L))

1 Kommodore[156]

1 adjutant

1 officer of the air signal units[157]

1 technical officer

4 clerks

---

[152] See Glossary: Dive-bomber wing (Sturzkampfgeschwader).
[153] "Stz.Kpf.Geschw" is the abbreviation of "Sturzkampfgeschwader, indicating "Dive-Bomber Gruppe".
[154] "Stab.Stz.Kpf.Geschw" is the abbreviation of "Sturzkampfgeschwaders", indicating "Command of the Dive-Bomber Geschwader".
[155] See Glossary: Table of organization and equipment (Kriegsstärkenachweisung).
[156] "Kommodore" was the name given to the Geschwader commander. Although translated it could be written as "Commodore", we have opted to retain the original German role name given the prominence of this position.
[157] See Glossary: Air signals units (Luftnachrichtentruppe).

3 drivers

1 motorcycle with a sidecar

1 medium car

1 medium cross-country truck

4 pilots

5 radio operators (gunner)

2 flight engineers (gunner)

1 aircraft master sergeant[158]

3 aircraft mechanics

1 ordnance master sergeant

1 aircraft ordnance personnel

1 airman armorer master sergeant

1 aircraft radio master sergeant

3 dive-bombers[159]

2 couriers[160] (1 = A/B1 and 1 = B2)[161]

1 transport aircraft.

Total authorized strength of a Sturzkampfgeschwader Command:

4 officers

26 NCOs and enlisted men

---

[158] Meant here is the crew chief.

[159] The original German word was "Frontflugzeug". The literal translation would be "frontline aircraft". Implied here is the Ju 87, although this word could be used interchangeably across fighter, bomber or other units to indicate the main aircraft used.

[160] See Glossary: Courier aircraft (Reiseflugzeug).

[161] See Glossary: Aircraft-class (Flugzeugklasse).

3 dive-bombers[162]

2 couriers

1 transport aircraft.

3. Employment Guidelines.

General Employment Guidelines[163].

163.) Employment must be carried out in consideration of the currently still limited flight range from airports that should be as close as possible to the frontlines.

As a rule, the dive-bomber is to be assigned only those targets which cannot be successfully engaged, or only with a disproportionately high expenditure of forces and ammunition, by bomber formations. (Sniper among the bombers.)

Since point targets can only be detected and attacked during daylight hours, the dive-bombers are employed only during daylight hours. Naturally, this does not exclude an approach at dawn or a return flight at dusk.

The principles for employment orders and reconnaissance are analogous to those applicable to the bombers, but, as a rule, the dive-bomber formations will not take off until the weather conditions at the target have been reported.

164.) The most favorable weather conditions are cloudless or with scattered cloud cover. Less favorable are those that force a flight in broken or overcast weather conditions, since orientation during the approach is more difficult due to poor or missing ground references.

165.) Unfavorable are weather conditions with low, multi-level and overcast cloud cover. In this circumstance, the approach and attack must be carried out in low-level flight, with the abandonment of the dive attack.

---

[162] The original German word was "Frontflugzeug". The literal translation would be "frontline aircraft". Implied here is the Ju 87, although this word could be used interchangeably across fighter, bomber or other units to indicate the main aircraft used.

[163] In the other chapters included in *Aerial Tactics: The Dive-Bomber*, the sub-sections found in *Employment Guidelines* were continuously sorted by a lettered breakdown, starting at a) with sequential alphabetical headers. In the dive-bomber chapter, this was not done and as such we also did not add additional alphabetical headers.

En-Route and Approach.[164]

166.) Special emphasis must be placed on the thorough preparation of the attack. Every crew must be precisely informed about the planned route, approach, departure and return flight route. Detailed study of the location and appearance of the target based on maps, target sketches or, if possible, photographs are essential, as are precise course calculations.

167.) The route [to the target] must be such that it remains undetected by enemy aircraft warning service[165], reconnaissance and fighter aircraft. The dive-bomber's strength is the surprise attack. Changing course and taking advantage of cloud formation deceive the enemy aircraft warning service. Known defensive areas should be avoided if possible. Air combat before the dive attack is to be avoided. Bad weather areas are to be flown around.

168.) In case of uncertain weather, the route [to the target] should not focus on the target itself, but at prominent landmarks (lake area, river section) that ease orientation. The course must be set towards the center of this area so that it can still be found even with a deviation from the intended course.

169.) The dive-bomber Staffel usually flies[166] in a loose flight line astern[167]. Employment of a single Kette[168] is generally sufficient to destroy a point target[169].

170.) About 10 km[170] before the target, the approach to the target begins. For this, a loose left or right echelon[171] is particularly suitable.

---

[164] Given the context, in German "Anmarsch" implies a longer distance, whereas "Anflug" suggests the final stretch to the target. As such, we have translated "Anflug" with "approach". While a possible solution would be translating "Anmarsch" to "approach march", this might be confusing and not exactly fitting as "march" generally has a ground-based connotation. Equally, the text often used the word "marsch" to signify movement of a flight or formation. Due to this and the constant changes in context, a repeated use of the English word "march" might be the cause of some confusion. As such, we have translated the text in such a way that we avoid the use of "march" and maintain a distinction from approach by translating "Anmarsch" with "en-route" or "route [to the target]".

[165] Ground based observers that spot and track incoming and outgoing flights. See for example the British Observer Corps during the Battle of Britain.

[166] The original German word was "marschiert", which translates to "marches". We have changed this to "flies" due to the ground-based connotation of the English word "march".

[167] See Glossary: Flight line astern (Kettenkolone).

[168] See Glossary: Flight (Kette).

[169] See Glossary: Point target (Punktziel).

[170] 6.2 miles.

[171] See Glossary: Echelon (Reihe).

The approach to the target is completed when the dive is initiated. Since an immediate dive is difficult to perform from high altitude (5000 – 6000 m[172]) due to the challenging target acquisition, the last part of the approach to the target is usually performed in stages and with a constant change of direction until the actual attack is initiated, which is at an altitude of about 2000 m[173]. See the sketch for the individual procedures.

To maintain surprise, the approach to the target may be made in a glide[174] with reduced throttle[175].

The Attack.

171.) When the approach to the target has been completed, the attack is carried out in a dive by the individual aircraft one after the other from the echelon[176] on the right or left. The bomb release is not made until the aircraft in front has cleared the target.[177]

The attack itself must be carried out with surprising speed, and with reckless, sacrificial bravado and it must deliver the direct hit. In the execution of the dive a distinction must be made between the

steep dive (60 – 85 degrees) and

shallow dive (45 – 60 degrees).

172.) The steep dive must be initiated from sufficient altitude. This gives the bomb the direction and speed of the airplane, which corresponds best to the nature of the dive attack and is therefore always to be attempted. The steep dive ensures the greatest accuracy and the greatest penetrating power of the bomb. The most favorable release altitude is about 600 m[178]. (See section: The minimum release altitude).

173.) The shallow dive is used if a low approach altitude (low cloud cover) precludes the steep dive, or if the target can no longer be reached in the steep dive due to an error in the initial attack. The most favorable release altitude

---

[172] 16400-19700 ft.
[173] 6600 ft.
[174] See Glossary: Glide (Gleitflug).
[175] The original German words was "gedrosselt", which could indicate throttling back, or running the engine in idle.
[176] See Glossary: Echelon (Reihe).
[177] Meant is most likely that the previously diving Ju 87 has released its bombs and commenced its pull-out.
[178] 2000 ft.

decreases as the angle of descent diminishes up to about 200 m. (See also section: The minimum release altitude).

174.) For the hit result[179], the correct choice of lead point[180] is of decisive importance. The lead point is always different, depending on:

wind direction and wind speed,

dive direction and dive angle,

diving speed and release altitude.

The lead point must be developed[181] by each pilot during his training.

Influence of Wind on the Diving Attack.

175.) During the diving attack, the aircraft drifts in the air flow. Bound to a stationary target via the sight, this results in a continuously uniform change of the dive angle to the target, the extent of which depends on the wind speed and direction.

Headwind causes a shallower, tailwind causes a steeper [dive]. The effect is proportional to time, hence the longer the dive continues without wind improvement, the more the initial angle changes from the target. Accordingly, if a specific angle is to be flown, a dive that corresponds to the wind speed and direction must be improved.

The Transition into the Diving Attack.

176.) The transition to the diving attack is made out of the approach. On the one hand, by briefly aiming at a target, an approach with a simultaneous reduction in altitude enables a rough verification of the wind's direction, and on

---

[179] See Glossary: Score/BDA (Trefferergebnis).

[180] See Glossary: Aiming point (Haltepunkt).

[181] The original German word was "erwerfen". The literal translation could be "done by throwing". This is a very interesting statement, as it implies that each pilot is required to acquire a personal ("gut") feeling and judgement to have an intuitive understanding of bombing with the Ju 87. We have opted to translate "erwerfen" to "developed", as the process of learning to acquire this personal judgement happens as through gaining practical experience with diving attacks. One example can be found in Rudel's memoirs, where he mentions that, in terms of understanding dive bombing "the penny dropped slowly" for him during the practice attacks. This might support the statement that next to the theory, personal intuition was important to dive-bombing. See Hans Ulrich Rudel, *Mein Kriegstagebuch – Aufzeichnungen eines Stukafliegers*, 2nd ed., Limes Verlag Niedermayer und Schlüter GmbH, München, Germany, 1987, see *Chapter 1 – Vom Regenschirm zum Stuka*.

the other hand it improves the poor visibility to the target and thus makes it easier to determine the final dive position[182].

The diving attack can be initiated by:

by rolling to the side,

through a half roll or

by pushing forward into a dive[183].

177.) When rolling to the side, the aircraft tends to drift. This tendency becomes more pronounced the greater the airspeed during the roll. If it is not possible to initiate [the dive] from a stall, depending on the altitude the drift can have an effect of up to 1 000 m.

178.) The transition into the diving attack from a half roll requires a clean execution of this flight maneuver and may require that the exact diving position be flown inverted. The poor visibility for the formation from aircraft to aircraft, as well as the fact that the inverted flight easily puts the radio operator out of action[184], make this transition into the dive seem less suitable for the Ju 87 type.

179.) The most favorable transition into the dive must be considered the forward dive in the direction of the target. It can be performed at any time without causing the airplane to drift and ensures the earliest possible target acquisition.

Dive Direction and Dive Altitude.

180.) Diving against and with the wind are the most favorable directions for carrying out the attack. In both cases there is little or no drift from the target. Due

---

[182] See Glossary: Dive position (Sturzansatzposition). Emphasis original, this might be a formatting mistake.

[183] Although nowadays the half roll or inverted roll is, also through the liberal use of German propaganda footage from the Second World War, synonymous with the Ju 87 diving attack, as we can see from the following paragraphs, there were various practical problems with this which make it questionable how often it was used in practice. On the one hand, the half roll could confuse the pilot and gunner as the aircraft is pushed into the dive, while also being dangerous even in a loose formation. Equally, the chance of drifting off during the roll, and the need for additional diving corrections is increased by a half roll. Additionally, on a technical side the use of the dive recovery system which automatically sets the aircraft to a nose-heavy trim just prior to the attack makes an attack out of a half roll impractical, as the aircraft has a completely wrong trim setting for this. It is thus likely that most diving attacks went with a more straight-forward, nose-down diving approach.

[184] The radio operator in the back of the Ju 87 is only secured in his seat with a basic buckle belt, rather than a shoulder harness.

53

to the large drift, a wind correction angle[185] must be used in the case of a crosswind dive, which complicates the procedure and the aiming.

After a good initiation of the dive and with a favorable dive direction, a dive altitude of 1,000 to 2,000 m[186] up to the drop is sufficient both to achieve a suitable release velocity[187] and for flawless aiming.

The Dive Angle.

181.) From a theoretical point of view, the vertical should appear to be the most favorable dive angle, since in the case of the vertical fall, there is no need to correct for the point of impact from the lead angle (the angle between the trajectory to the target and the sight picture).

Practically, however, it is not possible to make a vertical dive directly on the target, so as to bring or hold the airplane in a perpendicular motion to the target. The practical execution of shallow dives has shown that the better visibility to the target makes a dive easier, and that the direction to the target can be slightly corrected in case of drift. The disadvantage of the shallow diving angle is that the necessary lead exceeds both the visual range of the visor and the visibility across the engine cowling.

In present conditions and according to the available experience, the most favorable diving angle is 70°. This angle balances the advantages and disadvantages of the vertical and flat angle.

The Minimum Release Altitude.

182.) The minimum release altitude is technically determined by the permissible pull-out radius[188] of the aircraft, a safety margin based on experience, and by the effective blast radius of the thrown bomb.

The practical values for this are compiled in "L.Dv. 366: Luftwaffe Regulation 366 – Special Guidelines for Diving with the Hs 123[189] and Ju 87".[190]

Maintaining a certain release altitude is required for both safety and accuracy reasons and require that the altimeter is set to target altitude before the

---

[185] See Glossary: Wind correction angle (Luvwinkel).
[186] 3300-6600 ft.
[187] See Glossary: Bomb release speed (Auslösegeschwindigkeit).
[188] See Glossary: Pull-out radius (Abfangradius).
[189] See Glossary: Hs 123.
[190] See *L.Dv. 366: Luftwaffe Regulation 366 – Special Guidelines for Diving with the Hs 123 and Ju 87*.

attack[191]. In the case of large differences in air pressure between the airfield and the target area, it is desirable to know the air pressure in the target area.

183.) For <u>details</u> on the <u>technical execution</u> of the diving attack and the <u>training</u> of the dive-bombers, see: "Pamphlet for the Employment and Training of Dive-Bombers" and "L.Dv. 20/2: Luftwaffe Regulation 20/2 – Guidelines for Dive-Bombing Training".[192]

Departure and Return Flight.

184.) The departure is carried out by low-level flight, taking advantage of the ground layout and overhead cover. This expediently disables the ground defenses and the enemy aircraft warning service and leaves the enemy completely in the dark about the return flight. Enemy fighters will also have difficulty finding the low-flying aircraft, which are well camouflaged by multicolored paint.

Outside the area of enemy ground defenses, the Ketten gather on the ordered return course. The return flight is usually made in the Kette, taking advantage of cloud cover.

4. Cooperation.[193]

185.) The same procedure applies as described for the bombers[194].

[The following section is found in the same publication under I. Die Fliegertruppe, A. Der Kampflieger, 4. Zusammenwirken on pages 75 to 80. See point 185.]

a) With Dive-Bomber Formations.

145.) The joint employment of the bombers and dive-bombers must be such that they complement each other in their effect. Within this common task (see section 1[195]), the dive-bomber formations combat the point targets whose destruction must be guaranteed. When attacking heavily protected objects,

---

[191] As a practical example, assume that the airfield from which a Ju 87 operates is set at 100 m above sea level, while the target is at 400 m above sea level, giving a difference of 300 m. If the pilot does not manually adjust his altimeter for the ground altitude of the target, he might misjudge the drop altitude and end up either in a very strenuous pull-out, within the blast radius of the bombs or experience a very violent man-machine-ground interface.

[192] See *L.Dv. 20/2: Luftwaffe Regulation 20/2 – Guidelines for Dive-Bombing Training.*

[193] In this section, found within the chapters on bombers in TsAMO, F. 500 Op. 12452 D. 239: *Aerial Tactics: The Bomber,* the sub-section's alphabetical headers were retained.

[194] See Glossary: Bomber (Kampfflugzeug/ Kampfflieger).

[195] See section 1. *Tasks and Applications* in this Document.

dive-bombers may be used to hold down enemy ground defenses, but for this purpose very accurate photographic images must be made available.

146.) To avoid any mutual obstruction, an exact distribution of targets and possibly a clear schedule must therefore be drawn up before the attack. The dive-bombers' attack should immediately precede the bombers' attack or, if the target area and the weather conditions are such that both cannot interfere or endanger each other, they should attack at the same time. An attack immediately after the bombers have dropped their bombs will seldom be practical because smoke and fire in the target area will often make it impossible to locate the point targets.

When bombers and dive-bombers are employed together, unity of command must be ensured by the higher command post.

b) With Fighter Formations.

147.) The cooperation of the bombers[196] with fighter units extends essentially to ensuring their protection during employment. Since the light fighters[197] currently have a flight time of only about 1 1/2 hours, they are able to provide protection only when flying over the front and in the vicinity of the front. This requires that they be informed at an early stage of the bomber formations' intentions. They can then also engage enemy shadow aircraft[198].

148.) The protection of the bombers over particularly dangerous sections in the enemy territory is provided by the heavy fighters[199]. Their employment is not to be considered as an escort aircraft, but they protect a certain area for a certain time.

c) With the Army.

149.) In the center[200] of a decisive combat action, bombers can be used where artillery with sufficient range is lacking. Furthermore, they can be used against targets where the smaller bombs[201] of the close air support units[202] cannot be

---

[196] This section was originally written for the bombers but also applies to the dive-bombers.

[197] Meant here are single-engine fighters. See Glossary: Fighter unit (Jagdflieger).

[198] See Glossary: Shadow aircraft (Klebeflugzeug).

[199] Twin-engine, heavy fighters. See Glossary: Heavy fighter (Zerstörer).

[200] The original German word was "Brennpunkt". The literal translation could be "burning point". We translated it with "center" since it implies that combat is in full swing and could potentially be decided.

[201] The original German word was "kleinkalibrigen Bomben", which literally translates into "small caliber bombs".

[202] See Glossary: Close air support unit (Schlachtflieger).

effective. Here, too, bombers and dive-bombers must complement each other in their effectiveness.

The combat is directed mainly against the enemy's supply of material and personnel deep in the enemy's rear are[203]. By obstructing or even preventing all types of supply, the aim is to weaken the enemy's fighting strength.

150.) As the decisive battle[204] approaches, employment of combat forces near the front becomes ever more effective. Attacks against enemy headquarters introduce confusion into the sensitive intelligence network and disrupt signal and command communication. Destruction of the field airfields of enemy reconnaissance planes hinders enemy aerial reconnaissance.

151.) Against an unshakable ground force deployed at the front, or at a position, an attack from the air does not generally promise an effect corresponding to the cost of the operation[205]. In the climax of the battle and campaign decision, however, ruthless employment of all available combat forces may be called for.

152.) To accomplish these tasks, the closest possible cooperation with the army services and the reconnaissance aircraft assigned to the army is required, especially when employment is against fast-moving ground forces (motorized formations, armored formations and rail transports). In such cases, it may be necessary to have bombers or dive-bombers on standby so that an attack can immediately follow the reconnaissance.

If the enemy marches with mass on a few main roads, the weight of effort[206] will be attacks on choke points (bridges, dams and trails ways).

See also the "Pamphlet for the Employment of Bomber- and Dive-Bomber Units against Fast-Moving Ground Forces".

---

[203] See Glossary: (Battlefield) Air interdiction.
[204] Note that instead of "Entscheidungsschlacht", the original German word was "Entscheidungskampf". "Kampf" generally refers to a "combat" action, whereas "Schlacht" stands for "battle".
[205] The original German word was "Einsatz", which can be translated as "employment" or "operation". We opted to translate it with "operation" if it is part of a concrete action on a given day, and "employment" if the use is more general or abstract way, e.g., part of employment guidelines. In this case we wanted to ensure that the intended purpose of this sentences, the questioning of the cost-benefit balance of an attack against an unshakable point of resistance, is clear. See Glossary: Employment of the whole unit (Einsatz, geschlossen).
[206] See Glossary: Weight of effort (Schwerpunkt).

d) With the Navy.

153.) The uses of the bombers in naval warfare are limited. Combat is mainly limited to attacks against naval bases and harbor installations. Only the dive-bomber is capable of successfully attacking individually moving ships. Since dive-bombers are not capable of flying over large stretches of water for the time being, employment is initially restricted to land areas. The pressure effect of large-caliber bombs can sink larger ships even if they strike in the immediate vicinity of the ship. In all other respects, section c) on page 31 of L.Dv. 10 Part 1 applies[207].

e) With the Aircraft Warning Service.

154.) In order for the aircraft warning service to function properly, it is desirable that the take-off of all bomber formations down to the Staffel, and at night also of single aircraft, be reported by the airfields to the nearest filter center[208] together with an indication of the expected flight and the time of return.

---

[207] L.Dv.10 – *Aufgaben des Kampffliegers* is *Luftwaffe Regulation 10 – Tasks of the Bomber.*
[208] See Glossary: Filter center (Flugwachkommando).

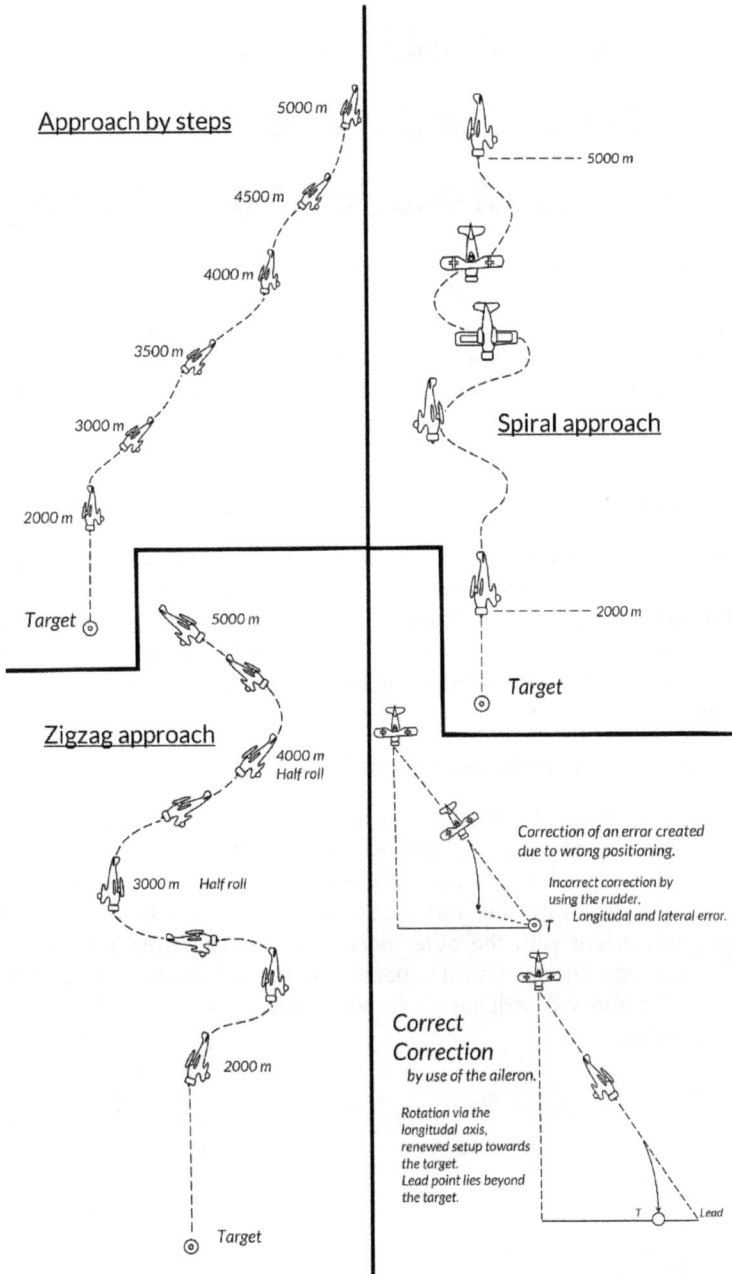

Approach by steps

5000 m
4500 m
4000 m
3500 m
3000 m
2000 m

Target

Spiral approach

5000 m

2000 m

Target

Zigzag approach

5000 m

4000 m
Half roll

3000 m   Half roll

2000 m

Target

Correction of an error created
due to wrong positioning.

Incorrect correction by
using the rudder.
Longitudal and lateral error.

T

Correct
Correction
by use of the aileron.

Rotation via the
longitudal axis,
renewed setup towards
the target.
Lead point lies beyond
the target.

T   Lead

59

Document: Pamphlet for the Employment of Bomber- and Dive-Bomber Units against Fast-Moving Ground Forces

This document is part of BArch, RH 19-XVI/3, *Pamphlet for the Employment of Bomber- and Dive-Bomber Units against Fast-Moving Ground Forces* and was referenced as one of the key documents pertaining to dive-bomber operations in *Aerial Tactics: The Dive-Bomber*. It provides details on the employment of dive-bomber units against fast-moving enemy ground elements such as motorized units or cavalry. It was written in September 1938 and was linked to a file describing the make-up of a Czechoslovakian motorized division.

Preliminary Notes / Source Situation, Actuality and Formatting

Throughout this volume, we aimed to retain some of the original formatting, yet the editorial focus lay on legibility. One of the main editorial changes was that, in order to present a clearer layout, we did not follow the original page count as this would have resulted in empty or near empty pages throughout the book. Instead, the text has been reformatted to follow a more conventional structure, page by page.

Please be aware of the following formatting decisions and changes:

- We corrected formatting mistakes in the original version (for example missing spaces, paragraph breaks or others).
- The original formatting sequence was retained, but we made some changes to transfer this document into a more legible layout that is consistent with the other documents found in this book. This also includes the deletion of unnecessary spacing between subs-sections.
- The annex describing a Czechoslovakian motorized division was not added.

Reich's Minister for Aviation   Berlin,   22.9.1938[209]
and Commander-in-Chief of the Luftwaffe[210]
Genst. 3. Abt.Nr.4300/38 geh. I.[211]   Number   309

Enclosed is the "Pamphlet for the Employment of Bomber and Dive-Bomber Units against Fast-Moving Ground Forces" as a guide for training.

To expedite the distribution, it is issued directly to the bomber and dive-bomber formations for immediate distribution to the Staffeln.

3 Appendixes

                                        I.A.[212]

                                signed v. Waldau[213]
                                        F.d.R.[214]

[A list of document recipients has been removed.]

---

[209] DD.MM.YYYY

[210] See Glossary: Reich's Minister for Aviation and Commander-in-Chief of the Luftwaffe (Reichsminister der Luftfahrt und Oberbefehlshaber der Luftwaffe).

[211] Generalstab 3. Abteilung Nr. 4300/38 geheim I.

[212] "I.A." is the abbreviation of "Im Auftrag", indicating "by proxy".

[213] General Otto Hoffmann von Waldau.

[214] "F.d.R." is the abbreviation of "Für die Richtigkeit". This is a declaration that the accuracy of the given information is confirmed by the signee.

Reich's Minister for Aviation   Berlin,   22.9.1938[215]
and Commander-in-Chief of the Luftwaffe [216]
Genst. 3. Abt.Nr.4300/38 geh. I.[217]

Pamphlet for the Employment of Bomber- and Dive-Bomber Units against Fast-Moving Ground Forces.

The employment of bomber and dive-bomber formations against fast-moving ground forces can, owing to their rapid marching speeds, only be successful if they can be caught quickly. An attack must follow reconnaissance as soon as possible.

This makes it necessary to keep bombers and dive-bombers on standby for a mission against such targets, so that they can be used immediately after combat reconnaissance.

In order to locate the reported enemy again, the shortest possible reporting route, the immediate reporting by the combat reconnaissance unit, the fastest possible transmission of the reconnaissance results to the commander responsible for the operation, as well as a short but accurate attack order are necessary.

In addition to the situation on the ground, the terrain provides clues for locating fast-moving enemy formations. Therefore, reconnaissance must be carried out especially against those areas through which the enemy units are most likely to have to pass (crossings, narrows, passes and similar).

Motorized units will mostly march at night. However, it will almost always be possible to detect the arrival and departure of such movements at dusk and dawn.[218]

---

[215] DD.MM.YYYY

[216] See Glossary: Reich's Minister for Aviation and Commander-in-Chief of the Luftwaffe (Reichsminister der Luftfahrt und Oberbefehlshaber der Luftwaffe).

[217] Generalstab 3. Abteilung Nr. 4300/38 geheim I.

[218] This most likely refers to the possibility to detect movement or the result of movement (tank tracks) from the air during the morning and evening lighting conditions. Interestingly, a related notice exists for tank units, where tank-attacks are meant to be initiated at dawn to "break into the enemy with the first 'hunting-light'". This lighting condition refers to German "Büchsenlicht" (literally translating into "rifle-hour") and is sometimes known

Large formations on large roads[219] will be detectable at night if weather conditions are favorable: this can be important in determining the whereabouts of the enemy in his assembly and resting areas for a daytime attack.

During the enemy's march, combat reconnaissance must be carried out especially to monitor the tips of enemy columns in order to detect in good time any diversion from the previous direction of march.

For the attack order, the speed of the march, i.e., the distance the enemy will have travelled, from the time of the combat reconnaissance report until he can be engaged, must be taken into account.

Essentially, there are 2 main scenarios to consider for the attack:

1.) The majority of the enemy marches on a few main roads. In this case the weight of effort[220] will be attacks on bottlenecks, (larger towns, bridges, forests, terrain difficult for the march, etc.).

2.) The enemy marches in small units on a broad front on small roads. In this case, the attack is to be carried out by deliberately abandoning the creation of a weight of effort[221] by dividing the attack forces into the smallest units (Kette[222]) against the individual parts of the enemy. This can paralyze the unified command of the enemy.

In both cases, the attack is to be conducted in depth, i.e., against the enemy's line of approach on a path leading toward the enemy.

Of the bomb types, the S.D.50 (later designation "P.C.50") bomb[223] promises the greatest effect against both motorized units and cavalry. In the absence of this bomb, the S.C.50 bomb is to be used.

More detailed information about Czechoslovakian fast divisions can be found in the appendices.

[Appendix has not been reprinted as it is not relevant to this book.]

---

nowadays as "golden hour" in photography. Tank units are to especially consider camouflage to prevent detection before this assault. See Bernhard Kast; Christoph Bergs, H.Dv. 470/7: Die Mittlere Panzerkompanie – The Medium Tank Company 1941, Bernhard Kast, Linz, Austria, 2019, p. 65, 67.

[219] The literal translation of "großen Marschstrasse" would be "large marching roads".

[220] See Glossary: Weight of effort (Schwerpunkt).

[221] See Glossary: Weight of effort (Schwerpunkt).

[222] See Glossary: Flight (Kette).

[223] See Glossary: Bomb types (Bombenarten).

Photo 3: A formation of Ju 87 B's flying over a beach, France 1940. Credit: Collection Roman Töppel.

Photo 4: Ju 87 B flying over a beach, France 1940. Two of the Stukas still carry their bomb loadout. Credit: Collection Roman Töppel.

Document: Pamphlet on Attacking AA-Defenses with Bombers

This document is part of BArch, RL 2-II/1029, *Pamphlet on Attacking AA-Defenses with Bombers*. It provides details about how bomber and dive-bomber units are to engage AA-positions and was referenced as one of the key documents pertaining to dive-bomber operations in *Aerial Tactics: The Dive-Bomber*. It was written in August 1938.

Preliminary Notes / Source Situation, Actuality and Formatting

Throughout this volume, we aimed to retain some of the original formatting, yet the editorial focus lay on legibility. One of the main editorial changes was that, in order to present a clearer layout, we did not follow the original page count as this would have resulted in empty or near empty pages throughout the book. Instead, the text has been reformatted to follow a more conventional structure, page by page.

Please be aware of the following formatting decisions and changes:

- We corrected formatting mistakes in the original version (for example missing spaces, paragraph breaks or others).
- The original formatting sequence was retained, but we made some changes to transfer this document into a more legible layout that is consistent with the other documents found in this book. This also includes the deletion of unnecessary spacing between subs-sections.

Reich's Minister for Aviation
and Commander-in-Chief of the Luftwaffe[225]
Genst. 3.Abt. Nr. 3550/38 g.(III).[226]

Berlin,   19.8.1938[224]

Proof.-Nr. 11

Secret

Due to several inquiries from the Fliegerdivisionen, the following leaflet

"Pamphlet on Attacking AA-Defenses[227] with Bombers" is enclosed, which is to be considered as a guide for training.

signed U e b e [228].

F. d. R.[229]

[A list of document recipients has been removed.]

---

[224] DD.MM.YYYY
[225] See Glossary: Reich's Minister for Aviation and Commander-in-Chief of the Luftwaffe (Reichsminister der Luftfahrt und Oberbefehlshaber der Luftwaffe).
[226] Generalstab, 3. Abteilung Nr. 3550/38 geheim (III).
[227] See Glossary: Open AA-positions (Flakstellung, offen).
[228] General Klaus Uebe.
[229] "F.d.R." is the abbreviation of "Für die Richtigkeit". This is a declaration that the accuracy of the given information is confirmed by the signee.

Reich's Minister for Aviation
and Commander-in-Chief of the Luftwaffe
Genst. 3.Abt. Nr. 3550/38 g.(III).

Berlin, 19.8.1938[230]

Pamphlet on Attacking AA-Defenses with Bombers.[231]

I.) Recognition Features of the Target.

a) An open, mobile heavy anti-aircraft battery is easier to recognize than a ground battery because of the required all-round view, which often prohibits its perfect adaptation to the terrain, because of its long barrels and gun carriages. As a rule, it forms a square with a gun located at each corner, with a distance of 100 m[232] per side, and, as long as it is not firing, it can only be made out by eye from medium altitudes[233] at most. From higher altitudes[234], aerial photography yields useful results. It is usually only recognized by its muzzle flash.

b) Light anti-aircraft[235] emplacements are only visible from low altitudes, since the individual guns adapt more easily to the terrain and are less conspicuous in their loose distribution. They are positioned close to or inside the protected object.

c) The 150 cm[236] anti-aircraft searchlights are placed in 2 - 3 circles - with the outer ring about 8 - 10 km[237] from the center of the protected object: the 60 cm[238] anti-aircraft searchlights are placed right next to the light anti-aircraft positions.

II.) The Purpose of Suppression.

The tactical purpose is achieved when, for the duration of the attack against the target, the enemy anti-aircraft defenses are distracted, divided, disrupted or paralyzed in such a way that their firing against the attacking force is interrupted

---

[230] DD.MM.YYYY
[231] The original heading was: "Angriffe von Kampfflugzeugen auf offene Flakstellungen".
[232] 330 ft.
[233] See Glossary: Altitude – low, medium and high (niedrige, mittlere und große Höhe).
[234] See Glossary: Altitude – low, medium and high (niedrige, mittlere und große Höhe).
[235] See Glossary: AA-defenses - light, medium and heavy (leichte, mittlere und schwere Flak).
[236] 59 in.
[237] 5 – 6.2 miles.
[238] 23.6 in.

or becomes inaccurate. Attack duration means the time during which the attacking aircraft move within the AA's defensive range. As a guide, the radius of the AA area is about 10 km[239] around the target. At an aircraft speed of 300 kph[240], the 10 km are flown through in 2 minutes. These 2 minutes are the most dangerous part of the approach to the AA area for the attacking bomber[241], because here a steady approach to the target must be made until the bomb is dropped, while immediately after the drop the aircraft regains their freedom to maneuver and takes advantage of it by changing course and altitude.

Against the smallest targets (guns, ballistic director[242], operating crews), a devastating effect cannot be expected.

III.) Ordnance.

a) Bombs.

1.) Bomber.

High-altitude attacks or attacks with cloud cover the prospects for hits are low.

Bomb type: 10 kg fragmentation bomb.

An interval bomb release[243] artificially increases the spread.

2.) Dive-Bombers.

Dive-bombers have considerably more favorable hit prospects when operating against heavy anti-aircraft batteries than bombers.

It is sufficient if a 250 kg bomb hits within the position of the battery during an attack by a dive-bomber Kette[244] against a heavy anti-aircraft battery. The blast can be expected to cause considerable disruption and damage, especially to the ballistic directors[245].

---

[239] 6.2 miles.
[240] 186 mph.
[241] Original German abbreviation was "K-Flugzeuge". Meant here are bombers (Kampfflugzeuge) and not reconnaissance aircraft. See Glossary: Bomber (Kampfflugzeug) and reconnaissance aircraft K (K- Aufklärungsflugzeug).
[242] See Glossary: Ballistic director (Kommandogerät).
[243] See Glossary: Interval bomb release (Reihenwurf).
[244] See Glossary: Flight (Kette).
[245] See Glossary: Ballistic director (Kommandogerät).

b) Guns (MG – and 2 cm-Cannons).

Firing with guns can only be considered from low altitudes during a low-level attack and has primarily a morale effect, especially due to tracer ammunition; the operating crews at the ballistic director and at the guns are unnerved, and increasingly disrupted. The ammunition consumption is to be limited to allow defense against fighter attacks, which may subsequently become necessary.

Against searchlights, machine gun fire is also useful from higher altitudes, even if the chances of hitting them are small. This action is carried out by the planes specially assigned for this purpose and by all the other planes already illuminated by searchlights. However, the aircraft not engaged in combat and not yet covered by searchlights must avoid giving away their position by machine gun fire (tracers).

c) Smoke Bombs.

The blinding of heavy AA batteries is accomplished by dropping a series of smoke bombs (burning time 3 - 5 minutes) windward[246] of the battery while flying low. The effect depends on wind strength, terrain and ground cover. Even a thin veil of fog is enough to make it impossible for the optical equipment[247] to work.

Against light AA, it is required to smoke the target itself as well as its immediate vicinity.

Visibility from above generally remains possible through a relatively thin veils of fog, so that the target remains recognizable to the attacking unit.

IV. Operation.

a) If enemy anti-aircraft positions are known, parts of the attacking formation are ordered to suppress them from the outset. The strength of these elements depends on that of the attacking formation as a whole and on the strength of the expected defense. It is to be calculated in such a way that the purpose of the attack is achieved in any case.

The detection and combatting of enemy anti-aircraft positions is all the easier the more accurate their position is known through prior reconnaissance (aerial photography!).

---

[246] See Glossary: Windward (Luv).
[247] AA-Defenses used optical range finding equipment to locate and establish the range to the target bombers, in order to calculate the correct lead for the guns and fuze setting for the ammunition.

b) If, despite previous reconnaissance, anti-aircraft positions are not known, but are suspected, parts of the attacking formation must also be assigned to combat them from the outset. These units carefully monitor the terrain near the target and engage the anti-aircraft defenses as soon as they are detected, which is usually not until their muzzle flashes are visible.

Detailed map and target study simplifies the finding of anti-aircraft positions and prevents unnecessary searching of areas unsuitable for AA use.

If no AA is detected during the bomber attack, the parts designated to engage it [AA] will participate in the attack of their formation. The mission and target assignment for this must have been given in advance, and the bomb load must have been made accordingly.

c) To protect against unexpectedly appearing anti-aircraft defenses at the target, a portion of the attacking formation is to be given advance orders to engage these anti-aircraft defenses in addition to the overall mission.

When anti-aircraft defenses are detected, this element leaves the rest of the formation without a special order and engages [the AA]. A simultaneous attack, carried out from different directions and altitude, is desired. This makes it difficult for the anti-aircraft defense to establish a target and to concentrate its fire, thus fragmenting and diminishing their effect.

Document: Guidelines for Dive-Bombing Training

This document is part of the BArch, RL 1/660 L.Dv. 20/2 *Die Ausbildung im Bombenwurf aus dem Sturzflug* and was referenced as one of the key documents pertaining to dive-bomber operations in *Aerial Tactics: The Dive-Bomber*. There it was referred to as *Guidelines for the Training in Bombing from the Dive*. This regulation details the training of dive-bomber pilots, as well as the mathematical theory and basis for accurate bomb drops. At the end of this document, the official training documents showing practice drops and accuracy requirements can be found. It was published in April 1940 and although it was marked as a "draft", it does not appear to have been substituted by a "final" version.

Preliminary Notes / Source Situation, Actuality and Formatting

Throughout this volume, we aimed to retain some of the original formatting, yet the editorial focus lay on legibility. One of the main editorial changes was that, in order to present a clearer layout, we did not follow the original page count as this would have resulted in empty or near empty pages throughout the book. Instead, the text has been reformatted to follow a more conventional structure, page by page.

Please be aware of the following formatting decisions and changes:

- Paragraphs and sections that referred uniquely to the Ju 88 were removed, as they usually only provided a slight adjustment to the values and information given on the Ju 87. Where the Ju 88 was mentioned within the text, this was retained.
- Due to the mathematical nature of this document, it is possible that certain phrases or elements could be lost in translation. Equally, a potential error in transcription cannot be fully ruled out. As such, this document is not to be taken as an educational reference for actual flying and dive bombing by the reader. Equally, due to the very detailed nature of the original text, we had to be flexible in our translation approach to this document to ensure good comprehension in English. As such, various sentences, phrases or entire paragraphs were more loosely translated than in our other documents.
- The original formatting sequence was retained, but we made some changes to transfer this document into a more legible layout that is consistent with the other documents found in this book. This also

includes the deletion of unnecessary spacing between sub-sections. A footnote has been added in case of a substantial change to the document, or when we had to change the format, layout and sentence structure of the original for a legible translation.

- We corrected formatting mistakes in the original version (for example missing spaces, paragraph breaks or others).
- In the 3rd section of this document *III. Bombing Training* we had to make one major translation change due to the German word of "werfen" and "der Wurf". Literally, these translate to "throwing" and "the throw" (noun) and would sometimes be used as part of a composite noun e.g., "Bombenwurf", a "bomb throw". Another use of these words was to signify the exercise of throwing bombs, e.g., "das Werfen". Due to this, we often translated this to "exercise" where it is contextually correct. This hopefully results in a more comprehensible English text, where the repeated use of "throwing" in all its variations might have been more confusing.
- Some mathematical symbols like "v" appeared capitalized and non-capitalized in the original. We assume that this distinction (see Section B. Terminology) was made for the velocity of the aircraft and the bomb, or a distinction between different assumed speeds. Sadly, in the text itself it appears that this was done in an inconsistent manner. As such we retained the original capitalizations in the flow text but used a non-capitalized version in the Figures. We hope to remain true to the originally intended meaning by doing so but can not eliminate the possibility of errors. The Luftwaffe also standardized on the non-capitalized "v" for velocity (speed) and used "V" either for volume or as the bomb lead factor, as can be seen in BArch, RL 1/641, L.Dv. 8/1 (Entwurf), *Der Bombenwurf, Teil 1, Grundbegriffe des Bombenwurfes*, April 1941, and BArch, RL 3/8233, *Lehrblätter für die technische Ausbildung in der Luftwaffe, mathematische und mechanische Grundbegriffe*, Berlin 1938.
- This document was written in the German "Fraktur" font, with the exclusion of the header "L.Dv. 20/2" on the cover and cover pages, as well as aircraft type and squadron designations.
- The first two pages of this document were removed, as they served only as covers, detailing the same information as the current first page.
- The original mathematical symbols and formulas were retained.

L. Dv. 20/2
Draft

Guidelines for Dive-Bombing Training (Ju 87 and Ju 88)

Berlin, April 1940

Printed in the Reich's Printing Office

Reich's Minister for Aviation
and Commander-in-Chief of the Luftwaffe[248]   Berlin, 1.5.1940[249]

The Chief of Education and Training
Department of Regulations and Instruction of the Luftwaffe Inspectorate 2[250]
    Nr. 1180/40

Subject: Draft of L.Dv. 20/2

The following draft of L.Dv. 20/2 has been compiled in cooperation with IV. (Sturzkampf-) Lehrgeschwader 1[251] and K.G.[252] 30.

In order to provide the formations with a basis for a standardized dive-bombing training until the final training regulations are available, this draft will be issued to the troops

The draft is to be used as a binding basis for dive-bombing training[253] until further notice.

Proposals for amendments based on practical experience are to be continuously submitted to the R.L.M.[254] L.In. 2[255], so that they can be used for the purpose of drafting of regulations.

With the appearance of this draft, the previous "Guidelines for Training in Dive-Bombing" are obsolete and to be destroyed.

                                                                I.A.[256]
                                                                Kühl[257]

---

[248] See Glossary: Reich's Minister for Aviation and Commander-in-Chief of the Luftwaffe (Reichsminister der Luftfahrt und Oberbefehlshaber der Luftwaffe).

[249] DD.MM.YYYY

[250] Department of Regulations and Instruction of the Luftwaffe Inspectorate 2 (Abteilung Vorschiften und Lehrmaterial Luftwaffen Inspektion 2). This inspectorate was the Inspectorate of the Bombers and Dive-bombers, named so in October 1939. Eventually: Inspectorate of the Bombers.

[251] This is the IV. Gruppe of the training wing 1 (Lehrgeschwader 1 [LG 1]) which was not a dive-bomber flight school but responsible for additional operational training of dive-bomber pilots. Additional groups of training wing 1 focused on fighter and bomber pilots. LG 1 also flew operational missions, for example during the invasion of Poland.

[252] See Glossary: Bomber wing (Kampfgeschwader).

[253] The original German word was "Wurfausbildung". The literal translation would be "throwing training". We have translated this into "dive-bombing training".

[254] See Glossary: Reich's Ministry of Aviation (Reichsluftfahrtministerium).

[255] Luftwaffen Inspektion 2 (Inspectorate of the Bombers and Dive-bombers, named so in October 1939. Eventually: Inspectorate of the Bombers).

[256] "I.A." is the abbreviation of "Im Auftrag", indicating "by proxy".

[257] General Ernst Kühl.

I. Bombing Theory[258]

A. Basic Physics for the Drop from the Dive

The basic laws of bombing theory define the factors that determine the flight curve of a bomb. Mastering the bombing theory and applying it appropriately by means of a suitable aiming procedure reduces the errors to a minimum.

When releasing a bomb from a dive, the critical factor to consider is the distance by which the impact of the bomb deviates from the initial direction of flight to the target. This value is denoted by ΔX[259] (trail distance[260]). (See under section I B and Figure 7.)

The following section[261] follows the simplest laws of gravity. For simplification, air resistance is not taken into account, hence it is assumed that the fall takes place in a vacuum.

1. Free Fall from a Balloon stationary in the Air.

In free fall from a balloon s t a t i o n a r y in the air, only the gravitational acceleration g acts on the bomb. It influences the fall in such a way that, according to the known laws of physics, the velocity v[262] of the bomb after a time of t sec is

<u>Figure 1</u>

$$v = g \cdot t$$

---

[258] The original German word was "Wurflehre". The literal translation could be "throwing teachings" or "throwing doctrine".

[259] Standing for "delta X", whereby "Δ" usually designates a change. As such "ΔX" indicates a "change in X". "Δ usually designates a change. "ΔX".

[260] See Glossary: Trail distance (Rücktriftstrecke).

[261] It should be noted that each statement in the following theoretical explanation builds upon the previous one. As such these examples apply purely to the described cases as they are presented here.

[262] Used to designate speed (velocity), "v" is sometimes written capitalized or non-capitalized in this document. Here it was non-capitalized, while the equation below had a capitalized "V". We have standardized around the non-capitalized "v". Although in this document the capitalized "V" was more common, we changed this to "v" for three reasons. First, it is closer to the modern international standard. Second, it prevents confusion with volume, usually denoted by a "V". Lastly, the Luftwaffe had also standardized on the non-capitalized "v", and used "V" for volume or as the bomb lead factor, as can be seen in BArch, RL 1/641, L.Dv. 8/1 (Entwurf), *Der Bombenwurf, Teil 1, Grundbegriffe des Bombenwurfes*, April 1941, and BArch, RL 3/8233, *Lehrblätter für die technische Ausbildung in der Luftwaffe, mathematische und mechanische Grundbegriffe*, Berlin, Germany, 1938.

75

The distance [s] traveled is thereby:

$$s = \frac{g}{2} \cdot t^2.$$

Every object would fall in the same way in a vacuum. Weight and shape of the body are without influence here.

2. Free Fall from an Aircraft flying horizontally at Speed v.

In the case of a free fall from an airplane flying horizontally at velocity v, at the moment of release the following forces act

Figure 2

the horizontal speed of the aircraft v

and the vertical gravitational acceleration g.

The interaction of both forces results in a parabolic fall curve.

The path traveled by the bomb in the horizontal direction is

$$s = v \cdot t,$$

where v = velocity of the aircraft per second

and t = time in seconds.

Since the vertical force[263] is always the same, the shape of the parabola changes only by a different speed of the airplane. Figure 2 shows that the smaller the velocity v, the more elongated the falling curve.

3. Falling from an Airplane moving vertically downward with Velocity v.

When falling from an airplane traveling vertically downward with velocity v, the bomb has the same falling curve as in case 1. However, it covers a greater distance at the same time. The distance traveled by the falling bomb after t sec is

Figure 3

$$h = \frac{g}{2} \cdot t^2 + v \cdot t.$$

Thus, the rate of descent depends on the vertical component of velocity of the aircraft at the moment of release.

To determine the influence of velocity v, the dive angle α and the release height h on the trail distance ΔX, these will vary in the following cases.

---

[263] Gravity.

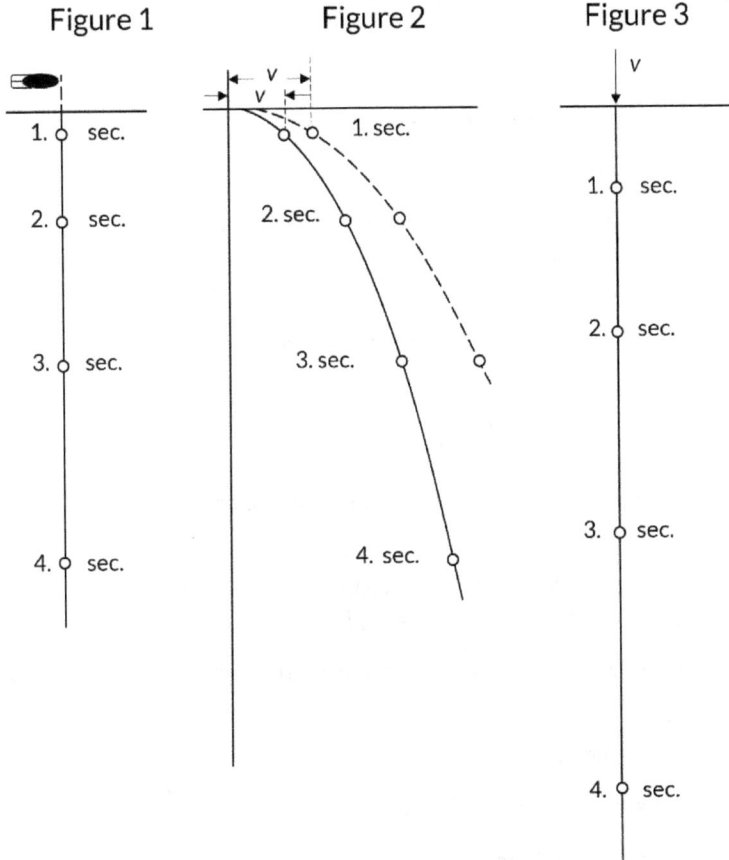

Figure 1   Figure 2   Figure 3

4. Fall from an Aircraft moving at Dive Angle α with Velocity v.

If, when falling from an airplane with dive angle α, the gravitational acceleration g acts on the bomb, the bomb's velocity at release v must be divided into a

vertical component v_1 and a

horizontal component v_2, which corresponds to the speed in Figure 2, but is smaller.

The paths of the bomb after t sec are

in vertical direction: $h = \frac{g}{2} \cdot t^2 + V_1 \cdot t$,

Figure 4

in horizontal direction: $s = V_2 \cdot t$.

This results in a parabolic fall curve.

In Figure 4 this parabola is drawn for two different release heights, h_1 and h_2. It can be seen that ΔX changes depending on the different release heights, according to the following principle:

The greater the release height, the greater the ΔX.

This results in the requirement:

Low release height.

5. Fall from an Aircraft moving with the same Velocity v, but with a changed Dive Angle α.

By increasing the dive angle α (70° compared to 45° in Figure 4) increases the vertical component while decreasing the horizontal component.

Figure 5 shows that the fall curve becomes stretched and ΔX becomes smaller. With a dive angle of 90°, $\Delta X = 0$.

Figure 5

This leads to the conclusion:

The larger α, the smaller ΔX

this results in the requirement:

Steep dive angle.

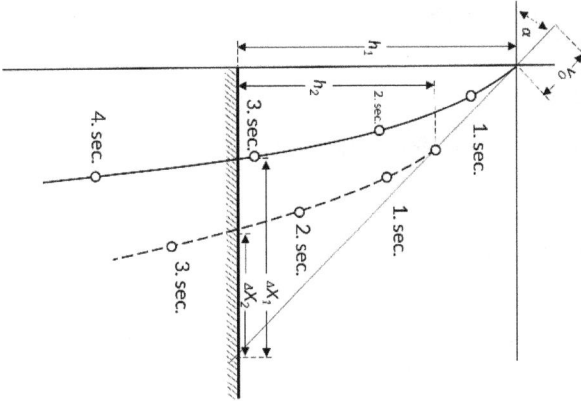

Figure 4

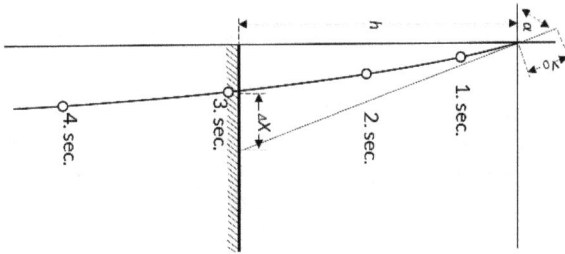

Figure 5

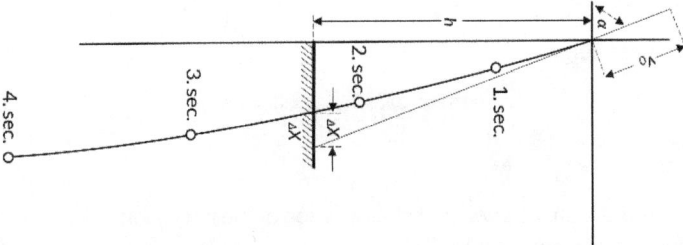

Figure 6

6. Fall from a moving Airplane at the same Dive Angle but with changed Velocity v.

By increasing the velocity v of the dropping airplane (double v compared to Figure 5), the vertical and the horizontal components increase proportionally.

This results in a more vertically stretched fall curve, hence for the same release height ΔX decreases.[264]

The ratio is therefore:

Figure 6

The larger v, the smaller ΔX.

This results in the requirement:

High dive velocity.

Air resistance changes these considerations only insofar as under its influence the drop time become longer and the fall curves more curved. The relationships between the quantities remain the same.

From Number 5 and 6 it can be seen that the same success occurs when either α or v are high.

A limit is set by the pull-out radius, hence the release height cannot be made arbitrarily small.

For a bomb to be thrown at a specific target, it is necessary to lead by the value of the trail distance ΔX at the moment of release. This lead is achieved by a corresponding lead angle in the sight.

To determine the lead angle, the following must be known:

dive angle,

dive velocity,

release height.

B. Terminology

Dive angle α

the angle difference between the depression of the aircraft at any point from the horizontal plane. (Figure 7).

Lead angle ε

---

[264] This is based on the given example which builds on top of the previously made statements regarding the behavior of a bomb. As such, this assumes a dive angle greater than 45°. In a dive shallower than 45°, ΔX would increase.

the angle difference between the longitudinal axis of flight and sight picture. (At the moment of release when there is no wind.) It is used to eliminate the trail of the bomb. (Figure 7).

Release angle α'

equal to the dive angle α reduced by the lead angle ε. An aircraft assumes this angle just prior to bomb release by correcting the aircrafts angle by the factor ε.

Wind correction angle[265] $\varkappa$

the angle, by which the longitudinal axis of the airplane must be corrected against the wind to compensate for the drift of the airplane by the wind. (Figure 8).

Lift or angle of incidence ϱ

the angle between the longitudinal axis of the airplane and the actual flight path caused by lift (Figure 9).

This value is negligible for Ju 87 and 88.

Release velocity v

is the velocity of the aircraft in the moment of bomb release.

Release velocity of the bomb V_0

the velocity of the bomb at the moment of release. It is equal to the release velocity.

Impact velocity of the bomb

the velocity of the bomb at the moment of impact.

Release altitude or drop altitude of the bomb h

the altitude of the release point above the target situated on the horizontal plane.

Throwing distance X

---

[265] See Glossary: Wind correction angle (Luvwinkel).

the distance on the horizontal plane between the vertical base of the point of release and the bomb impact point. (Figure 7, X can be found in L.Dv. 20/3).

Drop time T

the fall time of the bomb from release to impact in the target area (to be taken from L.Dv. 20/3).

Trail distance ΔX

the distance between the bomb impact point and the point at which the horizontal plane intersects with the extended flight line of aircraft during the dive (Figure 7).

Dive aiming point

the sight picture in the reflector sight[266], that is used during the d i v e .

Point of aim

the sight picture, which is taken just prior to r e l e a s e [of the bomb}.

Sight line

the line from the eye of the pilot over the dive aiming point and point of aim in the reflector sight to the target.

Lead point

the point on the target, on which the sight line is to be placed in the moment of the bomb release (influenced e.g., by the type of construction [of the target] or movement of the target).

Release point

the point on which the sight line was actually placed during the moment of bomb release.

---

[266] See Glossary: Reflector sight (Reflexvisier [Revi]).

Figure 7

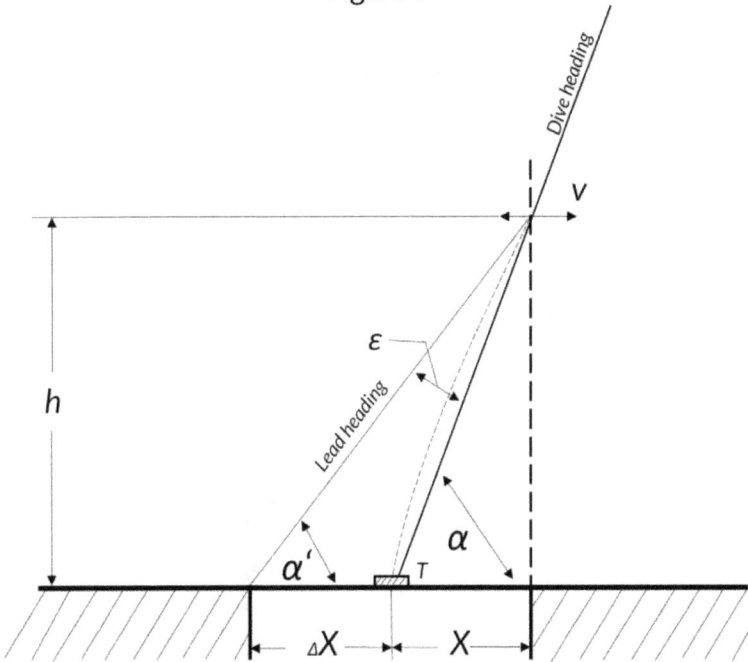

ε = Lead angle
(dependent on α and v and h)
α = Dive angle, α' = Release angle
ΔX = Trail distance
X = Throwing distance

C. The Influence of Wind on Bombing

With altitude, wind presents a sometimes unsteady current that changes in strength and direction. In general, wind strength increases by a factor of two up to about 500 m[267] of altitude, and less beyond that. The wind direction usually turns clockwise with increasing altitude. Measurements on the ground therefore only give an approximate indication.

Under the influence of the wind, the aircraft from which a bomb is to be dropped has a different flight path and a different speed relative to the earth than when

---

[267] 1600 ft.

there is no wind. Since the flight path and speed of the aircraft relative to the earth are decisive for the bomb drop, a straight flight path to the target must be achieved by eliminating the effect of the wind. Proper consideration of the wind effect is of the utmost importance for hitting the target.

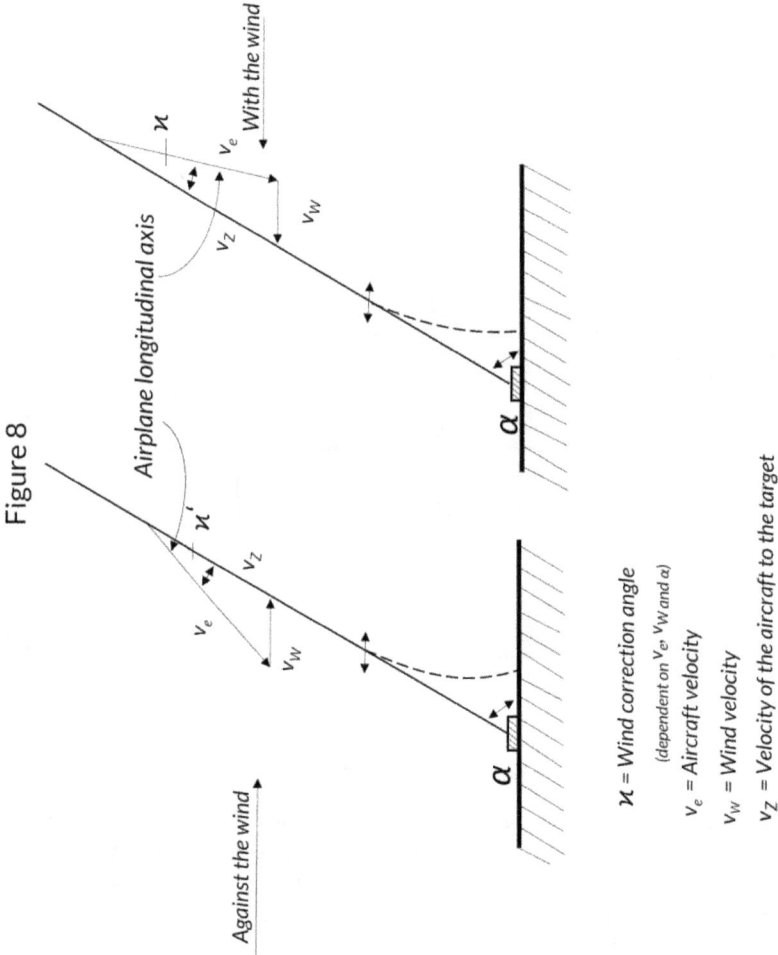

Figure 8

$\varkappa$ = Wind correction angle
(dependent on v_e, v_W and α)
v_e = Aircraft velocity
v_W = Wind velocity
v_Z = Velocity of the aircraft to the target

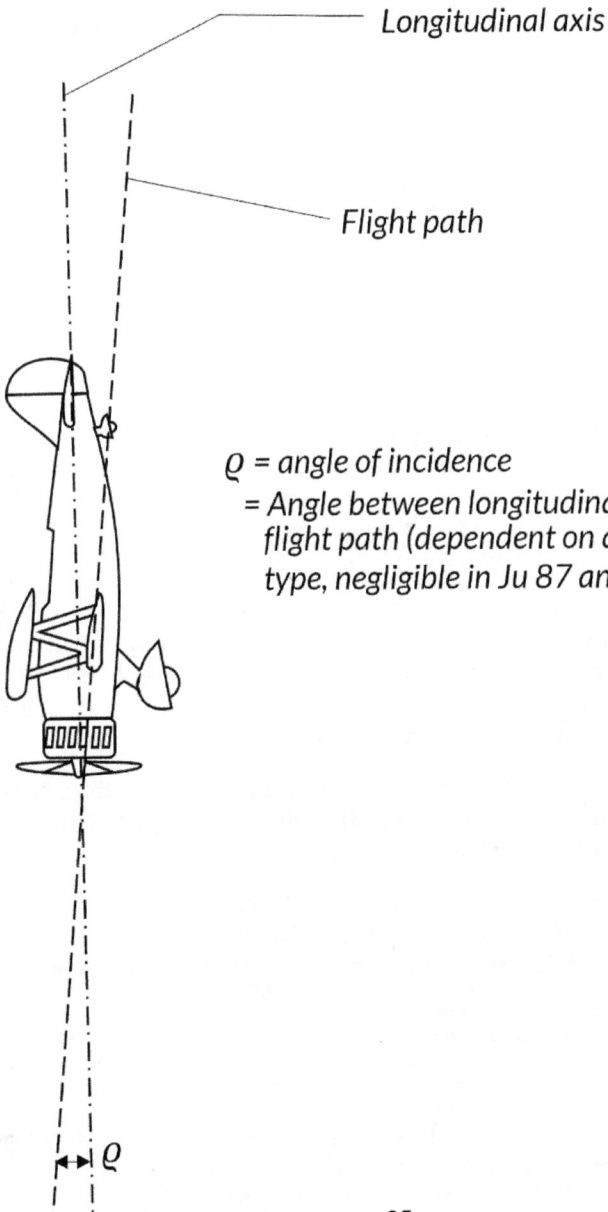

Figure 9

Longitudinal axis

Flight path

ϱ = angle of incidence
  = Angle between longitudinal axis and
    flight path (dependent on aircraft
    type, negligible in Ju 87 and 88)

ϱ

1. Influence of the Wind on the Dive.

During the diving attack, the aircraft drifts in the moving air flow. As it binds itself to a stationary target via the sight, this results in a uniformly progressive change of the dive angle to the target, the extent of which depends on the wind strength and the wind direction.

Headwind causes flattening, tailwind causes steepening, crosswind causes drifting. The effect is time-dependent, hence the longer the dive lasts without improvements of the wind [direction and strength], the more the initially assumed dive angle to the target changes.

Thus, if a certain dive angle is to be flown, corrections corresponding to the wind strength and direction must be made during the dive. The extent of the wind's influence can be determined by a wind triangle[268] or by calculation with the navigational calculator. In both cases the necessary wind correction angle[269] is obtained. The most common wind correction angles are listed in Table II.

At constant wind strength, the angular correction is independent of altitude throughout the dive. On the other hand, the margin of error [distance on the ground] is dependent on the length of the angle leg = release altitude (drop time of the bomb). The direction in which the wind correction angle is to be taken is always upwind from the target.

During a dive on a target, if the aircraft does not dive exactly against or with the wind, it is shifted to the side by the wind until it is pointed upwind. Only if the difference between dive direction and headwind direction is very small does it not have a practical effect. If the difference is greater, this effect manifests itself in a constant drifting of the sight line away from the target.

Furthermore, even when diving exactly against the wind, a drift in the sight line from the target occurs due to the fact that the wind direction generally changes [turns] with increasing altitude.

If a drift is detected during the attack, the target must be reacquired by applying aileron. This places the airplane in a better position to the wind. Towards the end of the dive or in the event of weak drift, the dive direction must be

---

[268] A wind triangle is used to describe the relationship between the wind and motion of an aircraft. It is broken down into four elements: air vector, ground vector, wind vector and the drift angle. The air vector describes the aircraft's true heading and true air speed (TAS), while the ground vector represents the actual motion over the ground, as well as the ground speed. The difference between these two vectors is called the drift angle. The wind vector describes the wind direction over the ground, and the wind speed.

[269] See Glossary: Wind correction angle (Luvwinkel).

continuously improved by control inputs around the longitudinal axis (= aileron). If the improvement cannot be completed, the remaining lateral drift must be considered.

A bomb released in windy conditions has the same drop curve in airspace as in calm conditions. However, different conditions prevail for the trajectory of the throw relative to the earth.

When thrown into the wind, the throwing distance of the bomb at the same release altitudes and velocities is less than that of the throw made in still air because the speed over ground at the release point is less than the airplane's own lateral speed.

When throwing with the wind, the speed over ground is composed of the airplane's own speed and the wind speed. The throwing distance is greater than when there is no wind because the ground speed at the time of release is greater than the airplane's own lateral speed.

In the case of crosswind, the bomb ['s trajectory] is influenced accordingly by distance and direction[270]. The drop curve is therefore no longer a flat curve. A spatial curve[271] develops, which is more pronounced the greater the wind angle at the moment of release.

The crucial impact of wind on generating a hit make it necessary that the direction and strength wind in the target area is determined before the unit attacks. It is desirable that the wind be determined at the altitude from which the drop is to be made, so generally between 2,000 m and 1,000 m[272] above ground or, depending on the weather, at lower altitudes.

Wind reconnaissance for the employment [of a formation] in enemy territory is conducted by the combat reconnaissance[273] as part of their general reconnaissance activities.

---

[270] The original German words were "Länge und Seite". The literal translation would be "length and side".

[271] Graphically, this would be displayed with a bomb trajectory on the z and y-axis (altitude and distance), as well as the x-axis (drift).

[272] 6600 – 3300 ft.

[273] See Glossary: Combat reconnaissance (Gefechtsaufklärer).

2. Influence of the Wind on a falling Bomb.

If a dive is made without a wind correction angle, the aircraft will experience considerable drift due to the wind, which is also inferred on the bomb at the time of the bomb release. On the other hand, the influence of the wind on the falling bomb after release is negligible (at a wind speed of 10 m/sec[274], the displacement of the falling bomb when thrown from 1 000 m[275] is less than 3 m[276]).

D. Sight and Aiming Method

When aiming, the angular values resulting from the different required improvements due to the throwing ballistics and the wind's influence are combined and produce a specific drop condition that is transferred to the sight[277].

Until the introduction of a gyro sight[278], which relieves the pilot of the task of calculating and compensating for the angular values[279], the reflector sight used for the fixed machine guns are used in the dive bomb aiming procedure.

The design of the reflex sight allows an aiming method that takes into account angular dimensions. Due to its infinite range[280], aiming is easier as the dive aiming point and the target are placed on the same plane.

The diameter of the aiming circle on the reflector sight corresponds to a distance of 10% of the target distance in each case, e.g., 10 m at 100 m[281] target

---

[274] 33 ft/sec.

[275] 3300 ft.

[276] 10 ft. This figure is an understatement as a wind speed of 10m/s would cause a far greater drift than a mere 3 m. The wind will have a similar effect on the falling bomb as on the diving Ju 87 which is not acknowledged here. This can be accounted for to a degree in the aiming procedure as will be shown later.

[277] A long-winded explanation stating that during the dive, the necessary corrections are made during the aiming procedure.

[278] A sight that could compensate for certain values affecting the trajectory of a weapon. In the Luftwaffe, these were generally known as "Kreiselvisier", which could be literally translating to "spinning top sight". A series of these were developed with mixed results and were known as "EZ-Visiere", EZ being the abbreviation for "Eigen- und Zielgeschwindigkeitsgesteuertes Visier", or "own and target speed controlled sight" in a literal translation.

[279] The original German word was "Fehlerwerte", which can be literally translated to "error values". We have stuck with "angular values" to provide a standardization with the previous paragraphs.

[280] Meant here is that the sight does not adjust for distance.

[281] 32 – 320 ft.

distance. The distances of the ends of the 3 crosshair lines[282] from the tip of the aiming post[283] each correspond to 1% of the target distance. Expressed in angular dimensions, the radius of the light circle[284] is 3°.

Due to the fact that at dive angles between 50° and 80° the total value of the lead and wind correction angle generally exceeds 3° would result in a calculated dive aiming point that lies outside the circle if the reflex sight is adjusted as for shooting. To remedy this, the reflector sight[285] used for bombing must be adjusted in such a way that when aiming via the aiming post[286], a lead angle corresponding to the average required angle is already used, or an adjustable reflector sight must be used.

In practice, it is advisable to base the adjustment for the Ju 87 on a lead angle of 3°. This means that a lead angle of 3° is always achieved when aiming via the aiming post, and a lead angle of 6° is achieved when aiming at the point where the circle intersects with the vertical axis [aiming post]. The upper intersection point of the vertical axis with the circle results in a sight line parallel to the adjustment axis and thus the sight line for shooting with the machine gun.

[Following sentences omitted as they refer to the Ju 88.]

The different corrections that must be considered during the aiming procedure are addressed below.

1. Effect of Lift.

In general, a diving aircraft has lift up to where the angle of incidence ϱ of the wings overshoots the vertical axis. The lift acts as forward motion, thus the airplane steadily drifts out in the direction of the upper wing surface. The factors of drift must be known by degrees and subtracted from the lead in the aiming procedure. (See Figure 9!)

---

[282] The original German word was "Hilfsstriche", which can be literally translated to "help strokes". For a visual representation of a sight, see Figure 12.

[283] The original German word was "Zielstachel", which can be literally translated to "target spike/sting". It has this name as the lower vertical line which was the main reference line sometimes tapered off to a spikey or pointy end. This design is generally referred to as a "German post sight".

[284] See Glossary: Circle (Lichtkreis).

[285] See Glossary: Reflector sight (Reflexvisier [Revi]).

[286] The original German word was "Stachelspitze", which can be literally translated to "spike top".

With extended dive brakes, this lift is not produced with the Ju 87 and 88. The lift moves around the zero value, probably due to the effect of the dive brakes, and can therefore be neglected in the target procedure.

2. Considering the Trail Distance ΔX.

A bomb thrown at a diving angle of less than 90° will trail rearward of the longitudinal axis direction of the aircraft by the trail distance ΔX. The value of the trail distance ΔX s taken into account during the aiming procedure by the lead angle ε.

The lead angles for different throwing conditions can be calculated as follows:

$$\varepsilon = 90 - \alpha - tg\ \varphi^{1})$$

$$tg\ \varphi = \frac{\text{Throwing distance}^{2})}{\text{Release altitude}}$$

Example: h = 950 m[287], v = 550 kph[288], $\alpha = 50°$.

From the table found in L.Dv. 20/3, 550 kph[289] at 50° diving angle and 950 m[290] release altitude result in a throwing distance of 640 m[291].

$$tg\ \varphi = \frac{640}{950} = 0.675 = 34° \qquad \text{(Conversion of tg 0.675}$$
$$\text{to 34° in tangent table)}$$

$$\varepsilon = 90° - 50° - 34° = 6°.$$

[One small paragraph and value were omitted as they refer only to the Ju 88.]

Lead angles for the most common dive angles and release altitudes are summarized in Table I.

3. Wind Compensation in the Reflector Sight.

From the information on wind direction and strength, the wind compensation angle for the dive is calculated.

---

[1]) See Appendix 3 for tangent table.
[2]) For throwing distances refer to L. Dv. 20/3 (bomb throwing tables).

---

[287] 3100 ft.
[288] 340 mph.
[289] 340 mph.
[290] 3100 ft.
[291] 2100 ft.

With wind compensation, the improvement is independent of the release altitude. For the pilot, there is no need to estimate aiming points; he uses the dive aiming point to aim directly at the center of the target or at a lead point resulting from the target movement.

The throw against the wind is the easiest to execute, since all corrections which have the purpose of taking or maintaining the correct direction are supported by the wind drift. The airplane, bound to the target by the sight line, hangs on it like a weathervane.

Throwing in a tailwind is more difficult in that the airplane, with a much higher ground speed, will be carried over or past the target very quickly if the wind direction is not quite right.

These disadvantages must be accepted and eliminated already in the training of the pilots by a lot of practice, because a throw with tailwind offers considerable tactical advantages due to the increased ground speed.

According to the different wind speeds, in order to obtain the correct dive angle in all cases, it is necessary, depending on the strength of the wind, to commence the dive later in the case of a headwind and earlier in the case of a tailwind.

In addition to the types of throws listed here, it is also possible to throw with a cross wind. The dive direction must be chosen so that it is approximately perpendicular to the wind direction, e.g., for a wind direction of 250° the dive direction must be either between 325° and 355° or between 145° and 175°. For wind directions that deviate more than 15° from the cross-direction, wind compensation is not feasible from an aeronautical point of view due to the difficulty of taking all movement components into account.

The crosswind is eliminated by the wind compensation angle in such a way that it is placed laterally in the reflector sight (see figures and practical examples).

To compensate for lateral drift of the aircraft, the approach and the dive position must be windward of the target equal to the amount of drift (which can be roughly estimated). The aircraft then dives onto the target with the longitudinal axis of the aircraft angled away from the sight line[292]. The additional trail of the bomb required due to an angular offset is negligible at the wind compensation angles that normally occur (at 50 kph[293] = 5°). Although the crosswind throw is the most difficult to perform from the air and requires practice, it will very often be tactically necessary, e.g., for targets which, due to

---

[292] See Figure 10.
[293] 31 mph.

91

their shape, require an attack in the longitudinal direction or obliquely to the longitudinal direction independent of the wind (ship targets, bridges).

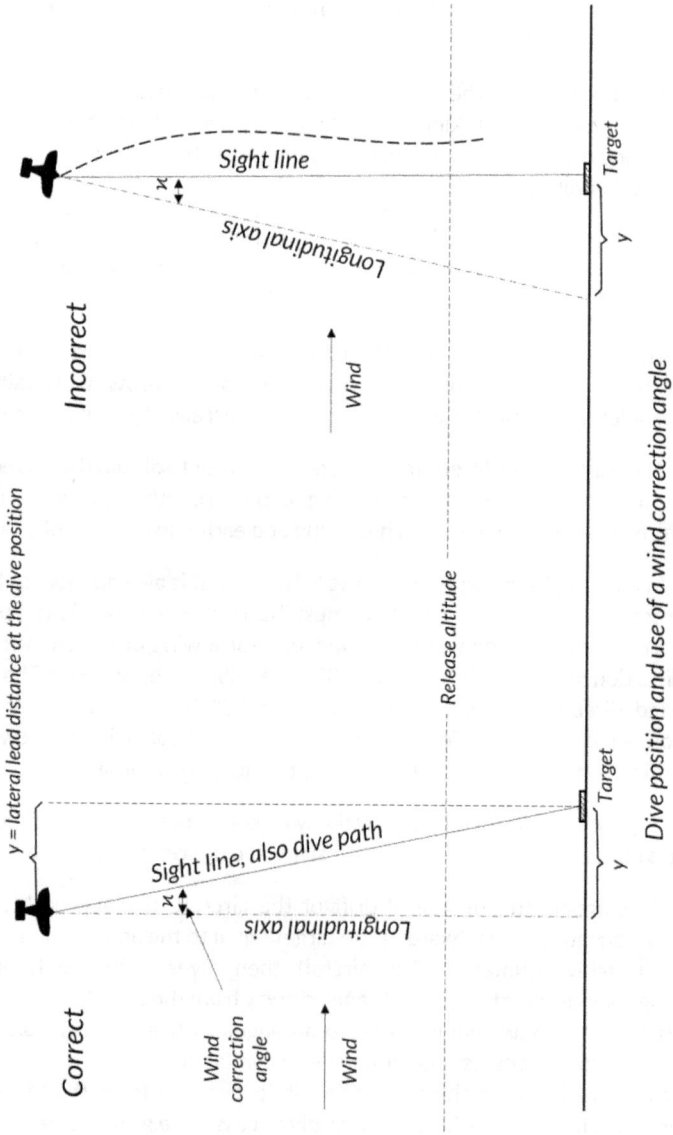

Figure 10

Bombing with crosswind (viewed in dive heading)

Incorrect

Sight line

x

Longitudinal axis

Target

y

Wind

Release altitude

y = lateral lead distance at the dive position

Correct

Sight line, also dive path

x

Longitudinal axis

Wind correction angle

Wind

Target

y

Dive position and use of a wind correction angle

Figure 11

Sideways view

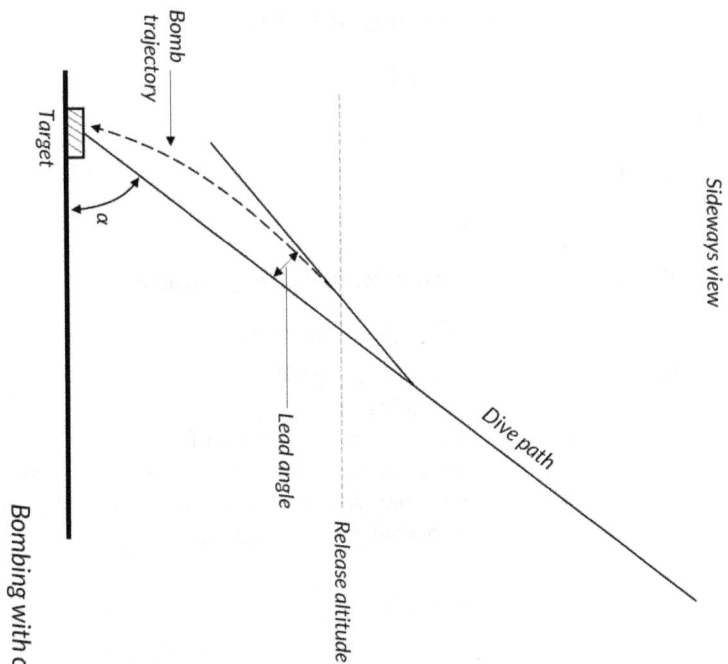

Bombing with crosswind

Bird's eye view

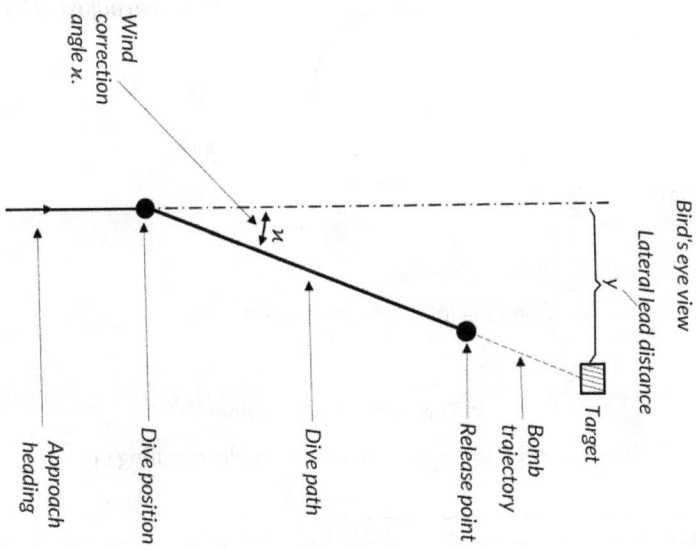

93

Practical Examples

a. Ju 87.

Dive angle α = 70°

release velocity v = 450 kph[294]

release altitude h = 700 m[295].

The lead angle (taken from Table Ia) is 2° for the values given above.

1. Throwing against the Wind:

An assumed wind from 270° of 25 kph[296] results in
directional dive heading 270°
wind compensation angle ϰ (Taken from Table IIa) = 3°
Consequently, the aiming point during the dive is – 3°, hence in this
case the sight post, with the dive aiming point for the drop – 5° (ϰ + ε),
2° below the post (see Figure).

Figure 12

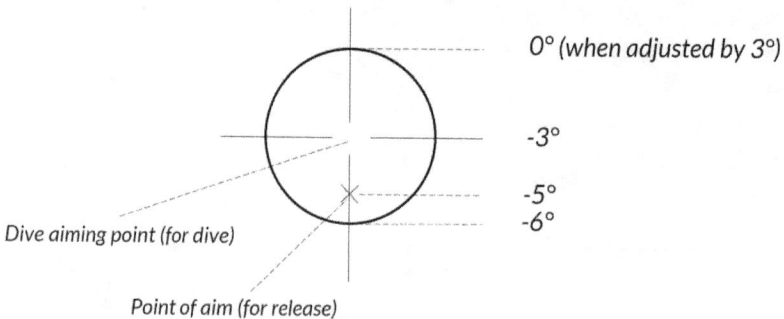

0° (when adjusted by 3°)

-3°

-5°
-6°

Dive aiming point (for dive)

Point of aim (for release)

Bombing into the wind (Ju 87)

2. Throwing with the Wind:

Wind assumed to be as in the first example, resulting in

---

[294] 280 mph.
[295] 2300 ft.
[296] 16 mph.

directional dive heading 90°
wind compensation angle $\varkappa = 3°$
lead angle $\varepsilon = 2°$.

The dive aiming point during the dive is + 3°, hence 3° above the circle[297], the dive aiming point for the drop is + 1° ($\varkappa - \varepsilon$), hence 1° above the upper intersection point [between the circle and the upper vertical post] (see Figure).

Figure 13

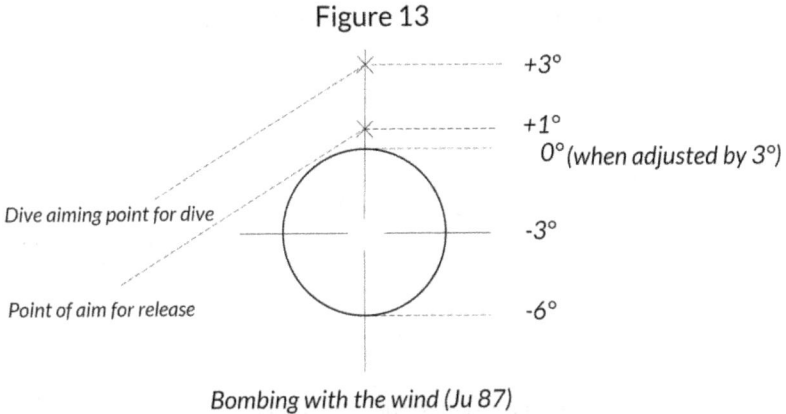

+3°

+1°

0° (when adjusted by 3°)

Dive aiming point for dive

-3°

Point of aim for release

-6°

Bombing with the wind (Ju 87)

3. Throwing with a Cross Wind:

Wind assumed to be as in the first example, resulting in a directional dive heading of

    either   180°
    or   360°.

In this case the direction 360° is chosen, resulting in a throw from the left.

    wind compensation angle $\varkappa = 3°$.

---

[297] See Glossary: Circle (Lichtkreis).

The dive aiming point is 3° to the right of the u p p e r intersection of post and circle on the reflector sight[298]. In this case it also lies above the right post and circle intersection.[299]

The dive aiming point for the dive is the same amount as the lead angle, hence 2° below the dive aiming point (see Figure).

For consideration of the lateral drift when starting the dive see section 3 paragraph 3 and following. Throw with a crosswind from the right has a corresponding wind compensation angle from the opposite direction.

Figure 14

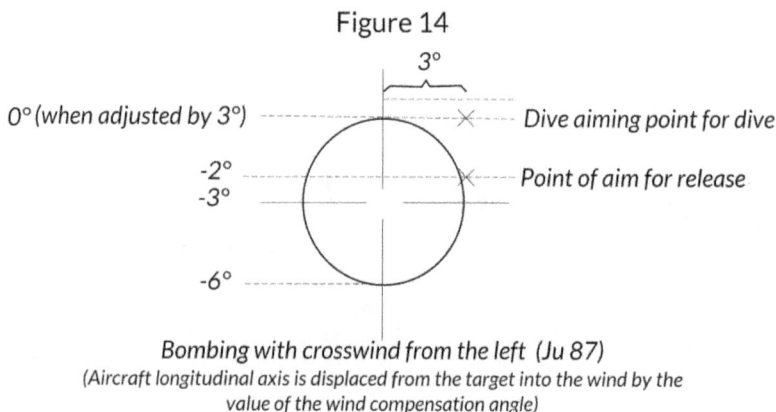

Bombing with crosswind from the left (Ju 87)
(Aircraft longitudinal axis is displaced from the target into the wind by the value of the wind compensation angle)

[Pages 24, 25 and parts of page 26 omitted as they refer to Ju 88.]

E. Techniques

1. The Transition into the Diving Attack.

The transition into the diving attack takes place from the approach.

The diving attack is entered by pressing [the control stick] in the direction of the target.[300]

---

[298] See Glossary: Reflector sight (Reflexvisier [Revi]).

[299] To make this short paragraph comprehensible in English, it had to be completely reformatted and split into two sentences. See Figure 14 for additional information.

[300] By moving the stick forward, the aircraft noses down directly into a dive. This was the most common advice when it comes to diving with the Ju 87 and is also the most straightforward operation of the aircraft given the technical workings of the dive-recovery system. The common depiction of Ju 87s rolling into a dive, often seen in propaganda reels,

This type of dive can be performed on any run without causing the aircraft to go into a sliding motion and ensures the earliest possible target acquisition.

[Paragraph omitted as it refers to Ju 88.]

The variometer must therefore be kept at 0.[301] When entering the area above the target, extend the dive brakes and enter the dive.

2. Dive Direction and Dive Altitude.

The most favorable dive directions for conducting the attack are dives with or against the wind. In both cases there is little or no drift from the target. A dive with crosswind requires a lateral wind correction angle due to the large drift and complicates the aiming procedure and the aiming.

After good dive initiation and with a favorable dive direction, a 1 000 to 2 000 m[302] dive is sufficient to achieve a usable release velocity and for perfect aiming.

3. Dive Angle.

From a theoretical point of view, the vertical would appear to be the most favorable dive angle, since in the case of a vertical dive there is no need to consider a diving angle.

Practically, however, it is not possible to dive vertically in relation to the target, so to bring or hold the aircraft in a vertical motion to the target according to the two planes[303].

The practical performance of shallow dives between 30° and 50° shows that the better visibility to the target is advantageous in the dive, and that, in addition, the direction of flight to the target can be slightly improved when the wind shifts. The disadvantage of the shallow diving angle is that the trail distance becomes very large and therefore the advantages of the throw from the dive are partly cancelled out.

---

can thus be considered to have been quite rare in actual combat. For additional information, refer to *Aerial Tactics – The Dive-Bomber*. See Glossary: Dive-recovery system (Abfangvorrichtung).

[301] The variometer measures the rate of climb and descent of an aircraft, in either m/s or ft/s depending on model, country and standardization. Ignoring all other factors, a measurement of "0" would indicate a horizontal flight, from which a dive should be executed.

[302] 3300 – 6600 ft.

[303] The horizontal and vertical plane.

Under current conditions and according to available experience, the most favorable dive angle is 70°. This angle combines and balances the advantages and disadvantages of the steep and shallow angle.

4. Minimum Release Altitude.

The minimum release altitude is technically determined by the permissible pull-out radius of the aircraft, a safety margin based on experience, and by the dangerous blast area of the bomb (see L.Dv. 20/3[304]).

Both safety and the dependence of achieving a hit rely on maintaining a certain release altitude above ground and thus make it necessary to set the altimeter to the target altitude before the attack. In the case of large differences in air pressure between the airfield and the target area, it is desirable to know the air pressure in the target area.

5. Aiming.

When using the reflector sight, a straight-line trajectory to the target is achieved if

in the absence of wind, only the lift angle ϱ,

with wind the lift angle ϱ and the wind correction angle $\varkappa$

are considered during aiming and the target is approached with the obtained dive aiming point.

If the lead angle ε is taken into account from the beginning of the diving attack, the flight path becomes steeper and steeper (hump[305]), hence the diving angle and thus the dive angle change continuously. The greater the lead angle and the dive altitude, the greater the effect of this error. See Figure 18.

Consequently, from the beginning of the dive, the corresponding correction of $\varkappa$ and ϱ must be taken with the dive aiming point

---

[304] *L.Dv. 20/3* is Luftwaffe Regulation 20/3. It is synonymous *with* L.Dv. 8/5, *Der Bombenwurf, Teil 5, Bombenwurftabellen*, which is Luftwaffe Regulation 8/5, *Bombing, Part 5, Tabular overview*. See BArch, RL 1/642, *L.Dv. 8/5 zugleich L.Dv. 20/3 Der Bombenwurf Teil 5 der LDv 8 bzw. Teil 3 der LDv 20*, January 1940.

[305] The original German word was "Hundekurve", which can be literally translated to "dog curve". This most likely originates from the curve running along a dog's back, for example a German shepherd, when it sits on its hind legs in an upright position.

aimed at the center of the target and shortly before dropping, the lead angle is pulled along the longitudinal axis[306].

Practical Example:

a) Ju 87.

The throwing parameters[307] for an attack are:

lead angle .... $\varepsilon = 3°$

wind compensation angle .... $\varkappa = 3°$

lift angle .... $\varrho = 0°$

After the transition into the diving attack, the target or aiming point is aimed at with the wind compensation angle $\varkappa = 3°$ (in this case = sight post[308]). Just before reaching the release altitude, the aircraft is pulled until the target appears above the lower intersection of the circle. At this point of aim, the target is held until release.

[One small paragraph and value were omitted as they refer only to the Ju 88.]

---

[306] See Figure 19.
[307] The original German word was "Wurfunterlagen", which can be literally translated to "throwing documents".
[308] In this example, the lower vertical (and main) post of the reflector sight.

99

Consideration of the ballistic lead angle

just prior to the bomb release

throughout the dive

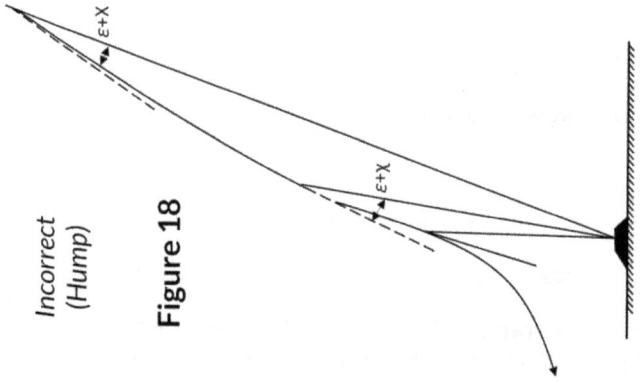

Incorrect
(Hump)

Figure 18

Correct

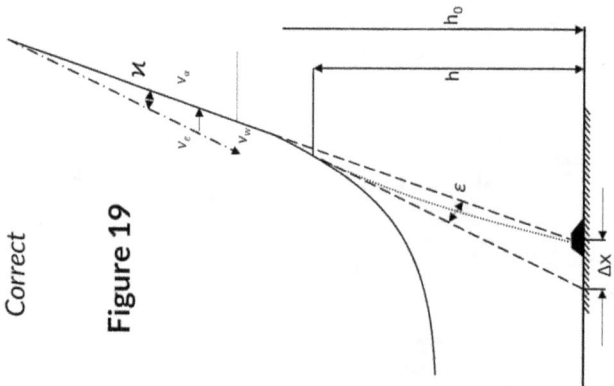

Figure 19

During the dive, the target is aimed with the reflex sight adjusted by 9° with the aiming point 1° above the upper edge of the light circle. Thus, the wind compensation angle of 5° (9° - 4°) is taken into account[309].

Shortly before reaching the release height, the lead angle of 7° is included so that the target now appears on the lower intersection point of the light circle. The target is held at this point until the bomb release.

6. Improvements in the Aircraft Attitude during the Dive.

Improvements in aircraft attitude during the fall will always be necessary, as it is seldom possible from the outset to adopt the desired dive angle and to fall exactly in the direction [or] against the wind.

Improvements to the dive angle can be achieved by pulling and pushing along the aircraft's longitudinal axis and, from experience, do not present any difficulty. If the pilot, after initiating the dive and acquiring the target or aiming point, recognizes that the angle is too shallow, he pulls on the longitudinal axis and then pushes again until the target appears at the desired angle. The reverse is true if the angle is too steep. A prerequisite for any improvement in the diving angle is, of course, that the pilot recognizes the factor of the required angle.

Experience has shown that improvements in the dive direction cause greater difficulties. Errors in the dive direction can be recognized as the target shifts after its acquisition.

At the beginning of the diving attack, the dive direction is improved by rolling [the aircraft] with the ailerons so that it heads to the target. The closer the dive approaches the release altitude, the more the target must be kept in sight by rolling with the ailerons.

Making improvements with the ailerons require a lot of practice and experience. This should therefore be taken into account as much as possible during training.

In principle, improvements to the aircraft attitude are easiest to make at the beginning of the dive. At the latest, at the moment of the bomb release, the aircraft must be at rest[310].

---

[309] Editorial notice: This paragraph was split into two sentences.
[310] Meant here is that at the point of the bomb release, the pilot is not adding additional corrections to the aircrafts heading and attitude, which could throw off his accuracy.

It is a mistake to make improvements with rudder, especially if an attempt is made to keep the target in sight by counter-holding with the rudder just before the drop. This results in a sliding movement, but it does not change the direction of movement of the aircraft.

As the airplane is operated over time, changes to the airframe occur which make it necessary to fly in each aircraft at regular intervals to adjust the rudder trim position. This is done by checking the position of the turn-and-slip indicator[311] during a dive. When the turn pointer deflects, the rudder trim is adjusted until the turn pointer remains in the 0 position. The flown 0-position is to be marked on the adjusting handle of the rudder trim.[312]

The lateral direction of the aircraft is also affected by the distribution of fuel in the wing tanks. It is therefore important to ensure that the fuel tanks are emptied evenly during the en-route.

II. Dive Bombing Training

A. General Notices

The dive and bombing training requires complete control of the airplane at high and low altitudes. The best basis for this is given to the pilot by a thorough training[313] in simulated combat flying.

Hereby he will learn to use the maneuverability of the aircraft for diving attacks and against ground defenses, as well as the disciplined integration of the single aircraft into the closed formation.

Practical training in dive and bombing must be preceded by a thorough theoretical preparation through the instruction in bombing theory. Only when the pilot has mastered the fundamentals of the theory, can he be expected to perform the required dive angles and maintain the necessary release

---

[311] A turn-and-slip indicator indicates both the rate of turn, as well as a slip in the aircrafts heading (for example due to extensive rudder input or an incorrect trim setting).

[312] This provides a visual reference to pilots where the 0-position on the rudder trim is on each respective aircraft, as this might be different between airframes and over time. It also prevents this setting of being "lost". As pilots would sometimes share different aircraft between them, this visual clue makes it easier to transition to an unfamiliar plane and find the proper trim setting. Also, future changes to the trim setting might take this reference as their starting point to make additional adjustments.

[313] See Glossary: Thorough training (Durchbildung).

altitude. Furthermore, the pilot must be made aware of the dangers of improper handling by the instruction in the operation of the aircraft and its stress limits.

B. Training Course

1. Acclimating to the Dive.

Practical training begins with the gradual familiarization of the pilot with the dive. Length and pitch are to be increased slowly, especially if physical discomfort occurs. Initially, pull-out altitudes should be set high enough to eliminate any danger of contact with the ground, even in the event of a gross misjudgment. Care must also be taken that the permissible stress limit is not exceeded during the pull-out procedure. Every airplane pilot tends to make this error during initial training.

2. Adhering to the Release Altitude.

Once the pilot is accustomed to the characteristics of the dive, he must learn to maintain specific release altitudes. This training is absolutely necessary both for achieving a successful hit and for safety reasons. It must be pursued until the pilot has acquired a feeling for altitude and thus becomes as independent as possible of the instruments.

Initially, the altimeter and contact altimeter[314] are available for this training.

Altimeter use is to be limited. It is to be remembered that its readout lags from 50 to 100 m[315] in a dive. Achieving certain release altitudes according to the altimeter alone distracts the pilot from the target just when the most precise aiming is necessary. If an altimeter with an acoustic signal[316] is not available, the standard altimeter provides only a rough estimate and should be used in conjunction with the pilot's feeling for the altitude to determine the release altitude.

[The last sentence of the paragraph was omitted as it referred only to the Ju 88.]

---

[314] See Glossary: Contact altimeter (Kontakthöhenmesser).
[315] 160 – 330 ft.
[316] In the Ju 87, after setting the contact altimeter to the desired altitude, an acoustic signal would alert the pilot that he passed this set altitude. See for example Junkers, *Betriebsanleitung Ju 87 B-2 Hauptabschnitt 90 Ausrüstung-Allgemeines*, Juni 1940, p. 12.

3. Flying specific Dive Angles.

If the instructor is satisfied that the pilot can maintain the release altitudes he is instructed to fly, then training in the flying of specific dive angles can commence.

The training method to be used must teach the pilot to set the dive angle in relation to the terrain, altitude and wind conditions. It must be chosen in such a way that the pilot can train himself.

The following procedure is recommended for this purpose, which is based on the theorem

"In a right-angled triangle the angle of the hypotenuse to a given horizontal cathetus[317] depends on the length (= height) of the other cathetus."

In training practice, this theorem can be applied as follows:

The instructor selects a route over an area according to a 1:25 000 scale map, the end points of which correspond to distinctive landmarks. The length must not exceed 1 km. The end points should be chosen appropriately:

a s   t h e   t a r g e t [318], a landmark clearly visible from the air, e.g., small water hole, small homestead, etc.,

a s   a   d i v i n g   p o i n t [319] o n   t h e   l i n e   o f   a p p r o a c h [320], a similarly recognizable landmark located where a parallel and perpendicular line [in reference to the line of approach] meet, e.g., intersection of two railroad lines, road intersections, etc.[321]

On the target, the desired dive angle is plotted on the chart, while a vertical line is to be established at the diving point. The extension of the angle leg at the point of intersection with the perpendicular gives the altitude from which the aircraft must descend to the target if the indicated dive angle is to be flown. S e e F i g u r e 20.

Based on this, the pilot is briefed on the target, the line of approach, the diving point and the altitude. When performing the exercise, he flies along the line of

---

[317] The "sides" of a triangle that are adjacent to the right angle are also called "legs".
[318] See Glossary: Target (Zielpunkt).
[319] See Glossary: Diving point (Abkipppunkt).
[320] See Glossary: Line of approach (Anfluglinie).
[321] Editorial note: This sentence had to be substantially revised from the German original in order to be marginally comprehensible in English.

approach and commences his dive on the target when it has passed through the bombing window[322]. After commencing the dive, he takes aim at the target and holds it in the dive aiming point.

Figure 20

Dive position
altitude 5500 m

Scale 1:2500

Dive angle 80°

Dive position 70°

Dive position
altitude 2750m

Dive position 60°

Dive position
altitude 1750m

Target

Diving point

Approach line

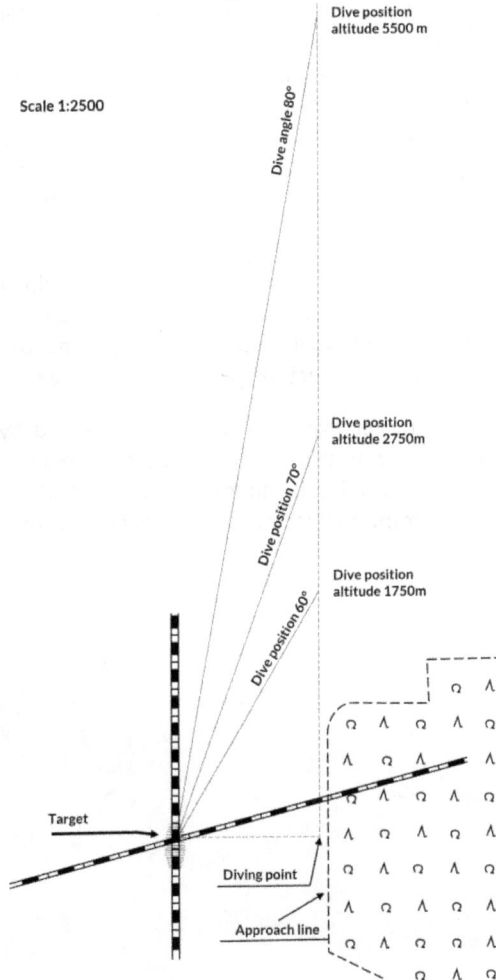

[322] On the Ju 87, the pilot could open a small window set between the rudder pedals. This allowed a measure of downward visibility and could be used for navigation (finding landmarks along the line of approach), or to judge the correct moment for the dive when attacking a target as explained here.

In order to check the dive angles and thereby eliminate errors made by pilots in estimating these angles during initial training, a dive angle protractor is used which can be easily and cheaply made in any air base workshop (See Figure 21). It consists of a sighting bar of 2 m[323] length equipped with a rear and front sight, which is mounted vertically on a rotating disc in such a way that its inclination can be read from 40° to 90°. The disk, which can be placed on a pole, and is mounted in such a way that it can be rotated in all directions with the sighting bar in the horizontal plane. It can thus be used to sight and measure dives from all directions. The dive angle protractor is positioned near a bombing cross made of white cloth or strips of paint, which serves as a target for the dives which angles are to be measured.

Through thorough practice on these fundamentals, the pilot will get a feel for the approach of the dive and for the most important dive angles. This will enable him to recognize a deviation from the desired dive angle and to evaluate it for the throw. He also learns how to detect the target and how to aim.

These introductory target exercises must be supported by instruction on maintaining a correct aircraft attitude and by briefings immediately after flight duty. Experience has shown that it cannot be assumed that the individual pilot will have the instinct for the correct improvements on his own.

---

[323] 6 ft.

Figure 21

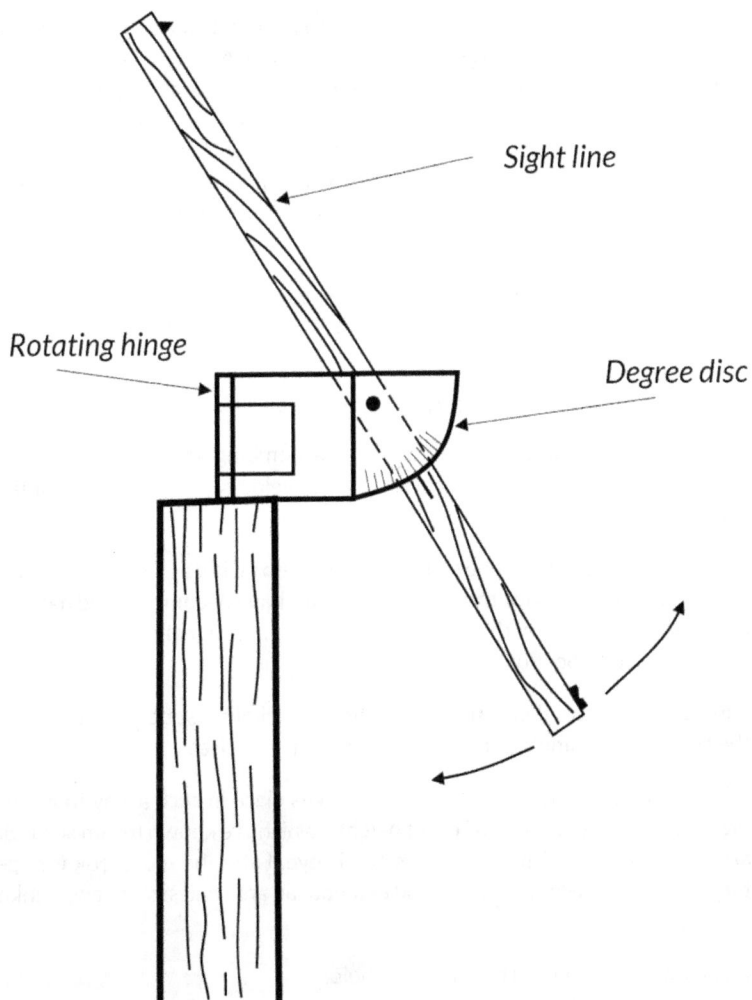

Sight line

Rotating hinge

Degree disc

Makeshift dive angle protractor

4. Flying specific Dive Angles in different Types of Wind while adhering to the ordered Release Altitudes.[324]

When the pilot's training has progressed to the point where he can perform the transition to dive and target acquisition flawlessly, the exercises are to be increased in such a way that he is instructed by the instructor to perform certain dive angles and release altitudes. While at first these exercises are to be conducted against weaker winds, later on more exercises must be flown against and with strong winds. In this way, the pilot should learn the degree to which the angle must be steeper in headwinds and flatter in tailwinds, depending on the height of the approach.

The best preparation for practical bombing is achieved when the diving angle of 50° or 70° is drilled into the pilot during basic training.

5. Training Bomb Aiming.

The final stage of preparations for practical bombing is the correct choice of the dive aiming point, which is determined by dive velocity, dive angle, wind influence and release altitude.

Here, too, training must be supported by theoretical instruction until the necessary factors for the dive aiming point have become second nature[325] to the pilot. It is necessary that the pilot has a perfect command of the basic laws of bombing theory (Section I).

In addition to this theoretical instruction, the pilot must be trained in selecting the correct dive aiming point through practical exercises.

The training in estimating target sizes takes place in such a way that the pilot first looks at targets from different heights, which are known to him according to area and size and memorizes them to his eye. Later, he must look for specific targets from a specified altitude and estimate an area and size that was unknown to him.

The following principle must be held:

---

[324] Yes, the title is that long in German too.
[325] The original German was "in Fleisch und Blut übergegangen", which can be literally translated to "transitioned into flesh and blood".

Before the student throws his first bomb[326], all the basics for this must be established through instruction and practical target practice. Only then will failures in practical bomb throwing be avoided. The instructor can verify the student's level of training by observing each approach from the target and he can, by using radio communications, immediately inform the student of any errors made.

6. Throwing a Bomb.

Training in practical bomb throwing is specifically covered in Section III (Bombing training[327]).

7. Principles for Approach, Release Altitude and Departure.

Soon after the bombing [training] begins, the attacks are to be carried out in a combat-like manner. This ensures that the pilot becomes accustomed at an early stage to approaching, diving and departing [from a target] under warlike conditions.

Under warlike conditions, a defensive force is to be assumed within a radius of 15 km[328] from the attacked target. The fact that defense must be expected in this radius forces pilots to take into consideration all possible opportunities to achieve surprise, such as exploiting the position of the sun, clouds and strong winds, and to arrange the approach, the release altitude and the departure in such a way that the effect of the defense is weakened in the event that the target cannot be surprised.

The possibilities of surprise remain unmentioned in the following, since they are not directly related to the bombing to be discussed here, but belong to tactics.

a. Defense on the approach and the required changes that result out of this to the approach.

The approach at high altitude lies within range of heavy defensive weapons (8.8 and 10.5 cm[329]).

---

[326] It is likely that a student is given the opportunity to practice diving with a training bomb first, before being allowed to drop these.
[327] The original German word was "Schulwerfen", which can be literally translated to "school throwing".
[328] 9.3 miles.
[329] See Glossary: AA-defenses - light, medium and heavy (leichte, mittlere und schwere Flak).

The use of these weapons is characterized by their long range (up to 12 km[330]), by the firing method with a ballistic director[331] and the spatial [blast and shrapnel] effect achieved by the delay fuze.

The long range results in projectile flight times of up to 25 sec. At short range, around 2 000 m[332], the flight time is 2 to 3 sec. Since the aircraft moves during the projectiles flight, a lead point is required in the firing procedure, the extent of which depends on the distance covered by the target during the flight time, the direction of flight and inclination of the target. Accordingly, effective engagement of a flying target is only likely if the target does not change the values for speed, flight direction and inclination on which the shot is based during the projectiles flight.

This gives the a t t a c k e r the possibility of at least hindering the effect of the heavy defensive weapons. This consists in changes of direction to such an extent that, depending on the flight altitude, the aircraft is shifted so far to the side that a lead point fired based on the previous flight direction is no longer effective. Due to the direct relation between the altitude and the projectile's flight time, only slight directional changes of a few degrees at irregular intervals of 10 to 20 sec are required when approaching at high altitudes (over 4 000 m[333]), but more rapid and significant directional changes are required at low altitudes (1 500 to 4 000 m[334]).

This consideration leads to a t y p e o f a p p r o a c h that takes into account the defensive effect and in the same way adapts the bomb throwing method.

As the aircraft enters the defensive zone, slight changes in direction are flown at irregular intervals with simultaneous changes in altitude. If the target appears to the pilot at an angle of view of 30° to 50°, altitude is also given up irregularly as the changes in direction become more severe. This approach, which ensures not only perfect visibility to the target but also good visibility within the formation, the aircraft flies towards the position from which it proceeds into the diving attack. S e e F i g u r e 22.

In addition to this type of approach, others in the form of spirals, straight-line stairs, etc. can be flown. In principle, however, the decisive factor for the type of approach is that any movement that places additional stress on man and material

---

[330] 7.4 miles.
[331] See Glossary: Ballistic director (Kommandogerät).
[332] 6600 ft.
[333] 13000 ft.
[334] 4900 – 13000 ft.

and perhaps at the same time disturbs visibility and the possibility of communication within the formation is wrong.

b. Defense during the dive, [and its] influence on the determination of the release altitude and defensive maneuvers[335] during the departure.

The dive on the target begins at an altitude at which the heavy defensive weapons no longer operate, and the light anti-aircraft weapons do not yet operate with effect. However, with decreasing altitude the dive enters into the most effective range for these weapons. For the time being, the departure lies within their most favorable range in all situations.

The combat method of the anti-aircraft guns is characterized by direct aiming with tracer use and a projectile that is effective only on impact. The aiming method is based partly on the spider-sight principle[336], partly on optical sights. Spatially, the majority of the anti-aircraft guns will be close to the target up to a distance of 1 500 m[337].

In both aiming methods, hitting the target depends not only on perfect aiming, which is made more difficult by the vibration of the weapon, but also, and above all, on the perfect acquisition of the lead point[338].

The greater the shooting distance, the greater the effect of a wrong lead point. Similarly, the greater the firing distance and thus the longer the bullet flight time, the more difficult it becomes to engage the target with the aid of the tracer. The sighting range of light anti-aircraft guns extends to about 1 000 m[339] for high elevation firing and decreases to about 700 m[340] on the horizontal. Within the sighting range, the projectile flight times are up to 1 sec.

---

[335] The original German word was "Abwehr", which can be translated to "defense". We have translated it to "defensive maneuvers" here, to make a distinction from its first use as Abwehr appears twice in this title. On the first mention, it signifies the use of defensive countermeasures on the side of the defender, like AA. We have retained this as "defense". The second use implies the use of defensive countermeasures by the aircraft during their departure from the area. To not conflate this with the defender or the defensive measures like AA, we opted to change it to "defensive maneuvers" as contextual information in the following section highlights the need for course changes and irregular flight paths when departing the area to present a more difficult target to AA.

[336] See Glossary: Spider-sight principle (Kreiskimmeprinzip).

[337] 0.9 miles.

[338] The original German word was "Schießunterlagen", which can be literally translated to "shooting documents".

[339] 3300 ft.

[340] 2300 ft.

For the attacker, this means that he must avoid the most effective area of action of these defensive weapons as far as possible or, once having thrown his bombs, he must withdraw [from the defenders] as quickly as possible.

During the diving attack on the target deliberate maneuvering to hinder the defense is not possible. Rather, the dive on the target must be performed on as straight a path as possible without regard to the defense. However, each new target correction means a drift of the target for the defense. If the possible defensive effect during the diving attack is to be limited, this can only be done by keeping the diving attack as short as technically possible.

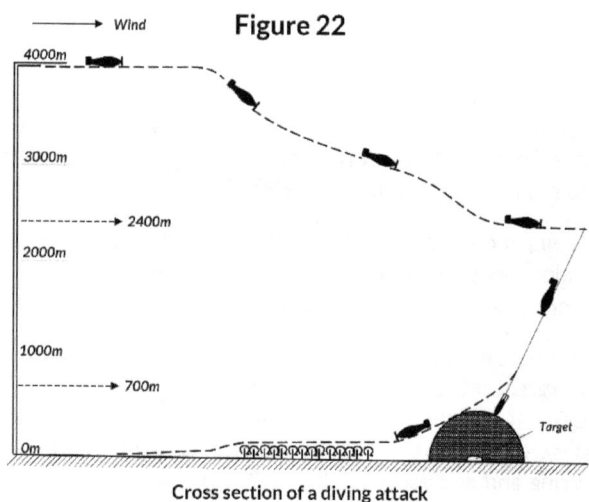

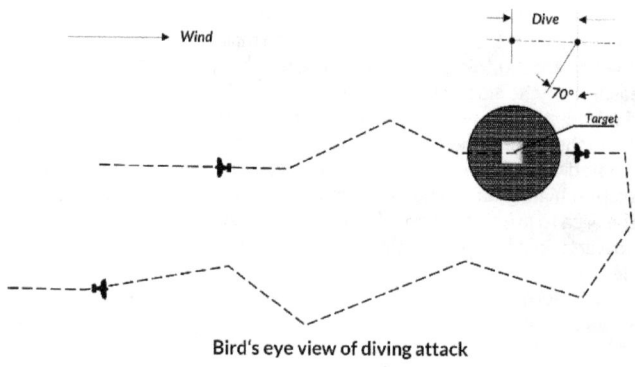

Figure 22

Cross section of a diving attack

Bird's eye view of diving attack

112

For the choice of the r e l e a s e   a l t i t u d e, it is necessary to balance the effect of the defense with the accuracy of the drop. For the time being, the release altitude of 1 000 m[341] can be considered as a release altitude that balances accuracy[342], the effectiveness of the defense, and the safety of the aircraft. The release altitude will increase as the experience of the pilots grows and the bombing sights improve[343].

During the d e p a r t u r e , the dive-bomber finds the best protection against defenses in its mobility. The direction is to be changed simultaneously with the pull-out following the bomb release. In the ensuing phase, while following a predetermined departure heading, the aircraft transitions to a low-level flight below obstacle height[344] with continuous, short-term, and coarse changes in direction and altitude. In many cases, departure through a climb[345] can also be advantageous.

After thorough preparation of the pilot in the courses on the employment and combat method of the ground defenses, it is the t a s k   o f   t h e   p r a c t i c a l t r a i n i n g to arrange the approach and departure so that maneuverability is practiced   by   frequent   and   supervised   exercises.   I t   w o u l d   b e i r r e s p o n s i b l e   f o r   a n   i n s t r u c t o r   t o   n e g l e c t   t h i s   t r a i n i n g b e c a u s e   h e   i s   p e r s o n a l l y   n o t   c o n v i n c e d   o f   t h e e f f e c t i v e n e s s   o f   g r o u n d   d e f e n s e s .

---

[341] 3300 ft.

[342] The original German word was "Treffen", which can be literally translated to "hit". We translated this to accuracy, since the contextual meaning of this sentences is to convey that a release altitude of 1000 m (3300 ft) presents a balance between the ability to score a hit, the effectiveness of the defense which increases the lower the release altitude is, and the requirement for a safety margin for the dive recovery pull-out.

[343] This refers to the anticipated introduction of a dive-bomber sight which would be able to account for the complexities of a dive-bombing attack (e.g., drift) unlike the generic reflector sight used. This new sight was never introduced operationally in Ju 87 units.

[344] This is most likely to allow the Ju 87 to break the line of sight from enemy AA-guns and thus prevent them from tracking and firing at the aircraft. This might not necessarily mean a descend to "tree-top level", but rather a low-altitude flight that at increasingly shallower angles places buildings, trees or hills between the guns and the aircraft.

[345] The original German word was "beweglichen Hochziehen", which can be literally translated to "movable pull-up". Meant here is most likely not a steady and thus predictable climb, but one that utilizes the gained speed during the dive to recapture altitude with a regular change in course and rate-of-climb. This could throw off the aim of light-AA guns, whose effectiveness not just decreases with range but whose aim also is more complex the more factors of lead (like fall of shot at altitude) have to be taken into account.

III. Bombing Training

A. General Notices

1. Good hit results can only be achieved through in-depth training.

At the present technical development stage, the bombing exercises necessary for training can have only a limited "conditional" character. Only the experience gained with bombing by a broad range of units and further the introduction of a usable dive-bomber sight will make it possible to define definitive bomb throw conditions.

2. The Staffel commander is responsible for the bombing training of the pilots. While respecting the independence of the Staffel commander, his superiors examine the training and intervene as soon as they notice any malpractice. Geschwader Kommodore and Gruppen commanders may schedule special bombing drills. When evaluating the performance, it is essential to consider the number of pilots who participated (in proportion to the unit's actual strength).

3. The training year[346] begins on October 1 and ends on September 30 of the following year after which it is named.

B. Type and Structure of the Exercises

1. The type of the training exercises must be largely adapted to the tactical necessities. It would be wrong, in order to increase the hit results, to carry out drops with concrete bombs[347] from release altitudes which are neither possible with live bombs[348] nor under warlike conditions (enemy defense).

Getting hits from low release altitudes in a dive presents no difficulties, but they are generally not practical in operational conditions[349].

---

[346] The original German word was "Wurfjahr", which can be literally translated to "throwing/litter year". See Glossary: Training year (Wurfjahr).
[347] See Glossary: Concrete bombs (Zementbomben [Ze.-Bomben]).
[348] This is due to the safety margins of the blast radius of live bombs, as well as the required pull-out altitude.
[349] The original German word was "unkriegsmäßig", which can be literally translated to "unwarlike".

On the other hand, the experience records available today prove that given appropriate training, sufficient success can be achieved even with the imperfect reflector sights[350] at the operationally usable release altitudes.

2. The s t r u c t u r e o f t h e e x e r c i s e s largely takes into account the different levels of difficulty, which are partly due to the aiming procedure with the reflector sight. It contains a training system that seems appropriate to train even the most simple-minded[351] pilot in throwing from the dive.

3. The exercises for the Ju 87 are divided into preparatory exercises, main exercises and unit exercises.

a) Preparatory exercises 1 to 5 are designed in such a way that the pilot only has to deal with the actual dive. All considerations for calculating the dive aiming point and the point of aim[352] are taken away from him by the instructor. The instructor commands the dive aiming point and the point of aim to be taken in the reflector sight. The pilot only has to follow the commanded instructions as well as the release altitude to follow the aiming procedure in an exact manner. Pre-determining the dive aiming point and the point of aim has the advantage that the novice pilot is not tempted to make blind corrections[353] due to poor hit success. These exercises give the instructor an indication of the student's level of training and thus the possibility of eliminating individual weaknesses through increased practice.

In p r e p a r a t o r y e x e r c i s e s 5 t o 8 , the pilot is also spared or assisted in selecting the dive aiming point and point of aim for the wind correction angle. However, the pilot is given the freedom to improve the point of aim at a commanded release altitude in accordance with the reached dive angle. On the basis of having obtained a feeling for a diving angle of 70° through the initial preparatory exercises, the student should judge whether the [flown] angle is steeper or shallower.

b) Of the m a i n e x e r c i s e s , 4 exercises are to be performed at operationally used altitudes and with different wind directions. The

---

[350] Again, this refers to the conventional reflector sight which was anticipated to be eventually replaced with a dedicated dive-bombing sight.
[351] The original German word was "einfach denkenden", which can be literally translated to "simple thinking".
[352] See Glossary: Point of aim (Abkommpunkt).
[353] The original German word was "blindem Tasten in der Korrektur", which can be literally translated to " blindly touching for a correction".

dive aiming point and point of aim are to be calculated by the pilot himself.

In the 3rd main exercise, the student should learn the difficulty of approaching [the target] at medium altitude followed by only a short dive with simultaneous aiming.

The 4th main exercise is a low altitude approach exercise.

c) The training exercises with the unit do not contain any changes with regard to the bombing procedure. They are intended to teach the student how to approach, attack and departure with formation in accordance with combat-like conditions.

C. Dividing the Instruction Groups

1. According to the increasing requirements, pilots are divided into:

II. Instruction group[354],

I. Instruction group.

Pilots in their 1st year of training follow the exercises of the II. Instruction group.

2. The Staffel commander may transfer the pilots to the I. Instruction group if he has completed all II. Instruction group exercises in one training year[355].

Reassignments to the II. Instruction group will be made in exceptional cases by the Staffel commander.

D. Execution of the Bombing Training

1. Bombing training is attended by all pilots.

2. If possible, each pilot should always use the same aircraft. If this is not possible due to overriding reasons, a note must be made in the "Remarks" column of the exercise in question inside the bomb score record[356].

3. Rushing through the exercises is just as harmful as longer interruptions.

---

[354] See Glossary: Instruction group I and II (Wurklasse I und II).
[355] See Glossary: Training year (Wurfjahr).
[356] See Glossary: Bomb score record (Wurfbuch), See also following pages for a representation based on the original print.

116

4. The information[357] necessary for the aim calculation are to be obtained from the air base meteorological office. Wind measurements made with balloons for the beginning and the end of the exercises is to be requested. The dive aiming point calculation is based on the respective average. It is to be noted in the bomb score notebook[358].

For wind detection near the target, combat reconnaissance[359] aircraft are used.

5. Before each bombing exercise, the dive aiming point is to be calculated by the exercise coordinator for each dive in a preliminary discussion with all pilots. This value is to be recorded in the bomb score notebook separately for lead and wind compensation angle. After completion of the throwing, the throwing results and faults during the throwing exercise are to be discussed with all pilots. The main points of this final discussion are to be recorded in the bomb score notebook.

6. An exercise is fulfilled only if the required result is achieved in one day in compliance with the required conditions.

---

[357] The original German word was "Unterlagen", which can be literally translated to "documents".
[358] See Glossary: Bomb score notebook (Wurfkladde).
[359] See Glossary: Combat reconnaissance (Gefechtsaufklärer).

E. Exercises (Ju 87)

1. Preliminary exercises

Number	Purpose of exercise	N° and type of bomb	Target	Approach altitude and direction	Dive initiation	Lead point	Dive angle	Release altitude	Dive heading	Departure	Conditions — II. Instruction group — Approach	Distance from target	Conditions — I. Instruction group — Approach	Distance from target
1	Exercise bombing from high altitude with ordered lead point	3 ZC 250	Practice target cross	3000 m into wind	Push nose down	As ordered	70°	700 m	Head wind	Pull-out straight, departure by discretion	By discretion	Never beyond 100 m, average distance not over 55 m	By discretion	~
2	As N° 1, but with defensive maneuvers	3 ZC 250	Practice target cross	3500 m into wind	Push nose down	As ordered	70°	700 m	Head wind	Pull-out straight, departure by discretion	By discretion	Never beyond 80 m, average distance not over 40 m	By discretion	Never beyond 70 m, average distance not over 30 m
3	As N° 1	3 ZC 250	Practice target cross	3000 m cross wind from the left	Defensive maneuvers to 2500 m, then by discretion	As ordered	70°	700 m	Cross wind	During the pull-out, turn away by 30-45°, dive to low altitude with a 30° dive	By discretion	Never beyond 100 m, average distance not over 55 m	By discretion	~
4	As N° 1, but with defensive maneuvers	3 ZC 250	Practice target cross	3500 m cross wind from the right	Defensive maneuvers to 2500 m, then by discretion	As ordered	70°	700 m	Cross wind	During the pull-out, turn away by 30-45°, dive to low altitude with a 30° dive	By discretion	Never beyond 80 m, average distance not over 45 m	By discretion	Never beyond 70 m, average distance not over 40 m
5	As N° 4	3 ZC 250	Practice target cross	3000 m 45° frontal cross wind	Defensive maneuvers to 2500 m, then by discretion	As ordered	70°	700 m	Cross wind (angle)	During the pull-out, turn away by 30-45°, defensive moves at consistent altitude	By discretion	Never beyond 80 m, average distance not over 45 m	By discretion	~
6	Exercise bombing from high altitude with defensive maneuvers and partially set lead point	3 ZC 250	Practice target cross	3500 m 45° rear cross wind	Defensive maneuvers to 2500 m, then by discretion	Lead points for 60 and 80° will be ordered	70°	700 m	Tail wind	During the pull-out, turn away by 30-45°, dive to low altitude with a 30° dive, while simultaneously flying defensive maneuvers	By discretion	Never beyond 80 m, average distance not over 55 m	By discretion	Never beyond 70 m, average distance not over 45 m
7	As N° 6	3 ZC 250	Practice target cross	3500 m tail wind	Defensive maneuvers to 2500 m, then by discretion	Lead points for 60 and 80° will be ordered	70°	700 m	Tail wind	During the pull-out, turn away by 30-45°, dive to low altitude with a 30° dive, while simultaneously flying defensive maneuvers	By discretion	Never beyond 80 m, average distance not over 50 m	By discretion	~
8	As N° 6	3 ZC 250	Practice target cross	4000 m tail wind then turn into wind to 45° head wind	Defensive maneuvers to 2500 m, then by discretion	Lead points for 60 and 80° will be ordered	70°	1000 m	Head wind 45°	During the pull-out, turn away by 30-45°, dive to low altitude with a 30° dive, while simultaneously flying defensive maneuvers	By discretion	Never beyond 90 m, average distance not over 50 m	By discretion	Never beyond 75 m, average distance not over 40 m

Notices: a) The exercises can be repeated twice to fulfill the requirements.
b) In all exercises 1 bomb can be added, if thereby the requirements are reached with the last 3 throws.

2. Main exercises

Number	Purpose of excercise	N° and type of bomb	Target	Exercise parameters — Approach altitude and direction	Exercise parameters — Dive initiation	Exercise parameters — Lead point	Bombing — Dive angle	Bombing — Release altitude	Bombing — Dive heading	Exercise parameters — Departure	Conditions — II. Instruction group — N° of approaches	Conditions — II. Instruction group — Distance from target	Conditions — I. Instruction group — N° of approaches	Conditions — I. Instruction group — Distance from target
1	Exercise bombing from high altitude with defensive maneuvers	3 ZC 250	Target cross	3000 m into wind	With defensive maneuvers to 2 5000 m, then by discretion	By own calculation	70°	700 m	Head wind	During the pull-out, turn away by 30–45°, transition to low altitude with defensive maneuvers	By discretion	Never beyond 70 m, average distance not over 30 m	5	Never beyond 70 m, average distance not over 35 m
2	As N° 1	3 ZC 250	Target cross	3500 m into wind	Push nose down	By own calculation	over 60°	600 m	Cross wind alternating	As N° 1	By discretion	Never beyond 80 m, average distance not over 40 m	5	Never beyond 70 m, average distance not over 40 m
3	Exercise bombing with an approach at medium altitude with defensive maneuvers	3 ZC 250	Target cross	3000 m cross wind from the left		By own calculation	over 60°	700 m	1 throw with head, cross and tail wind	As N° 1	By discretion	Never beyond 70 m, average distance not over 50 m	4	Never beyond 70 m, average distance not over 40 m (See Appendix A, throw with Fuze 15)
4	Exercise bombing from low altitude	3 SC 250	Target square 50x50 m	3500 m cross wind from the right	~	By own calculation	~	~	by discretion	Low altitude using ground cover		Never beyond 80 m, 1 hit in the target center	4	Never beyond 60 m, 1 hit in the target center
5	As N° 1 but with armed bombs	3 SC 250	Target square 50x50 m	3000 m 45° frontal cross wind		By own calculation	over 60°	850 m	As N° 3	As N° 1			4	Never beyond 70 m, 1 hit in the target center
6	As N° 5	2 SC 250 1 SC 500	As N° 5	3500 m 45° rear cross wind		By own calculation	over 60°	1150 m	As N° 3	As N° 1			4	Never beyond 70 m, 1 hit in the target center

Notices:

a) The exercises 1 – 4 can be repeated twice to fulfill the requirements, 5 – 6 are to be thrown only once. In exercises 3, 5 and 6 the additional bomb must be thrown from the same dive heading in relation to the wind.

b) In all exercises 1 bomb can be added, if thereby the requirements can be reached with the last 3 throws.

3. Unit Exercises.

The exercises are to be followed by predetermined Ketten, after the exercises of the II. Instruction group have been completed by all pilots of the Kette.

Training exercises in the unit

Number	Purpose of exercise	Nº and type of bomb	Target	Approach altitude and direction	Dive initiation	Lead point	Dive angle	Release altitude	Dive heading	Direction	Departure	Conditions
1	Exercise bombing by a Kette from high altitude in a loose echelon with defensive maneuvers	1x 3 ZC 250	Target cross	3500 m by discretion	With defensive maneuvers to 2 5000 m, then by discretion, distance between aircraft in the dive around 1000 m	Ordered by Ketten leader	By discretion but over 60°	700	Head or tail wind	Direction Ordered by Staffel leader from sun	During the pull-out, turn away by 30-45° in alternating directions, transition to low altitude with defensive maneuvers. Departure at low altitude in ordered heading rally on the return flight	Never beyond 80 m. average distance 50 m, bombing time of Kette 30 sec. (The bombing time is calculated from the impact of the first to the last bomb)
2	As Nº 1 but with armed bombs	1x 3 ZC 250	Target cross	5000 m by discretion				850	Cross wind			Never beyond 70 m, average distance 45 m, bombing time of Kette 25 sec.
3	Exercise bombing of a Staffel (minimum 7 aircraft) from high altitude in a loose echelon with defensive maneuvers	1x 3 SC 250	Target square 50x50 m			Ordered by Staffel leader		700 m	tail wind			Never beyond 70 m, 1 hit on target bombing time of Kette 30 sec.
4		7 to 9 ZC 250	3 random area targets 2500 / 1000 m, with 100 m² distance						from sun	Direction by Ordered by Ketten		Never beyond 70 m, 3 hit on target bombing time of Staffel 120 sec.
5	As Nº 4 but target division by Ketten											Never beyond 70 m from the target center 1 hit in each target bombing time of Staffel 60 sec.

The exercises 1, 2, 4, 5 can be repeated once to fulfill the requirements.
Exercise 3 is conducted just once per bomb training year.

7. In case of unfavorable weather conditions, the ordered approach altitude may be lowered to a minimum of 1 500 m[360] above the required release altitude.

8. Careful preparations must be made to ensure that each exercise is completed with the first bomb throw. If this is not successful and the required result is again not achieved after a single repetition, the Staffel commander may, in exceptional cases, repeat the exercise.

Exercises with live ammunition are not repeated.

9. If a bomb cannot be released due to technical defects, e.g., failure of the dive brake to extend, then the approach shall be repeated. If the failure to release the bomb is the fault of the pilot, the exercise is not fulfilled.

F. Exercise Regulations

1. Annual Instructions.

Every year, before the start of bombing training, the Staffel commander instructs the entire Staffel on

a) about the safety regulations and the running of the exercise. This instruction will be repeated if it appears necessary as a result of the reassignment of personnel or special incidents,

b) on the penal provisions of § 139 M. St. G. B.[361] for willful false reporting or recording of the exercise results.

Appropriate instruction of the evaluation team on the training site is carried out every month for the permanent staff or after a change of staff.

2. Exercise Operation.

a. The Exercising Staffel[362].

The exercise is supervised by officer as exercise coordinator[363].

He is assisted by the following auxiliary staff:

---

[360] 4900 ft.
[361] "M. St. G. B." is the abbreviation of "Militär-Straftgesetzbuch", the "Military penal code". See Glossary: Military penal code (Militär-Straftgesetzbuch [M.St.G.B.]).
[362] The original German title was "Werfende Staffel", which can be literally translated to "throwing Staffel".
[363] The original German title was "Leitender", which can be literally translated to "Director".

the aircraft sergeant major,

the ordnance master sergeant and

1 clerk.[364]

The exercise coordinator is responsible for the entire operation. He supervises the observance of safety regulations during the loading of bombs and readying of aircraft and regulates the order and sequence of the exercise.

He will not permit the exercise to begin until it is safe to do so in the training area[365].

The exercise coordinator also supervises the proper recording done by the clerk of the training area used by the pilots.

After the exercise has been completed, the exercise coordinator determines in writing the number of bombs thrown, the order and times of the individual drops and ensures that the information of the written report is copied into the bomb score notebook[366].

The clerk is given a place near the exercise coordinator. Following the report by each pilot, he enters the report into the bomb score record[367].

b. Service at the Observation Post during the Evaluation.

A non-commissioned officer shall oversee the observation post unless an officer or non-commissioned officer with sword knot[368] experienced in bomb throwing supervises the exercises at the target. (This must always be done for pilots new to bombing to determine each pilot's errors in diving angle and correction). The manning of the observation post is to be regulated depending on the local conditions and the evaluation procedure. However, in the interest of reliably recording the hits, it should be continuously manned.

The supervisor is responsible for the careful observance of the safety regulations and for conscientious determination and evaluation of the hit results. He checks the condition and set-up of the evaluation equipment and the

---

[364] See also *Aerial Tactics - The Dive-Bomber*.
[365] The original German title was "Wurfplatz", which can be literally translated to "throwing site".
[366] See Glossary: Bomb score notebook (Wurfkladde).
[367] See Glossary: Bomb score record (Wurfbuch).
[368] See Glossary: Non-commissioned officer with sword knot (Portepeeunteroffizier).

completeness of the evaluation team before the exercise. Having confirmed that the safety regulations are being followed, he reports the readiness of the observation post to the respective airport[369].

Before starting to exercise, he lays out the visual signs near the evaluation point, which indicate to the bombing unit whether it is possible to throw or not.

If, in special cases, the exercise must be interrupted, this must be reported by telephone to the airport and indicated by visual signals to the aircraft in the air.

The activities of the exercise are specified under "hit recording" in this regulation.

After the exercise is finished, he gives the order to dismantle the equipment and then checks whether the individual hits in the exercise area correspond with the evaluated result.

G. Record Keeping for the Exercise

1. Evaluation Notebook[370].

An evaluation notebook for even and odd days as well as an observation list for each of the two observation stands are kept at the training area.

The evaluation notebook is kept by the observation post supervisor. The supervision of an orderly operation is carried out by an officer assigned by the Gruppe.

Every day after the exercise, the Gruppe displays the evaluation notebook so that the results can be transferred into the bomb score notebooks of each Staffel.

The pages of the evaluation notebook shall be numbered consecutively. The number of pages shall be certified by the commanding officer or an assigned officer. Pages may not be removed. See Sample 1.

2. Bomb Score Notebook[371].

The Staffel transcribes the results to the bomb score notebook. The transfer must be certified by the Staffel's commander.

During the transcription, the individual throws of a pilot are added up together.

---

[369] Meant here is the airport where the Ju 87 used during the exercise will fly from.
[370] See Glossary: Evaluation notebook (Auswertekladde).
[371] See Glossary: Bomb score notebook (Wurfkladde).

S a m p l e 2 provides a reference for the record keeping in the bomb score notebook[372].

A comparison between the entries in the bomb score notebook with those in the evaluation notebook is facilitated by the fact that the number, page and consecutive number of the evaluation notebook are noted in the bomb score notebook.

Under "Remarks"[373] obvious errors of the pilot or the aircraft are to be recorded.

The average distance [from the center of the target] is to be calculated from all the bomb throws of a single exercise.

3. Bomb Score Record[374].

The Staffel keeps a bomb score record for each pilot. S a m p l e 3 provides a reference on how to organize the bomb score record.

The bomb score record acts as a certificate. Changes are therefore always to be countersigned by the Staffel commander.

The bomb score record remains in the possession of the pilot. He brings it with him to the exercise.

After a throw is made, the result is reported immediately to a clerk and is recorded by him.

The result is transcribed from the bomb score notebook to the bomb score record as soon as possible.

Upon transfer or reassignment of a pilot, the bomb score record is certified by the Staffel commanders signature and is transferred to the new duty station.

If a bomb score record is lost, a duplicate must be made using the exercise summary[375] and the bomb score notebook.

---

[372] See Glossary: Bomb score notebook (Wurfkladde).
[373] Editorial notice: Quotation marks added to emphasize that this is a special column in the bomb score notebook.
[374] See Glossary: Bomb score record (Wurfbuch).
[375] The original German title was "Wurfübersicht", which can be literally translated to "throwing overview".

4. Exercise Summary, Overview of Exercise Days and dropped Bombs.

The Staffel creates an exercise summary for each instruction group for each bomb training year. Preprinted forms can be used.

The summary should always be able to provide information about the current stage of the exercises, the performance of the individual pilot as well as the exercises attendance.

The exercise summary is to be recorded[376] on canvas and stored rolled up or folded. It must be possible to check the state of bombing training at a single glance.

The exercise summary is to be regarded as a certificate and stored accordingly. Duplicates can be displayed for general inspection.

In addition to the exercise summary, an overview of the exercise days and dropped bombs is also kept.

All summaries must always be kept up to date and certified by the Staffel commander at the end of the bomb training year. Then they are stored for another 3 years.

Stab units also carry their own summaries.

---

[376] The original German title was "aufzuziehen", which can be literally translated to "raise up".

Deckseite.

Auswertekladde

für gerade Tage

für den Bombenwurfplatz ....

Begonnen am: ....

Beendet am: ....

Dieses Buch enthält .... Seiten.

.... den .... 19......

....
Gruppenkommandeur

Lfd. Nr.	Kennzeichen des Flugzeuges oder Nummer im Verband	Uhrzeit des Aufschlages	Bombenfallzeit in sek.	Beobachtung		Auswertung		Bemerkungen
				I	II	Ablage in Meter	Richtung nach Sektor	

Wurfbuch

für

Dienstgrad

Name

Staffel

Anmerkung: Die Umschlagseite des Wurfbuches ist für die
I. Wurfklasse in roter Farbe
II. Wurfklasse in grüner Farbe
gehalten.

Übung ....

	Durchgang	Wurfanlage des Flugzeugführers				Wurfergebnis laut Wurfkladde b. St.			* Erfüllt oder nicht erfüllt und Seite der Zeile Wurfkladde	** Mittlere Ablage in Metern	Be-merkungen
		Ansatz-höhe	Sturzflug-winkel	Sturz-richtung	Auslöse-höhe	Ablage in Metern	Richtung nach Sektor	Auslöse-höhe nach Fallzeit			

Werf. nummer
Monat des Flug-zeuges
Tag
Jahr

Wiederholung

Abkommen nach Angabe des Flugzeugführers
Visierpunkt
Abkommenpunkt

Abkommen

W N S O

Errechneter Visier- und Abkommenpunkt

W N S O

Wind	
Richtung	
Stärke	

0 ——— 50 ——— 100 m

Einzeichnung für 1. Durchgang +   Einzeichnung für 2. Durchgang ○   Einzeichnung für 3. Durchgang ●   Bei Wiederholung: in roter Farbe

129

H. Hit Recording during Bombing Training using Concrete Bombs[377] with Guidance for the Employment of Tactical Radio Communication.

The fostering of the individual pilot's training requires that each individual hit result is accurately determined according to its direction and distance from the target, and that it be brought to the pilot's attention immediately after his throw.

Experience shows that estimates of the hit position from the air are by no means sufficient for a reliable evaluation of the single throw.

The following is a measurement procedure that can be set up by the troops themselves at little cost. The procedure has been tested in practical employment and ensures sufficient accuracy as well as rapid hit evaluation. For s a f e t y r e a s o n s , this procedure can only be used when dropping concrete bombs.

a . P r o c e d u r e .

At a distance of 300 m to 600 m[378] from the target cross, 2 observation stands are set up. They are set up in such a way that the connecting lines to the center of the target form a right angle and thus offer a complete view over the training area. See Figure 23.

From the observation posts, a sighting device (Picture 4 and 5) is used to assess the bomb impact point. The value obtained is recorded together with the time of impact and then transmitted by telephone to the evaluation post.

At the evaluation post, the drop time of the bomb and the time of impact are recorded, and the transmitted observations are evaluated. The evaluation is carried out on the basis of an evaluation table. It gives the distance of the hit [from the target] in meters and the direction in relation to North (Picture 1 and Picture 2, evaluation table Picture 3).

The evaluation result is entered into the evaluation notebook by a clerk under constant monitoring by the supervising NCO.

The method works with useful accuracy up to a radius of about 150 m[379] from the target center.

---

[377] See Glossary: Concrete bombs (Zementbomben [Ze.-Bomben]).
[378] 1000 – 2000 ft.
[379] 490 ft.

The time required for recording, evaluation and display is less than 1 minute from the impact of the bomb. The result of the throwing is transmitted to the pilot either by visual signals from a display panel (Picture 1 and 2) or by tactical radio communication.

b. Evaluation and Display Post.

The evaluation post must be equipped with the following devices:

Evaluation board, evaluation notebook (Sample 1), stopwatch, furthermore table, bench, clock, telephone for 2 men.

The display post has the following devices:

Display panels for aircraft numbers (numerical boards just like firing range signs) (attack sequence)

and offset in meters from target center (Figure 2) with Arabic numeric signs,

sector disk with pointer for direction indication (Figure 2),

2 red flags, cloths for displaying a blocking sign and a flare gun with red signal cartridges.

The evaluation post and the display post are located directly next to each other for reasons of cooperation and control (Figure 1).

Cooperation of the Evaluation Post and the Display Post.

At the evaluation post, the supervisor stops the drop time of the bomb from the moment of release to the moment of impact. The clerk records the stopped time and the time of the drop in the evaluation notebook.

The messages received from the observation posts are recorded by the clerk into the evaluation notebook. At the same time, the observations are evaluated by the operator of the evaluation post according to the evaluation board and orally[380] transmitted to the operator of the display post. The corresponding values are displayed on the display post so that the pilot can read the result as he flies past after this drop.

During the fly-by, the evaluation post reads the aircraft registration number and enters it in the evaluation notebook. In the case of a unit throw, the

---

[380] The original German title was "Zuruf", which can be literally translated to "call" or "shouting towards".

evaluation post also enters the serial number under which the aircraft threw within the unit.

The display post is continuously checked by the operator of the evaluation post for the correctness of the displayed values.

Figure 23

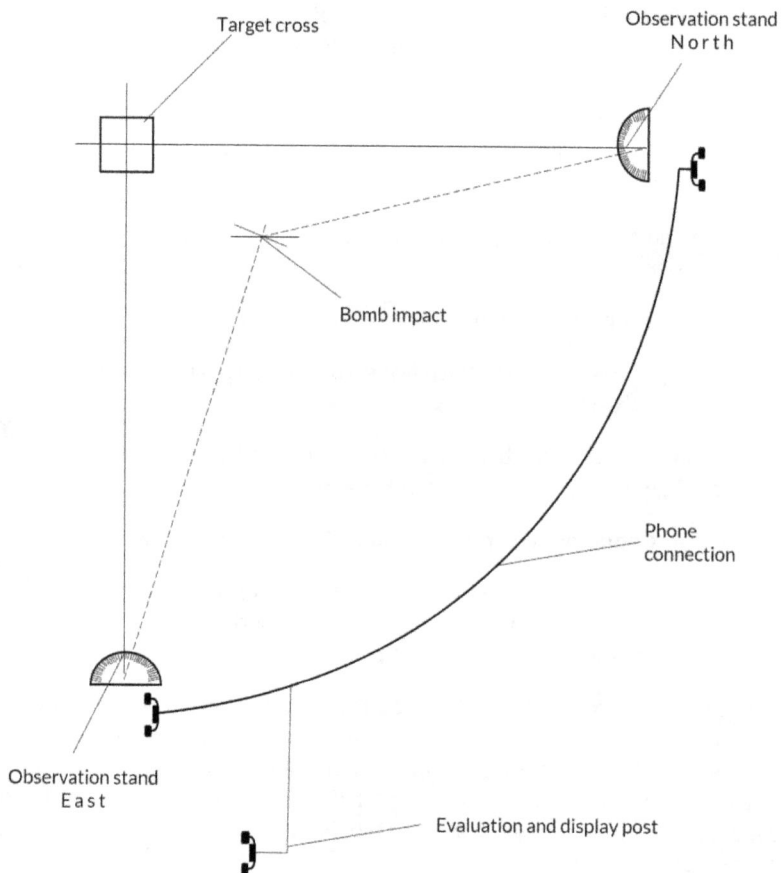

Target cross

Observation stand
North

Bomb impact

Phone
connection

Observation stand
East

Evaluation and display post

c. Transmission of the Evaluation Result to the Aircraft Pilot.

The transmission of the evaluation result to the pilot is done either by displaying it on the display post or by radio following the tactical radio communication procedure.

1. Showing the Result on the Display Post.

The consecutive numbering of the aircraft of a unit is shown on the left side of the display panel with numbers in the same manner as on a firing range (Figure 2).

The offset in meters from the target center is displayed with Arabic numerals (Figure 2).

The direction of a hit from the target is indicated on the sector disc with a direction arrow (Figure 2).

The size and arrangement of the signs shall be such that the pilot approaching the display post after the drop can read the evaluation results.

2. Transmission of Hit Results by the Tactical Radio Communication Procedure.

Employment of tactical radio communication for transmitting the hits has the purpose of training radio operators in tactical radio procedures and the physicality of dive-bombing operations and accustom the pilot to working with the radio operator.

In addition, the employment of radio communication gives the possibility of a simplified transmission of the result without approaching the display post. Furthermore, it is possible to transmit to the pilot complaints from the instructor or to convey instructions that serve the purpose of safety.

a. Necessary Equipment.

For the operation of tactical radio communication, a ground station is required, which is either set up directly at the evaluation stand or is telegraphed by the evaluation post. The radio can be a 1 kW-set or a Fu. G. III[381]. A radio operator trained in tactical radio communication joins the operating personnel.

---

[381] "Fu. G. III" is the abbreviation of "Funkgerät III", indicating "radio set III".

b. Preparation and Implementation of Radio Communication.

Since radio traffic is practiced alongside the bombing exercises in the usual training operations, the radio traffic connected with the exercise would be disturbed. It is thus necessary that a special frequency is assigned to the bombing exercise units.

Radio traffic shall be conducted in accordance with L. Dv. 421/4[382] in conjunction with the signal board as tactical radio traffic. During the approach to the drop, the dropping aircraft or, in the case of a unit drop, the leader aircraft shall establish communication with the ground station and report itself or the number of aircraft that will subsequently perform a dive attack.

During the dive, the aircraft report its call sign, so that the evaluation post can determine the exact sequence of the drops.

After the drop, or in the case of a formation drop, after all aircraft have dropped, the ground station will transmit the results by distance and direction offset to the aircraft or to the formation commander.

All radio messages given are encoded according to the principles of tactical radio traffic. The operating log is kept in accordance with L. Dv. 421/4, Annex 403.

If the codes[383] of the signal panel are insufficient, corresponding auxiliary signals[384] are to be used.

---

[382] L. Dv. 421/4, Funkvorschrift der Luftwaffe, Heft 4, Funkbetrieb der Kampfflieger is Luftwaffe Regulation 421/4, Signalling regulation of the Luftwaffe, Part 47, Signalling of the Bombers.

[383] The original German title was "Schlüsselgruppen", which can be literally translated to "key groups".

[384] The original German title was "Verfügungssignale", which can be literally translated to "availability signals".

c. Personnel Requirements for the Evaluation Post and the Display Post.

Supervisor... 1 NCO
(equally evaluation NCO.)

Evaluation post.. 1 NCO[385].

1 clerk

Display post.. 1 man

Observation post................................ each 1 man

For radio communications also............... 1 radio operator[386]

1 man
_____

1 NCO. 6 men,

including 1 clerk, 1 radio operator.

_____

[385] As indicated, this NCO doubles as the exercise's supervisor.

[386] The original German title was "Bordfunker", which can be literally translated to "onboard radio operator". As mentioned in the preceding text, this would be a radio operator trained in the use of air-to-air and air-to-ground radio communication. See also *Aerial Tactics – The Dive-Bomber*.

135

Picture 1

Picture 2

Picture 3

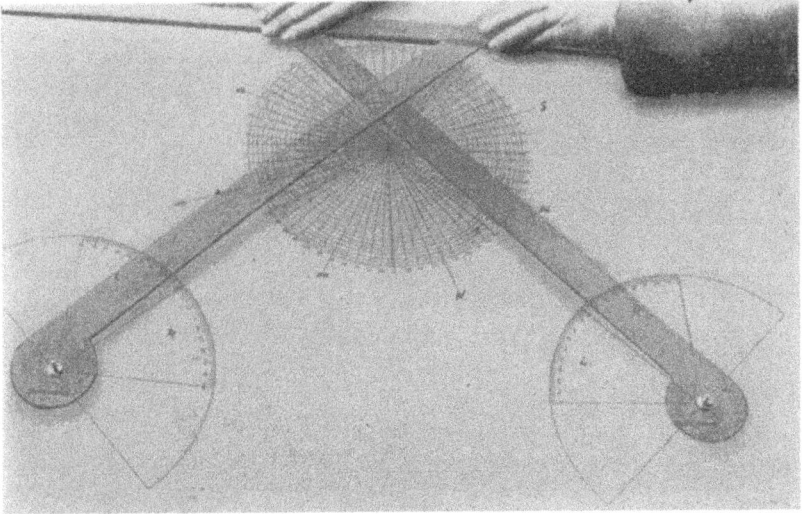

Picture 4

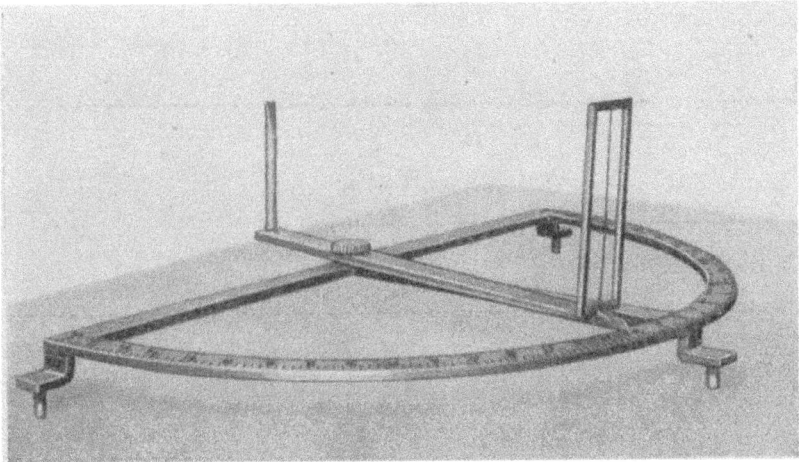

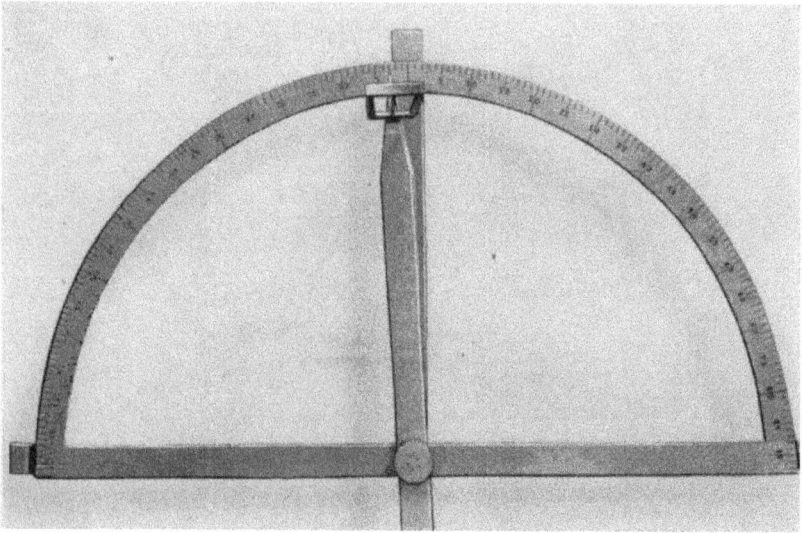

Table I

a. Lead angle for Ju 87

Auslösehöhe = 700 m	Auslösehöhe = 1000 m
Sturzflugwinkel α ==	Aufsatzwinkel ε
60° = 4° 70° = 2° 80° = 1°	60° = 5,5° 70° = 3 ° 80° = 1,5°

Aufsatzwinkel für Sturzflugwinkel 90° = 0°

Table II

a. Wind correction angle for Ju 87

Sturzflugwinkel α	Windgeschwindigkeit in km/h				
	10,8	18	36	54	72
60°	1,5°	2°	4,5°	6,5°	8,5°
70°	1,5°	2°	4,5°	6,5°	9 °
80°	1,5°	2°	4,5°	7 °	9 °

Tables for natural numbers of the trigonometric functions of tangent and cotangent

Appendix 3

Tangens.

°	0' 10' 20'	30'	40' 50' 60'		d.	P. P.
0	0, 0000 0029 0058	0087	0116 0145 0175	89	29	**29 30 31 32 33**
1	0175 0204 0233	0262	0291 0320 0349	88	39	1 2,9 3,0 3,1 3,2 3,3
2	0349 0378 0407	0437	0466 9495 0524	87	29	2 5,8 6,0 6,2 6,4 6,6
3	0524 0553 0582	0612	0641 0670 0699	86	29	3 8,7 9,0 9,3 9,6 9,9
4	0699 0729 0758	0787	0816 0846 0875	85	29	4 11,6 12,0 12,4 12,8 13,2
						5 14,5 15,0 15,5 16,0 16,5
						6 17,4 18,0 18,6 19,2 19,8
5	0, 0875 0904 0934	0963	0992 1022 1051	84	29	7 20,3 21,0 21,7 22,4 23,1
6	1051 1080 1110	1139	1169 1198 1228	83	30	8 23,2 24,0 24,8 25,6 26,4
7	1228 1257 1287	1317	1346 1376 1405	82	30	9 26,1 27,0 27,9 28,8 29,7
8	1405 1435 1463	1493	1524 1554 1584	81	30	**34 35 36 37 38**
9	1584 1614 1644	1673	1703 1733 1763	80	30	1 3,4 3,5 3,6 3,7 3,8
						2 6,8 7,0 7,2 7,4 7,6
						3 10,2 10,5 10,8 11,1 11,4
10	0, 1763 1793 1823	1853	1883 1914 1944	79	30	4 13,6 14,0 14,4 14,8 15,2
11	1944 1974 2004	2035	2065 2095 2126	78	30	5 17,0 17,5 18,0 18,5 19,0
12	2126 2156 2186	2217	2247 2278 2309	77	30	6 20,4 21,0 21,6 22,2 22,8
13	2309 2339 2370	2401	2432 2462 2493	76	31	7 23,8 24,5 25,2 25,9 26,6
14	2493 2524 2555	2586	2617 2648 2679	75	31	8 27,2 28,0 28,8 29,6 30,4
						9 30,6 31,5 32,4 33,3 34,2
15	0, 2679 2711 2742	2773	2805 2836 2867	74	31	**39 40 41 42 43**
16	2867 2899 2931	2962	2994 3026 3057	73	32	1 3,9 4,0 4,1 4,2 4,3
17	3057 3089 3121	3153	3185 3217 3249	72	32	2 7,8 8,0 8,2 8,4 8,6
18	3249 3281 3314	3346	3378 3411 3443	71	32	3 11,7 12,0 12,3 12,6 12,9
19	3443 3476 3508	3541	3574 3607 3640	70	33	4 15,6 16,0 16,4 16,8 12,2
						5 19,5 20,0 20,5 21,0 21,5
						6 23,4 24,0 24,6 25,2 25,8
20	0, 3640 3673 3706	3739	3772 3805 3839	69	33	7 27,3 28,0 28,7 29,4 30,1
21	3839 3872 3906	3939	3973 4006 4040	68	34	8 31,2 32,0 32,8 33,6 34,4
22	4040 4074 4108	4142	4176 4210 4245	67	34	9 35,1 36,0 36,9 37,8 38,7
23	4245 4279 4314	4318	4383 4417 4452	66	34	**44° 45 46 47 48**
24	4452 4487 4522	4557	4592 4628 4663	65	35	1 4,4 4,5 4,6 4,7 4,8
						2 8,8 9,0 9,2 9,4 9,6
						3 13,2 13,5 13,8 14,1 14,4
25	0. 4663 4699 4734	4770	4806 4841 4877	64	36	4 17,6 18,0 18,4 18,8 19,2
26	4877 4913 4950	4986	5022 5059 5095	63	36	5 22,0 22,5 23,0 23,5 24,0
27	5095 5132 5169	5206	5243 5280 5317	62	37	6 26,4 27,0 27,6 28,2 28,8
28	5317 5354 5392	5430	5467 5505 5543	61	38	7 30,8 31,5 32,2 32,9 33,6
29	5543 5581 5619	5658	5696 5735 5774	60	38	8 35,2 36,0 36,8 37,6 38,4
						9 39,6 40,5 41,4 42,3 43,2
30	0, 5774 5812 5851	5890	5930 5969 6009	59	39	**49 50 51 52 53**
31	6009 6048 6088	6128	6168 6208 6249	58	40	1 4,9 5,0 5,1 5,2 5,3
32	6249 6289 6330	6371	6412 6453 6495	57	41	2 9,8 10,0 10,2 10,4 10,6
33	6494 6536 6577	6619	6661 6703 6745	56	42	3 14,7 15,0 15,3 15,6 15,9
34	6745 6787 6830	6873	6916 6959 7002	55	43	4 19,6 20,0 20,4 20,8 21,2
						5 24,5 25,0 25,0 26,0 26,5
						6 29,4 30,0 30,6 31,2 31,8
35	0, 7002 7046 7089	7133	7177 7221 7265	54	44	7 34,3 35,0 35,7 36,4 37,1
36	7265 7310 7335	7400	7445 7490 7536	53	45	8 39,2 40,0 40,8 41,6 42,4
37	7536 7581 7627	7673	7720 7766 7813	52	46	9 44,1 45,0 45,9 46,8 67,7
38	7813 7860 7907	7954	8002 8050 8098	51	48	**54 55 56 57 58**
39	8098 8146 8195	8243	8292 8342 8391	50	49	1 5,4 5,5 5,6 5,7 5,8
						2 10,8 11,0 11,2 11,4 11,6
						3 16,2 16,5 16,8 17,1 17,4
40	0, 8391 8441 8491	8541	8591 8642 8693	49	50	4 21,6 22,0 22,4 22,8 23,2
41	8693 8744 8796	8847	8899 8952 9004	48	52	5 27,0 27,5 28,0 28,5 29,0
42	9004 9057 9110	9163	9217 9271 9325	47	54	6 32,4 33,0 33,6 34,2 34,8
43	9325 9380 9435	9490	9545 9601 9657	46	55	7 37,8 38,5 39,2 39,9 40,6
44	9657 9713 9770	9827	9884 9942°0000	45	57	8 43,2 44,0 44,8 45,6 46,4
45	1, 0000					9 48,6 49,5 50,4 51,3 52,2
	60' 50' 40'	30'	20' 10' 0'	°	d.	P. P.

Kotangens.

140

Tangens.

°	0′	10′	20′	30′	40′	50′	60′		d.
45	1,000	1,006	1,012	1,018	1,024	1,030	1,036	44	6
46	1,036	1,042	1,048	1,054	1,060	1,066	1,072	43	6
47	1,072	1,079	1,085	1,091	1,098	1,104	1,111	42	6
48	1,111	1,117	1,124	1,130	1,137	1,144	1,150	41	6
49	1,150	1,157	1,164	1,171	1,178	1,185	1,192	40	7
50	1,192	1,199	1,206	1,213	1,220	1,228	1,235	39	7
51	1,235	1,242	1,250	1,257	1,265	1,272	1,280	38	8
52	1,280	1,288	1,295	1,303	1,311	1,319	1,327	37	8
53	1,327	1,335	1,343	1,351	1,360	1,368	1,376	36	8
54	1,376	1,385	1,393	1,402	1,411	1,419	1,428	35	9
55	1,428	1,437	1,446	1,455	1,464	1,473	1,483	34	9
56	1,483	1,492	1,501	1,511	1,520	1,530	1,540	33	10
57	1,540	1,550	1,560	1,570	1,580	1,590	1,600	32	10
58	1,600	1,611	1,621	1,632	1,643	1,653	1,664	31	11
59	1,664	1,675	1,686	1,698	1,709	1,720	1,732	30	11
60	1,732	1,744	1,756	1,767	1,780	1,792	1,804	29	12
61	1,804	1,816	1,829	1,842	1,855	1,868	1,881	28	13
62	1,881	1,894	1,907	1,921	1,935	1,949	1,963	27	14
63	1,963	1,977	1,991	2,006	2,020	2,035	2,050	26	14
64	2,050	2,066	2,081	2,097	2,112	2,128	2,145	25	16
65	2,145	2,161	2,177	2,194	2,211	2,229	2,246	24	12
66	2,246	2,264	2,282	2,300	2,318	2,337	2,356	23	18
67	2,356	2,375	2,394	2,414	2,434	2,455	2,475	22	20
68	2,475	2,496	2,517	2,539	2,560	2,583	2,605	21	22
69	2,605	2,628	2,651	2,675	2,699	2,723	2,747	20	24
70	2,747	2,773	2,798	2,824	2,850	2,877	2,904	19	26
71	2,904	2,932	2,960	2,989	3,018	3,047	3,078	18	29
72	3,078	3,108	3,140	3,172	3,204	3,237	3,271	17	32
73	3,271	3,305	3,340	3,376	3,412	3,450	3,487	16	36
74	3,487	3,526	3,566	3,606	3,647	3,689	3,732	15	41
75	3,732	3,776	3,821	3,867	3,914	3,962	4,011	14	46
76	4,011	4,061	4,113	4,165	4,219	4,275	4,331	13	53
77	4,331	4,390	4,449	4,511	4,574	4,638	4,705	12	61
78	4,705	4,773	4,843	4,915	4,989	5,066	5,145	11	73
79	5,145	5,226	5,309	5,396	5,485	5,576	5,671	10	88
80	5,671	5,769	5,871	5,976	6,084	6,197	6,314	9	
81	6,314	6,435	6,561	6,691	6,827	6,968	7,115	8	
82	7,115	7,269	7,429	7,596	7,770	7,953	8,144	7	
83	8,144	8,345	8,556	8,777	9,010	9,255	9,514	6	
84	9,514	9,788	10,078	10,385	10,712	11,059	11,430	5	
85	11,430	11,826	12,251	12,706	13,197	13,727	14,301	4	
86	14,301	14,924	15,605	16,350	17,169	18,075	19,081	3	
87	19,081	20,206	21,470	22,904	24,542	26,432	28,636	2	
88	28,636	31,242	34,368	38,188	42,964	49,104	57,290	1	
89	57,290	68,750	85,940	114,59	171,89	343,77	infinit.	0	
90	infinit.								
	60′	50′	40′	30′	20′	10′	0′	°	d.

Cotangens.

P. P.

	6	7	8	9	10	11
1	0,6	0,7	0,8	0,9	1,0	1,1
2	1,2	1,4	1,6	1,8	2,0	2,2
3	1,8	2,1	2,4	2,7	3,0	3,3
4	2,4	2,8	3,2	3,6	4,0	4,4
5	3,0	3,5	4,0	4,5	5,0	5,5
6	3,6	4,2	4,8	5,4	6,0	6,6
7	4,2	4,9	5,6	6,3	7,0	7,7
8	4,8	5,6	6,4	7,2	8,0	8,8
9	5,4	6,3	7,2	8,1	9,0	9,9

	12	13	14	15	16
1	1,2	1,3	1,4	1,5	1,6
2	2,4	2,6	2,8	3,0	3,2
3	3,6	3,9	4,2	4,5	4,8
4	4,8	5,2	5,6	6,0	6,4
5	6,0	6,5	7,0	7,5	8,0
6	7,2	7,8	8,4	9,0	9,6
7	8,4	9,1	9,8	10,5	11,2
8	9,6	10,4	11,2	12,0	12,8
9	10,8	11,7	12,6	13,5	14,4

	17	18	19	20	21
1	1,7	1,8	1,9	2,0	2,1
2	3,4	3,6	3,8	4,0	4,2
3	5,1	5,4	5,7	6,0	6,3
4	6,8	7,2	7,6	8,0	8,4
5	8,5	9,0	9,5	10,0	10,5
6	10,2	10,8	11,4	12,0	12,6
7	11,9	12,6	13,3	14,0	14,7
8	13,6	14,4	15,2	16,0	16,8
9	15,3	16,2	17,1	18,0	18,9

	22	23	24	25	26
1	2,2	2,3	2,4	2,5	2,6
2	4,4	4,6	4,8	5,0	5,2
3	6,6	6,9	7,2	7,5	7,8
4	8,8	9,2	9,6	10,0	10,4
5	11,0	11,5	12,0	12,5	13,0
6	13,2	13,8	14,4	15,0	15,6
7	15,4	16,1	16,8	17,5	18,2
8	17,6	18,4	19,2	20,0	20,8
9	19,8	20,7	21,6	22,5	23,4

	27	28	59	62	63
1	2,7	2,8	5,9	6,2	6,3
2	5,4	5,6	11,8	12,4	12,6
3	8,1	8,4	17,7	18,6	18,9
4	10,8	11,2	23,6	24,8	25,2
5	13,5	14,0	29,5	31,0	31,5
6	16,2	16,8	35,4	37,2	37,8
7	18,9	19,6	41,3	43,4	44,1
8	21,6	22,4	47,2	49,6	50,4
9	24,3	25,2	53,1	55,8	56,7

	64	67	68	70	72
1	6,4	6,7	6,8	7,0	7,2
2	12,8	13,4	13,6	14,0	14,4
3	19,2	20,1	20,4	21,0	21,6
4	25,6	26,8	27,2	28,0	28,8
5	32,0	33,5	34,0	35,0	36,0
6	38,4	40,2	40,8	42,0	43,2
7	44,8	46,9	47,6	49,0	50,4
8	51,2	53,6	54,4	56,0	57,6
9	57,6	60,3	61,2	63,0	64,8

P. P.

Photo 5: A Ju 87 being loaded with a 250 kg bomb. For this, a small crane was used to hoist the bomb in position, before it was attached to the swinging bomb crutch in the centerline position. Original caption: France, near Arras during the Western Campaign. Frontline airfield, dive-bomber (Stuka) Junkers 87 is being loaded with a bomb. May 1940. Credit: BArch, Bild 101I-383-0313-22, Fotograf(in): Böcker.

Photo 6: Original caption: Belgium/ France – Pilots and crew of Ju 87 "Stukas" of Sturzkampfgeschwader 51 (9. Staffel) on a frontline aircraft next to a tent and Geschwader flag. May 1940. Credit: BArch, Bild 101I-383-0301-18A, Fotograf(in): Koster.

Document: L.Dv. 366: Luftwaffe Regulation 366 – Special Guidelines for Diving with the Hs 123 and Ju 87

This document is part of BArch, RL 1/1096, *L.Dv. 366: Luftwaffe Regulation 366– Special Guidelines for Diving with the Hs 123 and Ju 87* which outlines the special requirements of dive-bombing attacks. As it was published in 1937, the included information covers the first iteration of dive-bombers accepted by the Luftwaffe, namely the biplane Hs 123 and the early Ju 87 A. While the Hs 123 was eventually not considered as a dive-bomber, roughly 40 of these aircraft formed the nucleus of the first Schlachtgeschwader[387] the Luftwaffe deployed during the Second World War.[388] For future Ju 87 variants, a core information referred to in this document remain largely valid although the maximum dive speeds increased from 550 kph to 600 kph[389] with the later D-5 variant[390].

Preliminary Notes / Source Situation, Actuality and Formatting

Throughout this volume, we aimed to retain some of the original formatting, yet the editorial focus lay on legibility. One of the main editorial changes was that, in order to present a clearer layout, we did not follow the original page count as this would have resulted in empty or near empty pages throughout the book. Instead, the text has been reformatted to follow a more conventional structure, page by page.

Please be aware of the following formatting decisions and changes:

- We corrected formatting mistakes in the original version (for example missing spaces, paragraph breaks or others).
- The original formatting sequence was retained, but we made some changes to transfer this document into a more legible layout that is

---

[387] See Glossary: Close air support unit (Schlachtflieger).

[388] See Heinz J. Nowarra, *Die Deutsche Luftrüstung 1933-1945*, Bernard & Graefe Verlag, Koblenz, Germany, 1993, p. 22; and Karl-Heinz Völker, *Die Deutsche Luftwaffe 1933-1939 – Aufbau, Führung und Rüstung der Luftwaffe sowie die Entwicklung der deutschen Luftkriegstheorie*, DVA, Stuttgart, Germany, 1967, p. 89, 189.

[389] 340 and 370 mph.

[390] During a dive from higher than 2 km / 6600 ft. See Archiv Hafner, Werkschrift 2087 D-1 bis D-8, G-1, G-2, H-1 bis H-8/Fl, *Ju 87 D-1 bis D-8, G-1, G-2, H-1 bis H-8 Bedienungsvorschrift-Fl*, Teil II – Flugbetrieb, Februar 1944, p. 15.

consistent with the other documents found in this book. This also includes the deletion of unnecessary spacing between subs-sections.

- This document was written in the German "Fraktur" font, with the exclusion of the header "L.Dv. 366" on the cover and cover pages, as well as aircraft type designations.

L.Dv. 366: Luftwaffe Regulation 366– Special Guidelines for Diving with the Hs 123 and Ju 87.

Berlin 1937 • Printed in the Reich's Printing Office

[Table of Contents has been omitted since the document is short.]

Foreword.

The regulations contained in these guidelines must be observed under all circumstances. Under this condition, the Hs 123[391] with a reinforced leading edge[392] is once more certified for dives from higher altitudes.

The present special guidelines for dives with the Hs 123 and Ju 87 aircraft do not take into account tactical aspects (most expedient lines of approach and dive with regard to accuracy and ground defenses).

The guidelines apply only to the aeronautical and ordnance related aspects of the dive.

---

[391] See Glossary: Hs 123 (Henschel Hs 123).
[392] The leading edge is the frontal part of the wing and makes first contact with oncoming air.

I. General Guidelines.

(Valid for Hs 123 and Ju 87.)

1. It is not possible to construct an aircraft in such a way that it cannot be overstressed.
2. The level of stress (=acceleration) is determined solely by the dive velocity and the pull-out radius[393], irrespective of the type of aircraft. The higher the speed, the greater the required pull-out radius. Refer to curve sheet (see last page).
3. In isolated cases, each aircraft can still withstand stresses that will lead to certain failures in continuous operation.
4. In continuous operation the following applies:

> With Hs 123 not over 6 g
>
> With Ju 87 not over 6 g
>
> compare the dotted limiter line in the curve sheet.

> 1 g = Gravitational acceleration.

II. Special Guidelines for Hs 123.

Maximum achievable dive velocity is between 500 and 550 kph[394]. (Variations are possible due to loading, propeller pitch setting, idle engine power, etc.) This speed is harmless if sufficient care is taken during the pull-out.

With a final velocity of 550 kph, 6 g corresponds to a pull-out radius of 450 m.[395] Experience shows that 1-2 seconds elapse between bomb drop and the start of the pull-out. Within 2 sec. the airplane dives a further 250 m[396], which results in a safety limit for the release of 750 m[397], if the pull-out is to be completed at an altitude of 50 m[398].

---

[393] See Glossary: Pull-out radius (Abfangradius).
[394] 310 - 340 mph.
[395] 1500 ft.
[396] 800 ft.
[397] 2500 ft.
[398] 160 ft.

III. Special Guidelines for Ju 87.

1. Maximum achievable velocity with air brakes is around 480 kph[399]. Without air brakes this is around 700 kph[400], but a speed of 600 kph[401] m a y n o t be e x c e e d e d u n d e r a n y c i r c u m s t a n c e (diving without deployed air brakes is forbidden).

    In a 90° dive at 480 kph a permissible acceleration of 6 g corresponds to a pull-out radius of 350 m[402].

    Adding the above mentioned 2 second time span between bomb release and pull-out, this results in the lowest permissible drop height of about 650 m [403].

2. Before the dive[404]:
    a) the propeller is set to "cruise" (coarse pitch);
    b) air brakes are deployed.

        Reducing a diving speed that is too high during a dive by deploying the air brakes during the dive is not possible.

    c) retract flaps fully;
    d) set the supercharger to the low gear;
    e) close radiator cooling flaps.

3. After the dive:
    a) open radiator cooling flaps.
    b) retract air brakes (however, a continued flight with a deployed air brake extended is not dangerous).

---

[399] 300 mph.
[400] 435 mph.
[401] 370 mph. With the Ju 87 D-5, this was increased to 650 kph.
[402] 1150 ft.
[403] 2130 ft.
[404] It should be noted that more detailed instructions for the pre-dive preparations are found in the pilot manuals for each variant. However, the sequence described here remains pertinent to all Ju 87 types.

IV. Guidelines for Dropping Armed Bombs.

1. The aircraft must be outside the blast radius when the bomb detonates.

Bombs[405]	Fuze type	Blast radius[406]	
SC 50 o. V.[407] or m. V.[408] (0,05 Sec.)		250 m	
SC 250 o. V. or m. V. (0,05 Sec.)		500 m	Around the detonation.
SC 500 o. V. or m. V. (0,05 Sec.)		800 m[409]	

2. If the aircraft is expected to be outside the blast radius with o. V. or m. V. fuzes after its pull-out, bombs must be released from a safe release altitude.

Safe release altitudes for dives:

a)	Ju 87	for	SC 50	600 m[410]
		for	SC 250	825 m
		for	SC 500	1 090 m
b)	Hs 123	for	SC 50	750 m
		for	SC 250	975 m

This safe release altitude is based on the assumption that the smallest permissible pull-out radius is used.

---

[405] "SC" is the abbreviation of "Sprengbombe Cylindrisch", indicating a high-explosive bomb. The numbers correspond to the bomb weight in kilograms. See Glossary: Bomb types (Bombenarten).

[406] The blast radii of the here indicated bombs are not necessarily linked to the weight class. For example, unlike the SC 50, the SD 50 fragmentation bomb has an indicated blast radius of up to 500 m. BArch, RL 1/642, *L.Dv. 8/5 zugleich L.Dv. 20/3 Der Bombenwurf Teil 5 der LDv 8 bzw. Teil 3 der LDv 20*, January 1940. See Glossary: Bomb types (Bombenarten).

[407] "o.V." is the abbreviation of "ohne Verzögerung", indicating "without delay". See Glossary: Contact-fuze (Aufschlagzünder).

[408] "m.V." is the abbreviation of "mit Verzögerung", indicating "with delay". See Glossary: Contact-fuzes (Aufschlagszünder).

[409] Respectively: 820, 1640 and 2620 ft.

[410] Respectively: 1680, 2700, 3570, 2460 and 3200 ft.

3. **Prior to engine start:** Set altimeter, ASK[411], ZSK[412] and reflector sight[413] to "off" (With Ju 87 open the floor bombing window[414]).

4. **Prior to take-off:** Turn on reflector sight[415], adjust its luminosity, adjust the seat so, that eye is at same height as reflector sight.
    Set ZSK to o. V.[416] or m. V.[417] and to "dive" or "low altitude attack".

5. **Prior to the dive:** Turn on ASK, turn on ZSK (Hs 123 only: arm the bombs with the ASK).

6. **After the dive:** Turn off ZSK, ASK.

7. **Prior to landing:** Turn-off reflector sight, as it can be easily damaged.

V. Special Regulations.

1. A 90° dive may not be exceeded.

    The dive must be executed in such a way, that to retain the target during the dive, the airplane is not pushed above the 90° position under any circumstances (e.g., in case of tailwind). In such a situation, set a shallower dive than 90°.

2. Dive altitude as needed.

3. Ju 87 may not dive without air brakes.

4. The Ju 87's pull-out radius must not be less than 350 m[418]; this corresponds to a minimum drop height of 650 m[419] (for practice bombing).

---

[411] See Glossary: Bomb setting device (Abwurfschaltkasten).
[412] See Glossary: Fuze setting device (Zünderschaltkasten).
[413] See Glossary: Reflector sight (Reflexvisier).
[414] This was a small window set between the pilot's legs with a cover that could be opened manually. This allowed the pilot to look downwards, and just ahead of his aircraft. This not only assisted him in identifying terrain features, landmarks and the target, but also allowed him to judge the aircraft's relative position to the target, just prior to the dive.
[415] See Glossary: Reflector sight (Reflexvisier).
[416] "o.V." is the abbreviation of "ohne Verzögerung", indicating "without delay".
[417] "m.V." is the abbreviation of "mit Verzögerung", indicating "with delay".
[418] 1150 ft.
[419] 2130 ft.

5. The Hs 123's pull-out radius must not be less than 450 m[420]; this corresponds to a minimum drop height of 750 m [421] (for practice bombing).

6. It is prohibited to adjust the aircraft's trim during dive recovery.

    Dive and recovery must be made with a neutral trim setting[422]; or better, a slight nose-heavy trim setting.

7. Course corrections during the dive made with by aileron or rudder do not result in stress damage, as long as they are not made roughly.

---

[420] 1480 ft.
[421] 2460 ft.
[422] This was referred to as "Reisestellung" in the original document. The literal translation would be "travel setting" or "cruise setting". As such, this would not be necessarily a neutral setting in the strictest sense, but the setting used to maintain level flight.

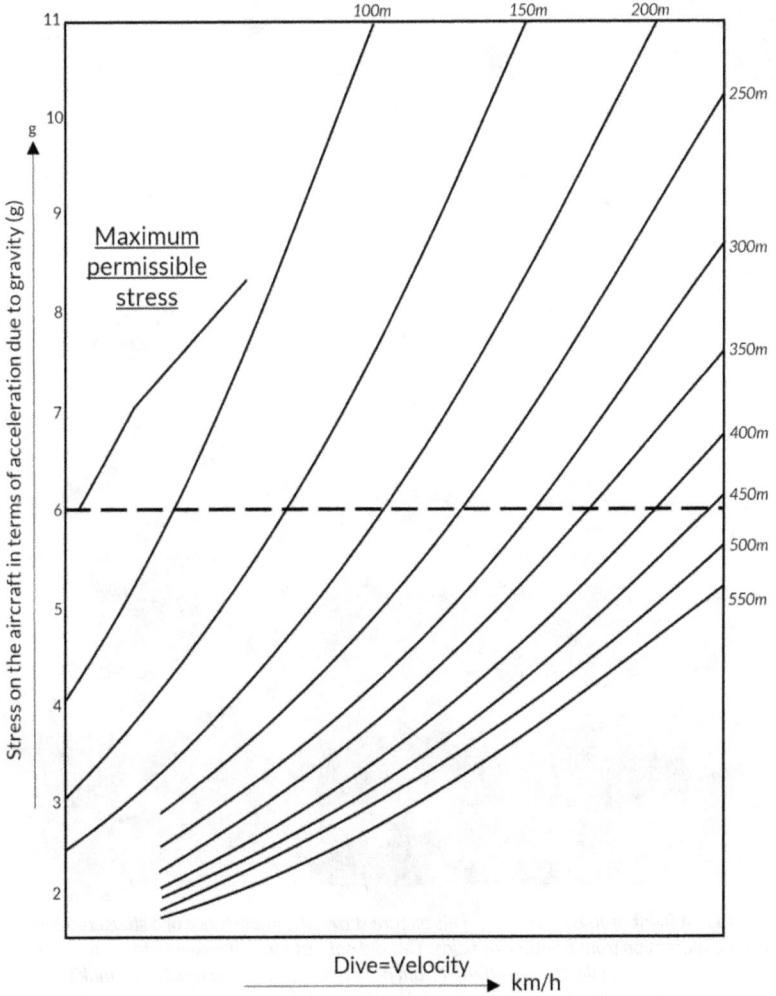

Curve sheet.

Pull-out radii

Stress on the aircraft in terms of acceleration due to gravity (g)

g

100m   150m   200m

250m

300m

350m

400m

450m

500m

550m

Maximum permissible stress

Dive=Velocity
km/h

Photo 7: A flight of Ju 87s takes off. This picture shows the importance of a staggered take-off in quick succession from frontline airfields. This did not just make it easier to form up in the air, but it also prevented pilots from suffering from poor visibility, and too much dust making it into the (filtered) engine air intakes. Original caption: Soviet Union, Battle of Stalingrad - Junkers Ju 87 taking off; approximately July-October 1942 Credit: BArch, Bild 116-489-01, o. Ang.

CHAPTER III

Experience Reports

Document: IV. Fliegerkorps - Mission Reports

In this chapter, a collection of Erfolgsmeldungen[423] or mission reports from the II./St.G. 77 attached to the IV. Fliegerkorps from 15th of May 1942, found in BArch, RL 10/473a, *Erfolgsmeldungen des IV. Fliegerkorps*. During this time, the Gruppe was flying missions in support of the counter-offensive during the 2nd Battle of Charkow in 1942. Throughout this battle, the Luftwaffe's IV. and VIII. Fliegerkorps provided support to the Axis ground forces between 1st to 31st May 1942, Ju 87 units from IV. Fliegerkorps flew 3 113 sorties (2 573 by St.G. 77 and 540 by St. G. 1).[424] During this time, the St.G. 77 flew its 20 000th sortie.[425]

The mission reports here were specially curated to provide a track record of over several days of activity, from the 18th to 23rd of May. This provides an overview of the type of missions flown throughout this time. With a wide variety of events, from a Geschwaderstab Ju 87 bombing friendly troops, over to a Ju 87 shot down by AA, the continuous interdiction attacks versus Soviet columns and bridges, an attempted attack versus a Soviet tank unit, as well as the effect of weather on mission parameters, this collection provides a lens into the "daily" sorties flown throughout this battle. Naturally, these reports reflect the account of the respective author and although they should be factual in theory, they can include errors, from subjective mistakes over to a more deliberate positive presentation of a strike. To provide a visual example of such a report, we have added a photo of a well conserved mission report at the start of our collection, dated 18th May 1942.

Considering the kill claims posted in these reports, it appears prudent to discuss the tendency of errors and number conflation within the chaotic nature of battle. The missions within this collection were flown around the time of the 2nd Battle of Charkow (12th to 28th May 1942). During this battle, the IV. Fliegerkorps reports 227 destroyed and 140 damaged tanks. The support provided to ground forces during this battle certainly appears significant, with General der Panzertruppe Paulus even specifically thanking the IV. Fliegerkorps for its attacks against Soviet tanks. In contrast, from the files available to the

---

[423] Literal translation: Success messages/reports.
[424] BArch, RL 10/473a, *Erfolgsmeldungen des IV. Fliegerkorps*; and BArch, RL 10/473a, *IV. Fliegerkorps, Übersicht über Einsätze, Erfolge und Verluste der Verbände des IV. Fliegerkorps v. 1-31.5.42*, 9. June 1942.
[425] BArch, RL 10/473a, *Sturzkampfgeschwader, Nachstehendes Anerkennungsschreiben des Kommandierenden Generals des IV. Flieger-Korps*, 21. June 1942.

authors, only a total of 122 destroyed and 79 damaged tank claims can be accounted for. 93 and 61 of these were credited to St.G. 77. Closer inspection of available reports shows that they only include 1,316 sorties with Ju 87s from a total of 2,573 sorties flown by St.G. 77. As such roughly half of the data set is missing. Within the available reports, tanks were the primary targets in only four attacks (8th, 15th, 22nd and 24th of May), totaling 124 sorties, of which the majority were cancelled and rerouted to secondary targets. As such, only 16 destroyed and 10 damaged tank claims can be found in the reports available to us from this timeframe, including those hit by collateral damage. It is thus not possible to verify the number of tank kills from the available mission reports, highlighting once again the difficulty in collecting data on such reported claims. On the whole, fixed targets, bridges and advancing as well as retreating columns (claims: 3038 destroyed and 462 damaged motorized vehicles) remained the most important targets, showing the continued use of the Ju 87 as an interdiction rather than close air support asset. This is also demonstrated within the enclosed mission reports on the following pages.[426]

Preliminary Notes / Source Situation, Actuality and Formatting

Throughout this volume, we aimed to retain some of the original formatting, yet the editorial focus lay on legibility. One of the main editorial changes was that, in order to present a clearer layout, we did not follow the original page count as this would have resulted in empty or near empty pages throughout the book. Instead, the text has been reformatted to follow a more conventional structure, page by page.

The following page provides a well-preserved example of a mission report in its original format. Many of these reports are either damaged, ripped, partially splattered with ink or oil, or badly legible. Our selection was therefore based on both the content, which showed a diverse mission set for Ju 87s, and those sheets that could be read in their entirety. For this document, please be aware of the following formatting decisions and changes:

- We corrected formatting mistakes in the original version (for example missing spaces, paragraph breaks or others).
- While the template provides consistency in its layout, these reports were often written by different individuals, contributing to some variation in how these were filled out. These differences are often inconsequential from a content perspective. Examples include using

---

[426] See BArch RL 10/473a, *IV. Fliegerkorps, Schreiben Paulus, 3. Juni 1942*; and BArch, RL 10/473a, *IV. Fliegerkorps, Übersicht über Einsätze, Erfolge und Verluste der Verbände des IV. Fliegerkorps v. 1-31.5.42*, 9. June 1942.

either "xxx" or "---" to strike off non-applicable rows like "secondary target" or "losses". To provide consistency, we have opted to complete such rows, as well as those left empty, with "[no entry]" instead.

- The original format of the template was a two-column layout, as can be seen from the picture showing an original sheet. To provide a more structured overview, we changed the format to a standard top-to-bottom layout.
- The format in which drop altitudes were written differed from entry to entry (either ascending or descending). The same applies to the placement of these figures, which was inconsistently placed on the "Mission" or "Results" entry. We have opted for an ascending format and placed these figures on the "Mission" row, as this was the more common style.
- Village and town names have only been translated where we could identify them with a degree of certainty.
- Be aware that we did not add a note for the different bomb types as those are explained in the Glossary.

Photo 8: This photograph gives some indications of the conditions on the Eastern Front which were far from ideal for aircraft. Original caption: Soviet Union – Dive-bomber (Stuka) Junkers 87 on a muddy frontline airfield. Bombs in the foreground. 1942. Credit: BArch, Bild 101I-394-1471-27, Fotograf(in): Schalber.

158

Mission Reports

Erfolgsmeldung 565 (198)
(Kampfverbände)

Tag: 18.5.42.
Stunde:
Melder:
Aufgenommen:

1. Korps: IV. Fliegerkorps
2. Verband: II./Stuka 77
3. Zahl: 17 (2 vom Gruppenstab
(4 von 4. Staffel
(6 von 5. Staffel
4. Typ: (4 von 6. Staffel
(1 vom Geschw.-Stab)
Ju 87
5. Startzeit: 13.30

6. Ldg.-Zeit: 14.20 - 14.25

Angr.-Zt.: 13.50 - 14.10

8. Auftrag:
Angriff auf zurückgehende
feindliche Kolonnen zwischen
P 233 und P 231,
P 233 und P 230,
P 232 und P 230.

(Anflughöhe 1500 m,
Auslösehöhe 500 - 600 m)

9. Erfolg:
Zwischen P 233 und P 231 und
bei P 231 vereinzelte Ansamm-
lungen von bespannten Fahrzeugen
und einige mot. Fahrzeuge ange-
griffen. 2 LKW und 5 bespannte
Fahrzeuge mit Sicherheit vernichtet, mehrere Pferde ge-
tötet und weitere Fahrzeuge beschädigt. Die Fahrzeugan-
sammlungen standen und machten
einen verlassenen Eindruck.
Im Hufeisenwald 4 km nordwestl.
P 233 wurden zwei mot und 2 besp.
Fahrzeuge zerstört. Im Wäldchen
am Ostrand Andrejewka (4 km
ostw. P 230) eine bespannte
Batterie und 5 bespannte Fahrz.
vernichtet.
Maschine des Geschwaderstabes be-
warf in Gegend 2 km südwestl.
P 234 eigene Truppen, ohne zu
treffen.

(signature) Major und Gruppenkommandeur.

10. Ausweichsziel:
xxxxxxxxxxxx

11. Abgebrochen:
a) Zahl: 1

b) Ursache: Motor ölt

12. Bomben (Zahl u. Art):
12 SD 250, 4 SD 250,
36 SC 50, 28 SD 50.

13. Abschüsse (Zahl u. Art):

14. Verluste (Zahl u. Art, durch):
(1 Maschine beschädigt durch
eigene Bombensplitter)

15. Abwehr:
nicht erkannt.

16. Sonstiges: Eigene Truppen haben Höhe
197,2 erreicht und stehen dort
in Feldstellung. Auf Flugplatz
westl. P 233 zwölf einmotorige
Flugzeuge, wahrscheinlich Mig.
(1 davon auf dem Rücken liegend)
erkannt. Eigene Panzer schossen
17. Wetter: Höhe 197,2 auf den Platz. Auf
dem Flugplatz war keine Bewegungen
zu erkennen, wahrscheinlich schon
verlassen. Zwischen P 232 und
P230 keinerlei Fahrzeugverkehr.
17. Wetter: Wolkenlos, Sicht 30-50km.

Original *Erfolgsmeldung*[427] of II./St.G. 77 from the 18th of May 1942. A
translation of this report is found on the following page. Source: BArch, RL
10/473a, *Erfolgsmeldungen des IV. Fliegerkorps*.

---

[427] The literal translation would be "success report".

Mission Report 565 (198)

Date: 18.5.42

1. **Korps:** IV. Fliegerkorps
2. **Unit:** II./Stuka 77
3. **Number:** 17 (2 from Gruppenstab, 4 from 4. Staffel, 6 from 5. Staffel, 4 from 6. Staffel, 1 from Geschwaderstab)
4. **Type:** Ju 87
5. **Take-off:** 13.30
6. **Landing:** 14.20 – 14.25
7. **Attack:** 13.50 – 14.10
8. **Mission:** Attack on enemy columns that are moving back between P 233 and P 231, P 233 and P 230, P 232 and P 230.
   (Approach altitude 1500 m, release altitude 500 - 600 m)

9. **Success:** Between P 233 and P 231 and at P 231 attacked scattered concentrations of horse-drawn carriages and some motorized vehicles. 2 trucks and 5 horse-drawn carriages destroyed with certainty, several horses killed and other vehicles damaged. The vehicle concentrations were stationary and made an abandoned impression. In the horseshoe shaped wood 4 km northwest of P 233 2 motorized and 2 horse-drawn carriages were destroyed. In the little forest on the outskirts of Andreyevka (4 km eastwest of P 230) one horse-drawn battery and 3 horse-drawn vehicles were destroyed. A machine of the Geschwaderstab bombed own troops in the area 2 km southwest of P 234 without hitting anything.
10. **Secondary target:** [no entry]
11. **Aborted:**
    a) **Number:** 1
    b) **Reason:** Oil leak in the engine
12. **Ordnance:** 12 SC 250, 4 SD 250, 36 SC 50, 28 SD 50.
13. **Aerial victories (Number and Type):** [no entry]
14. **Losses (Number and reason for):** (1 aircraft damaged by own bomb fragments)
15. **Defense:** not detected
16. **Misc:** Friendly troops reached height 197.2 and deployed in a hedgehog position. On airfield west of P 233 twelve single-engine planes, probably Mig, (1 of them on its back) detected. Friendly tanks fired on this airfield from height 197.2. No movements could be seen on the airfield, probably already abandoned. - Between P 232 and P 230 no vehicle traffic at all.
17. **Weather:** Cloudless, visibility 30 - 50km.

Mission Report 566 (199)

Date: 18.5.42

1. **Korps:** IV. Fliegerkorps
2. **Unit:** II./Stuka 77
3. **Number:** 17 (2 from Stab, 4 from 4. Staffel, 7 from 5. Staffel, 4 from 6. Staffel)
4. **Type:** Ju 87
5. **Take-off:** 17.50
6. **Landing:** 18.30 – 18.35
7. **Attack:** 18.10 – 18.20
8. **Mission:**
   1.) Attacking enemy vehicle concentration (500 vehicles) in Studenok (2 km west of P 243)
   2.) Destruction of the Bridge over the Donets at Studenok
   (Approach altitudes for target 1: 1800 m, for target 2: 3000 m. Release altitudes: 400 - 300 m)

9. **Success:**
   1.) Attack with 8 aircraft on the vehicle concentration at Studenok. Direct hits, strong fires observed. Destruction or damage of a large number of vehicles is to be expected, exact effect could not be observed due to heavy smoke.
   2.) 5 direct hits on Studenok pontoon bridge. Bridge destroyed. Some pontoons burned and floated away[428], on which probably some burning vehicles were standing
10. **Secondary target:** [no entry]
11. **Aborted:**
    a) **Number:** [no entry]
    b) **Reason:** [no entry]
12. **Ordnance:** 1 SC 500, 11 SC 250, 5 SD 250, 48 SC 50, 16 SD 50
13. **Aerial victories (Number and Type):** [no entry]
14. **Losses (Number and reason for):** [no entry]
15. **Defense:** Few heavy and medium anti-aircraft guns (firing poorly)
16. **Misc:** [no entry]
17. **Weather:** Cloudless, visibility 30 km.

---

[428] Some letters were not readable, yet the original word is most likely "wegget[ri]eben", which in the context would mean the pontoon segments floated away.

Mission Report 567 (200)

Date: 19.05.42

1. **Korps:** IV. Fliegerkorps
2. **Unit:** II./Stuka 77
3. **Number:** 17 (1 from Gruppenstab, 4 from 4. Staffel, 7 from 5. Staffel, 3 from 6. Staffel, 2 from Geschwaderstab)
4. **Type:** Ju 87
5. **Take-off:** 11.05
6. **Landing:** 12.05
7. **Attack:** 11.35 – 11.40
8. **Mission:** Attack on the Donets bridge near Protopopowka (C 223). (Approach altitude 3000 m, release altitude 300 - 600 m)

9. **Success:** 1 hit (250kg) on the eastern bridgehead, 1 hit (500kg) on the eastern part of the bridge (above water), probably 1 further hit on the western third of the bridge.
   Follow-up report based on the impact pattern: There are a total of 4 hits on the bridge, namely:
   1. eastward bridge joint destroyed,
   2. immediately next to this towards the west 50 m bridge destroyed,
   3. in the eastern third of the bridge over the river, two adjacent hits which destroyed a bridge length of up to 28 m.
10. **Secondary target:** [no entry]
11. **Aborted:**
    a) **Number:** [no entry]
    b) **Reason:** [no entry]
12. **Ordnance:** 3 SC 500, 14 SC 250, 66 SC 50
13. **Aerial victories (Number and Type):** [no entry]
14. **Losses (Number and reason for):** [no entry]
15. **Defense:** Poorly firing heavy and light anti-aircraft guns
16. **Misc:** Reconnaissance report: The attacked bridge was a very strong bridge[429], same construction as bridge at Bogorodichnoye. South between C 236 and C 223 4 other bridges of lighter, speedy construction, some still unfinished. No traffic recognized on all 5 bridges.
17. **Weather:** Cloudless, visibility 50 km.

---

[429] The original German word was "Kriegsbrücke". The literal translation would be "war bridge".

162

Mission Report 568 (201)

Date: 20.05.42

1. **Korps:** IV. Fliegerkorps
2. **Unit:** II./Stuka 77
3. **Number:** 17[430] (2 from Stab, 4 from 4. Staffel, 7 from 5. Staffel, 4 from 6. Staffel, + 1 Geschwaderstab)
4. **Type:** Ju 87
5. **Take-off:** 11.05
6. **Landing:** 12.10 – 12.15
7. **Attack:** 11.35 – 11.45
8. **Mission:** Attack on tanks and columns in the area C 245 - C 244 - C 230. (Approach altitudes 1200 - 2000 m, release altitude 400 - 500 m)

9. **Success:** 7 aircraft (5. Staffel): In the northern part of C 246 five camouflaged parked tanks and in the north-eastern part of C 245 34-T-tanks[431] attacked. Close hits on the tanks, some houses destroyed. Heavy losses among the observed accompanying infantry are assumed.
   4 aircraft (6. Staffel): In the orchards north of C 244 parked motorized vehicles and horse-drawn carriages attacked. No effect observed, destruction or damage of several vehicles to be expected.
   4 aircraft (4. Staffel): Destroyed a motorized radio station with 3 cars in the village 3 km north-eastward of C 242.
   3 aircraft (Gruppen- and Geschwaderstab). [?][432] trucks and 4 horse-drawn vehicles destroyed with guns. [?] Horse-drawn vehicles and 2 trucks, standing together destroyed by 500kg [bomb]. 1 tank on [road] 3 km east of C 242 probably damaged. (By two 50kg landing on either side)
10. **Secondary target:** [no entry]
11. **Aborted:**
    c) **Number:** [no entry]
    d) **Reason:** [no entry]
12. **Ordnance:** 1 SC 500, 16 SC 250, 1 SD 250, 62 SC 50, 10SD 50.
13. **Aerial victories (Number and Type):** [no entry]

---

[430] Note that the 2 + 4 + 7 +4 + 1 is actually 18 not 17. See also text.

[431] This should likely mean T-34 tanks. The German Army usually referred to them as "T 34", similarly how the Luftwaffe would refer to planes without a hyphen. The designation "34-T-Panzer" appears rather uncommon.

[432] The number of trucks destroyed as illegible as part of the page was missing. We assume it might have been "1".

14. **Losses (Number and reason for):** 4 aircraft hit by enemy fire, 1 of which made a smooth emergency landing on German territory approx. 2 km south of C 245.
15. **Defense:** M.G. and rifle fire and little heavy AA from far away.
16. **Misc:** Friendly infantry in defensive position (dug in) at 141.7 (2 km northeast C 246).
17. **Weather:** 2000 m 4/10, visibility 40 km.

Photo 9: Ju 87 fly over tanks from the SS-Panzer-Grenadier-Division "Totenkopf" during Operation "Citadel", July 1943. These Ju 87s are most likely on their return flight due to their heading, as they do not seem to carry any bombs, and are flying low. Credit: Collection Roman Töppel.

Mission Report 569 (202)

Tag: 20.5.42

1. **Korps:** IV. Fliegerkorps
2. **Unit:** II./Stuka 77
3. **Number:** 14 (1 from Stab, 4 from 4. Staffel, 7 from 5. Staffel, 2 from 6. Staffel) + 1 from Geschwaderstab
4. **Type:** [no entry]
5. **Take-off:** 15.15
6. **Landing:** 16.40
7. **Attack:** 15.45 – 16.05
8. **Mission:** Destruction of enemy forces in the form of armed reconnaissance in the area C 229 - C 215 - C 203 and on the road from 203 to the east.

9. **Success:** 8 aircraft (4. Staffel, 6. Staffel and Stab) eastward of C 226 and at C 201 attack on vehicle concentrations. 7 trucks, 2 towing vehicles, 2 cars put on fire with bombs or guns. One 250kg bomb between 2 four-horse carriages which can be assumed as destroyed. At airfield south-east of C 218 four Migs shot on fire.
   7 aircraft (5. Staffel) attacked at P 811 stationary concentration of motorized vehicles and tanks. Hits in the concentration. Due to heavy smoke and dust, the effect could not be recognized. Destruction of several vehicles is to be expected.
10. **Secondary target:** [no entry]
11. **Aborted:**
    a) **Number:** [no entry]
    b) **Reason:** [no entry]
12. **Ordnance:** 13 SD 250, 2 SC 250, 40 SD 50, 20 SD 50 [written by hand]
13. **Aerial victories (Number and Type):** [no entry]
14. **Losses (Number and reason for):** Ju 87 S2 + AN[433] with crew Stabsfeldwebel Kreb / Unteroffizier Stöver shot down in flames by a direct hit. Impact 5 km eastwards of P 811. Continued see reverse side!
15. **Defense:** 5. Staffel: Heavy, medium and light AA from area P 811 and P 809.
16. **Misc:** Worthwhile targets were found in the attacked area.

---

[433] Designated operational code of respective aircraft, usually painted on the side. The first combination, here S2, is the designation for the Geschwader. The second combination, AN is split in the aircraft's identification letter and Staffel code. A refers to the first individual aircraft letter, while N designates this aircraft as part of the 5. Staffel of II. Gruppe. See also Barry C. Rosch, *Luftwaffe Codes, Markings & Units 1939-1945*, Schiffer Publishing Ltd, Atglen, PA, USA, 1995, p. 8-12, 354-355.

17. Weather: 3500, 6 – 7/10, visibility 10 km, very hazy.

18. <u>Losses continued:</u>

Ju 87 S2 + DN[434] with the crew Unteroffizier Lannewers / Obergefreiter Bette missing. Was not seen by the unit after the attack. However, shortly before the Staffel reached the airfield, he reported through the radio as being on a return course[435]. It can be assumed that aircraft made an emergency landing on friendly territory.

Photo 10: Ju 87 attacking a pontoon bridge, Eastern Front, n.d. Credit: NARA.

---

[434] Designated operational code of respective aircraft, usually painted on the side. The first combination, here S2, is the designation for the Geschwader. The second combination, AN is split in the aircraft's identification letter and Staffel code. D refers to the first individual aircraft letter, while N designates this aircraft as part of the 5. Staffel of II. Gruppe. See also Barry C. Rosch, *Luftwaffe Codes, Markings & Units 1939-1945*, Schiffer Publishing Ltd, Atglen, PA, USA, 1995, p. 8-12, 354-355.

[435] The original German word was "Heimatkurs". The literal translation would be "course towards home".

Mission Report 570 (203)

Date: 21.5.42

1. **Korps:** IV. Fliegerkorps
2. **Unit:** II./Stuka 77
3. **Number:** 12 (2 from Stab, 3 from 4. Staffel, 5 from 5. Staffel, 2 from 6. Staffel)
4. **Type:** Ju 87
5. **Take-off:** 9.55
6. **Landing:** 11.00 – 11.20
7. **Attack:** 10.25 – 10.45
8. **Mission:** Attack on enemy columns falling back to the north on the road R 609 - R 610 - P 860 - P 846.
   (Approach altitudes 2500 - 3000 m, release altitudes 1000 - 500 m)

9. **Success:** On the road R 609 to P 860 horse-drawn carriages and in an orchard southwest of R 610 stationary horse-drawn carriages and motorized vehicles attacked. 2 trucks burned, 20 horse-drawn carriages destroyed with certainty. Damage to further vehicles is to be expected.
   At Chlebnoye station (south of 609) attacked standing freight train under steam and two single locomotives under steam. Close hit on the freight train, the two lone locomotives destroyed.
   On road 623 to the northeast M.G. strafing attacks on 5 trucks without observed effect.
10. **Secondary target:** [no entry]
11. **Aborted:**
    a) **Number:** [no entry]
    b) **Reason:** [no entry]
12. **Ordnance:** 7 SC 250, 5 SD 250, 38 SC 50, 10 SD 50.
13. **Aerial victories (Number and Type):** [no entry]
14. **Losses (Number and reason for):** [no entry]
15. **Defense:** Little light AA from the north of 624.
16. **Misc:** [no entry]
17. **Weather:** 10/10 in 3500 m, scattered clouds in 1800 m, visibility 20 km,

Mission Report 571 (204)

Date: 21.5.42

1. **Korps:** IV. Fliegerkorps
2. **Unit:** II./Stuka 77
3. **Number:** 10 (1 from Stab, 3 from 4. Staffel, 4 from 5. Staffel, 2 from 6. Staffel) + 1 Geschwaderstab.
4. **Type:** Ju 87
5. **Take-off:** 16.15
6. **Landing:** 17.15 – 17.20
7. **Attack:** 16.50
8. **Mission:** Attack on Donets bridge 20a between Ivanovka and Levkovka (14 km northwest of Izyum)
   Secondary target if cloud height below 2500 m:
   Northern part of C 209 or columns from there to the northeast.
   (Approach altitude 2700, release altitude 500 m)

9. **Success:** Due to bad weather over target (1500 m cloud height, rain and bad visibility) attacked north part C 209 according to given orders. Bombs lay scattered in the target. Special effect not recognized.
10. **Secondary target:** See under Success.
11. **Aborted:**
    a) **Number:** [no entry]
    b) **Reason:** [no entry]
12. **Ordnance:** 4 SC 500, 7 SC 250, 38 SC 50.
13. **Aerial victories (Number and Type):** [no entry]
14. **Losses (Number and reason for):** None.
15. **Defense:** Not observed.
16. **Misc:** Friendly troops 2 km northwest of C 209. The Donets bridge at C 223, destroyed by the group on 19.5.42, has not yet been rebuilt.
17. **Weather:** See under Success.

Mission Report 572 (205)

Date: 22.5.42

1. **Korps:** IV. Fliegerkorps
2. **Unit:** II./Stuka 77
3. **Number:** 12 (2 from Stab, 3 from 4. Staffel, 4 from 5. Staffel, 3 from 6. Staffel)
4. **Type:** Ju 87
5. **Take-off:** 6.55 – 7.00
6. **Landing:** 8.00 – 8.05
7. **Attack:** 7.40
8. **Mission:** Destruction of the Donets bridge 20 a between Ivanovka and Levkovka (14 km northwest of Izyum).
   (Approach altitude 3500 m, release altitudes 100-500m)

9. **Success:** Bridge destroyed by 5 direct hits.
10. **Secondary target:** [no entry]
11. **Aborted:**
    a) **Number:** [no entry]
    b) **Reason:** [no entry]
12. **Ordnance:** 1 SC 500, 9 SC 250, 2 SD 250, 30 SD 50, 8 SD 50.
13. **Aerial victories (Number and Type):** [no entry]
14. **Losses (Number and reason for):** [no entry]
15. **Defense:** No defense observed at the target. On approach in area C 234 friendly heavy AA. At C 234, a Russian[436] aircraft dropped bombs in a low-level attack, whereupon AA fired on friendly aircraft.
16. **Misc:** [no entry]
17. **Weather:** Cloudless, hazy, visibility 20 km.

---

[436] Although properly referred to as "Soviet" in today's literature, German sources from the time tend to refer to Soviet forces as "Russian". Major exception was the military intelligence organization Fremde Heere Ost (Foreign Armies East), which usually used "Soviet-Russian".

Mission Report 573 (206)

Date: 22.5.42

1. **Korps:** IV. Fliegerkorps
2. **Unit:** II./Stuka 77
3. **Number:** 10 (2 from Stab, 2 from 4. Staffel, 4 from 5. Staffel, 2 from 6. Staffel)
4. **Type:** Ju 87
5. **Take-off:** 9.25 – 9.30
6. **Landing:** 10.40
7. **Attack:** 9.50 – 10.10
8. **Mission:** Armed reconnaissance in the C 203 - C 202 - P 812 - C 215 area, with weight of effort[437] at C 203.
   (Approach altitudes: 1500 - 2000 m, release altitudes 400 - 500m)

9. **Success:** Eastward, southeastward and northeastward of C 203 attacked tanks, trucks and infantry moving backwards with bombs and M.G.s. Heavy damage to one tank and 4 trucks is expected. On two other tanks 1 close hit each and on one tank 2 close hits were scored, without observed effect. 1 motorcycle with a sidecar destroyed by M.G. fire and 4 horses killed by close hits on one horse-drawn carriage. Heavy casualties[438] among the infantry are to be expected.
10. **Secondary target:** [no entry]
11. **Aborted:**
    a) **Number:** [no entry]
    b) **Reason:** [no entry]
12. **Ordnance:** 5 SC 250, 5 SD 250, 22 SC 50, 18 SD 50.
13. **Aerial victories (Number and Type):** [no entry]
14. **Losses (Number and reason for):** None.
15. **Defense:** M.G. and rifle fire.
16. **Misc:** In the Razorennaya gorge southwest of C 200 horse-drawn carriages and motorized vehicles parked under trees. Position of German tank spearhead at Wolny height 182.3 (west of C 220).
17. **Weather:** 2 – 3/10 in 1200 m, visibility 10 km, Ground haze.

---

[437] See Glossary: Weight of effort (Schwerpunkt).
[438] The original German word was "blutigen Verlusten". The literal translation would be "bloody casualties".

Mission Report 574 (207)

Tag: 22.5.42

1. **Korps:** IV. Fliegerkorps
2. **Unit:** II./Stuka 77
3. **Number:** 10 (1 from Stab, 3 from 4. Staffel, 4 from 5. Staffel, 2 from 6. Staffel)
4. **Type:** Ju 87
5. **Take-off:** 12.15 – 12.20
6. **Landing:** 13.25 – 13.30
7. **Attack:** 12.45 – 12.50
8. **Mission:** Armed reconnaissance in area
   1.) P 860 – R 609 – R 611.
   2.) R 612 – R 624 – R 638.
   (Approach altitude 1700 - 2000 m, release altitude 400 - 500 m).

9. **Success:**
   1.) 5 aircraft:
   In Kolkhoz Swedloff (2 km southeastward of R 610) and in Swch. Kombajn (3 km northeast of R 610) horse-drawn carriages and horse-drawn guns were attacked. About 6 horse-drawn carriages destroyed, damage to others expected.
   2.) 4 aircraft:
   Motorized and horse-drawn carriage concentrations attacked in the area 1 - 2 km northwest of R 609. Destruction of 6 vehicles is to be expected, more damaged.
10. **Secondary target:** [no entry]
11. **Aborted:**
    a) **Number:** [no entry]
    b) **Reason:** [no entry]
12. **Ordnance:** 4 SC 250, 6 SD 250, 32 SC 50, 8 SD 50.
13. **Aerial victories (Number and Type):** None.
14. **Losses (Number and reason for):** None.
15. **Defense:** Not observed.
16. **Misc:** [no entry]
17. **Weather:** Cloudless, visibility 50 km, light ground haze.

Mission Report 575 (208)

Date: 22.5.42

1. **Korps:** IV. Fliegerkorps
2. **Unit:** II./Stuka 77
3. **Number:** 7 (1 from Stab, 3 from 4. Staffel, 3 from 5. Staffel)
4. **Type:** Ju 87
5. **Take-off:** 15.05 – 15.10
6. **Landing:** 16.20 – 16.25
7. **Attack:** 15.40 – 15.50
8. **Mission:** Attack on enemy troops near the base of the creek eastward of P 813 via P 812 and northwards until the village of Hf. Ljubizkije. (Approach altitude 2500m, release altitude 400 - 600m)

9. **Success:** 3 aircraft (5. Staffel): In Hf. Ljubizkije concentrations of trucks and tanks and infantry positions attacked. 4 trucks destroyed with certainty.
   4 aircraft (4. Staffel and Stab): In the area P 812 - C 200 - B 151 in the canyons parked vehicles attacked with bombs and M.G.. 3 trucks burned (ammunition) with certainty 2 more trucks destroyed. Damage to other vehicles is to be expected. One aircraft attacked vehicles parked in gardens at C 213 without observed effect.
10. **Secondary target:** [no entry]
11. **Aborted:**
    a)   **Number:** [no entry]
    b)   **Reason:** [no entry]
12. **Ordnance:** 7 SD 250, 26 SC 50, 2 SD 50.
13. **Aerial victories (Number and Type):** None.
14. **Losses (Number and reason for):** None.
15. **Defense:** Not observed.
16. **Misc:** In the area P 812 - C 200 - B 151 about 150 vehicles in total parked in columns in the ravines. In and around C 213 strong concentrations of motorized and horse-drawn vehicles.
17. **Weather:** 1/10 in 2000 m, visibility 50 km, light ground haze.

Mission Report 576 (209)

Date: 22.5.42

1. **Korps:** IV. Fliegerkorps
2. **Unit:** II./Stuka 77
3. **Number:** 12 (4 from 4. Staffel, 4 from 5. Staffel, 4 from 6. Staffel)
4. **Type:** Ju 87
5. **Take-off:** 18.00
6. **Landing:** 19.05 – 19.10
7. **Attack:** 18.30 – 50.
8. **Mission:** Attack on tanks in Nikolajewka, Tichopolje and Dmitrijewka (west and southeast C 229)
   (Approach altitude 1500 - 1800 m, release altitude 500 - 600 m)

9. **Success:**
   3 aircraft (4. Staffel)
   + 4 aircraft (5. Staffel)
   In the village of Nikolajewka no tanks detected. Single motorized vehicles at the houses. Most of the houses were destroyed. The destruction of around 4 motorized vehicles is to be expected.
   4 aircraft (6. Staffel)
   Village Dmitrijewka bombed in 4 attacks. Several fires in the village. Tanks not detected. Damage to several horse-drawn carriages possible.
   Tichopolje is not a village but only a small collective farm with orchards.
10. **Secondary target:** [no entry]
11. **Aborted:**
    a) **Number:** 1 (did not attack)
    b) **Reason:** Engine problems.
12. **Ordnance:** 7 SC 250, 4 SD 250, 34 SC 50, 10 SD 50.
13. **Aerial victories (Number and Type):** None.
14. **Losses (Number and reason for):** None.
15. **Defense:** Not observed.
16. **Misc:** 2 km east of Nikolajewka 1 moving tank detected.
17. **Weather:** Cloudless, heavy haze, visibility 20 km, approaching bad weather area from SW.

Mission Report 577 (210)

Date: 23.5.42

1. **Korps:** IV. Fliegerkorps
2. **Unit:** II./Stuka 77
3. **Number:** 13 (2 from Stab, 3 from 4. Staffel, 4 from 5. Staffel, 4 from 6. Staffel)
4. **Type:** Ju 87
5. **Take-off:** 8.05 – 8.15
6. **Landing:** 9.15 – 9.30
7. **Attack:** 8.35 – 8.50
8. **Mission:** Attack on troops in Pawlowka, Bakscharowka (south of C 216) and Nikolajewka.

9. **Success:**
   3 aircraft (4. Staffel)
   The village of Pawlowka was attacked. Bombs lay in vehicle concentrations (horse-drawn and motorized) which were parked camouflaged near houses and in gardens. Special effect not recognized. Damage to 5 - 8 vehicles is to be expected.
   4 aircraft (5. Staffel)
   Village Bakscharowka and Fedorowka attacked. 3 trucks set on fire with bombs, 2 - 3 other trucks put out of action.
   6 aircraft (6. Staffel + Stab)
   Village Nikolajewka, barely occupied, (no tanks) attacked. 1 towing vehicle with [attached] gun destroyed, several hits in houses and on parked vehicles.
10. **Secondary target:** [no entry]
11. **Aborted:**
    a) **Number:** [no entry]
    b) **Reason:** [no entry]
12. **Ordnance:** 10 SD 250, 3 SC 250, 44 SC 50, 8 SD 50,
13. **Aerial victories (Number and Type):** [no entry]
14. **Losses (Number and reason for):** None.
15. **Defense:** sporadic M.G. fire.
16. **Misc:** [no entry]
17. **Weather:** 8/10 in 2500 m, visibility 20 km (strong wind)

174

Mission Report 578 (211)

Date: 23.5.42

1. **Korps:** IV. Fliegerkorps
2. **Unit:** II./Stuka 77
3. **Number:** 10 (1 from Stab, 3 from 4. Staffel, 3 from 5. Staffel, 3 from 6. Staffel)
4. **Type:** Ju 87
5. **Take-off:** 11.35
6. **Landing:** 12.45 – 12.55
7. **Attack:** 12.00 – 12.15
8. **Mission:** Attack on areas C 214 - C 215 on detected enemy troop concentrations. Weight of effort[439] on the villages.

9. **Success:** In and near C 216 and C 215 as well as in Swjatuschury (1.5 km south of C 215) strong concentrations of troops and vehicles of all kinds attacked with bombs and M.G.. 5 trucks and 4 horse-drawn carriages destroyed with certainty. At least 10 - 15 vehicles disabled by damage. 10 horses killed. 5 men lay dead or wounded after the use of 50kg bombs with a contact-fuze[440] against enemy infantry that was moving back[441].
10. **Secondary target:** [no entry]
11. **Aborted:**
    a) **Number:** [no entry]
    b) **Reason:** [no entry]
12. **Ordnance:** 6 SC 250, 4 SD 250, 28 SC 50, 12 SD 50.
13. **Aerial victories (Number and Type):** None.
14. **Losses (Number and reason for):** None.
15. **Defense:** Not observed.
16. **Misc:** About 4 km southeast of C 251 a burned-out Bf 109 F with the marking G. - Enemy infantry in the canyons eastward of C 203. Moving back to the west. Friendly infantry in attack from area height 185.6 to the west.
17. **Weather:** 11/10 at 1000 m, about 6 - 8/10 at 1700 m, 9/10 at 2500 m, rain showers, visibility 10 km, visibility worsening in the showers.

---

[439] See Glossary: Weight of effort (Schwerpunkt).
[440] See Glossary: Contact-fuze (Aufschlagzünder).
[441] The original German word was "zurückgehen". The literal translation would be "walking back". As such it is not clear whether these troops are retreating, or rather due to their direction towards the west, are moving back towards the front lines.

Photo 11: A Junkers Ju 87 receives a new coat of paint for the winter months. Original caption: Eastern Front – Spraying a new white winter camouflage on to the wing of a Junkers Ju 87. December 1943. Credit: BArch, Bild 101I-665-6815-10A, Fotograf(in): Speck.

Photo 12: A Junkers Ju 87 just before take-off. Easy to recognize is the mix of ordnance. Conventional bombs are mounted on the wings, while the centerline features a receives a cluster munitions container. Original caption: Eastern Front – Junkers Ju 87 D just prior to take-off. December 1943. Credit: BArch, Bild 101I-665-6814-07, Fotograf(in): Speck.

Photo 13: This Junkers Ju 87 had its gear fairings removed, potentially to prevent mud from clogging up the wheel space. The aircraft in the back features a dotted winter camouflage. Original caption: Soviet Union - Junkers Ju 87 (2+NM)⁴⁴² or a muddy airfield. 1942/1943. Credit: BArch, Bild 101I-630-3562-20A, Fotograf(in): Wanderer, W.

---

[442] Designated operational code of respective aircraft, usually painted on the side. The first combination, a barely perceptible S with a clear 2, is the designation for the Geschwader, in this case St.G. 77. The second combination, NM is split in the aircraft's identification letter and Staffel code. N refers to the individual aircraft letter, while M designates this aircraft as part of the 4. Staffel of II. Gruppe. See also Barry C. Rosch, *Luftwaffe Codes, Markings & Units 1939-1945*, Schiffer Publishing Ltd, Atglen, PA, USA, 1995, p. 8-12, 354-355.

An Introduction to Anti-Shipping Operations with Ju 87s

The following documents are about anti-shipping operations. The first document, *Lecture on the Development of Navalized Dive-Bombers*, is a pre-war lecture held by the Kriegsmarine discussing the possible use of aircraft against ships, with the specific pages on dive-bomber developments and employment. The second document, *Methods of Attacking Naval Targets with Dive-Bombers*, is an overall experience report written post-war by Oberstleutnant i.G. a.D.[443] Helmut Mahlke. As a Staffelkapitän, Mahlke took part in the invasion of Poland and saw action at Dunkirk, before becoming Gruppenkommandant between June 1940 and September 1941. In this capacity, Mahlke commanded III./St.G. 1 during the Battle of Britain. The Gruppe was moved to the Mediterranean, where it saw action during the Invasion of Crete. It was later moved to the East to prepare for Operation Barbarossa, the attack on the Soviet Union in June 1941. Mahlke himself moved on to become Oberstleutnant im Generalstab. After the war, in 1955, he joined the West-German Bundeswehr, with a placement in the Luftwaffe as well as the Marineflieger[444].

The following essay is an introduction into the anti-shipping operations by German Ju 87s and of III./St.G. 1 in particular, to accompany the second source document with this section. Expanding on the Gruppe's experience in anti-shipping operations between 1940 to 1941 in Europe and the Mediterranean, the document occasionally sways from its own synopsis to a narrative that highlights minor details or claimed feats of arms that are difficult to verify more than 80 years after the fact. It is only in the second half of the document, that a clearer summary is given. This mix of tactical descriptions and field experience, with a lack of chronology, a tendency to jump between events and an inclination for storytelling is perhaps not surprising given the nature by which this account was drafted.

The document appears with a reference to the post-Second World War USAF Historical Divisions Study 163 *German Air Force Operations in Support of the Army* from June 1962, by General der Flieger Paul Deichmann. However, this study

---

[443] The rank of Oberstleutnant was roughly equivalent to Lieutenant Colonel in the USAAF or a Wing Commander in the RAF. The abbreviation "i.G." stands for "im Generalstab", indicating that the officer has successfully completed a special curriculum. "a.D." stands for "außer Dienst", literally translating to "out of service" and can be considered equivalent to the American (ret.) abbreviation for retired servicemen.
[444] The Marineflieger were the Naval Air Service of the German West-German Navy.

does not appear to reference Mahlke's document. Considering the distributor and content, it was most likely meant to add to Study 161 *The German Air Service versus the Allies in the Mediterranean*, by Helmuth Felmy (1955) rather than Study 163.[445] Considering all this, it appears prudent to focus on the passages that provide a general guide on Ju 87 anti-shipping operations appearing in the second half of the document and consider the more story-focused aspects with additional scrutiny.

To provide some additional context to Ju 87 anti-shipping operations that occurred in parallel to the dates and events stated in the document, the following summary endeavors to provide an overview of such missions between 1939 and late 1941, as well as an account of the documents author's own unit, III./St.G. 1.

III./Sturzkampfgeschwader 1

III./St.G. 1. had an unlikely origin. Anticipating the eventual completion of the Kriegsmarine's first carrier, the *Graf Zeppelin*, Germany kickstarted the development of a carrier-borne Ju 87 in July 1937. With some modifications to the Ju 87 B, this new variant became known as the Ju 87 C and underwent land trials the following year. To prepare for carrier operations, a special unit, the I./Trägergeschwader 186 was formed just before the German invasion of Poland.[446] Meant to be equipped with the Ju 87 C, the cancellation of the *Graf Zeppelin* prevented this unit and the aircraft from fulfilling its intended role. Eventually only between 5 – 7 Ju 87 C were completed.[447] Nevertheless, a possible use against ships in the future had been put into focus, and trials, both in dive-bombing (and later torpedo attacks[448]), against mock floating targets such

---

[445] Study 163 of the Air Force Project, also *AF-163 German Air Force Close Support Operations* by Hubertus Hitschold. It seems to have changed title and author to *German Air Force Operations in Support of the Army* by Paul Deichmann. Looking at the distributor list and content of this document, it is more likely it was meant to contribute to *AF-161* or *AF-162*, both titled *The German Air Force in the Mediterranean Theater* and edited by Helmuth Felmy. See W.S. Nye, *Guide to Foreign Military Studies 1945-54*, Headquarters United States Army, Europe, 1954, available at: https://www.ibiblio.org/hyperwar/Germany/FMS/FMS-1.html (last accessed 27.10.2021); and Air Force Historical Research Agency, *Numbered USAF studies 151-200*, available at https://www.afhra.af.mil/Information/Studies/Numbered-USAF-Historical-Studies-151-200/ (last accessed 27.10.2021).

[446] Barry C. Rosch, *Luftwaffe Codes, Markings & Units 1939-1945*, Schiffer Publishing Ltd, Atglen, PA, USA, 1995, p. 363-364.

[447] Manfred Griehl, *Junkers Ju 87 Stuka, Teil 1 – Die frühen Varianten A, B, C und R des Sturzkampfbombers der Luftwaffe*, AirDoc, Erlangen, Germany, 2006, p. 8-9.

[448] Although Germany did develop aerial torpedoes in the years leading up to 1939, it started out with a comparatively weak and ineffective design known as the Lufttorpedo LTF 5, usually shortened to F 5. Ineffective Luftwaffe and Kriegsmarine collaboration, as

as the decommissioned *Hessen*[449] gave some insight into the nature of hitting a floating target at sea at this early stage and later in the war. During the Invasion of Poland, I./Tr.G. 186 took part in the invasion as a regular Ju 87 unit. Throughout the campaign, German dive-bombers sank one destroyer and minelayer, as well as number of other smaller ships.[450] Following the campaign and the cancellation of the *Graf Zeppelin*, the orders for the Ju 87 C were cancelled. But while Germany's foray into carrier aviation had met with failure, the need for anti-shipping operations would only grow, as was evident during the aftermath of the invasion of Denmark and Norway and eventually the Low Countries and France. After the Armistice between France and Germany in late June 1940, the III./St.G. 1 was formed out of the I./Tr.G. 186[451], retaining its emblem of a red anchor on a white shield.

The first notable action against shipping in the Norwegian campaign saw the British heavy cruiser *HMS Suffolk* on the receiving end of I./St.G. 1, which scored a hit in the aft section of the ship, forcing her to retire to Scapa Flow. A successful attack on the destroyer *HMS Bittern* followed, resulting in her scuttling. In contrast to this success, throughout this campaign, identification of enemy ships

---

well as a preference for bombs in the former, torpedoed the chances for Germany to acquire a competitive aerial torpedo before hostilities commenced. Development and production were brought to an unglamourous halt in November 1939 with an existing inventory of just over 100 torpedoes in September 1939. Modifications to the F 5, front line success and the use of Allied and Japanese air services gave this issue new urgency. With Italian input, improvements were made to the German torpedoes and by 1941 Ju 87s were conducting torpedo trials in Grosseto, Italy but did not use it operationally. For further information on German torpedoes during the Second World War, consult Friedrich Lauck, *Der Lufttorpedo – Entwicklung und Technik in Deutschland 1915-1945*, Wehrtechnische Handbücher, Bernard & Graefe Verlag, München, Germany, 1981.

[449] The SMS *Hessen* was a *Braunschweig* class pre-dreadnaught battleship and one of the few ships retained by Germany following the Treaty of Versailles. Converted into a training ship for the Kriegsmarine in the mid-1930s, she eventually became a remote-controlled target ship and Icebreaker. She survived the war and was ceded to the Soviet Union in 1946. See Erich Gröner; Peter Mickel; Franz Mrva, *Die deutschen Kriegsschiffe 1815-1945. Band 1: Panzerschiffe, Linienschiffe, Schlachtschiffe, Flugzeugträger, Kreuzer, Kanonenboote*, Bernard & Graefe Verlag, 1982, Koblenz, Germany, p. 42.

[450] Ships sunk include the destroyer ORP *Wicher* (1 500 t), the mine layer ORP *Gryf* (2 200 t), as well as the smaller torpedo boat ORP *Mazur*, diver's tender ORP *Nazur* and the *Gdansk, Gdynia, Newa* and *Komendant Pilsudski*. See also Jürgen Rohwer & Gerhard Hümmelchen, *Chronik des Seekrieges 1939-1945*, Bibliothek für Zeitgeschichte, Württembergische Landesbibliothek, Online-Ausgabe 2007, available via: https://www.wlb-stuttgart.de/index.php?id=250 (last accessed 15.03.2022).

[451] Barry C. Rosch, *Luftwaffe Codes, Markings & Units 1939-1945*, Schiffer Publishing Ltd, Atgeln, PA, UK, 1995, p. 350.

proved difficult and fraught with error, showing limited experience with ship models among the crews of the Sturzkampfgeschwader. This seemingly resulted at one point in Kriegsmarine officers flying with them to assist with target identification.[452]

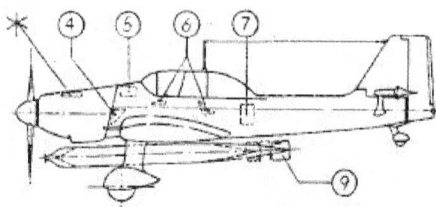

Original schematic of a Ju 87 D with a torpedo.
Source: Archiv Hafner, Werkschrift 2087 D-1 bis D-8, G-1, G-2, H-1 bis H-8/Fl, Ju 87 D-1 bis D-8, G-1, G-2, H-1 bis H-8 Bedienungsvorschrift-Fl, Teil II – Flugbetrieb, February 1944

Misidentifications could never be ruled out however, as on the 3rd May 1940 I./St.G. 1 claimed a battleship and cruiser sunk at Trondheim. Instead, the victims were the French and British destroyers Bison and HMS Afridi.[453] Although the correct identification of the attacked targets in the heat of battle left something to be desired, I./St.G. 1 managed to adapt to this role quickly. It remained in Norway during Fall Gelb, when Germany thrust westwards into the Low Countries and thus was not available to strike against Allied shipping at Dunkirk.

It was the operation at Dunkirk that proved that the Ju 87 could inflict a heavy toll on Allied shipping. Throughout the evacuation, bad weather prevented continuous strikes over a series of days, limiting the Sturzkampfgeschwaders to strike on only two-and-a-half days instead of the full nine.[454] Considering this, the achieved result was an exceptional success for the Luftwaffe. Gruppen from St.G. 1, 2, 51, 76 and 77 all took part in the attacks. Together they sank multiple destroyers and passenger ships, as well as damaging seven destroyers on 29th alone, and a further four destroyers and ten merchant ships on 1st June with eleven losses.[455] Mahlke describes the operations at Dunkirk as the first attack against shipping by III./St.G. 1. Claiming the destruction of the harbor lock, the attacks are summarized on page three and four, with a paragraph expanding on the "mine" effect of a bomb exploding underneath a merchant ship. It should be

---

[452] Eddie J. Creek, Junkers Ju 87 – From Dive-Bomber to Tank-Buster 1935-1945, Classic: Ian Allen Publishing, Hersham, UK, 2012, p. 133.

[453] Eddie J. Creek, Junkers Ju 87 – From Dive-Bomber to Tank-Buster 1935-1945, Classic: Ian Allen Publishing, Hersham, UK, 2012, p. 133.

[454] Next to bad weather, Feldmarschall Herman Göring had also issued a series of conflicting orders that prevented a concentration of forces throughout this time.

[455] Eddie J. Creek, Junkers Ju 87 – From Dive-Bomber to Tank-Buster 1935-1945, Classic: Ian Allen Publishing, Hersham, UK, 2012, p. 141.

remembered that III./St.G. 1 was based at close to maximum range from Dunkirk throughout this time.

The Ju 87 had proven its ability to successfully complete anti-shipping operations, but the operations also highlighted the ever more pressing issue of the aircrafts lack of range, a critical factor in these and later operations. The Belgian and French coast lay close to the maximum operational range for various Ju 87 units. Even after being relocated closer, they had great difficulty in striking the French defenses around Dunkirk, and the actual British evacuation. This deficiency had been identified and remedied somewhat with the longer ranged R-variant that slowly appeared with drop tanks. Likewise, the majority of ships at this time featured only a limited anti-aircraft suite, which made things easier for the German pilots.

In the opening phases of the Battle of Britain, III./St.G. 1 flew anti-shipping operations in the English channel. Based on Mahlke's statements, the first attack on a solitary ship by II./ and III./St.G. 1 resulted in failure due to the impact of wind on the diving Stukas. This experience introduces a longer segment on how III./St.G. 1 changed tactics in order to compensate for adverse weather conditions. This included the shift over to shallow dives if the target permitted this, as well as the creation of specific target zones in each convoy for the individual flights that attacked. Considering the description, they appear to have been conducted against various formal training regulations (see for example wind conditions) that are outlined in the document L.Dv. 20/2: Luftwaffe Regulation 20/2 – Guidelines for Dive-Bombing Training, emphasizing the difference between formal procedures and practical reality. Additional footnotes are provided throughout this segment, where further information can also be found on the given claims regarding sunk shipping.

The "Kanalkampf" was moderately successful for the Ju 87 units employed, although the use of the Ju 87 during the Battle of Britain is often considered to having been close to a disaster. Aiming to close off the English Channel, Ju 87s started to fly dedicated anti-shipping operations against naval targets around Britain. In this capacity they were able to retain operational strength from July through mid-August, losing only 12 aircraft in July 1940. In the two first weeks of August, the Luftwaffe had just under 300 Ju 87 operational, indicating that operational readiness since Poland had not fallen that drastically.[456] In the

---

[456] Eddie J. Creek, *Junkers Ju 87 – From Dive-Bomber to Tank-Buster 1935-1945*, Classic: Ian Allen Publishing, Hersham, UK, 2012, p. 145.

second half of August, due to mounting losses and changing targets in the second half of the month, the Ju 87 were withdrawn from the Battle of Britain.[457]

In the second half of 1940, III./St.G. 1 was one of the few units that resumed anti-shipping operations around the southern coast of England. Attacks on the 1st, 8th and 11th November are described in this document, although some care should be taken considering the claims made. Around the same time, Germany moved Ju 87s to the Mediterranean, where the Italians had already started using this plane against Malta and British shipping after acquiring a limited number of Ju 87.

Perhaps the most famous early attacks on shipping occurred when the Royal Navy moved Force "H" with the carrier *HMS Illustrious* came into striking distance of the Ju 87s based in Italy. Tasked to protect a convoy, Force "H" was first attacked on 8th January 1941 by Italian Ju 87s, and a larger attack by German dive-bombers followed two days later. Multiple near misses and a single hit failed to sink the carrier. On the next day, the heavy cruiser *HMS Southampton* was hit and later scuttled, while *HMS Gloucester* was damaged during a surprise attack.[458]

Operations against Malta continued in Spring 1941, with III./St.G. 1 now joining before transferring to North Africa in early April. From this period, Mahlke highlights an attack on a "Monitor"[459], taking it as an example of how military ships are to be attacked. Although not specifically mentioned in the document, the Battle of Crete in May-June 1941 also once again puts into focus the Stuka as a capable anti-shipping dive-bomber.[460] This battle would be the last instance of III./St.G.1 attacking shipping for some time. Moved to central Europe in preparation of Operation Barbarossa, III./St.G. 1 would operate in the central sector under Luftflotte 2. Periodically it would strike at Soviet shipping and its fleet in the Baltic Sea and Leningrad, before being redesignated as III./SG 1 in late 1943.

---

[457] Richard Overy, *The Battle of Britain*, Carlton, London, UK, 2014 (EBook edition); see also Falko Bell, *Britische Feindaufklärung im Zweiten Weltkrieg - Stellenwert und Wirkung der "Human Intelligence" in der britischen Kriegführung 1939-1945*, Ferdinand & Schönigh, Paderborn, Germany, 2016, p. 120.
[458] J.J. Colledge; Ben Warlow, *Ships of the Royal Navy*, 3rd Ed. Chatham Publishing, London, UK, 2006, p. 326.
[459] A monitor was a type of warship that was relatively small and slow, but carried large guns for its size.
[460] Further information on the operations at Crete can be found in *Air-Sea Battle of Crete on the 22nd May 1941*.

Document: Lecture on the Development of Navalized Dive-Bombers

This document contains a shortened version of a lecture held by Oberst Coeler on the 9th November 1937 on the development of equipment and aircraft for the Seeluftstreitkräfte. It is included in BArch, RM 7/2383, *Entwicklungsstand des Materials der Seeluftstreitkräfte (State of Development of the Equipment for the Naval Aviation Force)*. The lecture focuses the main challenges and trails for naval aviation and strike aircraft, their proposed designs and the necessity to develop certain, specialized types. The pages presented here focus on the development and use of dive-bombers in an anti-shipping capacity.

Preliminary Notes / Source Situation, Actuality and Formatting

Throughout this volume, we aimed to retain some of the original formatting, yet the editorial focus lay on legibility. One of the main editorial changes was that we, to present a clearer layout, did not follow the original page count as this would have resulted in empty or near empty pages throughout the book. Instead, the text has been reformatted to follow a more conventional structure, page by page.

Please be aware of the following formatting decisions and changes:

- This is an abridged version of the original lecture, taken from pages 16 to 28[461], collecting all information on the use of dive-bombers against ships.
- We corrected formatting mistakes in the original version (for example missing spaces, paragraph breaks or similar issues).
- The original numbered sequence was retained, but the beginning of each paragraph was aligned directly with the referenced number to make the best use of the available space. Overall, these changes allow us to transfer this document into a more legible layout that is consistent with the other documents found in this book.
- The original formatting sequence was retained, but we made some changes to transfer this document into a more legible layout. This also includes the deletion of unnecessary spacing between subs-sections and the introduction of new paragraphs.

---

[461] This corresponds to page 60 to 72 with the Bundesarchiv enumeration. The cover page is page number 42.

- The first word of the following page was written on the bottom right of the preceding page and was underlined. This was a common practice at the time for unbound documents, but we did not follow this standard.
- There were some markings and notes with a blue and regular pencil, which we omitted.
- The stamp of the OKM[462] on the cover page was omitted.

---

[462] Oberkommando der Kriegsmarine.

Flottenkommando[463]   Kiel, 29th November 1938.

B.-Nr.[464] 129052/38. g.Kdos.[465]

"Top Secret [Stamp]"

To

The High Command of the Kriegsmarine

Berlin,

Subject: Presentation Oberst Coeler.

Refers to: O.K.M. B.Nr. AIL 18/38 gKdos.[466] from 6.I.38.[467]

Enclosed is the lecture – Oberst Coeler - given on 9.11.37 on the state of development of the material of the Naval Air Forces.

On behalf of!

[Signature]

---

[463] In Fraktur pre-printed.

[464] "B.-Nr." is the abbreviation of "Bearbeitungsnummer", indicating "processing number". In Fraktur pre-printed.

[465] "g.Kdos.." is the abbreviation of "Geheime Kommandosache", indicating "top secret military document". This is the highest secrecy level for documents in the Wehrmacht.

[466] Oberkommando der Kriegsmarine Bearbeitungsnummer AIL 18/38 geheime Kommandosache.

[467] DD-MM-YYYY. It is uncommon to see a roman numeral designating the month.

[...]

Until a few years ago, bombs were dropped exclusively, depending on weather conditions, from more or less high altitudes. The success of these bombing attacks during the war[468] on large targets, such as cities, large ammunition depots, large industrial plants, etc., was in line with expectations. On small targets the successes were certainly negative, as on the smallest, like ships, hits have hardly been achieved. However, there are a lot of airmen from the war claimed to have had success even on such targets. However, there are only a few bombs that hit. The effect on the target on vehicles and ships was = zero, because the used bombs of 10 kg - at the end of the war larger calibers were added - had of course no success. This way of attacking targets from high-flying aircraft by means of more and more improved bomb sights or aiming devices was considered the only possible way until the Americans dropped bombs from an airplane actually built as a twin-seat fighter in a vertical dive on target ships or targets on land. This idea then very quickly gained a foothold in all other nations, was then again discarded, and today is found most prominently in the German Air Force.[469]

The consideration of the advantages and disadvantages of both attacks results in the following: A unit attacking at high altitude is likely to be seen from a distance and exposed to the effects of AA at great distances, provided that the weather conditions in our latitudes allow it to attack at an operational[470] altitude of 4 000 m[471] and above. Depending on the training of the AA operators, [the bomber] will be forced to risk a lot before he drops his bombs or aborts his attack. In any case, [the bomber] has the possibility to do the latter. If, however, [the bomber] manages to get in position over the target despite AA defenses and fighters, it will try to hit the ship. [The bomber] is not able to fly large defensive maneuvers, because in the last 30 seconds or so it has to calculate[472] the bomb release. AA and fighters will have a rewarding target at these moments. Even if it drops the bomb with the greatest accuracy and within a fraction of a second, [the bomber] does not know whether the bomb will hit. Theoretically, it should hit, but in practice it mostly does not. Various reasons speak against it:

---

[468] As this lecture was given in 1937, this refers to the First World War.

[469] Editorial notice: Added paragraph break.

[470] The original German wording was "kriegsmäßiger Höhe". The literal translation would be "war-like altitude".

[471] 13100 ft.

[472] The original German wording was "Unterlagen für seinen Wurf erfliegen". The literal translation could be "fly to acquire the documents for the throw".

1.) The bombardier[473] is not able to determine the absolute altitude of his aircraft because his altitude determination is barometric.

2.) The ballistics of the bomb are not so accurate that one falls like the other. Slight oscillations of the bomb during flight, caused by invisible bending of the stabilization fins, the irregular release from the bomb's mounting etc. result in scattering.

3.) Each increase of the aircraft's speed when flying with the wind or each decrease of speed when flying into the wind cause a different bomb trajectory.

4.) All errors of the pilot and thus movements of the aircraft around it's longitudinal, lateral[474] and vertical axis give the bomb substantial deviations from the imagined and desired impact point.

The experience gained in recent years confirms this, for of the probably total of 500 and more bombs dropped in recent years by the Seeluftstreitkräfte[475], only 3 bombs have hit, which means that not even 1% of the bombs hit. Even the bombing exercises held by Lehrgeschwader Greifswald[476] in June of this year did not achieve more than 2% hits. I therefore stand on the point of view that the high-altitude attack on point targets, meant are ships, does not stand in any proper proportion to the achieved effect on the target. The bombs were dropped on the slow moving and therefore badly manoeuvring "Zähringen"[477]. If one considers that the bombed targets are capable of very energetic defensive maneuvers at maximum speed, the futility of this type of attack becomes even more obvious. In the near future, too, there will hardly be any aircraft capable of carrying more than two 500 kg bombs for use in naval warfare in order to increase the probability of hits with the release of multiple bombs at an interval.

---

[473] The original German wording was "Beobachter". The literal translation could be "observer".

[474] Editorial: The lateral axis was added as a hand-written notice.

[475] The German Naval Air Service was a part of the Kriegsmarine until January 1939, when it was folded into the Luftwaffe.

[476] A "Lehrgeschwader" is usually translated as "training wing" and usually responsible for additional operational training of dive-bomber pilots. "Greifswald" refers to the location it was based around to conduct its training.

[477] This refers to SMS Zähringen a pre-dreadnought battleship of the Wittelsbach class that was converted to a remote-controlled target ship 1926/1928. The speed for the original ship was noted as 17.7 knots. She was sunk in 1944, recovered and used as a block ship in 1945. Hildebrand et al: Die Deutschen Kriegsschiffe, Band 8, Koehlers Verlagsgesellschaft mbH, Hamburg, Germany, p. 125.

The situation is different for dive-bombers. Even a closed cloud cover at 2 000 m[478] of altitude is no obstacle for a dive-bomber. Any other type of cumulus or stratocumulus cloud, which would be an obstacle to the attack in horizontal flight, favors the Stuka attack. A Stuka attack from multiple sides and multiple aircraft is more difficult for anti-aircraft defenses. During the attack, the Stuka pilot, unlike the others [bombers], is unlikely to be able to break off his attack without remaining at danger of being shot down. The faster he gets the bomb to the target, the greater the prospects for his survival[479].

In favorable weather conditions, the Stuka will approach from an altitude of at 3 – 4 000 m[480]. From this altitude the dive is made at about 70° and the bomb is dropped from about 1 000 m[481]. The advantages of this type of attack are

1.) that the aircraft passes quickly through the AA defenses,
2.) the velocity given to the bomb by the dive,
3.) elimination of all sources of error that occur in the trajectory of the bomb when released at high altitude, and more accurate aiming, since the drop is made from a low altitude.

If dive-bombers are noticed during their approach and fired upon by AA, defensive movements in the form of spirals, etc., are possible.

At the request of the Flieger-Inspektion Seeflieger[482], the Lehrgeschwader has this year carried out a bombing exercises on the "Zähringen" off Tromper Wiek[483], at the E-Stelle off Sylt[484] and in the Bay of Kiel. All these exercises resulted in a hit percentage of 40%. These figures prove the superiority of the Stuka for bombing over the conventional bomber and the inappropriateness of continuing to carry out high altitude bombing attacks on protected point targets. The Flieger-Inspektion Seeflieger will submit an appropriate request in a timely

---

[478] 6600 ft.
[479] The original German wording was "Rettung". The literal translation could be "rescue". Instead of "survival", one could also translate this with "salvation" as within the context of the text, the dive-bombers pilot is almost described as finding his own preservation and lifeline in his speed and the direct attack of the target.
[480] 9900 – 13100 ft.
[481] 3300 ft.
[482] Flieger-Inspektion Seeflieger, also known as Inspektion der Seeflieger (L. Jn. 8). In February 1939, it was renamed to Luftwaffen Inspektion der Marineflieger (L. In. 8), and eventually Luftwaffen Inspektion des Seeflugwesens. This can be translated to Inspectorate of Naval Aviation. Karl-Heinz Völker, Die Deutsche Luftwaffe 1933 – 1939, DVA, Stuttgart, Germany, 1967; and Horst Boog, Die deutsche Luftwaffenführung 1935-1945, DVA, Stuttgart, Germany, 1982, p. 570.
[483] The "Tromper Wiek" is a bay to the north-east of Germany in the Baltic Sea.
[484] A German island in the North Sea, just on the height of its border with Denmark.

manner. With the discontinuance of high-attack bombing, there will be substantial simplifications in training and substantial improvements in equipment requirements for the general-purpose aircraft[485]. This should also change the use of the 6 naval long-range bombing Staffeln in naval warfare. The Luftwaffe[486] has also come to the same conclusion, which is having the effect on the development of long-range, 2-engine dive-bombers.

With regard to the further development of bombs, the Flieger-Inspektion Seeflieger[487] is of the opinion that the effect on a heavily armored ship is of primary interest and that armor-piercing bombs should therefore be developed as a matter of priority. Although the 250 kg bombs with 130 kg of explosives available today and the reinforced 500 kg bomb with the same explosive charge can achieve considerable effects on a deck's superstructure, a devastating effect will only be achieved by the armor-piercing bomb. The 250 kg bomb, as well as the 50 kg bomb, will continue to be provided for anti-submarine warfare in both naval[488], reconnaissance[489] and general-purpose aircraft[490]. The development of the bomb also dates from the years [19]28 - 32. For production and deception reasons[491], the bomb was made of 3 parts and welded together at that time. This production method did not prove successful in that the bomb, thrown with delay, broke on impact and as a result did not detonate. The newer bombs with the designation "J"[492] are pressed bombs[493].

In agreement with the OKM[494], the following program has been drawn up on the basis of these considerations.

---

[485] See Glossary: General-purpose aircraft (Mehrzweckfluzgzeug [Mz.-]).

[486] The original German word was "Landluftstreitkräfte". The literal translation could be "land air force".

[487] Flieger-Inspektion Seeflieger, also known as Inspektion der Seeflieger (L. Jn. 8). In February 1939, it was renamed to Luftwaffen Inspektion der Marineflieger (L. In. 8), and eventually Luftwaffen Inspektion des Seeflugwesens. This can be translated to Inspectorate of Naval Aviation.

[488] See Glossary: Naval aircraft (Marine Flugzeug [M.-]).

[489] See Glossary: Reconnaissance aircraft F (F-Aufklärungsflugzeug) [F.-]).

[490] See Glossary: General-purpose aircraft (Mehrzweckfluzgzeug [Mz.-]).

[491] Since Germany had heavy restrictions on the development of aircraft and was prohibited to have an air force after the First World War, developments of the time had to be disguised to varying degrees of success.

[492] The original designation in the text was "J". We are unsure to which bomb this refers and whether the designation was not supposed to be "i", as "J" was often used to designate an "i" in German abbreviations and documents of the time. One example would be the Army's "Infanteriegeschütz", which would usually be abbreviated "J.G.".

[493] The original German wording was "gezogene Bomben". The literal translation could be "pulled bombs", referring to the casing that was made out of one piece of metal.

[494] Oberkommando der Kriegsmarine.

The following are being developed and provided[495]

1.)   50 kg bombs

2.)   250 kg bombs

3.)   500 kg bombs

4.)   if necessary 1 000 kg-bombs.

Referring to 1.) 50 kg bombs with a wall thickness of 4 mm and about 50% explosive are intended for anti-submarine warfare and for occasional attacks on small vessels[496]. Bombs smaller than 50 kg can hardly be used successfully against naval targets. A recent requirement by the Flottenkommando[497] to carry ten 10 kg bombs in place of two 50 kg bombs as intended for the naval[498] and reconnaissance[499] aircraft, is not considered appropriate. The 10 kg bomb, with its low explosive content, promises no effect on submarines, while the 50 kg bomb can already be expected to have greater psychological effect.

Referring to 2.) The 250 kg bomb with 6 mm wall thickness and 130 kg explosive will continue to be used in the general-purpose aircraft[500] for anti-submarine warfare even after the elimination of the high-altitude attack. The new general-purpose aircraft[501] will carry two such bombs.

Referring to 3.) For the development of the 500 kg bomb, there are two different directions:

a)   A thick-walled 500 kg bomb of non-alloy steel is being developed, and will be available for testing at the end of [19]37. The explosive content of this bomb will be 130 kg, approximately the same as the thin-walled 250 kg bomb. The performance requirements are as follows:

---

[495] See Glossary: Bomb types (Bombenarten).
[496] The original German word was "Fahrzeuge". The conventional translation would be "vehicles", but it is unclear whether small naval craft (e.g., PT-boats or similar) are also meant by this. Considering the context, this is a possibility.
[497] Fleet Command.
[498] See Glossary: Naval aircraft (Marine Flugzeug [M.-]).
[499] See Glossary: Reconnaissance aircraft F (F-Aufklärungsflugzeug [F.-]).
[500] See Glossary: General-purpose aircraft (Mehrzweckflugzeug [Mz.-]).
[501] It is unclear which exact aircraft is being referred to.

Schiffbaustahl II[502] V_z[503]   = 200 m/sec. = 70 mm

= 280 m/sec. = 115 mm.

Panzerblech Wh[504] V_z = 200 m/sec. = 60 mm

= 280 m/sec. = 100 mm.[505]

b)   Since higher impact velocities of 200 - 220 m/sec. cannot be achieved when dropping the bomb even in a high-altitude attack, and these impact velocities are not sufficient to break through the horizontal armor with the available bomb weight, a bomb with additional propulsion is currently being developed which is increase the impact velocity to 380 m/sec. The total weight of the bomb is 500 kg, of which 170 kg is required for the rocket propulsion system, leaving a bomb weight of 330 kg with a correspondingly thick wall and an explosive content of about 14.5 kg. Despite the low explosive content, the requirement for this bomb was set up because one wants to penetrate the deck armor under all circumstances. This bomb is expected to penetrate armor decks with a total thickness of up to 200 mm. This bomb is only intended for use by the dive-bomber[506]. Of the bombs mentioned so far, the thin- or thick-walled 250 kg and 500 kg bombs are also suitable for causing hull damage when dropped directly next to the ship. However, the effect decreases very rapidly with distance from the hull, so that an effect can no longer be expected at a distance of 10 m from the ship.

Referring to 4.)[507] The 1 000 kg bomb made of non-alloy steel with 130 kg of explosives is expected to perform as follows:

---

[502] Literally translated "Schiffsbaustahl" means "ship construction steel". Type I was used for material that was welded, type III for special material and type for normal material according to a table in Johow-Foerster, *Hilfsbuch für den Schiffbau*, Erster Band, Fünfte Auflage, Springer-Verlag, Berlin, Germany, 1928, p. 487.

[503] V_z means impact velocity, whereas "Z" likely refers to "Ziel" meaning "target".

[504] Literally translated "Panzerblech" means "armor sheet metal", whereas "Wh" refers to "Wotan hart" which literally translates to "Wotan hard". In contrast, "Ww" stands for "Wotan weich", or "Wotan soft" in English. Note that "Wotan" is the Richard Wagner's name for the Germanic god "Wodan"/"Woden" generally known as "Odin". This is an interwar armor that was used widely as for horizontal, sloped and vertical armor plates on German warships. See NavWeaps.com, *German Krupp "Wotan" Steels*, http://www.navweaps.com/index_nathan/metalprpsept2009.php#%22Wotan_H%C3%A 4rte%22_%28Wh%29 (last accessed 31.12.2021).

[505] Respectively: 2.7, 4.5, 2.3 and 3.9 inch.

[506] This development did not result in a bomb that was used operationally.

[507] Unlike the previous entries, this one was not underlined.

Schiffbaustahl II[508] V_z[509] = 200 m/sec. = 100 mm

= 280 m/sec. = 160 mm.

Panzerblech Wh[510] V_z = 200 m/sec. = 90 mm

= 280 m/sec. = 140 mm.[511]

Up to now, only the electric impact fuze has been used as a detonator for naval purposes. This has the advantage that the setting could be adjusted to "without delay" (not sensitive) or "with delay" shortly before release from the aircraft. After the electric detonator Az[512] 5 has been discontinued, the electric detonator Az 15 is in use, which differs from the former in that after the detonator has been turned 180° when inserted into the bomb, the detonator can be used with a delay of 0.05 sec. or 8 sec. after impact. This device is practically meaningless for naval use. With the new Zünder 28, the delay is 0.15 sec. This fuze was created mainly to achieve underwater hits against the bottom of ships and against diving submarines. It is an interim solution until the Naval Fuze[513], which can be set by a variable delay, is ready for operational use. The problems with this fuze are not yet solved.

For the thick-walled bombs, a mechanical tail fuze will have to be used, since a weakening of the bomb's casing due to the installation of an electric fuze can lead to premature failure of the bomb.

Since the electric side fuze[514] is not highly sensitive when thrown without a time delay, the Navy continues to emphasize the development of a highly

---

[508] Literally translated "Schiffsbaustahl" means "ship construction steel". Type I was used for material that was welded, type III for special material and type for normal material according to a table in Johow-Foerster, *Hilfsbuch für den Schiffbau*, Erster Band, Fünfte Auflage, Springer-Verlag, Berlin, Germany, 1928, p. 487.

[509] V_z means impact velocity, whereas "Z" likely refers to "Ziel" meaning "target".

[510] Literally translated "Panzerblech" means "armor sheet metal", whereas "Wh" refers to "Wotan hart" which literally translates to "Wotan hard". In contrast, "Ww" stands for "Wotan weich", or "Wotan soft" in English. Note that "Wotan" is the Richard Wagner's name for the Germanic god "Wodan"/"Woden" generally known as "Odin". This is an interwar armor that was used widely as for horizontal, sloped and vertical armor plates on German warships. See NavWeaps.com, *German Krupp "Wotan" Steels*, http://www.navweaps.com/index_nathan/metalprpsept2009.php#%22Wotan_H%C3%A4rte%22_%28Wh%29, (last accessed 31.12.2021).

[511] Respectively: 3.9, 6.3, 3.5 and 5.5 in.

[512] See Glossary: Contact-fuze (Aufschlagzünder).

[513] The original German word was "Wasserzünder". The literal translation would be "water fuze".

[514] A fuze that would be installed in the side of the bomb, rather than on its tip.

sensitive contact fuze[515], possibly with a fuze extender[516], or a connection of the electric side fuze to a contact fuze, which would also have to be equipped with a fuze extender. The possibility of retrofitting such a device to the existing thin-walled bombs has not yet been tested.

The existing means of aiming still have so many disadvantages that, as experience shows, the success of a bomb release cannot be predicted. A distinction is made between mechanical and optical aiming devices. For the Seeluftstreitkräfte[517], only optical sights are useful, since additional reference landmarks[518], as required for mechanical sights, are not available at sea. Optical aiming has the disadvantage of a reduced luminosity in the optic and are therefore difficult or impossible to use at night. The latest Zeiss aiming device has the advantage over the Görz-Boykow Rohr, which has been used up to now, that changes in the speed of the target are compensated for up to the moment of the release by adjusting the aiming mark. With this target device, no distance is measured as a whole, but when following the measurement path, the position of the target is continuously brought into alignment with the device's indicator. In dive bombing, the target is attacked with the Zeiss reflector sight[519], which is also in use for fixed weapons. During a low altitude attack, i.e., on submarines, small vessel[520], at a height of 300 - 100 m[521], bombs are released without the aid of a sight. One of the first tasks of the Lehrstaffeln will be to develop a type of auxiliary sight called "Prenzlauer Marken" for naval aircraft[522].

[...]

---

[515] The original German word was "Kopfzünder". The literal translation would be "head fuze". It refers to a conventional fuze installed in the tip of the bomb.

[516] The original German word was "Stössel". The literal translation would be "muddler/tapper". We assume that this refers to a fuze extender or a spike. The former is an extension which places the fuze, or a mechanism activating the fuze further out from the bomb. This could result in an airburst effect or prevent a late detonation. A spike would provide a chance for the bomb to lodge itself in the object (like deck plating of a ship) at angles where it would otherwise bounce off.

[517] The German Naval Air Service was a part of the Kriegsmarine until January 1939, when it was folded into the Luftwaffe.

[518] The original German word was "Hilfsziele". The literal translation would be "helping targets".

[519] See Glossary: Reflector sight (Reflexvisier [Revi]).

[520] The original German word was "Fahrzeuge". The literal translation would be "vehicles".

[521] Respectively: 1000 - 330 ft.

[522] We were so far unable to find out what exact sight or aiming method is meant by this. It is possible that this is a method utilizing reference markers on the aircraft or on the sight. This method was sometimes used, for example seen in some Soviet Ilyushin IL-2s that used bomb reference lines on the upper engine cowling and on the front windscreen. These corresponded to set release altitudes-speeds and had to be aligned during flight.

Document: Methods of Attacking Naval Targets with Dive-Bombers

This document was originally written by Oberstleutnant i.G. a.D.[523] Helmut Mahlke and can be found in BArch, RL 10/512, *Einsatz England und Mittelmeerraum 1940/41*. It was a contribution to the Historical Studies series on the German Army[524]. As a Staffelkapitän, Mahlke took part in the invasion of Poland and saw action at Dunkirk, before becoming Gruppenkommandant between June 1940 and September 1941. In this capacity, Mahlke commanded III./St.G. 1 during the Battle of Britain and when the Gruppe was moved to the Mediterranean, where it saw notable action during the Invasion of Crete. It was later moved to the Eastern Front for the imminent Operation Barbarossa. Mahlke would later author a book on his experiences during the Second World War.[525]

Expanding on the Gruppe's experience in anti-shipping operations between 1940 to 1941 in Europe and the Mediterranean, the document switches between synopsis to adding minor details or events that are difficult to verify more than 80 years after the fact. Due to the mixing of events and a lack of chronology, as well as Mahlke's inclination for "storytelling" is perhaps not surprising given the nature by which this account was drafted post-war. As with any first-person account, especially considering the distance between the events and the writing

---

[523] The rank of Oberstleutnant was roughly equivalent to Lieutenant Colonel in the USAAF or a Wing Commander in the RAF. The abbreviation "i.G." stands for "im Generalstab", indicating that the officer has successfully completed a special curriculum. "a.D." stands for "außer Dienst", literally translating to "out of service" and can be considered equivalent to the American (ret.) abbreviation for retired servicemen.

[524] Although Study 163 is indicated, this might be a victim of mislabeling. Study 163 of the Air Force Project, also *AF-163*, was titled *German Air Force Close Support Operations* by Hubertus Hitschold. It seems to have later changed title and author to *German Air Force Operations in Support of the Army* by Paul Deichmann. Looking at the distributor list and content of this document, it is more likely that Mahkle's document was meant to contribute to *AF-161* or *AF-162*, both titled *The German Air Force in the Mediterranean Theater* and edited by Helmuth Felmy. See W.S. Nye, *Guide to Foreign Military Studies 1945-54*, Headquarters United States Army, Europe, 1954, available at: https://www.ibiblio.org/hyperwar/Germany/FMS/FMS-1.html (last accessed 27.10.2021); and Air Force Historical Research Agency, *Numbered USAF studies 151-200*, available at https://www.afhra.af.mil/Information/Studies/Numbered-USAF-Historical-Studies-151-200/ (last accessed 27.10.2021).

[525] In English: Helmut Mahlke, *Memoirs of a Stuka Pilot*, Frontline Books, Barnsley, UK, 2013.

of this report, the reader should be cautious about the accuracy of the text, especially in those instances where success claims are made. Nevertheless, various technical aspects and operational experiences found here can be considered fairly accurate as they often recount standardized procedures.

Preliminary Notes / Source Situation, Actuality and Formatting

Throughout this volume, we aimed to retain some of the original formatting, yet the editorial focus lay on legibility. One of the main editorial changes was that, in order to present a clearer layout, we did not follow the original page count as this would have resulted in empty or near empty pages throughout the book. Instead, the text has been reformatted to follow a more conventional structure, page by page.

Please be aware of the following formatting decisions and changes:

- We corrected formatting mistakes in the original version (for example missing spaces, paragraph breaks or others).
- The original formatting sequence was retained, but we made some changes to transfer this document into a more legible layout that is consistent with the other documents found in this book. This also includes the deletion of unnecessary spacing between subs-sections.
- The first word of the following page was written on the bottom right of the preceding page and was underlined. This was a common practice at the time, but we did not follow this standard.
- The document contains various markings with pencil, including underlines, lines on the side or boxes. We omitted these.

Property of
Historical Division[526]
Hq USAREUR
- Air Force Project -

Return after completion of work.

---

[526] The Foreign Military Studies Program of the Historical Division, United States Army, Europe commissioned a large number of studies, predominantly from high-ranking officers of the German Armed Forces following the end of the war. By collecting, editing, summarizing and finally disseminating the experiences of the German Army, this project collected a wealth of information on German operations during the war. At the same time, the information within each summary remained subjective and was initially often poorly translated or labelled. See W.S. Nye, *Guide to Foreign Military Studies 1945-54*, Headquarters United States Army, Europe, 1954, available at: https://www.ibiblio.org/hyperwar/Germany/FMS/index.html (last accessed 27.10.2021).

[527] A veteran of the First World War, Hans Speidel eventually became the General Chief of Staff of Army Group B in 1944. After the unsuccessful 20th July 1944 assassination attempt on Hitler, Speidel was placed under house arrest. After the war, he authored multiple studies for the Historical Division and in 1955 joined the West German Armed Forces until his retirement in 1964. See Dieter Krüger, *Neue deutsche Biographie*, Band: 24, Stader, Berlin, Germany, 2010, p. 648-649, available at: https://daten.digitale-sammlungen.de/0008/bsb00085893/images/index.html?seite=672 (last accessed 27.10.2021).

[528] As one of the authors of Luftwaffe Regulation 16, Hellmuth Felmy was a prominent General Staff officer in the Luftwaffe. He was briefly forced to retire following the January 1940 "Mechelen Incident", during which two of his staff officer's emergency landed in Belgium with detailed invasion plans for the upcoming Western campaign. He later returned to the Luftwaffe as it transitioned into the Mediterranean in mid-1941. After the war he was on trial in Nuremberg and given a sentence of 15 years in 1948, later reduced to 10. He was released early in 1951.

[529] We were so far unable to find out which collection, institution or person is meant by this.

[530] Most likely indicating a single copy to be filed as storage.

Methods of Attacking Naval Targets with Dive-Bombers. (Experiences from the Operations of the II/St. G. 1[532][sic!] England and Mediterranean.)

v. Oberstltn.i.G.a.D.[533] Helmut Mahlke.

The unique nature of engaging naval targets, based on operational experience, led to the development of special attack procedures that ensured the greatest possible effectiveness with the lowest risk of loss during subsequent employments.

This development of the attack procedures is to be shown here by example of the employment of the III./St.G.1 against naval targets.

(III./St.G.1 was the Stuka-Gruppe originally intended for the aircraft carrier[534]. Most of the flying personnel had been drawn from the Navy. Therefore, in its

---

[531] This study number appears to be mislabeled. Study 163 of the Air Force Project relates to *AF-163 German Air Force Close Support Operations* by Hubertus Hitschold. It later seems to have changed title and author to *German Air Force Operations in Support of the Army* by Paul Deichmann. Looking at the distributor and content of this document, it is more likely it was meant to contribute to *AF-161* or *AF-162*, both titled *The German Air Force in the Mediterranean Theater* and edited by Helmuth Felmy. See W.S. Nye, *Guide to Foreign Military Studies 1945-54*, Headquarters United States Army, Europe, 1954, available at: https://www.ibiblio.org/hyperwar/Germany/FMS/FMS-1.html (last accessed 27.10.2021); and Air Force Historical Research Agency, Numbered USAF studies 151-200, available at https://www.afhra.af.mil/Information/Studies/Numbered-USAF-Historical-Studies-151-200/ (last accessed 27.10.2021).

[532] II./Sturzkampfgeschwader 1. This is a typo, Mahlke's account focuses on the III. Gruppe.

[533] The abbreviation "i.G." stands for "im Generalstab", indicating that the officer has successfully completed a special curriculum. "a.D." stands for "außer Dienst", literally translating to "out of service" and can be considered equivalent to the American (ret.) abbreviation for retired servicemen.

[534] The *Graf Zeppelin* was to be the first carrier of the Kriegsmarine. Its keel was laid in December 1936 at the Deutsche Werke Kiel AG, following the launch of the *Gneisenau*. It was 85% completed when war broke out, but work halted in mid-1940. Her sister ship, much less advanced in construction, started being broken up at this point and *Graf Zeppelin* herself lost part of her guns that were shipped away to serve as coastal batteries in Norway. Between 1942 and 1943 the idea was floated to resume construction but after a brief

employment against England[535] and in the Mediterranean Sea (Sicily, Africa) the Gruppe was preferentially used against naval targets, even after the original Naval Air Service core [of the Gruppe] had melted down to individual crews due to personnel losses, while the mass of junior crews - due to the usual Stuka pilot training - had gone without special training for combatting naval target.

Employment of the III./St.G. 1 against naval targets came for the first time at Dunkirk. Here it was important to prevent or delay the evacuation of the encircled armies by sea by destroying the means of transportation. On 29.5.1940 the Gruppe first destroyed the locks of Dunkirk, so that the use of the inner harbor was made impossible for the enemy. On 1.6.1940 the Gruppe flew 3 times against ships off Dunkirk.[536]

The ships assembled for the evacuation of the enemy troops were mostly small units, sometimes also trawlers towing 2 - 3 prams, which were to be found in large numbers in the sea area from Dunkirk all the way to the English south coast. Accordingly, the approach followed the usual attack procedure at an altitude of about 3 500 m[537] above a broken cloud cover. Over the target area, the group split up to attack in Ketten. The individual Ketten set off in free target selection against the largest sighted ship units for the attack in a steep dive (through the broken cloud cover); release altitude 500 m[538] fuze setting "mV"[539]. With favorable wind conditions - light, steady winds, no wind shifts at altitude - accuracy was generally good and the success satisfactory.

In one case, the mine effect[540] of a 500 kg bomb was observed. After the cloud cover had fallen, a Staffelkapitän saw that a Kette was attacking the same target next to him. He changed targets in a staircase dive[541] and attacked a steamer of about 3 000 t which was running at high speed. Due to the target change, the release altitude had become so low that the fuze did not respond with the set

---

period, these plans were cancelled. *Graf Zeppelin* was scuttled in March 1945, before being raised by the Soviet Navy, only to be sunk again in weapons tests in 1947. See Siegfried Breyer, *The German Aircraft Carrier: Graf Zeppelin*, Schiffer Publishing, West Chester, UK, 1989.

[535] It is common among German speakers and primary sources around this time to refer to the United Kingdom or the British Empire as "England".

[536] Due to the limits in the Ju 87 range, as well as the metereological conditions and other operational requriemenets, the German Ju 87 force was only used on about three days against the evacuation that lasted from May 27th to June 4th, 1940.

[537] 11500 ft.

[538] 1600 ft.

[539] "mV" is the abbreviation of "mit Verzögerung", indicating "with delay". See Glossary: Contact-fuze (Aufschlagzünder).

[540] Blast effect. See Glossary: Bomb types (Bombenarten).

[541] For a visualization of this, see *Aerial Tactics - The Dive-Bomber*.

delay, but an additional delay. The impact lay sharply in front of the bow of the ship, which passed over the impact point at high speed. As a result of shallow water, the explosion occurred below midship, so that the ship was torn apart and whole sections of the superstructure flew through the air[542]. Such an effect could not be observed in later attacks in deep water. Such hits must also be considered coincidental, since according to all later experience no such effect is obtained even with minor lateral offsets. Damage to the submerged part of the hull, which could result in the sinking of a ship, was only possible with hits close to the ship's side (under 3 to at most 5 m from the ship).

On 11.7.1940 the Gruppe was deployed with the II. Gruppe of the Geschwader for a joint attack against a reported convoy on the English south coast (Channel area, west of the Isle of Wight). Airfield Théville. Instead of a convoy, only 1 steamer was sighted in the whole Channel area and was eventually attacked. As a result of a strong wind shear at 1 000 – 1 500 m, strong corrections had to be made in the steep diving attack shortly before the release altitude, so that the aircraft released the bombs partly turning, partly drifting or with an inaccurate point of aim[543]. Not a single aircraft of III./St.G. 1 scored even one hit on the steamer!

Thereupon the II./St.G. 1 attacked the same target as "easy prey". But the II. Gruppe did not score a hit either! This devastating result gave pause for thought. The wind shear[544] at altitude and the inaccurate wind position reports of the weather forecast were the cause for this "failure". These error possibilities were also to be taken into account for future employment, since exact wind determinations by drift measurements were not possible during longer overseas flights from the Ju 87 due to the lack of equipment necessary for this. In addition, the hits had to be made in such a way that the attacked ship was sunk by direct hits, not merely damaged. Thus, an attack procedure had to be found that eliminated all sources of error in the aiming procedure. For this, 2 solutions were

---

[542] As the Luftwaffe attacked multiple ships on the 1st of June 1940 that resemble this description, it is not possible to confirm to which exact ship Mahlke refers to here. Even though the ship was identified here as a steamer of about 3 000 t, it is possible that in the confusion of combat, both size and type of the ship were misidentified. It is most likely that the ship in question is the TSS Scotia, a passage-steamer of about 3 500 t. Alternatively, the following ships could be meant: The British HMS Havant (H32), a H-class destroyer of about 2 000 t, or HMS Kieth, a B-class destroyer of 1 800 t, Foudroyant, a French L'Adroit-Klasse of 2 000 t although this would require the ship to have been misidentified as a non-military vessel. Wrecksite, SS Scotia, available at: https://www.wrecksite.eu/wreck.aspx?42 (last accessed 02.01.2021).
[543] See Glossary: Point of aim (Abkommpunkt).
[544] See Glossary: Wind shear (Windsprung).

201

found, which were subsequently applied depending on the defensive situation at the target and in each case led to complete success, namely

1.) a shallow dive[545] when faced with light AA defense by the target (merchant ships!)

2.) a steep dive[546] against strongly defended naval targets (warships!)

With the shallow dive method, the sinking of a trade ship of any size could be guaranteed by a Kette of Ju 87 (500 kg + 4 x 50 kg bombs[547]). As an example, for this 3 attacks of III/St.G. 1 against convoys in the outer Thames estuary on 1.11.40, 8.11.40 and 11.11.1940[548], in which 18 to 21 aircraft of the group were used in each case; sinking figures: Sinking figures: 28 000 t, 18 000 t and 37 000 t thus a total of 83 000 t of merchant shipping tonnage, with own losses (by fighter defense!) of a total of 3 Ju 87.[549]

The attack[550] took place at normal approach altitude (3 500 m[551], without oxygen equipment) as a Gruppe. The large convoys, which were sighted entering

---

[545] See Glossary: Shallow dive (Flachsturz).
[546] See Glossary: Steep dive (Steilsturz).
[547] This loadout is not included in the official ordnance loading plan of the Ju 87 B which would have been used around this time. While a single centerline 500 kg bomb exists as an option, the additional wing-mounted 50 kg are only included as an additional loading for a single 250 kg centerline bomb. Because the Ju 87 B was also rated for a single 1 000 kg bomb, it appears plausible that 1x 500 kg + 4 x 50 kg is technically possible, but perhaps not officially sanctioned. Whether the Gruppe used this loadout option or a confusion with a single 250 kg bomb is made here, is unclear.
[548] It is not clear which convoy is referenced although it appears to be either FS 22 and FS 32 running from Methil to Southend in the Thames Estuary arriving on the 1. and 11. November 1940 respectively, and FN 29 and FN 32 running the opposite route departing on the 8. and 11. November. During these attacks the SS *Letchworth* (1 300 t) of FS 22 was sunk on 01.11.1940. Interestingly, the convoy report describing the sinking of the *Letchwood* indicated dive-bombers as the cause, but that the attack happened unobserved. Additionally, the SS *Garesfield* of FN 29 is reported to have been lightly damaged on 08.11.1940. SS *Corsea* and SS *Colonel Crompton* of FN 32 were damaged on 11.11.1940 with the latter being put under tow by HMS *Vimera* of FS 32, while three Ju 87s were shot down according to British reports in the same attack. It appears that both FN and FS 32 were attacked on the same day, potentially around the time they passed each other. See TNA, ADM 199/39, M022061/40 *Report of HMS Vanity*, 4.11.40; and TNA, ADM 199/39, M 022639/40 *Report of HMS Vimiera*, 12.11.40, and TNA, ADM 199/32, TD(C) 1296/40 FN 29, 18.11.40; and TNA, ADM 199/32, TD(C) 66/41 FN 32, 21.11.40.
[549] As the previous footnote shows, these figures are likely exaggerated. It appears that only a single ship was sunk, with one more damaged. British reports do also indicate 3 Ju 87 shot down.
[550] In a later paragraph, this attack is dated as 11.11.1940.
[551] 11500 ft.

and leaving the Thames estuary during these attacks (50 to 80 ships!), were divided into 3 parts according to the briefing, of which each Staffel had to spot the 3 largest ships in "its third" and attack them Kette by Kette in by dividing the corresponding targets. This attack of the individual Kette of the unit pulled the otherwise strong [enemy] fighter defense apart. This gave a considerable moment of weakness in terms of defense [against fighters], but this was outweighed by the potential success that could be achieved, when following the procedures for the attack itself (not flying into the bomb explosions of the preceding Ju 87).

After this basic division of targets, the individual Ketten (in limited "free target choice") attacked the target groups assigned to them in a steep dive. Direction of attack: Without regard to the wind direction (!) from behind in the direction of travel of the ship. In the steep dive, an imaginary point was attacked about 1 000 m to 1 500 m behind the ship. At an altitude of about 1 000 m, the steep dive would be aborted and the stern of the ship was approached in a steep glide or "shallow dive" of about 30 - 45°[552]. Here, the ship's stern AA was fired at (AA or machine guns on merchant ships are always mounted on the stern and bow), in order to make the ship's anti-aircraft gunners "nervous" and to interfere with their effective firing against "aircraft on attack approach". This strafe was continued by firing over the ship's upper deck, with the weapons focusing briefly on the bow gun (flight altitude now about 200 to 150 m[553]). The strafe was pulled through, until the rounds whipped into the sea in front of the ship's bow, and at this moment the bomb button [should be] pressed. (Ship here no longer in the sight but covered by engine cowling!).[554]

In this attack and bombing method, the bomb had to hit just behind the bridge superstructures in the center of the ship! Aiming errors were no longer possible. Missed drops or bomb impacts in the water were observed only in exceptional cases, which were probably due to the fact that individual bombs bounced off the ship at an unfavorable point of impact. This possibility was compensated for by the use of one Kette against each ship, the bomb load of which - even in the case

---

[552] See Glossary: Shallow dive (Flachsturz) and steep dive (Steilsturz).

[553] The altitude indicated here appears very low for a pull-out. While technically possible from a shallow dive, it appears more likely that a pilot would be focusing on recovering his plane, rather than purposely attempting to strafe the target with an aimed burst while doing so.

[554] The British report on this attack only includes one reference to strafing by machine gun fire on the SS *Corsea*. It also indicates that the attacking formation broke up into smaller groups (assumed reason being AA fire), and dove at an angle of "about 45°". TNA, *ADM 199/39, M 022639/40 Report of HMS Vimiera*, 12.11.40; and TNA, *ADM 199/32, TD(C) 66/41 FN 32*, 21.11.40.

of individual "ricochets" - was sufficient to sink the ship in any case. Success: see above the attack with 21 Ju 87 against convoys in the Thames estuary on 11.11.1940 (loadout 1 x 500 kg SC, 4 x 50 kg SC, fuze m.V.[555]) [556] whereby after evaluation of the visual observations of the unit 37 000 t of enemy merchant shipping were reported as sunk. This tonnage figure was confirmed[557] as accurate by the photographic analysis of the Luftwaffe's long-range reconnaissance, which had captured these convoys in aerial photographs before and shortly after the attack.

(Experience has shown that the difficulty of estimating tonnage from the air, even with the best knowledge of ship types, can best be overcome by the rule of thumb: 1 000 GRT[558] per cargo hatch or cargo beam; large differences from this rule of thumb could not occur).

The greatest moment of weakness in these widely dispersed attacks of the individual Ketten was the rallying of the unit to a sufficiently strong defensive force against enemy fighters, which, despite strong and good friendly fighter protection (in the aforementioned attacks in the Thames estuary 2 Jagdgeschwader, respectively under the command of Mölders[559] and in another

---

[555] "m.V." is the abbreviation of "mit Verzögerung", indicating "with delay". See Glossary: Contact-fuze (Aufschlagzünder).

[556] As mentioned previously, this loadout is not included in the official ordnance loading plan of the Ju 87 B which would have been used around this time. Whether the Gruppe used this loadout option or a confusion with a single 250 kg bomb is made here, is unclear.

[557] Considering this as well as British reports, the description of this attack on 11th November 1940 appears accurate to a point, although with some exaggeration and the usual mistakes found in kill claims. Given that 21 Ju 87s took part (later on Mahlke changes this to 19 Ju 87s), the majority of III./St.G.1 seems to have been employed in the attack. Given Mahlke's description, each *Kette* would operate against a single ship. This would theoretically place up to seven vessels into the crosshairs. With the assumption that the convoys in question are FS and FN 32 who appear to have passed each other as the attack occurred. The following ships are reported to have been damaged but not sunk: SS *Corsea* and SS *Colonel Crompton*, both of FN 32. FS 32 indicated that it observed the attacks, but was not attacked itself. If these convoys are the ones Mahlke references, which is given the similar descriptions of both sides very likely, this counters Mahlke's description of the tonnage sunk as not a single British ship sank. Interestingly, Mahlke goes on explaining that evidence was also gathered from other units that confirmed the claimed tonnage as sunk. As mentioned previously, the validation of claims during an action was a business fraught with error. See also TNA, *ADM 199/39, M 022639/40 Report of HMS Vimiera*, 12.11.40; and TNA, *ADM 199/32, TD(C) 66/41 FN 32*, 21.11.40.

[558] Gross Registered Tonnage.

[559] Werner Mölders, commanding Jagdgeschwader 51 (JG 51).

employment under the command of Galland[560]) always managed to punch through to the Stuka unit, albeit only with a few single aircraft.

The time from the attack to the rallying of the unit had to be reduced. For this purpose, the unit leader flew with wide horizontal turns on the ordered return course with the engine at a very low throttle setting (less than 200 kph) and gave "rallying signals" by wobbling his wings. However, this was not yet a perfect solution[561], since in hazy weather (limited visibility under a cloudless blue sky) it happened that - generally the youngest crews - had lost connection with the unit and were looking for it on the return course at higher speeds. This resulted in all other aircraft of the unit trying to rally on this aircraft, assuming that this must be the unit leader. The low performance of the Ju 87 made rapid rallying impossible in such cases, since the last planes could not catch up even when throttling up to their maximum speed. The best solution was found on the basis of an order of the higher command, which ordered in this time that, to avoid too high unit leader losses (the replacement of unit leaders had probably encountered difficulties) the flying of the unit leader at the head of their units was forbidden and that the unit leader had to choose another position in the unit, from which he could lead the unit without particularly conspicuous exposure to himself.[562]

III./St.G. 1[563] refused to carry out this order, since the unit was led only by visual signals, which could only be given from the front, and radio silence was ordered in principle, except in cases of sea emergencies[564], since experience had shown that every radio message immediately alerted the enemy's fighter defense. In addition, Gruppenkommandeure and Staffelkapitäne considered to be in a much better position to hold their own against a larger number of attacking enemy fighters because of their greater flying experience than what could be expected of an inexperienced crew. The above-mentioned order thus triggered the opposite reaction: the aircraft of the Gruppenkommandeure and the Staffelkapitäne were marked in a particularly conspicuous manner, namely Gruppenkommandeure: both landing legs of the aircraft sprayed yellow, Staffelkapitäne: one landing leg sprayed yellow. This was intended to attract the

---

[560] Adolf Galland, commanding Jagdgeschwader 26 (JG 26).
[561] The original German word was "Patentlösung". The literal translation would be "patented solution".
[562] Editorial notice: Paragraph break added. This paragraph continued along multiple pages. As such we have broken it up here to present a more legible text.
[563] Handwritten correction from II. Gruppe to III. Gruppe.
[564] Most likely when a friendly aircraft was spotted ditching to immediately alert the search and rescue service.

enemy's fighter defense, and encourage them to attack these conspicuously marked aircraft in order to spare and relieve the younger crews.[565]

Experience in air combat had shown in many cases that the Ju 87 could outmaneuver up to 5 simultaneously attacking Spitfires, if the pilot had enough experience to observe all attackers sufficiently and to take the necessary defensive measures at the right moment; this was generally: lowest possible speed, counter-turns to counterattack with fixed weapons against the approaching fighter (although no shooting successes could be expected with the 2 fixed machine guns, the "massive" looking Ju 87, when flying stubbornly on a ram course against the fighter, always had such an impressive effect that the fighter preferred to turn away before he could aim and shoot properly). The most difficult thing was to outmaneuver several fighters when they launched their attacks from different directions at the same time. They all had to be watched at the same time to catch the moment when one of them, in firing position, was about to open fire and achieve a sure hit; at that moment, a quick yank on the control stick was enough to make a "jump" so that the fighter's fixed weapons barb passed under the Ju 87.[566]

Since flying away was out of the question due to the low speed of the Ju 87 compared to the fighter, the Ju 87 had to "counter" until the fighters had expended their ammunition. In this context, it should be mentioned that in many cases after such a dogfight - when they had expended their ammunition - the British fighters flew close to the Ju 87 in parallel flight and signed off with a sporty "military" salute before waving off to head back home. In these dogfights, the Ju 87s usually brought home more or less heavy damage, but they were sturdy enough to give the experienced pilot an absolute feeling of security in aerial combat. In one case, a Ju 87 of a Staffelkapitän came back without any hits, even after an entire Spitfire Staffel[567] (apparently less experienced crews) had expended all their ammunition on this plane in the air combat.

The yellow paint on the landing gear of the aircraft of the commander and Staffelkapitäne made it much easier for all crews to rally after the attack. The only order to rally was to follow the "yellow legs", crews that flew past the marked aircraft of the unit leader during the departure were threatened with punishment. With these recognition aids the gathering of the unit was ensured in the shortest possible time (approx. 3 minutes) even in the case of the unit splitting up into individual attacks. Rallying and departure as well as the return

---

[565] Editorial notice: Paragraph break.
[566] Editorial notice: Paragraph break.
[567] The original German word was "Spitfirestaffel". It is possible that this either refers to a flight (generally 6 aircraft) or, more likely, a section (generally 3 aircraft).

flight were carried out in at <u>low altitude</u> in case of attacks on naval targets, with the formation called "an unorderly assembly of pigs[568]". Due to the flight at low altitude, a fighter attack from the defensive blind spot of the Ju 87 (from the rear below) was not possible. The formation, which was very characteristically called "unorderly assembly", was the most effective protection against fighter attacks from the most favorable attack direction for fighters, namely the rear. The last aircraft of the formation was most exposed to fighter attacks ("the dogs catch the slowest one"![569]), since the weak defensive armament (1 MG 15[570]) of the other aircraft of the unit could only be brought to bear against an attacker to a limited extent and at longer firing distances[571].

The formation was therefore intended to ensure that - as long as enemy fighters were to be expected - no aircraft was tied to the position as the "last one in the formation". In the event of a fighter attack, the best possible mutual support of the aircraft of the formation could be provided for the defense against the fighter attack.[572] The implementation of the formation "unorderly assembly" was carried out in this way: the unit leader flew on a return course with a throttled back engines (200 to 220 kph[573]), so that all aircraft had ample speed reserves (50 to 80 kph[574]) [to catch up].

If an enemy fighter attacked one of the last planes of the unit, it throttled up, flew over the other planes of the unit and then dove down into the center of the formation, here again changing to low-level flight. If the fighter did not break off its attack against this aircraft, this brought other aircraft of the unit into firing positions for the fixed weapons.

The fighter escaped this situation by turning and aborting the approach, usually before he had even fired. If the enemy fighter, in order to avoid such situations from the outset, changed targets during his approach, his firing became so inaccurate that - apart from very isolated exceptions - he could not succeed in firing, especially since the aircraft of the unit that was now being targeted had space to freely maneuver. Thus the chances for attacking fighters against the

---

[568] The original German word was "Sauhaufen". The literal translation would be "sow heap". This refers to a less than organized formation pattern, where planes were staggered in the horizontal and vertical at uneven intervals. In future mentions, we will call this formation an "unorderly assembly".

[569] The original German wording was "den Letzten beissen die Hunde". The literal translation would be "the dogs bite the last one".

[570] The MG 15 was a light machinegun (7.92x57mm).

[571] Most likely to void hiting the friendly aircraft being attacked.

[572] Editorial notice: We have cut this sentence in two to provide a more legible text.

[573] 125 - 135 mph.

[574] 30 - 50 mph.

"unorderly assembly" formation was very small, as long as the attacking fighters could not force all aircraft of the unit to engage in turn fights through numerical superiority.[575] The latter, however, only came into question in the case of numerical superiority of a factor of 3 to 5, since in such a case it was easier to outmaneuver attacking fighters in a turn fight by individually dogfighting Ju 87s, than to direct the attention to the mutual support within the unit. However, such air battles against such strongly superior enemy forces were exceptional cases, which could only occur if the own fighter protection did not function properly or recognized the situation too late. (e.g., air combat in the Dover-Calais canal area on 14.11.1940, in which each aircraft of the unit was involved in turn fights against at least 5 – 5 [sic!][576] Spitfire at the same time; duration of the air combat approx. 15 minutes; losses apart from heavy strafing damage - up to 130 hits per aircraft - 2 Ju 87 total loss, one of them by AA near Dover).

Individual enemy fighters or fighter Schwärme[577], that had broken through friendly fighter protection could not achieve any success against a unit flying in an "unorderly assembly" formation.

As the most impressive result for the attack guidelines of Stukas against naval targets carried out according to the above principles, reference is made again to the attack of the III./St.G.1[578] on the 11.11.1940 at noon against convoys in the Thames estuary: (To the knowledge of the reports author [Mahlke] this was the last day attack which was flown by a entire German unit against England[579]). 19 Ju 87[580] of the III./St.G.1 were employed under strong fighter protection (2 Geschwader led by Galland[581]). Approach to the target at 3 500 m[582]. Very strong

---

[575] Editorial notice: We have cut this sentence in two to provide a more legible text.

[576] In the original text the quoted number was 5 – 5 as shown here. We assume this is a typo and that 3-5 aircraft were meant, in line with the preceding text. It should also be noted that it is very common to, due to the chaotic nature of air combat, count the wrong number of enemy aircraft and inflate their numbers.

[577] A Schwarm was generally a formation of four aircraft. It is likely that Mahlke refers to small formations of fighters that broke through the friendly fighter defense, perhaps in Section strength (generally 3 aircraft), rather than a specific number of aircraft.

[578] Handwritten correction from II. Gruppe to III.Gruppe.

[579] It is common among German speakers and primary sources around this time to refer to the United Kingdom or the British Empire as "England".

[580] Mahlke's earlier description indicated 21 Ju 87s. The repeated attention this event received throughout this document is perhaps a reflection of Mahlke's conviction that this was a successful attack which stands out from all the sorties he and his Gruppe flew.

[581] Since Galland did not command two Geschwaders, it could be that Mahlke meant two Gruppen or that Galland was in overall command of an escort that included fighters from multiple Geschwader. Likewise, it should be mentioned that the simultaneous employment of a full Geschwader was rare.

[582] 11500 ft.

208

enemy fighter defense in the target area was bound by excellent friendly fighter protection (staggered[583] around the unit [of Ju 87s]), so that only enemy fighters rarely penetrated the formation during the approach to the target, but they did not succeed [in shooting down an aircraft]. Attack in a steep dive, changing to a shallow dive[584] (low altitude attack). Followed by a low altitude flight. Return flight at low altitude in an "unorderly assembly". Success: 37 000 GRT sunk[585]. Losses of the III/St.G.1: None! The latter result deserves special attention since even during the departure and return flight there were continuous attacks by individual enemy fighters which had broken through to the unit, but which could be rendered ineffective without exception by the behavior of the unit described above.

This very successful attack procedure (steep dive followed by shallow dive) for the destruction of merchant ships was not applicable in every case for the following reasons:

1.)   In attacks against <u>warships</u>, this method could not be expected to produce a sufficient bombing effect, since the angle of impact of the bomb - due to the low release altitude during the shallow dive or glide - was so shallow that the bomb could not penetrate the horizontal armor with which at least the most important parts of all newer types of warships were protected against attacks from the air. A bomb striking this horizontal armor at a flat angle would either shatter ineffectively or destroy and damage only the superstructure above the horizontal deck armor. The bomb's penetration through the horizontal deck armor, necessary for the sinking of a warship, required the bomb to be released in a very steep dive. (80 - 85°, as close as possible to the 90° dive).

2.)   In addition, when attacking warships, there was a very strong, massed anti-aircraft defensive fire of all calibers in the center of the target, which shot particularly well in all navies, but especially in the Royal Navy, and which had favorable hit chances against a "target on its attack dive" that did not maneuver in the dive on the target.

For these reasons, only the usual <u>steep dive</u> attack method was considered for attacking warships. The aiming errors possible due to incorrect aiming were rendered harmless by disciplined unit attack as follows:

---

[583] The original German word was "Käseglocke". The literal translation could be "cheese cloche".

[584] See Glossary: Shallow dive (Flachsturz).

[585] As mentioned previously, this success claim is exaggerated.

According to the weather forecast, the attack and lead angle and the release altitude were ordered in the briefing with the crews.[586] Furthermore, the bridge or the mast was considered as the best aiming points on the ship. With these aiming points the commander attacked the target and dropped his bomb exactly according to the ordered aiming and lead point - even if he had found out during the flight that these points had been changed by shifting winds and thus his bomb would miss the target. The following Ketten corrected the aiming point according to the offset of the first bomb's impact, but otherwise kept exactly to the ordered aiming procedures and release altitudes. With this disciplined adherence to the attack order, theoretically all further bombs had to be on target because of this hold point correction. This was also largely the case.

The nature of this procedure required the attack of several aircraft on the same target to guarantee its sinking (at least 1 Staffel).

Example: Employment in Africa on 18.4.1941 against an enemy battleship reported by the Army, which fired on friendly positions near El Alamein from the sea with the heavy caliber guns. Departure from Derna at 09.45 with 12 Ju 87's. After surveying the enemy-free sea area near El Alamein, the unit encountered an older coastal armored ship (Monitor) of approx. 8 000 GRT north of Sollum Bay.[587] The wind report of the weather forecast was outdated, since almost calm winds had set in. Therefore, the bombs of the leading Kette thrown with the ordered values lay 20 - 30 m to the front left of the ship. The entire bomb load of the following Kette of the Staffelkapitän hit with an appropriate correction the foreship and pressed this under water. The next Kette hit the stern with the entire bomb load. The last Kette returned to the port of operations with bombs,

---

[586] Editorial notice: We have cut this sentence in two to provide a more legible text.

[587] Considering the geographical description, it is possible that this extract refers to *HMS Fiona*. It was the only ship that was sunk North of Sidi Barrani in the Bay of Sollum (named after the coastal town El Salloum) on the 18th April 1941 by German and Italian Ju 87s. It is possible that this attack happened with a larger number than the 12 indicated machines, that appear only to account for the III./St. G. 1. This example shows once again how difficult the correct estimation of ship size and type was during these operations, as *HMS Fiona* was not a coastal monitor but rather a much smaller than indicated repurposed passenger ship, built in the 1920s. It was armed with two 4" (101.6mm) guns as its main armament, one 12pdr (76.2mm) and four .303 (7.7mm) machine guns for aircraft defense. *HMS Fiona* sank with the loss of 51 sailors, including Captain Arthur Harold Hildreth Griffiths. Considering the limited AA-defense and size of the attacking Ju 87 force, this result does not necessarily surprise if we can trust Mahlke's description of the accuracy achieved during the attack. See Wrecksite, *HMS Fiona*, available at https://www.wrecksite.eu/wreck.aspx?140064 (last accessed 27.10.2021).

as the target was already underwater during the dive (loss of a monitor confirmed by the British Admiralty according to intelligence services)[588].

The release altitude was determined by the strength of the anti-aircraft defenses at the target. The dive on the target itself was carried out without any consideration of the anti-aircraft defenses of all calibers (without defensive movements of the aircraft to enable proper aiming). However, the strength of the anti-aircraft defense from the target had to be taken into account insofar as the release altitude was to be set higher in the case of particularly strong anti-aircraft concentration than in the case of low defense (highest release altitude 700 m, lowest release altitude 300 m[589] or a low altitude drop described previously).

This measure was based on the consideration that the combat mission could only be fulfilled if the bomb was released and "armed" before the Ju 87 itself exploded![590] (The effect of higher release altitudes on aiming errors had to be accepted and compensated for by the above-mentioned aiming point corrections of the following aircraft). The sober reality of this consideration can only be appreciated by those who have flown a diving attack against such massed light and medium AA-fire[591] from the target. When the tracer bullets ("flatirons"[592]) coming from the center of the target streaked past the pilot's cabin in such concentrations to the right, left, above and below the fuselage at a distance of less than 1 m that the pilot had the impression that he was flying into an increasingly narrowing tube, and when he was taken under fire by this AA at an altitude of 2 500 m and had to fly through this defensive fire up to 1 000 m, and when further tracers came from different directions before and behind the own airplane, then the moment comes, where also the most stubborn Stuka pilot

---

[588] Without more information and relevant files, the identity of this "monitor" remains unclear. Looking at the operational area, one attack on a British monitor of the Erebus-class happened two months prior to the sinking of the HMS Fiona on 23rd February 1941 referenced in the above footnote. Damaged and subsequently scuttled by the crew, HMS Terror roughly fits the description by Mahlke. It is possible that Mahlke mixed up the dates in this post-war report, or otherwise confuses two separate attacks. However, this remains speculation. See also Wrecksite, HMS Terror (I-03), available at https://www.wrecksite.eu/wreck.aspx?98977 (last accessed 27.10.2021); and uboat.net, HMS Terror (I 03), available at https://uboat.net/allies/warships/ship/5460.html (last accessed 27.10.2021).

[589] 2300 and 1000 ft respectively.

[590] It is unclear if Mahlke refers here to the isolated incidents in which a bomb malfunction is said to have destroyed a Ju 87, or whether he refers to the aircraft getting hit. The latter appears more likely as he goes on talking about strong AA-defenses.

[591] See Glossary: AA-defenses - light, medium and heavy (leichte, mittlere und schwere Flak).

[592] The original German word was "Bügeleisen". Likely personal or Gruppe/Geschwader-specific slang.

means: " Now surely I get hit"! And before he gets "hit" he must just press the bomb button, so that the whole thing has had a meaning. - This has nothing to do with questions of "courage", because pressing the bomb button does not switch off the AA: the pilot still has to go through it anyway! However, from that moment on, he does not have to concentrate on the aiming process anymore, but could devote his attention to the enemy defense, and take appropriate countermeasures.[593]

-.-.-.-.-.-.-.-.-.-

In principle, in the case of attacking naval targets, the aim had to be to attack the ships at sea (in motion under steam), since then a sinking can be achieved with far greater certainty (with fewer expended resources and personal risk) than with ships in port. In the case of ships at sea, the explosive effect of the bombs is often intensified by boiler explosions. In the case of underwater damage at sea, the effect of taking water is also much greater, while ships in port can often still be secured and docked for repair in the event of heavy damage by tugs and auxiliary craft.

In the case of attacks against ships in port (e.g., La Valetta on Malta, Tobruk), the actual success of the attack could not be clearly determined, because the ships attacked were severely damaged by direct hits and partially grounded, but the final destruction or the degree of damage could not be determined with certainty.

The attack on ships at sea was also to be attempted because a sinking also destroys the ship's cargo before it reaches its port of destination and could be unloaded.

In addition, the execution of a Stuka attack against naval targets[594] in the harbor was far more difficult and associated with greater operational risk for the attacking aircraft due to the incomparably stronger air defenses. Since the strongest and best air defenses of the enemy were concentrated precisely at the most important supply ports, surprises regarding the type, strengths and positions of the defenses always had to be expected.[595]

---

[593] While the previous section of this document jumped between events and provided a less organized account, the upcoming second half will be summarizing the made experiences in a clearer fashion.

[594] The original German word was "Schiffsziele". The literal translation would be "ship targets".

[595] In the original document, this whole paragraph was a single sentence. For legibility reasons, we split this sentence into two sentences.

212

When attacking a naval target on the high seas, the expected anti-aircraft defenses of the attacked ship group could be clearly identified. The attack could be timed in the approach and departure in such a way that these anti-aircraft weapons could only be fired for a limited time.

In contrast, when attacking naval targets in harbors, several AA-defense lines had to be broken through, whose positions were not always known in advance. Anti-aircraft weapons of all calibers, usually positioned in several belts far around the harbor area, could act simultaneously on the attacking formation over a much longer period of time and from different (sometimes surprising) directions.[596]

The behavior of the unit had to be adapted accordingly to the respective defensive situation. In this context, the following principles had emerged through experience, which limited the risk of loss to the unavoidable minimum.

1.)   The approach to the target against heavily defended targets was made at altitudes above the range of the light and medium anti-aircraft guns (generally at altitudes of 3 000 to 3 500 meters[597]). Before reaching the firing zones of the heavy AA, the closed approach formation was broken up into a Gruppen line, in order to be able to exploit the maneuverability of the single aircraft as its best defense against the heavy AA and to enable well-aimed single dives of the aircraft. As soon as the first muzzle flash of the heavy AA was detected, some sharp turns (serpentines) were flown, which made even the best firing solutions of the AA ineffective due to the flight time of the projectiles. Then, as soon as the blast points of the first AA salvos could be seen in front of the unit, the aircraft would steer towards them, since hardly ever a second shell hits the same place as its predecessor. (According to the old infantry rule: the best cover in a barrage is the last opened shell hole!). This method of defense against heavy AA was also based on the general observation that AA usually tended to cover larger "sky areas" with explosive clouds during "barrage shooting", as if an AA explosive cloud were still an obstacle for the approaching aircraft. The British heavy AA, e.g., at La Valetta on Malta, where it was concentrated in particular strength, presented the intervening Stuka unit with 3 such barrages, which were staggered in altitude. The first barrage was located at about approach altitude, the second barrage just after the start of the dive about 500 to

---

[596] In the original document, this whole paragraph was a single sentence. For legibility reasons, we split this sentence into two sentences.
[597] 9900 – 11500 ft.

213

800 m[598] lower (thus in front of the diving unit), the 3rd barrage was again about 1 000 m[599] lower than the second. All these barrages were easily outmaneuvered by approaching the last blast points. A successful hit resulting in a downed aircraft by the heavy AA could only be done by chance and only one such case is known to the author during the employment of the unit (over La Valetta). It remains unclear whether the explosion of a Ju 87 (in the middle of the unit) was caused by heavy AA hits or by other influences[600].[601]

2.)   The <u>dive on the target</u> itself was done without any consideration to the caliber of the AA-defense (see above: Release altitude).

3.)   <u>The departure:</u> As soon as the bomb was released - and the attacks with fixed weapons that were given in the orders for the attack were accomplished - the only principle governing the behavior of the single aircraft and the unit in regard to the defense was to, if possible, bring the aircraft "home safely". Since, after pulling out of the dive, the aircraft was at its most exposed to light and medium AA at low speed, a low altitude departure from the target was generally the safest and best defense during harbor attacks, by which at least part of the enemy's defensive weapons could be avoided by "flying under" their firing arcs. In addition, the target departure had to be done in such a way that the light AA firing zones could be traversed by the shortest route, since the light and medium AA firing from forward positions was much more difficult to outmaneuver by defensive maneuvers of the aircraft than the projectiles shot at the aircraft from behind. As soon as the light AA positions were passed, so that the tracers came from behind, the aircraft pilot could control them. Improvements of the light AA lead could be recognized by a bend in the tracer pattern. If this bend pointed toward the own aircraft, the bullet trajectory had to be "skipped over" with a short pull on the control stick. The flight time of the projectiles gave a few pilots enough time to do this.

4.)   <u>Return flight:</u> Depending on the situation, the unit usually rallies outside the area of effect of the light AA. Departure and return over sea at low altitude ("unorderly assembly" see above).

---

[598] 1600 – 2600 ft.
[599] 3300 ft.
[600] There are some reports that premature detonations of bombs on Ju 87s could occur in rare moments after the bombs were armed during the flight.
[601] The last sentence was separated from the previous sentences for legibility reasons.

214

-.-.-.-.-.-.-.-

signed. Helmut Mahlke

Oberstlt.i.G.a.D.

[Originally attached pictures not added due to their very poor quality.]

Photo 14: Ju 87 D on the Eastern Front, January 1944. Original caption: "There she stands without any fuel...". Credit: Collection Roman Töppel.

An Introduction to Night-Bombing in the Ju 87

This document was compiled through the experiences of St.G. 1 and 3, operating in the English Channel, against Malta and in the North African theater. It is noteworthy in so far, that night bombing incidents with the Ju 87 have naturally not attracted the same amount of attention as the more conventional attacks by Sturzkampfgeschwader. Given their own account, St.G. 1 had only flown 250-night missions between July 1940 to July 1942. The overall significance of these attacks is thus low but provides experience in a form of attack that Ju 87s would be conducting in future years.

This is especially noteworthy as before Autumn 1942, there had been no direct endeavor to establish dedicated units for frontline night bombing, an impetus that is often brought in connection with the German experience on the Eastern Front where front-line units suffered harassing attacks at night by light soviet aircraft. These Behelfskampfstaffeln[602], later named Störkampfstaffeln[603], were small units, living a nomadic lifestyle, flying an assortment of light and/or outdated aircraft, mirroring those on the Soviet side. The inflicted material damage of these units appears low, although given their purpose was harassment as the name implied, rather than direct material damage, the actual impact is hard to quantify. It was only with the reorganization of the Luftwaffe's close air support arm in early 1943 that the now christened Nachtschlachtgruppen[604] (N.S.Gr.) would emerge, of which the majority would operate on the Eastern Front. Nevertheless, various units like N.S.G. 9 would operate with Ju 87s against the Western Allies in Italy between early 1944 to April 1945.[605]

It is in this context that the following document provides an excellent entry point into the complexities of using a Ju 87s at night. The documented experiences with this alternative form of attack, acquired years before it before an operational requirement for it was set, provide a summary for the reasons, challenges and tactical applications of night bombing attacks by Ju 87s, that remained largely relevant until the end of the war.

---

[602] Can be loosely translated to "auxiliary bombing Staffeln".
[603] Can be loosely translated to "disruption bombing Staffeln".
[604] Can be loosely translated to "night attacker Gruppen".
[605] Nick Beale, *Ghost Bombers – The Moonlight War of NSG 9: Luftwaffe Night Attack Operations from Anzio to the Alps*, Classic Publications, Manchester, UK, 2001, p. 9-15.

While most bomber aircraft had, due to their size and requirements the necessary equipment, the Ju 87 had not been built with night missions in mind. Falling outside the domain of the Sturzkampfgeschwader as described in *Lufttaktik*[606], dive-bombers were to act at daytime, eliminating targets that required a heavy bombload and accuracy. Equally, the Ju 87 was to provide support to the German Army, and this required a use throughout the day when ground forces were the most active and coordination was easier. In the operations against Britain and in the Mediterranean, its use shifted away from interdiction and operational support to anti-shipping, and destruction of ports and military installations. Given the growing threat of enemy fighter aircraft, experimental night sorties sought to alleviate this threat. Naturally, most sorties remained daytime missions but with the years, became ever more perilous. The Luftwaffe continued to use the Ju 87 in its envisioned role, flying targeted interdiction and support missions just beyond the front lines on the Eastern Front until mid-1943, yet by this point it had long admitted that a similar use was "worthless in the West".[607] It was only by exploiting the supposed safety of darkness that Ju 87 crews were able to offset the Luftwaffe's disadvantage in the air and the aircrafts vulnerability, thus allowing it to play to its strengths.

For this to occur, the Ju 87 needed to be made ready for night operations which required additional equipment and changes to the aircraft. Of special interest here is the documents account on the reliance crews have on the lunar phases for natural light and what additional equipment and modifications to the aircraft (e.g., artificial horizon, modified sight illuminations, contact altimeters and exhaust mufflers)[608] are required to allow for this new mission set. The erstwhile technical limitations of the Ju 87 restricted it to mainly coastline use at night, as these are more easily navigated due to the natural reflections of moonlight. Specialized training as well as the introduction of new navigational equipment, for example the Peilgerät offering radio-transmitted direction-finding built into the Ju 87 D-model as a factory standard allowed the crews to include areas more distant from coastlines.

The complexities and equipment requirements for night flying did not stop with the aircraft and crew. As such, special note should be made of the basing issues described in the document. Airfields required the necessary equipment for illumination, search lights, radio direction finding, clear communication and

---

[606] See *Aerial Tactics – The Dive-bomber*.
[607] BArch, ZA 3/282, *Jagdbomber, Sturzkampf- und Panzerbekämpfungsflugzeuge, Transporter, Sonderflugzeuge*.
[608] In later Ju 87 models, the airbrakes would often be removed from the aircraft if it was used by a N.S.Gr. as dives took place from lower altitudes (2-3 000m), or at less steep angles.

coordination between flying and Flak-units, and up-to-date meteorological data[609].

Comparing the later night-time attacks over Italy and on the Western Front with the general procedure described in the document, we see a near identical approach both from navigating via coastlines, rivers and train tracks, as well as the use of flares in the lead aircraft to illuminate the target area to the remaining unit. Here, Nachtschlachtgruppen operating Ju 87 seem to employ similar tactics to that of the first experimental sorties. Naturally, the Allies had learned to counter this threat and the use of night fighters in Italy provided a response to these night intrusions, inflicting continuous losses upon N.S.Gr. 9. Again, the defensive corkscrew already described in the document remained the most usual move in order to shake a night pursuer. With an authorized strength of 60 Ju 87 for the purposes of night mission, it usually did not field more than half this number operationally, losing 75 dive-bombers between January 1944 to April 1945.[610] The inflicted damage as usual is up to debate, as the majority of attacks were small-scale attacks against supply convoys.

On the Eastern Front, the absence of a viable Soviet night fighter allowed Ju 87 operating units such as N.S.G. 4 and N.S.G. 8 more operational freedom. These ranged from small attacks of two Ju 87 against convoys, all the way to larger units of up to 40 aircraft, dropping a mixture of high-explosive and cluster munitions.[611] These tactics had also been collected in a 1943 pamphlet on night bombing with close air support aircraft, differentiating between solitary, nuisance and unit attacks at night[612]. At least in one of these attacks, a high number of machine gun rounds were also reported to have been expended, indicating good enough light conditions for strafing runs.[613]

---

[609] Of interest is both the veiled criticism towards meteorological units in the document, as well as the additional difficulties noted regarding to the African climate.

[610] Nick Beale, *Ghost Bombers – The Moonlight War of NSG 9: Luftwaffe Night Attack Operations from Anzio to the Alps,* Classic Publications, 2001, p. 198-199.

[611] Most often used ordinance appear to be SC/SD and AB 250 as well as SC/SD 70 and 50 bombs. See BArch, RL 7-6/14, *Tagesabschlußmeldung* and *Nachtabschlußmeldung* of Lft.Kdo. 6. Februar 1945, March 1945.

[612] BArch, RL 2-II/142, *Merkblatt: Die Nachtschlachtflieger-Verbände,* March 1943, p. 8.

[613] BArch, RL 7-6/14, *Nachtabschlußmeldung Lft.Kdo. 6 vom 19.2.1945,* 20. February 1945, p. 2 detailing the use of 1 900 rounds of 7.9 mm rounds and 20 rounds 2 cm, indicating a mixed use of Ju 87 D-3 and D-5 in the attack.

Document: Pamphlet on Night-Bombing with the Ju 87

This document from 1942 can be found in BArch, RL 16-2/6, *Merkblatt für den Nachteinsatz mit Junkers Ju 87*, providing an overview of early night-time operations with the Ju 87.

Preliminary Notes / Source Situation, Actuality and Formatting

Throughout this volume, we aimed to retain some of the original formatting, yet the editorial focus lay on legibility. One of the main editorial changes was that, in order to present a clearer layout, we did not follow the original page count as this would have resulted in empty or near empty pages throughout the book. Instead, the text has been reformatted to follow a more conventional structure, page by page.

Please be aware of the following formatting decisions and changes:

- We corrected formatting mistakes in the original version (for example missing spaces, paragraph breaks or others).
- The original formatting sequence was retained, but we made some changes to transfer this document into a more legible layout that is consistent with the other documents found in this book. This also includes the deletion of unnecessary spacing between subs-sections and the removal of colons in the headings.

Reich's Minister for Aviation   Berlin,   27.7.1942[614]
and Commander-in-Chief of the Luftwaffe [615]
Lw.Fü.St.Ia[616] / Gen. of the Bombers
L.In.2 Nr. 2925/42 geh.[617]

Enclosed is the

"Pamphlet on Night-Bombing with the Ju 87"

I.A.[618]
signed [Signature]

---

[614] DD-MM-YYYY

[615] Reich's Minister for Aviation and Commander-in-Chief of the Luftwaffe (Reichsminister der Luftfahrt und Oberbefehlshaber der Luftwaffe).

[616] "Lw.Fü.St." is an abbreviation for Luftwaffe operations staff while Ia designates the role of the Operational Chief of Staff. See Glossary: Operational Chief of Staff (Führungsgruppe [Ia]) and Operations staff (Führrungstab).

[617] Luftwaffe Inspectorate 2 Nr. 2925/42 secret. L.In.2 was the Inspectorate of the Bombers and Dive-bombers, named so in October 1939. Eventually: Inspectorate of the Bombers).

[618] "I.A." is the abbreviation of "Im Auftrag", indicating "by proxy".

Pamphlet on Night-Bombing with the Ju 87

(Collected based on the experience of St.G.1 and 3 over the English Channel, Malta and the African theater of war.)

A. General Notices

Employment of the Ju 87 at night makes it possible to engage even those targets that are most heavily protected by fighters and AA. While losses must always be expected during daytime missions on these targets, no losses due to enemy action have occurred, for example, during the 250 night missions flown by St.G.1 to this date. Against all enemy defenses (night fighters, AA, searchlights, barrage balloons), the Ju 87 has proven itself due to its good flight characteristics, its great maneuverability and its small size.

However, this great advantage which night operations offer over day operations can only be exploited in very specific situations and under special conditions.

B. Required Conditions

Night operations of the Ju 87 are subject to the following conditions:

1.) Targets

So far, experience has been gained primarily in the employment against naval targets[619] and targets in the immediate vicinity of the coast. Naval targets are easily identified by their wake; the coastline stands out clearly from the water even in poor lighting conditions, so that there are no major difficulties in navigating.

Employment against land targets, which require a longer approach over land, present a greater navigational challenge. Since the Stuka aircraft does not have the radio equipment required to locate its target by means of dead reckoning[620] in conjunction with radio navigation[621] - and Stuka crews have not yet been

---

[619] The original German word was "Schiffsziele". The literal translation would be "ship targets".
[620] See Glossary: Navigation by dead reckoning (Koppelnavigation).
[621] See Glossary: Radio navigation (Funknavigation).

trained in this - such navigational difficulties arise during such employment and misidentification becomes unavoidable. The risk of misidentification is usually so great that before each night mission it must be checked whether it stands within an acceptable ratio to the bombing effect that could be achieved.

Consequently, it will seldom be possible to engage a target with longer approaches over land. Only during a night with a full moon and in good visibility conditions should attacks be considered promising, and if the target is close to the coast, a lake, a large river or other conspicuous landmarks.

This means that night missions with Ju 87s can only be carried out under the most basic navigational conditions.

2.) Meteorological Conditions

The weather is decisive for the employment. Only from the 1st quarter to the beginning of the last quarter of the lunar phase are attacks possible in the time between moonrise to moonset[622]. During the rest of the time, no night attacks can be carried out since it is then impossible to find the target. During this time, only twilight attacks are possible, in which a last, pale light shines over the target at the time of the attack.

3.) Special Equipment for the Aircraft

Blackout curtains for the cabin[623], installation of an artificial horizon (Sperry[624]), installation of a low-light red bulb in the reflector sight[625], darkening[626] of the aircraft, installation of exhaust flame mufflers, dimming of all bright light sources in the aircraft, installation of contact altimeters[627].

C. Execution

1.) Ground Organization

Sufficiently large airfields must be available for conducting night operations with Ju 87s. The field airfields generally used by Ju 87 units are in many cases

---

[622] This refers to the lunar phrase of the first quarter, over the full moon to the last quarter, and is thus roughly about half of the lunar phase.
[623] Most likely similar in style to some instrument flying hoods used during the training of pilots, also on modern aircraft.
[624] See Glossary: Sperry.
[625] See Glossary: Reflector sight (Reflexvisier [Revi]).
[626] The original German word was "Berußung". The literal translation would be "sooting".
[627] See Glossary: Contact altimeter (Kontakthöhenmesser).

inadequate for night operations. The airfield must have a conventional illuminated runway and illuminated obstructions. It has been proven expedient to separate the electrical installation of the illuminated runway and remaining light sources on the airfield. In the case of a simultaneous enemy attack, illumination of only the runway has proven to be sufficient as a landing aid. An artificial horizon is not absolutely necessary as a takeoff and landing aid, since the lighting and visibility conditions during the employment of the Ju 87 do not require the use of the artificial horizon. Hand lamps[628] must be provided in case of a failure of the electrical system. Additionally, in such a case, the creation of a searchlight dome or the use of illumination guns[629] must be requested from the AA-defenses by the airfield's air traffic control, so that the airfield can be found. In order to ensure smooth cooperation between the AA and the air traffic control, the air traffic controller and the commander of the AA unit must be consulted during the briefing. The command of all ground units involved in the employment must be done from a single command post.

2.) Meteorological Conditions

In the briefing, the meteorologist first discusses the weather and assesses the suitability of the weather for attacks with Ju 87s. The leader of the flying unit makes the decision whether to take-off to carry out the ordered attack. The visibility conditions indicated by the meteorologist are usually too good, since the higher-lying haze layers, which cannot be seen from below, considerably impair oblique visibility. It is therefore advisable to carry out a meteorological flight in the direction of the target about one hour before take-off. If the weather situation is not entirely perfect, the unit leader is the first to take-off in time so that, if necessary, the employment can be aborted in good time via a friendly ground radio station.

3.) Take-off

Take-off is done individually at timed safety intervals without position lights. In case of particularly good visibility conditions, it is also possible to launch in Rotten and Ketten with time intervals of 3 - 5 minutes. This depends on the training level of the crews. In any case, the launch time is set according to the attack time determined by the lighting conditions. During the lunar phase (from the 1st quarter to the beginning of the last quarter) it is determined by moonrise

---

[628] The original German word was "Panzerhandlampen". The literal translation would be "tank hand lamps". These are small lamps, used as hand lights on landing strips, by mechanics or in buildings. They usually include a hook on the top, by which they could be hanged or carried.

[629] See Glossary: Illumination guns (Lichtspucker).

or moonset. During the rest of the time, the start is to be set in such a way that a last pale glow shines over the target when the unit arrives in the attack area (twilight attack).

4.) Identifying the Targets

a) Naval

Naval targets are perfectly silhouetted against the moonlight. Without the moon, Naval targets can only be made out when the last, pale glow on the western horizon dully illuminates the sea surface during the attack. This dull light is no longer sufficient for silhouetting. The ships can then be made out primarily by the wake of the fast-moving escort boats, with the wake interrupting the pale reflection of the water surface. In near-total darkness, the wake can be seen only at altitudes below 1 000 m[630]. Locating a convoy of ships in such lighting conditions is only promising if the location is correctly indicated by Freya[631], observation, etc. Under these lighting conditions, naval targets can be detected during high cloud cover at a visibility of up to 4-5/10.

The attack is best launched with a target marker[632]. When the target marker has found the target, he drops flares as a homing point for the following Ju 87s. Depending on the circumstances, the Ju 87s take-off after the target marker. It is best that the target marker indicates by radio when he is at the target. Radio communication between the target marker and the following Ju 87s must be ensured so that further flares can be dropped by the target marker on request. The target marker is equipped primarily with flares.

During an employment on naval targets without a target marker, the Ju 87s will be patrolling a region in which the target is assumed to be. All aircraft are to be equipped with a sufficient quantity of flares. Armed patrol reconnaissance then begins in the indicated region. The altitude of the individual aircraft must be staggered so as to avoid the danger of collision. Radio communication among them must be ensured. When the first aircraft has found the target, it fires 2 flares at 5-minute intervals. At the request of the following aircraft, further flares must be fired. The first aircraft remains at the target as a target marker until it is relieved by another Ju 87.

---

[630] 3300 ft.
[631] See Glossary: Freya (Freya-Gerät).
[632] See Glossary: Target marker (Fühlungshalter).

b) Coastal Targets

Coastal targets are easy to spot in all lighting and weather conditions that were also mentioned as favorable for naval targets, since the coastal outline is always silhouetted against the water. Distinctive lines such as harbor piers[633], headlands, etc. allow the commanded targets to be perfectly identified and detected by the reflector sight[634] in the dive. In poor visibility conditions, approaching the coast is facilitated by the activity of red flashing navigational lights, whose location must be known, and by searchlight activity.

c) Land Targets

Little experience has been gained in this area, as primarily ship and coastal targets have been attacked at night. This is due to the more difficult navigational conditions for night approaches over land. Railroad installations have occasionally been attacked with success on clear moonlit nights.

Experience in Africa has shown that even in light haze it is not possible to find a point target from the normal approach altitude of 2 - 3 000 m[635]. In this weather condition, the approach is made at low altitudes from which ground orientation is still possible. Clear, moonlit nights provide sufficient ground orientation. If the approach leads over terrain that is difficult from a navigational standpoint, the briefing should order the approach over prominent navigational aids, such as lakes, rivers, cities, railroads, etc. Targets located near such prominent terrain features are relatively easy to spot.

5.) Direction of Attack

In moonlight, ship and coastal targets are attacked against the moon, since they then stand out most against the illuminated water and can be detected perfectly by the reflector sight. Before and after the lunar phase[636], attacks are made in the last light provided by the sun set, if possible, in a longitudinal direction to the target, since the greatest light scattering can be expected in this direction. Both types of attack allow perfect dive recovery due to the horizon still being present. The attacks out of the darkness offer the advantage that enemy defenses can only acquire the aircraft very late.

---

[633] See Glossary: Harbor mole (Hafenmolen)
[634] See Glossary: Reflector sight (Reflexvisier [Revi]).
[635] 6600 - 9900 ft.
[636] Meant here is most likely the previously indicated favorable first to last quarter lunar phase.

6.) Diving Angle and Release Altitude

Ship targets are attacked in a diving attack with an angle of 30 to 50°, coastal targets with a diving angle of up to 70° and 80° in good lighting conditions. Release altitudes for naval targets are 300 - 500 m[637], and for coastal targets 800 - 1 000 m[638]. For targets protected by barrage balloons, higher release altitudes are to be ordered. Immediately after the pull-out, if possible, move away into the dark or against a wall of clouds, so that the aircraft does not stand out against the bright horizon.

7.) Enemy Defenses

The following enemy defenses must be expected during night attacks:

From naval targets: MG, AA of all calibers, barrage balloons and night fighters guided by ground control[639].

From Land: MG, AA of all calibers, light and heavy searchlights, barrage balloons, night fighters guided by searchlights or ground control[640].

a) The Defense of Naval Targets

When attacking ships that are escorted, strong anti-aircraft defenses of light and medium caliber[641] must always be expected. The protection of convoys by barrage balloons at night must also be expected (however, so far only one barrage balloons has been detected in a large, escorted convoy at an altitude of 500 to 600 m[642]). As a defensive measure against AA, strong maneuvers are made during the attack and departure in response to the enemy AA fire indicated by the tracers.

b) The Defense on Land

In the case of coastal targets, because of the greater approach altitude (around 3 000 m[643]), the defense does not appear to the same extent as in the attack on convoys. Even numerous searchlights do not impair the approach and the execution of the attack. According to previous experience, the attacking aircraft

---

[637] 1000 – 1600 ft.
[638] 2600 – 3300 ft.
[639] See Glossary: Nightfighter (Nachtjäger - dunkel / hell).
[640] See Glossary: Nightfighter (Nachtjäger - dunkel / hell).
[641] See Glossary: AA-defenses - light, medium and heavy (leichte, mittlere und schwere Flak).
[642] 1600 – 2000 ft.
[643] 9900 ft.

are always captured [by searchlights] only for a short time, if the following defensive measures are applied; small course changes on approach to the target area, significant changes to the throttle setting and altitude and sharp turns before the attack, in addition simultaneous presence of several aircraft in the target area.

According to experience, the searchlights turn off during the dive and turn on again during the departure. If the aircraft is caught in a search beam, sharp turns with simultaneous altitude changes eliminate the possibility of being kept in the search beam for a long time.

c) Night Fighters

When attacking in target areas protected by night fighters, night fighters directed by searchlights or ground operators must be expected[644]. Based on previous experience, it has been determined that the searchlights are switched on too early. This allows for early detection [of the presence of night fighters]. The most successful defense against enemy night fighters after they have been detected consists of an immediate turn[645] with a significant loss of altitude.

d) Barrage Balloons

According to the experience of St.G.1, barrage balloons are clearly detected during the attack, but so late that evasion seems questionable.

8.) Landing

The approach to the airfield up to the passing of the identification lights[646] should be made at an altitude of about 400 m[647], and if there are obstacles in the vicinity of the airfield, correspondingly higher. According to the situation, locally specified signals are to be agreed upon for the request of the runway illumination; among other things, flashing with the on-board searchlight or firing of E.S.N.[648] The position lights are turned on only when turning in for a landing. Landing should be made on the grass to the right of the light path at airfields equipped with concrete runways. This allows the airplane to touch down softly and has a considerably shorter roll-out distance.

---

[644] See Glossary: Nightfighter (Nachtjäger - dunkel / hell).
[645] Turning into the direction of the attacker. The original German word was "Gegenkurven". The literal translation would be "counter-turning".
[646] See Glossary: Identification lights (Kennfeuers).
[647] 1300 ft.
[648] "E.S.N." is the abbreviation of "Erkennungssignale", indicating "identification signals". These were signal flares, fired from a signaling pistol in single shot, single color cartridges.

9.) Navigational Aids

A strong transmitter and a large shortwave receiver are used at the airfield for handling the radio traffic. The following navigational aids are to be used:

a)   a small light beacon near the airfield;

b)   a red warning light installed for example on a church tower or a similar structure located in the vicinity of the airfield which is turned on continuously during night flight operations;

c)   a small radio beacon for D/F homing using the Peil G IV[649].

Distributor: Being drafted.

I. A. [650]
signed Meister
Oberst i.G.

F.d.R.d.A.[651]
signed [Signature]
Major.

---

[649] See Glossary: Direction-finding equipment (Peilgerät).
[650] "I.A." is the abbreviation of "Im Auftrag", indicating "by proxy".
[651] "F.d.R.d.A." is the abbreviation of "Für die Richtigkeit der Angaben". This is a declaration that the accuracy of the given information is confirmed by the signee.

Ju 87s during the Poland Campaign and Crete Operations

Throughout the Polish campaign, Luftwaffe air attacks successfully disrupted Polish troop and supply movements. Yet throughout the operation it discovered that there was a need to operate much closer to the frontlines than anticipated. This caused unforeseen problems to dive- and bomber units, as these planes were not suited for this role.[652] Nevertheless, the experiences gained in Poland, especially with the unit of the Nahkampfverband[653] under General von Richthofen, served the Luftwaffe well for the coming campaigns.[654]

The Luftwaffe's operation over Poland would also give rise to international outcry as the indiscriminate nature of many attacks on civilians, either in cities or those retreating eastwards are inseparable from the Luftwaffe's wider operations during the campaign. For example, one of the first attacks flown was on the city of Wieluń.[655] Repeatedly bombed with no discernable military reason on the 1st September by the order of General von Richthofen[656], in the war diary of I./St.G. 77 no military targets were indicated and the attack purpose was simply described as the "destruction of the eastern part of Wieluń". Wieluń was reported "burning" by 6am in the morning.[657]

Except for one instance concerning the bombing of Warsaw, where I./St.G. 1 refers to attacks made against "whole city districts"[658], little reference is made to

---

[652] BArch, RL 7-1/12, *Erfahrungsberichte der Verbände der Luftflotte 1 im Polenkrieg*, 2 Ausfertigung.
[653] Can be loosely translated to close air support unit.
[654] James S. Corum, *The Luftwaffe – Creating the Operational Air War, 1918-1940*, University Press of Kansas, Lawrence, USA, 1997. p. 272–275.
[655] Roger Moorhouse, *First to Fight: The Polish War 1939*, Vintage, London, UK, 2020.
[656] Hans-Erich Volkmann, *Wolfram von Richthofen, die Zerstörung Wieluńs und das Kriegsvölkerrecht*, Militärgeschichtliche Zeitschrift 70, Potsdam, Germany, 2011, p. 287–328.
[657] BArch, RL 10/348, *Polenkrieg Kriegstagebuch I./Stuka 77*,1939, p. 3.
[658] The original German wording was "ganze Stadtteile". The bombing of Warsaw in 1939, next to Guernica (1937), Coventry (1940) and Rotterdam (1940) are the most well-known early terror bombing attacks carried out by the Luftwaffe. Although other towns like Wieluń also suffered, Warsaw became the international symbol of the German air campaign. The referenced attack here, with the clear description of attacks on large areas within the actual city, once again highlights the indiscriminate air assault on the city. It should also be noted that, next to an international media outcry, the Luftwaffe and Germany itself took the destruction of Warsaw as an example of its capabilities to pressure other governments. See Richard Overy, *The Bombing War*, Penguin Books, London, UK,

such types of attacks in the coming two experience reports by I./St.G. 1 and III./St. G. 2. Instead, a more general operational and technical description is given, providing a summary of how attacks were conducted and what (military) success was achieved. It is possible however, when reading through the reports, to find examples where attacks on urban centers or potentially civilian targets are referenced almost in passing [See section II. 6. and II. 7. of I./St.G. 1 and Number 4) in the report of III./St.G. 2]. In those sections where attacks on cities like Warsaw are mentioned, we have included additional information on the attack.

In the second document, a post-war report on the activities of St. G. 2 during the air-sea battle of Crete on the 22nd May 1942 is given. Written as a summary for the Historical Division, this document focuses on the attacks and observations by Ju 87 crews against the Royal Navy. This official English translation is not a direct translation but a summary that condense rather than directly relays the information[659]. In our translation we will endeavor to remain as close to the original in content and meaning.

While the Luftwaffe enjoyed some success in the operation, it was largely a failure for the Axis landing forces as the British naval force was able to successfully thwart this seaborne landing operation. The report here is included with some comparisons to the Royal Navy Naval Staff History of the Second World War, *Naval Operations in the Battle of Crete*[660], to combine the accounts and supply additional data to the reader.

Before reading these experience reports, it is recommended to having read or consulted the Documents *Aerial Tactics – The Dive-Bomber*, as well as *L.Dv. 20/2: Luftwaffe Regulation 20/2 – Guidelines for Dive-Bombing Training*. Both are included in the first chapter of this book. These explain the operational thinking for the employment of the dive-bombers, as well as explain how a dive-bombing attack is to be made, including various keywords found in the following experience reports. This provides a good contrast between the "theory" and "practical reality" of the dive-bomber units.

1994, p. 64; similar attacks are also referenced in the mission reports of, for example, I./Sturzkampfgeschwader 77 on the 25th of September 1939. See BArch, RL 10/350, *Kriegstagebuch Polenkrieg I. /Stuka 77 Anlagen, 1939.*

[659] NARA, M1035 Fiche 0614, B-640, *2nd Stuka Wing in the Crete Operation*. By Generalmajor Oscar Dinort and Generalmajor Hubertus Hitschhold, 1947.

[660] B.R. 1736 (2) Naval Staff History, *Naval Operations in the Battle of Crete 20th May-1st June 1941* (Battle Summary No. 4), Admiralty, 1960.

Document: Poland and Crete Report

This section consists of two reports, reproduced here in chronological order. The first provides a summary of the experiences by I./St.G. 1 and III./St. G. 2. from the Invasion of Poland in 1939. The second is a 1947 report from the Air-Sea Battle of Crete (22nd May 1942), authored by ranking officers who experienced this battle when part of St.G. 2. The original files can be found in BArch, RL 7-1/12, *Erfahrungsberichte der Führungsstellen und unterstellten Verbänden über den Einsatz in Polen* and BArch, ZA 1/993, *Dinort, Oskar; Hitschhold, Hubertus: See-Luft-Schlacht um Kreta am 22.5.1941: Sonderbericht des Sturzkampfgeschwaders 2 "Immelmann"* respectively.

Preliminary Notes / Source Situation, Actuality and Formatting

Throughout this volume, we aimed to retain some of the original formatting, yet the editorial focus lay on legibility. One of the main editorial changes was that, in order to present a clearer layout, we did not follow the original page count as this would have resulted in empty or near empty pages throughout the book. Instead, the text has been reformatted to follow a more conventional structure, page by page.

Please be aware of the following formatting decisions and changes:

- We corrected formatting mistakes or inconsistencies in the original version (for example missing spaces, paragraph breaks or others).
- The original formatting sequence was retained, but we made some changes to transfer this document into a more legible layout that is consistent with the other documents found in this book. This also includes the deletion of unnecessary spacing between subs-sections and the removal of colons in the headings.
- The first word of the following page was written on the bottom right of the preceding page and was underlined. This was a common practice at the time, but we did not follow this standard.
- The Poland experience report had a few words that were crossed out with a series of "x". These are usually not reprinted.
- The Crete report's short title "MS # B-640" was in the header on every page. For consistent formatting we omitted it.

Transcript: (excerpt)

I./Sturzkampfgeschwader 1[661]   Insterburg, 3. Oct. 1939[662]

Abt.Ia Nr. 795/39 geh.[663]

Document: Experience Report of the Employment of the Gruppe in the Polish Campaign from 1.9. – 27.9.39

I. General Tactical Experience

1.) En-Route

When en-route to the target the Gruppe formed up in almost all employments as a loosened Gruppe column (Sequence: Stab, 1.,2.,3. Staffel). It was carried out in a straight line until about 30 km[664] before the objective. For reaching the operational altitude of 4-6 000 m[665], a climb with 3-4m/sec. at 200 kph[666] on the air speed indicator[667] and 0.9 atü [sic!][668] boost pressure proved to be sufficient in terms of time. Using these performance values, the above-mentioned unit reached 4 000 m in 20 minutes and 6 000 m in 30 minutes. The altitude flown en-route to the target was strongly dependent on the weather conditions. Heavy haze and cloud layers often reduced visibility to such an extent that ground orientation was completely lost, and the group had to fly to the target more or less blind. Often the Vistula and Bug lowlands[669] proved to be a weather barrier

---

[661] I./Sturzkampfgeschwader 1 was stationed in East Prussia (today the Russian Kaliningrad enclave) prior to the invasion and thus could fly into Poland from the Northeast.

[662] DD.MM.YYYY

[663] Abteilung Ia Nr.795/39 geheim. See Glossary: Operational Chief of Staff (Führungsgruppe [Ia]).

[664] 18.6 miles.

[665] 13100 – 16700 ft.

[666] 120 mph.

[667] The original German word was "Staudruckmesser", which could be translated into "pitot gauge".

[668] Meant is most likely ata. See Glossary: ata.

[669] The Vistula and Bug are both rivers in Poland. The Vistula meanders from the southern Polish-Czech-Slovakian border (current borders) northwards through Warsaw, before flowing into the Baltic Sea at Gdańsk. The Bug originates in Ukraine, flowing along the

when approaching from the north, e.g., after passing the river courses the weather cleared up and there was often a cloudless sky or at least significantly better visibility over the target (Warsaw).

Employment of short-range reconnaissance aircraft K[670] for weather reconnaissance and a thorough navigational preparation [for the attack], as well as flying by set timings, proved exceptionally effective in this regard.

2.) Approach

After reaching the target area, the approach was made by breaking up the Gruppen column into attack groups, if there were several targets, or into a line. The approach was selected in such a way that AA and areas protected by fighters, which were known from previous employment, were avoided if the location of the target permitted this. In the process, each aircraft flew with vigorous defensive maneuvers. In heavy haze and when approaching from the sun, the approach was not detected by enemy AA, but when approaching under a closed cloud cover, it was always answered with barrage AA-fire. Casualties did not occur in the approach during any operation.

3.) Direction of Attack

When en-route towards the target, the direction of attack was chosen from the sun if possible. These attacks were usually detected only after the bombs had been dropped. However, the defenses missed their target here as well, since the aircraft departed in the direction of the sun with vigorous defensive maneuvers. For the most reliable targeting conditions in the dive, the direction of the attack against the wind is to be demanded without regard to any safety measures (position of the sun). It turned out that in the case of dives with the wind or in a crosswind, accuracy was considerably worse than in the case of dives against the wind. In the case of dives with the wind, the planes usually started the dive too late and were then carried too steeply and out of the target by the tail wind, resulting in drops with a considerable long trail. With crosswinds, the planes were usually pushed out of the sight line to such an extent that smooth and safe aiming was no longer assured and the throws were far to the left or right of the target. This difficulty was particularly noticeable in attacks on bridges, which permit only 2 directions of attack.

---

present border of Poland and Belarus where it passes Brest, before meeting with the river Narew and flowing into the Vistula northwards of Warsaw.
[670] See Glossary: Reconnaissance aircraft K (K-Aufklärungsflugzeug).

4.) Release Altitude

During the first operations, the bombs were released at the altitudes of 1 000 - 700 m[671] used during training exercises, so that the aircraft had an altitude of only 500 - 300 m[672] after dive recovery and were thus exposed to the enemy's light anti-aircraft defense to a greater extent. During further operations, this experience was taken into account and the release altitude was increased to 1 800 – 1 500 m[673]. It became apparent that even with correspondingly larger lead angles, the hit situation was just as good as with the low release altitudes. The pilots felt more confident and therefore aimed more calmly and accurately. The release altitude for targets that were not protected by strong anti-aircraft defenses, such as railroad lines and railroad transports, was 700 - 400 m[674], which naturally had a considerable effect on these targets.

During the last operations on Warsaw, release altitudes of 2 000 m[675] proved to be sufficient, since it was a matter of attacking whole city districts[676], e.g., area targets of considerable extent.

[Section 5.) and 6.) are missing in the original.]

7.) Departure

The type of departure depended on the strength of the enemy AA or enemy fighter attacks. With strong anti-aircraft defenses and a good blast cloud [from the bombs], the best way to escape enemy fire was to turn the aircraft upside down[677] and fly away at the highest possible speed while making strong

---

[671] 3300 – 3000 ft.
[672] 1600 – 1000 ft.
[673] 5900 – 4900 ft.
[674] 3000 – 1300 ft.
[675] 6500 ft.
[676] The original German wording was "ganze Stadtteile". The bombing of Warsaw in 1939, next to Guernica (1937), Coventry (1940) and Rotterdam (1940) are among the most well-known early terror bombing attacks carried out by the Luftwaffe. Although other towns like Weilun also suffered, Warsaw became the international symbol of the German air campaign. The referenced attack here, with the clear description of attacks on large areas within the actual city, once again highlights the indiscriminate air assault on the city. It should also be noted that, next to an international media outcry, the Luftwaffe and Germany itself took the destruction of Warsaw as an example of its capabilities to pressure other governments. See Richard Overy, *The Bombing War*, Penguin Books 1994, p. 64; similar attacks are also referenced in the Mission reports of, for example, I./Sturzkampfgeschwader 77 on the 25th of September 1939. See BArch, RL 10/350, *Kriegstagebuch Polenkrieg I. Stuka 77 Anlagen.*
[677] The original German wording was indeed "dass man die Maschine auf den Kopf stellte", which could be translated as "putting the aircraft on its head". We are not sure

defensive movements and constantly changing altitude. Pulling up when under heavy enemy fire, with only 200 kph[678] on the airspeed indicator gauge in the first few minutes, proved not to be favorable, since, especially in overcast conditions, one was presenting a perfect target for the enemy AA. With this method, the enemy firing groups were often in precarious proximity to the aircraft, so that minor damage was caused by fragmentation. Even when attacked by fighters, the method of gaining the outermost speed while diving while maintaining strong defensive maneuvers proved to be the best, so that no more losses by fighters occurred later on. As soon as the planes were out of the danger zone[679], they went back to 3 000 m[680] altitude over enemy territory, flying around AA-protected areas Serock, Modlin, Puttusk).

8.) Returning to Base

When flying back to the base, preset courses and altitudes that allow the planes to rally were ordered for the individual Staffeln, so that they could arrive as united as possible back at the airfield. Rallying usually lasted until 15-20 minutes after the attack, since the strong anti-aircraft defense forced the Staffeln to scatter after the bombs had been dropped.

9.) Reconnaissance Activity

As mentioned earlier, the group's reconnaissance aircraft were used with success for weather and target reconnaissance. Defense reconnaissance was mostly unsuccessful because enemy AA usually did not fire on individual aircraft. Wind measurement over the target by the reconnaissance aircraft was absolutely necessary for calculating the lead angle and proved very useful.

If a report on the wind conditions could not be obtained during a rapid employment, the accuracy achieved was significantly worse.

Photographic reconnaissance before and after the attack was poor due to insufficient training of the crews and could not be utilized in most cases.

---

what is meant by this, as an inverted flight appears less than plausible. It is possible that this means that the aircraft was put in another dive after the recovery to gain more speed, so that it could leave the area quicker, break line of sight and/or have the speed required to pull defensive maneuvers and have additional speed for a rapid change of altitude. The following sentences seem to support this interpretation.

[678] 120 mph.
[679] See also: Kenny Loggins, *Danger Zone*, 1986.
[680] 9800 ft.

II. Effect of the Attack

1.) Bridges

The Gruppe repeatedly attacked the Vistula bridges between Warsaw and Praga[681], as well as at Modlin, Wyszogród and Płock.

During these attacks, which were evaluated through photographs, it turned out that a lasting destruction of the bridges themselves was almost impossible. However, it was possible to achieve a lasting effect by placing the weight of effort[682] on the bridgeheads, thus rendering the bridge unusable for a long time.

Photographic analysis of railroad and road bridges that had been hit with 500 kg with delay-fuzed bombs[683] showed that these bombs had sometimes only torn pieces out of the bridge or had simply fallen through the bridge leaving a more or less large hole without causing the bridge to collapse, which was the actual goal of the attacks.

As already mentioned under section I, direct hits on bridges can only be achieved with some certainty when a dive against the wind is possible and no or only little AA defenses allow for a low release altitude.

As the photographic analysis proves, numerous 250 and 50 kg bombs[684] destroyed the railroad platforms and tracks. A 500 kg bomb hit right next to the armored transport train in Łochów lifted it of the tracks by the blast pressure.

The effect of these attacks proves that dive-bomber units can be used with great success on railroad lines and transport trains, since they can drop from relatively low altitudes due to the limited ability to defend [against this attack] and can thus achieve the greatest possible effect with good hit accuracy.

3.) Roads and Town Exits

The group was deployed several times against roads and exits of the suburb of Praga and performed this task with good success. The bombs were dropped without delay and, even if they fell next to the streets and exits, caused considerable damage by demolishing houses. The debris fell on the street and thus fulfilled the purpose of blocking it.

---

[681] The Praga district opposite the center of Warsaw on the east bank of the Vistula.
[682] See Glossary: Weight of effort (Schwerpunkt).
[683] See Glossary: Contact-fuze (Aufschlagzünder).
[684] See Glossary: Bomb types (Bombenarten).

4.) Gas, Electricity and Water Works

Attacks on gas and electricity plants have proved very effective in 3 of the group's employments (Tczew electricity plant, Warsaw gas plant). Such targets are excellent Stuka targets, on which a good effect can always be achieved. The Tczew power plant was completely destroyed by 500 kg bombs during the group's first raid, as was the Warsaw gas plant (target No. 521[685]) in its vital parts (gas holder burned out, tar tower hit[686]).

The effect of two attacks with parts of the Gruppe on the waterworks (Warsaw Target No. 531) could not be clearly recognized even by photographic analysis. Whether vital parts of the plant were actually hit can only be determined on the spot.

5.) Radio Station

The group targeted the Mokotów and Babice radio stations twice. In the process, the Mokotów transmitter was set on fire and the transmitter towers were knocked over. The effect on the Babice transmitter could not be determined properly. According to our own visual reconnaissance, hits were in the immediate vicinity of the transmitter building, so that it can be assumed that at least some underground connections were disrupted. None of the 11 transmitting towers of this station were hit, since the towers were difficult to see when attacking[687] from an altitude of 3 000 m[688], and the transmitter building could not be identified without problems.

6.) Fortifications

The two attacks of the Gruppe on the bunker line in front of Mława have shown that direct hits on bunkers can only be achieved by chance. The nearest impacts were about 5 meters from the bunkers. Even if the bunkers themselves were not destroyed, according to statements of officers of Generalkommandos I.A.K. [689] the effect on the bunker crews by the blast pressure of the detonation seems to

---

[685] This number was corrected multiple times and is thus not fully legible. It might be incorrect.

[686] Tar is a by-product from the coal gas production during the coking process. This tower would most likely be linked to this step in the production of coal gas. Tar could be used in other products, e.g., by the chemical industry for dyes.

[687] The original word was "Sturmes", which translates to "storm". We assume that this refers to a "Sturz", so "dive".

[688] 6500 ft.

[689] "I.A.K." is the abbreviation of "I. Armeekorps", indicating "I. Army Corps". It was subordinate during the Poland campaign to the 3rd Army (3. Armee).

have been considerable, since several crews were apparently found incapacitated by the bomb effect when the bunker line was taken. The bombs were released at an altitude of 500 m[690].

The effect of the attacks on the Modlin fortifications could not be determined.

7.) Artillery Positions and Marching Columns

The Gruppe was set to destroy artillery positions near Modlin on the south bank of the Vistula on 26.9.39[691]. The positions were reconnoitered by reconnaissance planes. Because of the weather conditions, the group had to approach at 1 200 m[692] altitude and carry out the attacks in shallow dives. Only 50 kg bombs were used as ordered. The bombs were well located in the target area. However, only one battery was properly detected, in which considerable detonations, accompanied by columns of smoke and fire, indicated the destruction of munitions. After the bombs were dropped, the positions were strafed in low-level flight with M.G. fire. Actual effect could not be determined to this day.

Recognized marching columns after attacking roads and town exits were attacked independently by the Gruppe with low-level M.G. fire. The marching columns were hindered in their forward movement by taking up air cover and, as far as could be determined by visual reconnaissance, suffered casualties. No friendly losses, but numerous hits by light AA-machine guns on the aircraft.

8.) Fuze Settings

When attacking live targets (fire positions, marching columns, troop concentrations) fuze setting: o.V.[693]

Railroad transport m.V.[694], to destroy tracks at the same time. In the case of stone bridges, fuze setting m.V. only makes holes in the bridges, fuze setting o.V. does not cause stone bridges to collapse either.

On railway bridges, a fuze setting of o.V. results in the destruction of the tracks and such the inoperability of the bridge.

---

[690] 1600 ft.
[691] DD.MM.YYYY
[692] 3900 ft.
[693] "o.V." is the abbreviation of "ohne Verzögerung", indicating "without delay". See Glossary: Contact-fuze (Aufschlagzünder).
[694] "m.V." is the abbreviation of "mit Verzögerung", indicating "with delay". See Glossary: Contact-fuze (Aufschlagzünder).

All other targets, such as bridgeheads, fortifications, radio transmitters, gas works, electric power plants and water works are most effectively attacked with firing position m.V..

In attacks on urban centers, mixed fuze settings to achieve blast and fragmentation effects.

[Chapter III. missing in the original.]

Signed. Hozzel,

F.d.R.:[695]   Hauptmann and deputy Kommandeur.

signed [Signature],

Hptm. i. Genst.[696]

[End of experience report by I./St.G. 1. The following report is by III./St.G. 2.]

Photo 15: A Ju 87 B over Poland. Easy to recognize is the old-style canopy that changes with the later Ju 87 D model. Original caption: Poland - bomber aircraft Junkers Ju 87 in the air. September 1939. Credit: BArch, Bild 101I-320-0946-32A, Fotograf(in): o. Ang.

---

[695] "F.d.R." is the abbreviation of "Für die Richtigkeit". This is a declaration that the accuracy of the given information is confirmed by the signee.

[696] Hauptmann im Generalstab.

Excerpt. Transcript !   Secret !   3. Version.

III./Stuka "Immelmann" 2[697]   Langensalza, 24.9.1939.[698]

<u>Br.B.Nr. 7/39 geh.</u>[699]

<u>Referring to:</u> Flieger Division 1,

   SSD Nr. 18423/39.

<u>Subject.:</u> Experiences of the Polish campaign.

   To Fliegerdivision 1, Berlin.

Regarding the above mentioned reference the III./Stuka 2 reports:

[Paragraph 1.) is missing in the original.]

2.) The Gruppe has very little experience cooperating with the Army. The operation at Lviv[700] has shown that the ground troops must be required to mark their front lines during operations of the Luftwaffe in support of the Army without fail and must fire the recognition signals. It is impossible to recognize from the air during a Stuka attack whether there are enemy or friendly troops at the indicated area of attack. In this case, to be on the safe side, the attack had to be conducted further inland of the enemy's own line than originally intended.

3.) The Gruppe's achieved the most success in attacks against railroads. Of 30 bombs dropped, 28 were on target. In all operations, railroad lines and stations were destroyed, making it impossible to put railroad facilities into operation for a long time. Good success was achieved in diving attacks on columns. Attacks at low level or at a shallow dive were not so convincing. Also, in this case, almost all aircraft received hits from ground fire.

---

[697] III./Sturzkampfgeschwader 2 was stationed in the Northern part of the main German-Polish border. It later transferred to Slovakia to assist the German army in the southern front region.

[698] DD.MM.YYYY

[699] "Betriebsberichtnummer 7/39 geheim" stands for "Report number 7/39 secret".

[700] Nowadays Lviv is in the Ukraine. During the Second World War the city was Polish and known as Lwów, or Lemberg in German.

4.) The group flew an operation against a city[701]. It was dropped 500 kg bombs with mine detonation[702]. The effect of the bombs was very good, since the bombs apparently fell far inside the house and only then detonated.

[Paragraph 5.) through 8.) are missing in the original.]

Further perceived as burdensome by the group during the operation:

[Paragraph 1. is missing in the original.]

2. In the event of crash landings, etc., the Gruppe requested the scrapping [of the aircraft] in each case. However, the Gruppe was never informed whether and where the aircraft were repaired. Thus, the unit never had an overview, which airplanes would come back into its possession. It is hereby requested that in future, when aircraft breakdown, the unit be notified as to when the aircraft will be dismantled, where it will be transferred to, and when the repaired aircraft can be expected back at the group.

[Paragraph 3. is missing in the original.]

Signed. [Signature],

Hauptmann and Gruppenkommandeur.

---

[701] It is not clear which city is referred to here by III./St.G. 2. It is possible that the city was Warsaw.
[702] Most likely a SC 500. See Glossary: Bomb types (Bombenarten).

Garmisch, 5. May 1947

Document: Air-Sea Battle of Crete on the

22nd May 1941

(Special report Sturzkampfgeschwader "Immelmann" 2)

MANUSCRIPT DATA SHEET

I.   Author: Oscart Dinort, Generalmajor
                             Hubertus Hitschold [sic!], Generalmajor

II.   Title of report: Air-Sea battle[703] of Crete on the 22nd May 1941)*
                             (Special report Sturzkampfgeschwader
                             "Immelmann" 2)

III.   Commissioned on: 15 March 1947

IV.   Sources:
       A. Authors: None.   Transcribed from memory[704].
       B. Documents: None.   Transcribed from memory.

)*   Contribution to the main study:

The operation of the VIII.Fliegerkorps in the occupation of Greece and Crete in the spring of 1941.

---

[703] The original German word was "Seeluftschlacht". As such "Air-Sea battle" is a literal translation. We added a hyphen to differentiate it from "AirSea battle" doctrine.
[704] While certainly a useful tool in the study of history, relying too heavily on the "memory" of eyewitnesses can sometimes lead to errors as the relevant actors misremember or confuse events. As this report was written relatively recently after the war, this is less likely in this case. To provide an external comparison to the report, we have accessed various aspects with the official British report on the operation. B.R. 1736 (2) Naval Staff History, *Naval Operations in the Battle of Crete 20th May-1st June 1941* (Battle Summary No. 4), Admiralty, 1960.

242

<u>Operational airports[705] of the Geschwaders:</u>

Geschwaderstab with Stabstaffel (Reconnaissance)

I./Stuka 2	Molaoi
I./Stuka 3	Argos

1 reinforced Staffel III./Stuka 2

1. Report of Geschwader's early morning reconnaissance[706] (22.5.41 approx. 6.15 am.). Enemy warships (some cruisers and several destroyers) in area south of Milos[707] fire on friendly troop transports[708] (see Illustration).

(Appendix 1)

2. Report of the early morning reconnaissance (22.5.41 approx. 6.30 am).

Strong enemy fleet with 2 battleships, several cruisers and about 18 destroyers southwest of Kythera on northeast course (see Illustration).[709]

(Appendix 1)

[Operation on the 22nd May 1941]

<u>Order of the VIII. Fliegerkorps</u> based on the reconnaissance results: Immediate attack against enemy fleet north of Crete in area south of Melos.

---

[705] The original German word was "Absprunghafen". The literal translation could be "drop port" or "jump-off port".

[706] The original German word was "Frühaufklärung". The literal translation could be "early reconnaissance".

[707] In the original report, this island was referred to as "Molos". This is a typo, as the island in question would be "Melos" in German (Milos in English). It continuous to appear as "Melos" in the German original. The island Molos is too close to the Greek mainland to be correct.

[708] Force "C" under command of Rear-Admiral King: Cruisers HMS Naiad, Calcutta, Carlisle, (HMAS) Perth and destroyers, Kandahar, Kingston and Nubian. See B.R. 1736 (2) Naval Staff History, Naval Operations in the Battle of Crete 20th May-1st June 1941 (Battle Summary No. 4), Admiralty, 1960, p. 40.

[709] The size of the fleet appears to be exaggerated if this refers to Force "A" under command of Rear-Admiral Rawlings: Battleships HMS Warspite, Valiant and destroyers Napier, Hereward, Decoy, Hero and Hotspur. See B.R. 1736 (2) Naval Staff History, Naval Operations in the Battle of Crete 20th May-1st June 1941 (Battle Summary No. 4), Admiralty, 1960, p. 40.

Operation

Friendly recon planes remain in permanent contact with the enemy fleet.

Ongoing Stuka attacks against enemy fleet in the area north of Crete (area south of Melos) to protect friendly troop carrier movements from Melos to Crete.[710]

For the Stuka attacks every available unit of the Geschwader, even in the smallest units (i.e., also single Ketten) were used immediately after refueling, loading with bombs and ammunition (employed about 5 times[711]).

Friendly Success

Some hits on cruisers and destroyers, one cruiser put on fire,[712] a destroyer probably sunk.[713]

Turning of the enemy fleet first to the south, shortly afterwards to the west in the direction of Antikythera, single ships heading southeast(?), in the direction of the Strait of Kasos[714].[715]

The German transport movement Melos - Crete could continue, unhindered by enemy fleet units.

---

[710] Force "C" reported the first air attack at 0700h. See B.R. 1736 (2) Naval Staff History, *Naval Operations in the Battle of Crete 20th May-1st June 1941* (Battle Summary No. 4), Admiralty, 1960, p. 11.

[711] About 5 missions were flown.

[712] Possibly the cruiser *HMS Gloucester* which was heavily bombed and on fire in the afternoon, around 1550. See B.R. 1736 (2) Naval Staff History, *Naval Operations in the Battle of Crete 20th May-1st June 1941* (Battle Summary No. 4), Admiralty, 1960, p. 13.

[713] Hits were scored against *HMS Naiad* and *Carlisle*.

[714] The islands of Antikythera and Kasos lie to the west and east of Crete respectively.

[715] By this point, Force "C" had expended a considerable amount of its AA ammunition, having been subject to continuous air attacks and the force was limited to 21 knots. Rear-Admiral King's decision to swing his force towards the west was later subject to much criticism: "The situation was undoubtedly a difficult one for him, as this attack was certainly on a majestic scale, but it appears that no diminution of risk could have been achieved by retirement, and that, in fact, the safest place for the Squadron would have been among the enemy ships." See B.R. 1736 (2) Naval Staff History, *Naval Operations in the Battle of Crete 20th May-1st June 1941 (Battle Summary No. 4)*, Admiralty, 1960, p. 12.

244

Enemy Success

Destruction of several makeshift transports and turning back of some makeshift transport ships to Melos. Detached rafts (loaded with anti-aircraft guns) drifting freely in the sea.

Observation from the Air by Commander of I./Stuka 2:

(Report Hitschhold (Eyewitness)).

During the approach, the turning away of the enemy fleet, which had come within firing distance of the troop transport fleet, and fires and explosions on one of the English[716] ships was observed. Only one Italian torpedo boat was recognized protecting the troop transport fleet. When the enemy fleet turned westward, an enemy cruiser(?) trailed by about 5 kilometers[717] behind. This [cruiser(?)] was unsuccessfully attacked by the Stuka-Gruppe (without a Staffel[718]) and a Staffel of I./Stuka 3, because it was maneuvering in a tight full circle. Its anti-aircraft defense was light[719]. After the Stuka attack on this cruiser(?), 9 ships of the enemy fleet were observed in closed formation (see illustration) heading west [720].

(Appendix 2)

---

[716] It is common among German speakers and primary sources around this time to refer to the United Kingdom or the British Empire as "England".

[717] This was most likely the light cruiser HMS Naiad which had been unable to rejoin the formation due to continuous evasive maneuvers. The sustained hits forced her to drop speed to 16 – 19 knots. See B.R. 1736 (2) Naval Staff History, Naval Operations in the Battle of Crete 20th May-1st June 1941 (Battle Summary No. 4), Admiralty: 1960, p.12.

[718] Possibly referring to a group, rather than a Gruppe, of Ju 87 that attacked together, without belonging to the same formation.

[719] Force "C" had expended the majority of its AA-ammunition throughout the early morning.

[720] While HMS Naiad and Carlisle had been hit at this point, Force "C" had not yet lost a ship. It had a total 7 ships, 4 light cruisers and 3 destroyers, against the estimate of 3 cruisers and 6 destroyers as indicated in Annex 1.

Morning of 22nd May 1941 the VIII. Fliegerkorps gave the following Order to Stukageschwader 2

Continuous attacks against enemy fleet northwest of Crete, remain in contact with enemy fleet north of Crete by continuous reconnaissance. (Target marker[721]).

Operation

Initially, employment in Gruppen or Staffeln. Then rolling employment of all forces of the Geschwader (in the order in which they were ready for employment) against fleet west and southwest of Cythera, which turned south after the Stuka attacks and came between Cythera and Antikythera to join the fleet coming from the area north of Crete[722]. This entire assembled fleet was observed at noon (exact time not remembered)[723] waiting in the assembly area, bow to the east, by a Stuka unit designated to attack. Shortly before the Stukas attacked, the aforementioned fleet started moving eastward. After ongoing attacks by the Stukas and probably other combat units, the enemy fleet was reported to have changed course to the south-southwest. In the late afternoon (time not remembered) friendly air reconnaissance reported that the departing fleet divided in the height of Crete (western tip) - bulk of the enemy fleet departing with general south-west course, weaker parts with general southern course. The latter was attacked with bombs for the last time in the area southwest of Crete (western tip).

Success

Enemy fleet leaves the sea area near Crete; thus, further supplies to Crete by sea are secured.[724]

---

[721] See Glossary: Target marker / pathfinder (Fühlungshalter).

[722] Force "A" steered towards Force "C", after having united with Force "B" and "D" around noon. See B.R. 1736 (2) Naval Staff History, *Naval Operations in the Battle of Crete 20th May-1st June 1941* (Battle Summary No. 4), Admiralty, 1960, p. 12.

[723] The reinforced Force "A" and "C" met around 1330h. See B.R. 1736 (2) Naval Staff History, *Naval Operations in the Battle of Crete 20th May-1st June 1941* (Battle Summary No. 4), Admiralty,1960, p. 13.

[724] At the same time, the Royal Navy successfully prevented the German seaborne landing on this day.

One cruiser sunk, one destroyer sunk, bomb hits on other ship units, wide oil trail behind southbound fleet.[725]

In the course of the rolling attacks from the air, the enemy anti-aircraft defenses weakened so noticeably that the assumption had to be made that the enemy had shot themselves dry.[726]

(Hitschhold[727])

Sinking of an English destroyer by the 2./Stuka 2 took place direct north of Antikythera, where it was found dead in the water.[728]

Observation from the Air by Commander of I./Stuka 2

An English cruiser, which came into sight direct north of Antikythera on course west, was attacked about three kilometers northwest of Antikythera and received 5 direct hits with 500 kg bombs. Thereupon it lay with a strong list, it had only offered light anti-aircraft defense. (According to reconnaissance reports it sank after about 35 minutes).[729]

Somewhat off to the west of the attacked cruiser, several English ships were observed sailing in unclear formation and on different courses.[730]

---

[725] The sunk destroyer indicated here was most likely the destroyer *HMS Greyhound* who had separated from the formation to sink an Italian transporter. She was struck by two bombs at 1351 and sank within 15 min. During the rescue operation, the destroyer *HMS Kingston* was damaged by near misses. Additionally, the light cruiser *HMS Gloucester* was abandoned after sustaining heavy damage at 1550. The battleship *HMS Warspite* was reported hit by a bomb dropped by a fighter-bomber Bf 109, damaging the starboard 4 in and 6 in guns, as well as the engines, reducing her speed, at 1332. The battleship *HMS Valiant* received two hits at 1645. See B.R. 1736 (2) Naval Staff History, *Naval Operations in the Battle of Crete 20ᵗʰ May-1ˢᵗ June 1941* (Battle Summary No. 4), Admiralty, 1960, p. 13-14.

[726] Overall, this was a correct assessment. On the morning of the 22ⁿᵈ May, the following AA-ammunition state was reported: *HMS Warspite* 66%, *Valiant* 80%, *Gloucester* 18%, *Fiji* 30%, *Dido* 25%, *Orion* 38% and *Ajax* 40%. By 1413 Rear-Admiral King asked his counterpart Rawlings for additional AA support, indicating that Force "C" was running dry. See B.R. 1736 (2) Naval Staff History, *Naval Operations in the Battle of Crete 20ᵗʰ May-1ˢᵗ June 1941* (Battle Summary No. 4), Admiralty, 1960, p. 13.

[727] It is not clear if this refers to General Hitschhold signing the above with this entry, or indicating that the following section was written by him. Considering the first eyewitness entry, the latter seems more likely.

[728] Likely the destroyer *HMS Greyhound.*

[729] Likely the abandoned light cruiser *HMS Gloucester.*

[730] Combined Royal Navy force retiring southwards. The light cruiser *HMS Fiji*, previously sailing with light cruiser *HMS Gloucester*, was sunk at 2015 after being hit by a Bf 109

Assessment of the Situation by Kommodore Stukageschwader 2. (Molaoi) on the Morning of the 22nd May 1941

1. It is obvious that the enemy intends to cut off the supply to Crete.

Reinforcement of the British garrison of Crete and additional support to destroy the landed German airborne troops likely.

2. The enemy may have the intention to land also on the Peloponnese [mainland[731]] or to take the airfield Molaoi under naval gunfire. The situation seemed dangerous, since there were no known Army troops in the vicinity.

Preparatory Measures of the Stukageschwaders 2 based on the above Assessment of the Situation

1. All personnel not essential to aircraft maintenance are assigned to ground combat. Marching readiness of these parts on motorized vehicles.

2. Assignment of maintenance personnel to existing shelters against artillery fire; in addition, reconnaissance of further dispersal positions for aircraft not ready for take-off.

Inspection of protected storage of gasoline and oil supplies.

3. Assignment of I./Stuka 3 (Argos) for ground deployment of dispensable ground personnel not required for aircraft maintenance and preparation for marching readiness on motorized vehicles.

Meteorological Conditions on 22.5.41

Cloudless, light wind, best visibility (80 - 100 kilometers visibility). Towards evening visibility decreased to 10 km.

---

fighter-bomber. See B.R. 1736 (2) Naval Staff History, *Naval Operations in the Battle of Crete 20th May-1st June 1941* (Battle Summary No. 4), Admiralty, 1960, p. 14.

[731] The Peloponnese is a large peninsula that makes up the southern geographical region of Greece. It is connected to the central part of Greece via a small land bridge known as the Isthmus of Corinth.

Technical Readiness (Stukageschwader 2)

Many engines had exceeded the normal permissible operating hours of 100 hours. Airframes were in normal condition.

Condition of the Personnel (Stukageschwader 2)

A large part of the flying and ground personnel was not fully able to perform their tasks due to the effects of the climate and difficulties with nutrition, as well as due to the efforts of the previous Greek campaign.

Losses: (only from Memory) Stukageschwader 2

Two Ju 87 - crews total. About a quarter of the planes suffered damage from guns, some planes (2 - 3 planes) had to make an emergency landing before they could reach their airfields.[732]

Supplementary Details

I. Employment of Stukageschwader 2.

(Hitschhold[733])

a. Approach altitude: 3 000 – 4 000 m

b. Approach when anti-aircraft defense is deployed: Used defensive maneuvers (flying with constant change of altitude and direction of flight).

c. Direction of attack: Generally, in the longitudinal direction of the ship to be attacked.

d. Diving attack: At an angle of 60 – 80 degrees down to 400 – 800 meters, from this altitude bombs are dropped as the planes attacked in the closest permissible sequences and release their entire bomb load at the same time.[734]

---

[732] Royal Navy estimates amounted to shot down: 2 (certain), 6 (probable) and 3 (damaged). This estimate can include aircraft of other types. See B.R. 1736 (2) Naval Staff History, *Naval Operations in the Battle of Crete 20th May-1st June 1941* (Battle Summary No. 4), Admiralty, 1960, p. 44.

[733] It is not clear if this refers to General Hitschhold signing the above with this entry, or indicating that the following section was written by him. Considering the previous entries, the latter seems more likely.

[734] Refer to *An Introduction to Anti-Shipping Operations with Ju 87s* for more information on anti-shipping tactics by dive-bomber units.

e. Departure: After the pull-out defensive maneuvers were flown, [the aircraft] rallied as quickly as possible outside the AA-zone at the pull-out altitude on their return course.

f. Navigation: No special navigation preparations were made, since the sea area was known and visibility was excellent on 22.5.41.

g. Target allocation: In principle by free decision of the unit commander, only one ship was attacked by the whole unit from the air.

II. Communication Link

a. From the reconnaissance aircraft (target marker[735]) only to the ground-based radio station of the Geschwader: Fu G III (morse code) according to signal board and using code names (code names no longer remembered).

b. There was no direct radio communication from the reconnaissance aircraft (target marker) to the approaching dive-bomber unit.

c. From aircraft to aircraft (air to air[736]) of the flying Stuka unit radio communication by Fu G VIII. As far as I remember, there was no radio communication from the airborne Stuka unit to the Geschwader's ground radio station.

d. From the Geschwader command post (ground) to the commanding station (VIII. Fliegerkorps (ground) telephone and Fu G III or Fu G X (morse code)).

III. Aircraft Type

1 a. Stuka unit equipped fully with Ju 87 B. The Argos-based parts of the Geschwader (I/Stuka 3 and one Staffel III/Stuka 2) were equipped with the additional range system[737] (additional tanks under the wings).

b. Bomb load: Per aircraft (Ju 87 B) 1 heavy bomb (250 kg or 500 kg) centerline, 4x50 kg bombs 2 per wing (on the Ju 87 B equipped with additional range system with attached tanks the 4x50 kg bombs were not used).

---

[735] See Glossary: Target marker / pathfinder (Fühlungshalter).
[736] The original German wording was "Bord zu Bord". The literal translation would be "onboard to onboard".
[737] The original German wording was "Reichweitenanlage". The literal translation would be "range system".

c. Armament: 2 fixed MG 17 mounted outside the propeller arc in the wings (operated by pilot), 1 flexible MG 15 (one barrel) for the gunner for rearward defense.

2 a. Reconnaissance aircraft (reconnaissance Staffel of the Stuka Geschwader, the so-called "Stabsstaffel"). Equipped with Do 17 (model type not remembered) and Me 110.

b. Bomb load none (bomb storage removed).

c. Armament: probably 3 flexible MG[738] (model and exact number not remembered).

IV. Bombs and Fuzes used

a. Almost all of them were SD 500 (thick-walled high-explosive bombs) and SD 50. Some SC 500 (mine bombs) were used because there were not enough SD bombs available and because there was uncertainty about their effectiveness. (Explosive filling of aforementioned bombs not remembered).[739]

b. Fuzes: Electric fuzes used, the same as for employment against ground targets (Fuze 15). Mixed use of delay and contact-fuze.

V. Strength of Sturzkampfgeschwaders "Immelmann" 2

a. Personnel.

Ground crew strength approximately 70 % of the authorized strength.

Flying crews as authorized strength.

b. Aircraft.

Geschwaderstab	3 Ju 87 B
Stabsstaffel	approx. 2 Do 17 and 2 Me 110
I./Stuka 2	approx. 33 Ju 87 B
I./Stuka 3	approx. 35 Ju 87 B/R
1 Staffel III/Stuka 2	approx. 15 Ju 87 B/R

signed DINORT

---

[738] This refers to the Dornier Do 17.
[739] See Glossary: Bomb types (Bombenarten).

Appendix 1

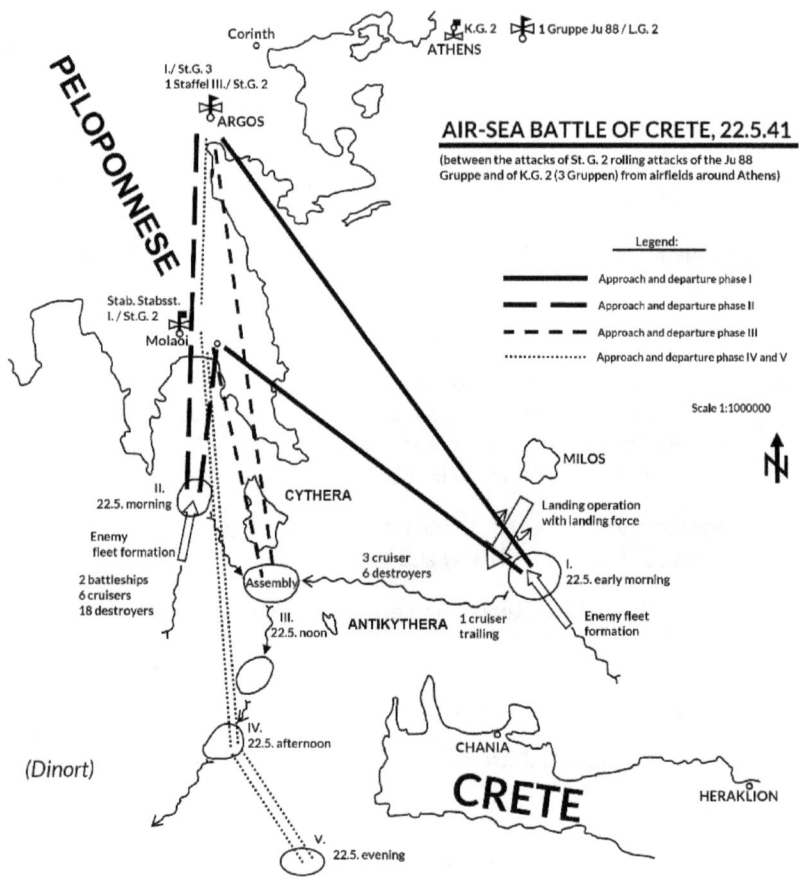

Corinth
ATHENS
K.G. 2   1 Gruppe Ju 88 / L.G. 2

I./ St.G. 3
1 Staffel III./ St.G. 2
ARGOS

PELOPONNESE

AIR-SEA BATTLE OF CRETE, 22.5.41

(between the attacks of St. G. 2 rolling attacks of the Ju 88
Gruppe and of K.G. 2 (3 Gruppen) from airfields around Athens)

Legend:

Approach and departure phase I

Approach and departure phase II

Approach and departure phase III

Approach and departure phase IV and V

Scale 1:1000000

Stab. Stabsst.
I. / St.G. 2
Molaoi

MILOS

II.
22.5. morning
CYTHERA

Landing operation
with landing force

Enemy
fleet formation

3 cruiser
6 destroyers

Assembly

I.
22.5. early morning

2 battleships
6 cruisers
18 destroyers

III.
22.5. noon   ANTIKYTHERA

1 cruiser
trailing

Enemy fleet
formation

IV.
22.5. afternoon
CHANIA

(Dinort)

CRETE

HERAKLION

V.
22.5. evening

252

Sketch of the English fleet formation moving from the region south of Milos to the West.

(Based on memory from observations made by Commander I. /St. G. 2 from the air)

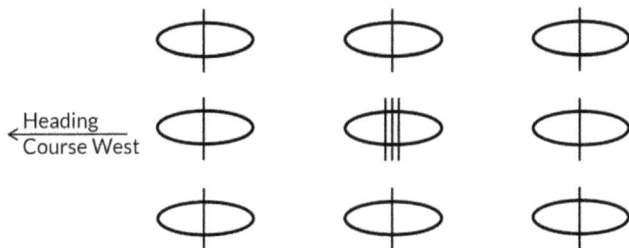

Heading
Course West

(Dinort)

CHAPTER IV

Data Sheets and Special Equipment

Documents: Engine Data Sheets

The following data on engine performance originates from the following files:

- Archiv Hafner, Junkers Flugzeug- und -Motorenwerke, *Junkers Flugmotor JUMO 211 B u. D – Baureihe 1 – Betriebsanweisung und Wartungsvorschrift*, 2. Ausgabe, March 1940.
- Archiv Hafner, Junkers Flugzeug- und -Motorenwerke, *Junkers Flugmotor JUMO 211 B und D – Baureihe 1 u. 2, Kurz-Betriebs- und Wartungs- Anweisung*, 3. Ausgabe, February 1940.
- Archiv Hafner, Junkers Flugzeug- und -Motorenwerke, *Junkers Flugmotor JUMO 211 F u. J – Baureihe 1 – Motoren-Handbuch*, August 1941.
- Archiv Hafner, Junkers Flugzeug- und -Motorenwerke, *Junkers Flugmotor JUMO 211 F u. J – Baureihe 1*, Auszug, 2. Ausgabe, September 1941.

Provided are the basic details on the engine, fuel, liquid and oil-cooling requirements, as well as performance figures. It should be noted that the data on engine performance shown here reflects the figures of the manufacturer. As such it should be taken as a guideline only, as performance might vary slightly or drastically from a newly produced engine, or one that has already been used in a field.

Preliminary Notes / Source Situation, Actuality and Formatting

Throughout this volume, we aimed to retain some of the original formatting, yet the editorial focus lay on legibility. One of the main editorial changes was that, in order to present a clearer layout, we did not follow the original page count as this would have resulted in empty or near empty pages throughout the book. Instead, the text has been reformatted to follow a more conventional structure, page by page.

Please be aware of the following formatting decisions and changes:

- We corrected formatting mistakes in the original version (for example missing spaces, paragraph breaks or others).
- We have collected information out of two manuals for each engine. As such the formatting only partially resembles that of the originals and was edited to be as consistent between the two engines as possible.

256

Engine Data Sheets

Jumo 211 D

Engine Reference Chart

a) **Type**   Liquid-cooled petrol aero-engine with direct fuel injection

Working method   Four-stroke

Cylinder arrangement   Two 6-cylinder rows in inverted V configuration[740]

Cylinder numbering
View from above

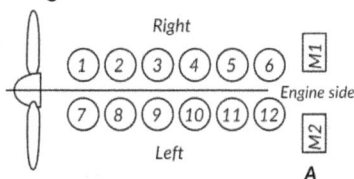

A

b) **Details**

Bore	150 mm
Stroke	165 mm
Displacement per cylinder	2.914 l
Total engine displacement	34.97 l
Compression ratio	1 : 6.5
Rotation	
Crankshaft left	} Perspective from engine
Propeller right	

Valve times

Inlet opens	15° before TDC[741]
Inlet closes	46° after BDC
Outlet opens	46° before BDC
Outlet closes	31° after TBC

---

[740] A more common designation of the cylinder arrangement would be "inverted V-12". However, in the original document this engine is described as having "Zwei 6-Zylinderreihen in hängender V Form", literally translating to "two 6-cylinder rows in hanging V shape".

[741] The German original abbreviations were "o.T." and "u.T.", standing for "oberem Totpunkt" and "unteren Totpunkt". In English, this is known as top dead center (TDC) and bottom dead center (BDC) respectively. The dead center refers to the position of the piston at which it is either closest to (BDC), or farthest (TBC) from the crankshaft.

Valve timing with the engine cold:

Inlet valve lift	0.8 mm
Outlet valve lift	1.0 mm
Firing order	1-9-4-11-2-7-6-10-3-8-5-12

Coolant capacity in the engine jacket	33 l
Coolant capacity in the header tank	10 l
Sparkplugs	Beru F 220/a 19 m
Injection start point	60° after dead center[742]

c) Design
Jumo 211 D

Engine with two-speed supercharger until 5.0 km rated altitude[743] during the climb.

Automatic manifold pressure control.

Automatic supercharger boost control and mixture control.

1548 propeller RPM at 2400 crankshaft RPM Reduction ratio 1.55:1.

Operating Fluids

a) Fuel
Leaded petrol (knock-rating of 87 octane per C.F.R., measuring procedure[744]).
Fuel purity, with no dilution by water is mandatory[745].
Caution with open wounds! Leaded petrol is toxic!

---

[742] The dead center refers to the position of the piston at which it is either closest to, or farthest from the crankshaft.

[743] The maximum altitude up to which the Jumo 211 supercharger can maintain an intake manifold pressure that is equal to that at sea level (without the use of a supercharger). Critical altitude also known as full throttle height, which refers to the altitude up to which a specific manifold air pressure can be maintained at a set RPM.

[744] Motor-Oktanzahl (MOZ) in German. The CFR procedure is named after the Cooperative Fuel Research (CFR) Committee of the American Society of Automotive Engineers.

[745] The German original wording was "selbstverständliche Voraussetzung", which could be literally translated to "self-evident prerequisite".

b) Oil

Aero Shell "medium" or Intava Rotring or Intava 100. These types are suitable for summer and winter operation.

Oil change. Oil should if possible be replaced with that of the same brand and type. If, during a cross-country flight, this type of oil is not available, another of the aforementioned types can be used. Using a type of oil that is not approved for the JUMO 211 is out of the question under any circumstances.

Lubricant consumption in cruise flight at 2100 RPM and 1.20 ata[746] manifold pressure around 9.5 kg = 10.6 l/h.

Lubricant
>   Minimum pressure: at 2500 RPM and 60 to 70°C.
>   Temperature: at sea level 5.5 atü[747], not above 9 atü at critical altitude (high gear) 4 atü.
>   Maximum intake temperature 90°C.
>   Optimal cruising temperature 60 to 70°C, during cold weather not under 50° C.

c) Cooling liquid

Clean, soft water, a high lime content leads to scale build-up - very poor cooling effect.

To prevent corrosion in the cooling system, add 1.5% Schutzöl[748] 39.

In winter add 50 parts by volume of glycol as antifreeze: this provides frost protection down to approximately minus 35°C.

---

[746] See Glossary: ata.
[747] See Glossary: atü.
[748] "Schutzöl", can be literally translated to "protection oil".

Performance and Fuel Consumption Figures

Performance at sea-level

Naming	Manifold pressure ata	Authorized RPM	Power hp	Authorized duration (Min.)	Altitude km
Take-off power	1.35	2400	1200	1	0
Climb and combat power	1.15	2300	930	30	0
Max. continuous	1.10	2100	790	continuous	0

Performance at rated altitude of supercharger (low-gear)

Climb and combat power	1.15	2300	1030	30	1.8
Max. continuous	1.10	2100	860	continuous	1.8

Performance at rated altitude of supercharger (high-gear)

Climb and combat power	1.15	2300	930	30	5.0
Max. continuous	1.10	2100	800	continuous	4.5

Fuel consumption at maximum continuous power
n_{kw} = 2100 RPM and 1.10 ata manifold pressure

Altitude in km	0	0.5	1.8	3	4.5	6
Outside temperature in °C (INA)	+15	+12	+4	-4.5	-15	-24
Mixture control at setting "rich"	262 l/h	267 l/h	280 l/h	258 l/h	275 l/h	240 l/h
Mixture control at setting "lean"	224 l/h	228 l/h	238 l/h	218 l/h	233 l/h	200 l/h
	Low-gear			High-gear		

Engine Connections

1. Engine suspension points
2. Engine support points
3. Leveling points
4. Support feet on the cylinder heads
5. Support feet on the oil filter
6. Grommets (cannot be removed)
7. Tapped holes on gearbox cover

[8-9 were missing in the original.]

10. Propeller connection flange
11. Coolant pump inlet
12. Coolant outlet at the header tank
13. Leakage point at the coolant pump
14. Connection for cooling circuit gauge
15. Connections for equalizing and venting line (double valve)
16. Coolant filler neck
17. Oil inlet
18. Thermometer connection oil inlet
19. Oil outlet
20. Thermometer connection oil outlet
21. Oil pressure gauge connection
22. Oil starter fitting on the filter
23. Pressure oil connection for propeller governor
23a. Return oil connection from propeller governor
24. Lubricant relief valve

[25 was missing in the original.]

26. Ratchets for lubricant gap filter
27. Oil filter for reduction gear
28. Oil reservoir air vent
29. Swivel connection for compressor
30. Oil filter cover
31. Suction connections on the fuel feed pump
31a. Pressure regulator on the fuel feed pump
32. Connection for fuel pressure gauge
33. Fuel vent line to the supply tank
34. Primer line
34a. Primer nozzles
35. Fuel drain on bottom of injection pump (2 pieces)
36. Air vent fuel filter
37. Exhaust port (cylinder 4)

38. Air vent for engine housing
39. Throttle control
39a. Limiter screw for full throttle position
40. Lever on automatic transmission
40a. Limiter [on automatic transmission]
41. Supercharge suction port
[42 was missing in the original.]
43. Pressure gauge for supercharger air
44. Venting line on the air line
45. Bypass outlet on the supercharger
46. Supercharger air extraction (for rapid tank draining)
47. Connection for Bosch inertia starter motor
48. Bosch magneto GE 12 BR (outer spark plugs connected to M 2)
49. Starter ignition cable
49a. Clamp 1 (2) on both ignition magnetos
50. Generator outlet (generator with elastic axis)
51. Output for compressor or suction pump
52. RPM measurement sensor or tachometer output
53. RPM measurement sensor output
54. Special drive [if engine mounted weapon is fitted]
55. Output for propeller governor
56. Oil cover (crankshaft) for mounting a degree disc
57. Motor housing tension rods 8 pieces (never loosen)
58. Coolant control holes (one hole on the right and left side of the engine for each cylinder)
59. Oil filter for transmission
60. Device connection for propeller regulator or engine weapon
61. Drag switch
61a. Adjustment of the drag switch
62. Outside air inlet for automatic gearbox
63. Ventilation line for boost pressure regulator box
64. Screw plug for oil level check in supercharger regulator housing
65. Small filter in oil pressure line for injection pump (211 G/H only)
66. Small filter in oil pressure line for supercharger regulator (211 G/H only)
67. Solenoid for mixture control
68. Inductive transducer for fuel consumption measurement

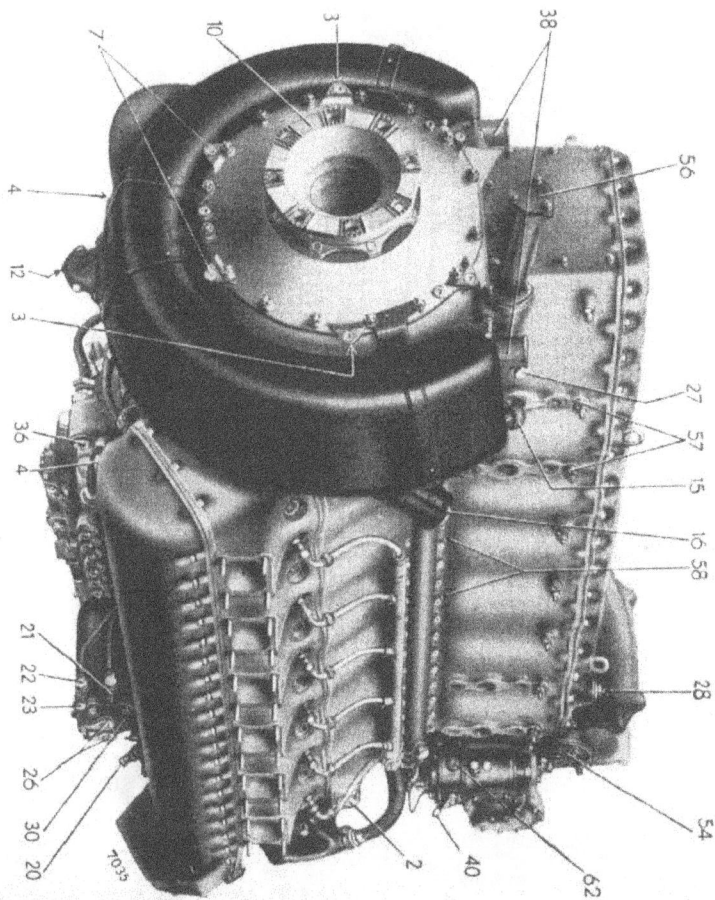

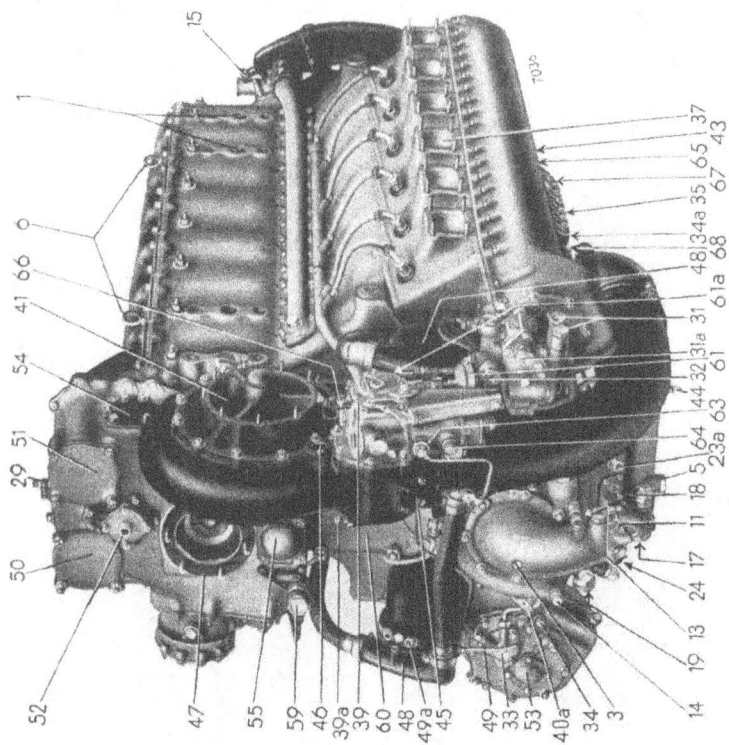

264

Jumo 211 J

Engine Reference Chart

a) Type   Internal combustion engine with direct fuel injection and pressurized liquid cooling

Working method   Four-stroke

Cylinder arrangement   Two 6-cylinder rows in inverted V configuration[749]

Cylinder numbering
View from above

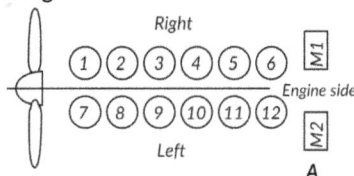

Right

(1)(2)(3)(4)(5)(6) M1

Engine side

(7)(8)(9)(10)(11)(12) M2

Left

A

b) Details

Bore   150 mm
Stroke   165 mm
Displacement per cylinder   2.914 l
Total engine displacement   34.97 l
Compression ratio   1:6.5
Rotation:
Crankshaft left   } Perspective from engine
Propeller right
Coolant capacity engine tank   33 l

Valve times

Inlet opens   30° before TDC[750]
Inlet closes   42° after BDC
Outlet opens   70° before BDC
Outlet closes   46° after TBC
Valve timing with the engine cold:

---

[749] A more common designation of the cylinder arrangement would be "inverted V-12". However, in the original document this engine is described as having "Zwei 6-Zylinderreihen in hängender V Form", literally translating to "two 6-cylinder rows in hanging V shape".

[750] The German original abbreviations were "o.T." and "u.T.", standing for "oberem Totpunkt" and "unteren Totpunkt". In English, this is known as top dead center (TDC) and bottom dead center (BDC) respectively. The dead center refers to the position of the piston at which it is either closest to (BDC), or farthest (TBC) from the crankshaft.

Inlet valve lift	0.5 mm
Outlet valve lift	0.5 mm
Firing order	1-9-4-11-2-7-6-10-3-8-5-12
Ignition timing	M 1 has 35° pre-ignition.
	M 2 has 40° pre-ignition.
Injection timing	30° after induction dead center.

c) Design
Jumo 211 F[751]

Engine with two-speed supercharger[752] until 5.0 km rated altitude[753] during the climb.

Automatic manifold pressure control. Automatic supercharger boost control and mixture control.

1418 propeller RPM at 2600 crankshaft RPM.

Reduction ratio 1.833:1.

Jumo 211 J like Jumo 211 F, but with provisions to add an intercooler.

Operating Fluids

Fuel and lubricant according to the Fuel and Lubricant Regulations for Aircraft Engines from January 1, 1940.

a) Oil change
Oil should if possible be replaced with that of the same brand and type. If, during a cross-country flight, this type of oil is not available, another of the aforementioned types can be used. Using a type of oil that is not approved for the JUMO 211 J/F is out of the question under any circumstances.

b) Cooling liquid
Clean, soft water (a high lime content leads to scale build-up - very poor cooling effect).

---

[751] Equal to Jumo 211 J but without the provision for an intercooler.

[752] The German original words were "Boden- u. Höhenlader", which can be literally translated as "Ground loader and altitude loader".

[753] The maximum altitude up to which the Jumo 211 supercharger can maintain an intake manifold pressure that is equal to that at sea level (without the use of a supercharger). Critical altitude also known as full throttle height, which refers to the altitude up to which a specific manifold air pressure can be maintained at a set RPM.

To prevent corrosion, add 1.5% Schutzöl[754] 39 (Fl. 44400[755]) to the cooling liquid.

In winter add 50 parts by volume of glycol as antifreeze: this provides frost protection down to approximately minus 35°C.

Operating Figures

a) Fuel
Fuel is delivered from the tank to the injection pump by a JUMO 2135 (gear pump) or 2017 (piston pump) double pump. A pressure-maintaining pump (gear pump) is arranged immediately in front of this.

Flow rate: JUMO 2135 delivers 1000 l/h,
                JUMO 2021 delivers 1000 l/h,
                    at 2600 crankshaft RPM.

Fuel pressure:
        Double pump (feeder pump) 0.3 to 0.4 atü[756] (not displayed).
        Low-pressure feed pumps 1.0 to 1.5 atü on the ground with fuel tank pump up to 2.0 atü in flight.

b) Oil
Pumping by means of a gear pump from the fuel tank to the motor. Circulation rate at 2400 RPM = 3500 to 4000 kg/h.
Pressure: at ground level at full throttle at least 5.5 atü, not above 9 atü. Minimum pressure at critical altitude at 2250 n_{Kw}[757] and 60 to 70°C lubricant temperature is 4.0 atü.

---

[754] "Schutzöl", can be literally translated to "protection oil".
[755] The Luftwaffe attributed an identification number to essentially every piece of equipment in its catalogue, from instrument gauges, weapons, over to tools and more. These were known as the "Fl-Nummer", standing for "Flieg-Nummer", literally translating to "flying number".
[756] See Glossary: atü.
[757] "n_{Kw}" is the abbreviation for revolutions per minute (n = RPM) and kilowatt (Kw).

Intake temperature   when warming up minimum 20°C,
                        when throttling back[758] minimum 30°C.

Maximum intake temperature 105°C.
Consumption in cruise at 2250 RPM and 1.15 ata[759] approximately 12 l/h.
Heat dissipation through the lubricant approximately 17 kcal/PS$_e$h.

c) Liquid Cooling
Circulation   Main flow 10.5 to 11 l/sec,
                 Auxiliary flow 0.5 l/sec.

Temperature outlet at sea-level: 115°C.
Maximum temperature in flight:

Altitude km	0	1	2	3	4	5	6	7	8	9	10
Out temp.°C	115	112	109	106	103	100	97	94	91	88	85

so 3°C difference each 1 000 m[760],
provisionally 120° C authorized at all altitudes.

Outlet temperature when warming up at least 50 to 60°C.
During cruise: see chart displaying maximum temperatures in-flight.
Heat dissipation: 250 to 260 kcal/PS$_e$h at rated power altitude in supercharger low-gear (climbing power).

---

[758] The German original word was "abbremsen", which can be literally translated as "braking". It is likely that this simply means that when throttling back, a minimum temperature of 30° should be maintained.
[759] See Glossary: ata.
[760] 3300 ft.

268

Performance and Fuel Consumption Figures

Performance at 50% temperature reduction of the boost air after the supercharger (with intercooler).
Performance at sea-level.

Naming	Manifold pressure ata	Authorized RPM	Power hp	Fuel consumption g/PS$_e$h	Altitude km
Take-off power	1.4	2600	1420	240	0
Climb and combat power	1.25	2400	1190	230	0
Max. continuous	1.15	2250	960	210	0

Supercharger low-gear performance at rated altitude

Climb and combat power	1.25	2400	1260	226	1.5
Max. continuous	1.15	2250	1080	205	2.0

Supercharger high-gear performance at rated altitude

Climb and combat power	1.25	2400	1180	243	4.9
Max. continuous	1.15	2250	1020	218	5.1
Above rated altitude	1.15	2400	1030	224	5.6

Engine Connections

Engine mounting
1. Engine suspension points
2. Engine support points
3. Leveling points

Motor installation and heating
4. Support feet on the cylinder heads
5. Support feet on the oil filter
6. Grommet (cannot be removed)

Engine cowling fastenings
7. Tapped holes on gearbox cover
8. Hook connector on engine hood (back)
9. Hook connector on engine hood (center)

Airscrew hub
10. Connection flange

Cooling
11. Main flow cooling inlet at the pump
12. Main flow cooling outlet at the cooling lines
13. Leakage connection to coolant pump
14. Gauge connection for cooling circuit
15. Bypass cooling inlet
16. Bypass cooling outlet
16a. Leakage connection to bypass pump

Lubrication
17. Oil inlet
18. Thermometer connection oil inlet
19. Oil outlet
20. Thermometer connection oil outlet
21. Oil pressure gauge connection
22. Oil starter fitting
[23 not identified in manual, see 19.]
24. Relief valve
25. Check valve
26. Ratchets for lubricant gap filter
27. Oil filter for reduction gear
28. Oil reservoir vent
29. Swivel connection for compressor
30. Oil filter cover

Fuel
31. Suction connections on the fuel feed pump
31a. Pressure regulator on the fuel feed pump
32. Connection for fuel pressure gauge
33. Fuel vent line to the supply tank

34. Primer line
34a. Primer nozzles
35. Fuel drain on injection pump
36. Air vent fuel filter

Exhaust
37. Exhaust ports

Motor housing ventilation
38. Air vents

Engine operation
39. Throttle control
40. Lever at the gear box
40a. Limiter

Supercharger
41. Flange for suction
42a. Air outlet from charger (radiator connection) (Jumo 211 J only)
43. Pressure gauge for supercharger air
44. Venting line on the air line (Jumo 211 F only)
44a. Air intake to the engine (Jumo 211 J only)
45. Bypass outlet on the supercharger
46. Supercharger air extraction

Starter
47. Bosch inertia starter

Ignition
48. Bosch magneto
49. Plug for starter ignition cable (M 2) Jumo 211 J only
49a. Plug for ignition switch Jumo 211 J only

Drives
50. Connection for Bosch generator
51. Output for compressor or suction pump
52. Connection for RPM electric measurement sensor or tachometer output
[53 was missing in the original.]
54. Special drives right and left
55. Propeller governor
55a. Sheave on the propeller governor
55b. Connection for electric reversible motor
55c. Pressure reducing valve on propeller regulator
56. Oil cap (only removed when a degree disc is fitted or during a partial overhaul).
57. Motor housing tension rods 8 pieces (never loosen)
58. Coolant control holes (two times 6 holes)
59. Oil filter for transmission
61. Drag switch
61a. Adjustment of the drag switch

271

62. Outside air inlet for automatic gearbox
63. Ventilation line for boost pressure regulator box
64. Screw plug for oil level check in supercharger regulator housing
65. Small filter in oil pressure line for injection pump (211 G/H only)
66. Small filter in oil pressure line for supercharger regulator (211 G/H only)
67. Solenoid for mixture control
68. Inductive transducer for fuel consumption measurement
69. Idling valve

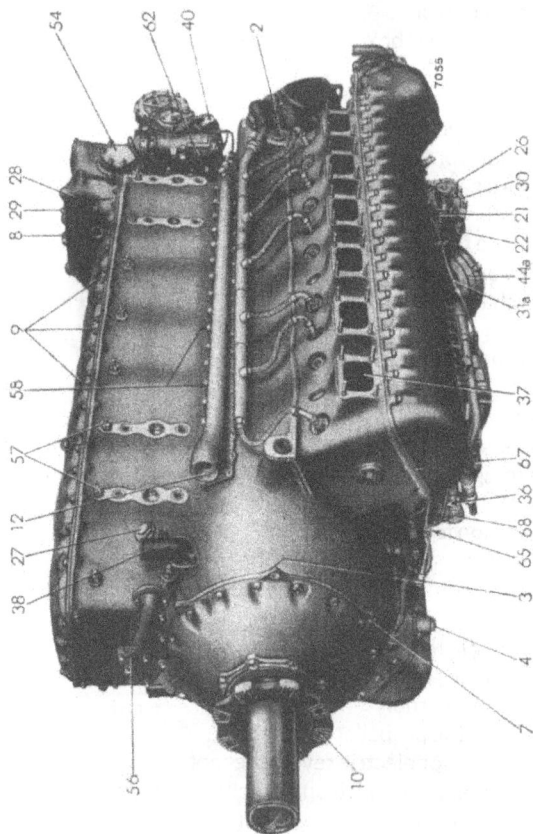

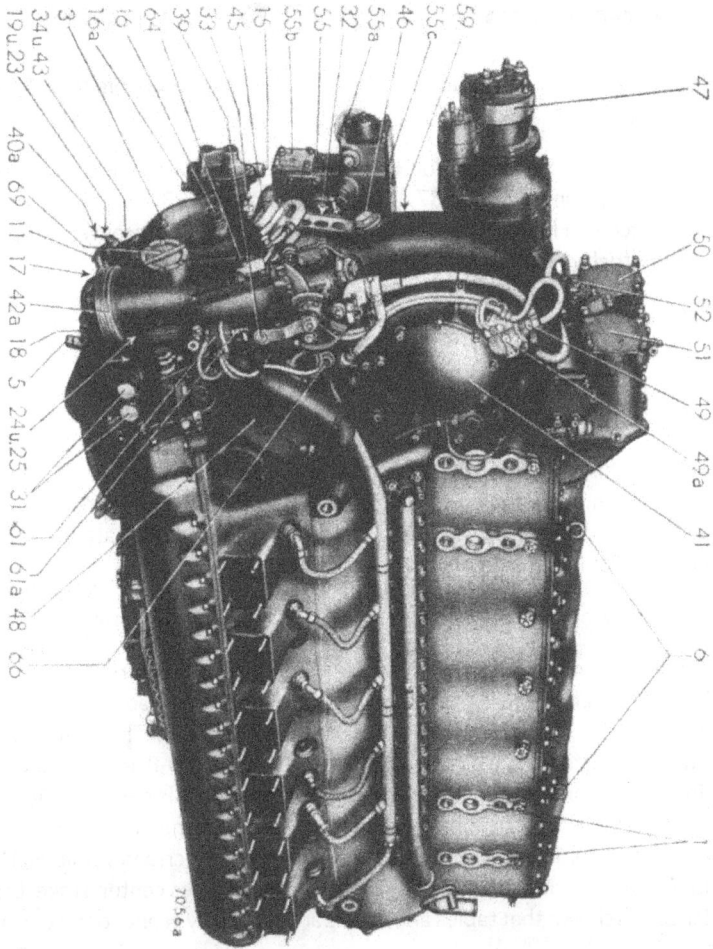

47

59
55c
46
55a
32
55b
55
55b
15
45
33
39
64
16
16a
3
34u43
19u23
40a
69
11
17
42a
18
5
24u25
31
61
61a
48
66

50
52
51
49
49a
41
6
7

7056a

273

Documents: Aircraft Data Sheets

The following are the official aircraft data sheets originating from the following files:

- Archiv Hafner, Junkers Flugzeug- und -Motorenwerke, *Betriebsanweisung Ju 87 A-1* III. Entwurf, July 1937.
- Archiv Hafner, Junkers Flugzeug- und -Motorenwerke, *Kurz-Betriebsanleitung Ju 87 B-2*, June 1940.
- Archiv Hafner, L. Dv. T. 2087 R-2 /Fl, *Ju 87 R-2 Bedienungsvorschrift-Fl*, May 1941.
- Archiv Hafner, Werkschrift 2087 D-1 bis D-8, G-1, G-2, H-1 bis H-8/Fl, *Ju 87 D-1 bis D-8, G-1, G-2, H-1 bis H-8 – Bedienungsvorschrift-Fl*, February 1944.

Provided within them are the basic performance figures of the aircraft and supplementary information on the engines. It should be remembered that these figures are based on the manufacturer's information, most likely attained from a clean aircraft, not laden with bombs or external stores.

Preliminary Notes / Source Situation, Actuality and Formatting

For the aircraft data sheets we have collected a set of nine reference cards, detailing performance figures of the Ju 87 A through G. We made the decision of transcribing three data sheets (A, B-2 and D-1 to D-4). These serve as a translation template for the remaining sheets (R-2, D-5 to D-8 and G-1 to G-2) as these follow the same style. There are four reasons for this decision. First, this allows the originals to be shown as references. Second, these sheets are templates, and their layout is easy to follow with the transcribed versions. Third, it is within the spirit of this book to put the primary sources center-stage. Lastly, experience has shown that tables and charts are especially prone to transcription errors.

Please be aware of the following formatting decisions and changes:

- We corrected formatting mistakes in the original version (for example missing spaces or values, paragraph breaks or others).
- The information included is presented in the same layout as in the original datasheets, but some elements might vary due to formatting or size restrictions.

Aircraft Data Sheets

Junkers Ju 87 A

Ju 87

Stress group H 5

Engine:	JUMO 210 D
Propeller:	Ju HPA 20° III automatic
Pitch range:	18°÷38°
Fuel type:	87 Octane
Lubricant:	Rotring or A S M

Fuel and oil

Capacity:	{ Fuel:	440 l
	{ Oil:	32 l
Consumption:	{ Fuel:	180 l/h
	{ Oil:	9 l/h
Flight time:	Approx. 2 ½h	

		min.	max.
Temperature:	{ Fuel:	45°C	95°C
Sea-level	{ Oil:	45°C	95°C
Pressure:	{ Fuel:	0.25 atü	0.30 atü
Sea-level	{ Oil:	4.00 atü	6.00 atü

RPM and manifold pressure

Standing with low-gear "start"

RPM		Man. pres. ata		Duration (min)
min.	max.	min.	max.	
2600	2700	1.25	1.30	

Flight at rated altitude approximately 2.7 km

	RPM		Man. pres.		Duration
Take-off	2640	2700	1.23	1.27	5
Increased continuous	2450	2550	1.16	1.20	30
Continuous	2450	2550	1.05	1.09	∞
Dive V_{max} = 450 km/h	3200				

Junkers Ju 87 B-2

Front

Stress group:	H 5 k at 4500 kg H 3 at 5600 kg			

Engine performance limits

		Dura tion	Man. pres.	RPM under 6 km min.	RPM over 6 km
Stationary		-	1.35	2200	-
Take-off	normal	1'	1.35	2300	-
Take-off	Overload	-	-	-	-
Flight		-	-	-	-
Flight		~30	1.15	2300	2300
Flight	Cont.		1.10	2100	2300
Supercharger gear change	Automatic			2.5 km	
Supercharger gear change	Manual			3.5 km	
Glide and dive	Maximum RPM: 2400				
Glide and dive	V_w max = 600 km/h				

Flight time and distance

At maximum continious with **480 l** fuel
(without mixture control)

Flight altitude km	0	4.0	5.2
Supercharger Throttle position	Low Retracted	Low Full throttle	High
Manifold pres. ata	1.1	0.92	1.1
RPM	2100	2100	2100
Fuel consumption l/h	275	245	275
TAS kph	295	325	350
Flight time (total) h'	1³⁵	1⁴⁵	1³⁵
Range (total) km	470	505	465

Front

Back

Plane	Ju 87 B-2	
Designation Werk-Nr.		
Engine	Jumo 211 D	
Propeller	Type: Junkers VS 5	Lowest pitch 20°

Maximum indicated airspeed (IAS) in a dive

Altitude	V_a
0 km	600
2 km	550
4 km	490
6 km	440

Liquid cooling system temperture

Altitude	Max. Out
0-3 km	95°
4 km	90°
6 km	85°
8 km	80°

Oil temperature

	In	Out
min	30°	-
max	90°	95°
short	-	-

Oil pressure

norm.	4-6 atü
min.	3.5 atü

Fuel pressure
1.0 - 1.5 atü

Oil:	Aero Shell mittel, Intava 100 Rotring	Written on fuel cap

Fuel: Octane 87

Version: 1	Date: 14.6.40	E'Stelle Re

Airspeed Indicator

Engine guages

These figures are to be marked on the relevant instruments before this reference card is stored away.

Back

276

Junkers Ju 87 R-2 with Jumo 211 D

Beanspruchungsgruppe: Hk 5 bei 4700 kg / H 4 bei 4850 kg / H 3 bei 5600 kg

Motor-Belastungsgrenzen

		zul. Zell	Ladedruck	Drehzahl bis km	über km
Stand		—	1,35	min. 2200	—
Abflug	norm.	—	—	—	.
Abflug	Überlast	min. 1	1,35	2300	~
		—	—	—	~
Flug		min. 30	1,15	2300	—
		dauernd	1,10	2100	—

Lader-schalthöhe	Automatik	2500
	Hand-verstellung	3500
Gleit- und Sturzflug	Höchstdrehzahl:	2400
	Vw max: 600 km/h	

Flugzeit und Flugstrecke

bei höchstzulässiger Dauerleistung für 1080 l Kraftstoffmenge

Flughöhe	km	0	4	5,2
Laderschaltung Drosselhebelstellg.		BL gedr	BL Vollg.	HL Vollg.
Ladedruck	ata	1,10	0,90	1,10
Drehzahl	U/min.	2100	2100	2100
Kraftstoffverbrauch	l/h	275	238	282
Wahre Geschwindigk.	Hin km/h / Rückfl.	285/305	290/330	320/350
Gesamt-Flugzeit	h'	345	415	350
Gesamt-Flugstrecke	km	1120	1255	1160

Vorderseite

Muster	Ju 87 R-2
Zulassung	
Werk-Nr.	
Motor	Jumo 211 D/1
Luftschraube	Muster: Junkers VS 5 kleiner Anschlag: 20°

Höchstzulässige, angezeigte Geschw. b. Bahnneigungsflug

Höhe	Va
0 km	600
2 km	550
4 km	490
6 km	440

Kühlstoff-Temperatur

Höhe	max. Austr.
0-3	95
4	90
6	85
8	80

Schmierstoff-Temperatur

	Eintritt	Austritt
min.	30	—
max.	90	95
kurzzlg.	—	—

Schmierstoffdruck

norm.	4-6	oder 5,5-9 bei n = 2200
min.	3,5 in 7 km	oder 4,0 in 5,5 km bei n = 2300

Kraftstoffdruck

1,0 — 1,5

Schmierstoff:	Aero Shell mittel / Intava 100 / Intava Rotring	Beschriftung auf Einfülldeckel
Kraftstoff: A2 u. B4 Okt. 87		

Ausgabe: 2	Tag: 14.1.41	E'Stelle Re.

Fahrtmesser — Triebwerks-Überwachungsgeräte — Diese Werte sind durch Marken an den entsprechenden Geräten vor dem Einstecken der Karte zu kennzeichnen.

Rückseite

Betriebsdatentafel Ju 87 R-2 mit Jumo 211 D Motor

Junkers Ju 87 R-2 with Jumo 211 H

Beanspruchungs-gruppe :	Hk 5 bei 4700 kg H 4 bei 4850 kg H 3 bei 5600 kg		
Motor-Belastungsgrenzen			

	zul. Zeit	Lade-druck	Drehzahl bis km	über km
Stand	—	1,35	min. 2200	—
Abflug norm.	—		—	—
Abflug Überlast	min. 1	1,35	2300	—
Flug	—		—	—
Flug	min. 30	1,15	2300	—
	dau-ernd	1,10	2100	
Lader-schalthöhe	Automatik	2500		
	Hard-verstellung	3500		
Gleit- und Sturzflug	Höchstdrehzahl:	2400		
	Vw max — 600 km/h			

Flugzeit und Flugstrecke				
bei höchstzulässiger Dauerleistung für 1080 l Kraftstoffmenge				
Flughöhe	km	0	4	5,2
Laderschaltung Drosselhebelstellg		BL gedr	BL Vollg.	HL Vol g.
Ladedruck	ata	1,10	0,90	1,10
Drehzahl	U/min.	2100	2100	2100
Kraftstoff-verbrauch	l/h	275	238	282
Wahre Geschwndigk.	Hin-km/h Rückfl.	285— 305	290— 330	320 350
Gesamt-Flugzeit	h	345	415	350
Gesamt-Flugstrecke	km	1120	1255	1160

Vorderseite

Muster	Ju 87 R-2	
Zulassung		
Werk-Nr.		
Motor	Jumo 211 H	
Luftschraube	Muster: Junkers VS 5 od. VS 11 kleiner Anschlag : 20°	
Höchstzulässige, angezeigte Geschw. b. Bahnneigungsflug		
Höhe	Va	
0 km	600	
2 km	550	
4 km	490	
6 km	440	
Kühlstoff-Temperatur		
Höhe	max. Austr.	
0—3	95	
4	90	
6	85	
8	80	
Schmierstoff-Temperatur		
	Eintrit	Austrit
min.	30	—
max.	90	95
kurzztg.	—	—
Schmierstoffdruck		
Am Boden bei n = 2200 U/min c min — 5,5 ; p max — 9		
In 5,5 km Höhe bei n — 2300 c min — 4,0		
Kraftstoffdruck		
1,0 — 1,5		
Schmier-stoff :	Aero Shell mittel Intava 100 Intava Rotring	Beschriftung auf Einfüll-deckel
Kraftstoff: A 2 u. B 4 Okt. 87		
Ausgabe: I	Tag : 10.2.41	E'Stelle Re.

Rückseite

Betriebsdatentafel Ju 87 R-2 mit Jumo 211 H Motor

(rotated text, right margin) Fahrmesser — Diese Werte sind durch Marken an den entsprechenden Geräten vor der Karte zu kennzeichnen. — Triebwerks-Überwachungsgeräte

Junkers Ju 87 D-1 to D-4 with Jumo 221 J

Stress group:	H 5' with lower load multipler
Engine performance limits	

	Dura tion	Man. pres.	RPM under 6.5 km	RPM over 6.5 km
Stationary	-	1.4	approx 2500 see B.V.-FI-Part 1	
Take-off normal	1'	1.4	2600	-
Take-off Overload	1'	1.4	2600	-
Flight	-	-	-	-
Flight Climb & combat power	30'	1.25	2400	2400
Flight Max. cont. power		1.15	2250	2400
Supercharger gear change	Automatic		2500 m ± 300	
Glide- and dive	RPM$_{max}$ = 2250			

Flight time and range at maximum continious power

Altitude m	300	2500	5000
Supercharger	Low	Low	High
Manifold pressure ata	1.15	1.06 Vg	1.11 Vg
RPM	2250	2250	2250
Fuel consumption l/h	310	305	320
For 770 l fuel without drop tank (For 1370 l fuel with drop tank)			
True Air Speed (mean) in kph	335 (325)	365 (355)	395 (385)
Total flight time h'	2^h 15' (4^h 10')	2^h 20' (4^h 15')	2^h 15' (4^h 10')
Range km	750 (1350)	820 (1480)	820 (1535)

Front

Plane	Ju 87 D-1 to Ju 87 D-4 with intercooler.
Designation	
Werk-Nr.	
Engine	Jumo 211 J with intercooler
Propeller	Type: VS 11 Standard setting: 25°

Maximum indicated airspeed (IAS) in a dive	
Altitude (km)	(V$_a$ km/h)
0-2	600
over 2	550

Liquid cooling temp. max 120°

Altitude	Normal maximum temp.
1	110°
4	100°
8	90°

Oil temperature	
In	
min	30°
max	105°

Oil pressure	
Sea-level	p$_{min}$ = 5.5 p$_{max}$ = 9
At 5.5 km altitude P$_{min}$ 4.00	

Fuel pressure	
1.0 - 2.0	

Oil:	Rotring Shell mittel Intava 100	Written on fuel cap

Fuel: 87 Oct.		
Version 1	Date: 15.12.41	E'Stelle Re

Air speed indicator

Engine instrument gauges

These figures are to be marked on the relevant instruments before this reference card is stored away.

Back

Junkers Ju 87 D-5 to D-8 with Jumo 211 J

Beanspruchungsgruppe	H 5 mit abgeminderten Lastvielfachen		
Motor-Belastungsgrenzen			
	Zul. Zeit	Lade-druck	Drehzahl bis 6,5km / über 6,5km
Stand	—	1,4	$n = ca.$ 2500 s. 3-V.-Fl. Teil I
Abflug normal	1'	1,4	2600 / —
Abflug Überlast	1'	1,4	2600 / —
	—	—	—
Flug Steig-Kampfl.	30'	1,25	2400 / 2400
Höchstzu'. Dauerleis'.		1,15	2250 / 2400
Lader-umschalthöhe	Automatik	2500 m — 300	
Gleit- und Sturzflug	$n_{max} = 2250$		

Flugzeit und Flugstrecke bei höchstzulässiger Dauerleistung

Flughöhe	m	300	2500	5000
Laderschaltung		BL	BL	HL
Ladedruck	ata	1,15	1,06 Vg	1,11 Vg
Drehzahl	U/min	2250	2250	2250
Kraftstoff-verbrauch	l/h	310	295	305

Für 770 l Kraftstoff ohne Abwurfbehälter und ohne Lasten

Wahre mittlere Geschwindigkeit	in km/h	320	340	370
Gesamt-flugzeit	h'	2h 15'	2h 25'	2h 25'
Reichweiten	km	715	800	835

Muster	Ju 87 D-5 bis D-8 / Ju 87 H-5 bis H-8 mit Ladeluftkühler
Zulassung	
Werk-Nr.	
Motor	Jumo 211 J mit Ladeluftkühler
Luftschraube	Muster VS 11 Grundeinstellung: 25°

Höchstzulässige angezeigte Geschwindigk. bei Bahnneigungsflug

Höhe (km)	Va (km/h) mit Sturzflug-Bremse	ohne Sturzflug-Bremse
0–2	600	650 *)
über 2	550	600 *)

*) Für alle Flugzeuge D-5 bis D-8, die nicht 4 Querruderlager, Querruder-Massenausgleich sowie verstärkte Bodensichtfenster haben, gelten die Werte „mit Sturzflugbremse"

Kühlstofftemperatur max 120°

Höhe	Normale Höchsttemp.
1	110.8
4	100°
8	90°

Schmierstoff-Temperatur

Eintritt	
min	30°
max	105°

Schmierstoffdruck

Am Boden	$p_{min} = 5,5$ $p_{max} = 9$
In 5,5 km Höhe	$p_{min} = 4,0$

Kraftstoffdruck

1,0—2,0

Schmierstoff:	Rotring Shell mittel Intava 100	Beschriftung auf Einfülldeckel
Kraftstoff	Okt. 87	
Ausgabe 3	Tag: 29.12.43	JFM-FTV Dru

Fahrtmesser — Triebwerks-Überwachungsgeräte — Diese Werte sind durch Marken an den entsprechenden Geräten vor dem Einstecken der Karte zu kennzeichnen

Betriebsdatentafel Ju 87 D-5 bis D-8, H-5 bis H-8

Junkers Ju 87 D-5 to D-8 with Jumo 211 P

Left table

Beanspruchungsgruppe	H 5 mit abgeminderten Lastvielfachen			
Motor - Belastungsgrenzen				
	Zul. Zeit	Lade-druck	Drehzahl bis 6,5 km	über 6,5 km
Stand	—	1,45	n = ca. 2600	
Abflug normal	1'	1,45	2700	—
Abflug Überlast	1'	1,45	2700	—
	—	—	—	—
Flug Steig·Kampfl.	30'	1,32	2500	2500
Höchstzul. Dauerleist.		1,15	2250	2400
Lader-umschalthöhe	Automatik	2500 m ± 300		
Gleit- und Sturzflug	nmax = 2250			

Flugzeit und Flugstrecke bei höchstzulässiger Dauerleistung

Flughöhe	m	300	2500	5000
Laderschaltung		BL	BL	HL
Ladedruck	ata	1,15	1,06 Vg	1,11 Vg
Drehzahl	U/min	2250	2250	2250
Kraftstoffverbrauch	l/h	310	295	305

— Für 770 l Kraftstoff ohne Abwurfbehälter und ohne Lasten

Wahre mittlere Geschwindigkeit	in km/h	320	340	370
Gesamtflugzeit	h'	2h 15'	2h 25'	2h 25'
Reichweiten	km	715	800	835

Right table

Muster	Ju 87 D-5 bis D-8 / Ju 87 H-5 bis H-8 mit Ladeluftkühler
Zulassung Werk-Nr.	
Motor	Jumo 211 P mit Ladeluftkühler
Luftschraube	Muster VS 11 Grundeinstellung: 25°

Höchstzulässige angezeigte Geschwindigk. bei Bahnneigungsflug

Höhe (km)	Va (km·h)	
	mit	ohne Sturzflug-Bremse
0—2	600	650 *)
über 2	550	600 *)

*) Für alle Flugzeuge D-5 bis D-8, die nicht 4 Querruderlager, Que ruder-Massenausgleich sowie verstärktes Bodensichtfenster haben, gelten die Werte „mit Sturzflugbremse"

Kühlstofftemperatur max 120°	
Höhe	Normale Höchsttemp.
1	110°
4	100°
8	90°

Schmierstoff-Temperatur	
Eintritt	
min	30°
max	105°

Schmierstoffdruck	
Am Boden	Pmin = 5,5 / Pmax = 9
In 5,5 km Höhe Pmin = 4,0	
Kraftstoffdruck 1,0—2,0	

Schmierstoff:	Rotring Shell mittel Intava 100	Beschriftung auf Einfülldeckel
Kraftstoff 87 Okt.		

Ausgabe 4	Tag: 29.2.1944	JFM-FTV Dru

(Randbeschriftung rechts) Fahrtmesser — Triebwerks-Überwachungsgeräte — Diese Werte sind durch Marken an den entsprechenden Geräten vor dem Einstecken der Karte zu kennzeichnen

Betriebsdatentafel Ju 87 D-5 bis D-8, Ju 87 H-5 bis H-8
mit Jumo 211 P Motor.

Vorderseite — Rückseite

281

Junkers Ju 87 G-1 to G-2 with Jumo 211 J

Beanspruchungsgruppe:	H 5 mit abgemind. Lastvielfachen			
Motor-Belastungsgrenzen				
	Zul. Zeit	Lade-druck	Drehzahl bis 6,5 km	über 6,5 km
Stand	—	1,4	n = ca. 2500 s.B.V.-Fl.87 Du.G Teil 1	
Abflug normal	.1'	1,4	2600	—
Abflug Überlast	1'	1,4	2600	—
	—	—	—	—
Flug Steig-Kampfl.	30'	1,25	2400	2400
Höchstzul. Dauerl.		1,15	2250	2400
Lader umschalthöhe	Automatik		2500 m ± 300	
Gleit- und Sturzflug	n max = 2250			

Flugzeit und Flugstrecke bei höchstzulässiger Dauerleistung

Flughöhe	m	300	2500	—
Laderschaltung		BL	BL	—
Ladedruck	ata	1,15	1,06 Vg	—
Drehzahl	U/min	2250	2250	—
Kraftstoffverbrauch	l/h	310	305	—
I Für 770 l Kraftstoff II Für 620 l Kraftstoff III Für 480 l Kraftstoff				
Wahre mittlere Geschwindigkeit	km/h	300	330	—
Gesamtflugzeit I	h'	2 h 15'	2 h 20'	
Gesamtflugzeit II		1 h 45'	1 h 47'	—
Gesamtflugzeit III		1 h 18'	1 h 19'	
Reichweite I	km	675	770	
Reichweite II		525	590	—
Reichweite III		390	430	

Muster	Ju 87 G-1, G-2 mit Ladeluftkühler
Zulassung	
Werk-Nr.	
Motor	Jumo 211 J mit Ladeluftkühler
Luftschraube	Muster: VS 11 Grundeinstellung: 25°

Höchstzulässige angezeigte Geschwindigkeit b.Bahnneigungsfl.

Höhe (km)	Va (km/h)
0—2	600
über 2	550

Kühlstofftemperatur max 120°

Höhe	norm.Höchstemperat.
1	110°
4	100°
8	90°

Schmierstoff-Temperatur

	Eintritt
min.	30°
max.	105°

Schmierstoffdruck

Am Boden	P min = 5,5 P max = 9
In 5,5 km Höhe	p min = 4,0

Kraftstoffdruck

1,0 – 2,0

Schmierstoff:	Rotring Shell mittel Intava 100	Beschriftung auf Einfülldeckel
Kraftstoff:	87 Okt.	
Ausgabe: 2	Tag: 27.11.43	JFM-FIV Dru

(rechte Randbeschriftung:) Fahrtmesser — Triebwerks-Überwachungsgeräte sind durch Marken an den entsprechenden Geräten vor dem Einstecken der Karte zu kennzeichnen. Diese Werte

Vorderseite **Betriebsdatentafel Ju 87 G-1, G-2** Rückseite

Junkers Ju 87 G-1 to G-2 with Jumo 211 P

Left table:

Beanspruchungsgruppe:	H 5 mit abgemind. Lastvielfachen		
Motor-Belastungsgrenzen			
	Zul. Zeit	Lade- druck	Drehzahl bis 6,5 km / über 6,5 km
Stand	—	1,45	n = ca. 2600
Abflug normal	1'	1,45	2700 / —
Abflug Überlast	1'	1,45	2700 / —
	—	—	— / —
Flug S'eig-Kampfl.	30'	1,32	2500 / 2500
Flug Höchstzul. Dauerl.		1,15	2250 / 2400
Lader- umschalthöhe	Automatik		2500 m ± 3CO
Gleit- und Sturzflug	n max = 2250		

Flugzeit und Flugstrecke bei höchstzulässiger Dauerleistung

Flughöhe	m	300	2500	—
Laderschaltung		BL	BL	—
Ladedruck	ata	1,15	1,05 Vg	
Drehzahl	U/min	2250	2250	—
Kraftstoff- verbrauch	l/h	310	305	
I	Für 770 l Kraftstoff			
II	Für 620 l Kraftstoff			
III	Für 480 l Kraftstoff			
Wahre mittlere Geschwindigkeit km/h		300	330	—
Gesamt- flugzeit h' I		2 h 15'	2 h 20'	
II		1 h 45'	1 h 47'	—
III		1 h 18'	1 h 19'	
Reich- weite km I		675	770	
II		525	590	—
III		390	430	

Vorderseite	**Betriebsdatentafel Ju 87 G-1, G-2**

Right table:

Muster	Ju 87 G-1, G-2 mit Ladeluftkühler
Zulassung	
Werk-Nr.	
Motor	Jumo 211 P mit Ladeluftkühler
Luft- schraube	Muster: VS 11 Grundeinstellung: 25°

Höchstzulässige angezeigte Geschwindigkeit b. Bahnneigungsfl.

Höhe (km)	Va (km/h)
0—2	600
über 2	550

Kühlstofftemperatur max 120°

Höhe	norm. Höchsttemperat.
1	110°
4	100°
8	90°

Schmierstoff-Temperatur

Eintritt	
min.	30°
max.	105°

Schmierstoffdruck

Am Boden	P min = 5,5 P max = 9
In 5,5 km Höhe p min = 4,0	

Kraftstoffdruck
1,0 – 2,0

Schmierstoff:	Rotring Shell mittel Intava 100	Beschriftung auf Einfülldeckel
Kraftstoff:	87 Okt.	
Ausgabe: 3	Tag: 1.3.44	JFM-FTV Dru

(vertical text, right margin) Fahrtmesser — Diese Werte sind durch Marken an den entsprechenden Geräten Triebwerks-Überwachungsgeräte vor dem Einstecken der Karte zu kennzeichnen.

The Siren – A Trumpet that never was

Perhaps no aspect of the Ju 87 is more widely known than the so-called "Jericho-trumpet". As the arch-typical cliché of the "Stuka", the siren featured consistently in German propaganda, as well as in post-war documentaries and movies. Its name too, "Jericho-trumpet", continues to be used in reference to the siren, although so far, we have not found a single primary source that uses this word for the sirens of the Stuka.

In German official documentation, the siren was referred to as "Lärmgerät", which literally translated means "noise-device". Colloquially it was simply known as "Sirene". It is so far unclear when, why and how exactly the siren became known as the "Jericho-trumpet". We do however know the origin of this word, which might give a glimpse as to at least the why of the aforementioned questions. The Luftwaffe developed a small whistle that, attached to the tail fins of a bomb, would shriek as the bomb tumbled to the ground[761]. Developed to be a psychological warfare tool, this whistle – which came in at least two iterations – was known as the "Jericho-Gerät", or "Jericho device" and even appears in Allied documentation where it was described as follows:

> "One type is a black cardboard tube, shaped like an organ pipe. The other model is an adapted bayonet scabbard, with an attachment for fastening it to one of the vanes of the bomb. Both models are approximately 14 in. in length and 1½ in. in diameter, the vent being about 4 in. from the closed end[762], which is rounded."[763]

A closer inspection of photographs also shows the former described whistles attached to the tail fins of bombs. Furthermore, as one picture is dated Finland - June/August 1944, this might be an indication that these whistles were also used during the late stages of the war.

---

[761] See for example: Wolfgang Thamm, *Fliegerbomben*, Bernard & Graefe Verlag, Bonn, Germany, 2003, p. 148; or Roman Töppel, *Kursk 1943: The Greatest Battle of the Second World War*, Helion and Company, Warwick, UK, 2018, p. 158. See also Tinus Le Roux, in conversation with Ju 87 pilot Dr. Heinz Migeod, *Stuka pilot interview 45: Diving sirens of the Ju-87*, published on YouTube 10th July 2010, available at: https://www.youtube.com/watch?v=K-CQ5Sko3mk (last accessed: 05.10.2021).
[762] 35.5 cm (length), 3.8 cm (diameter) and 10 cm (vent to closed end).
[763] Ministry of Home Security, Civil Defence Training Pamphlet No. 2 (3rd ed.), *Objects dropped from the air*, His Majesty's Stationery Office, London, UK, 1944.

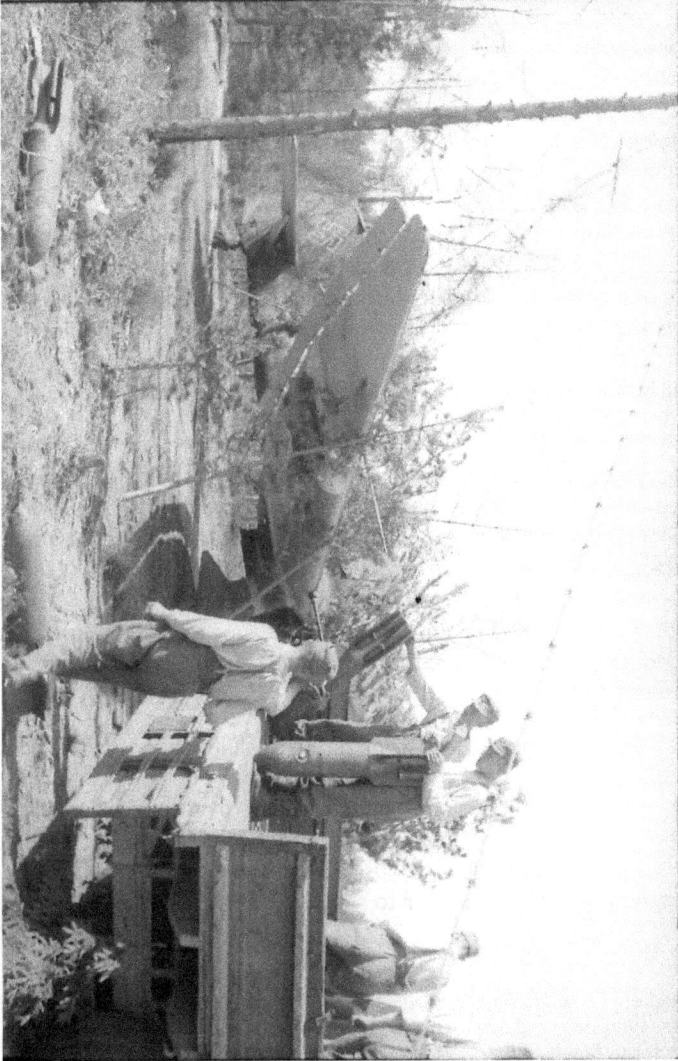

Photo 16: Junkers Ju 87 in Finland. Notice the small whistles known as "Jericho-Gerät" attached to the bombs being loaded from the truck. Original caption: Finland, Airfield Immola. Gefechtsverband Kuhlmey. Soldiers unload bombs for an aircraft (Junkers Ju 87 in the background) from a truck. Approximately July/August 1944. Credit: BArch, Bild 101I-727-0297-17A, Fotograf(in): Doege.

The "siren" came in two main iterations. The first, as an ad hoc field kit, appeared with the early Ju 87 variants and was mainly used by the B-type. It was a simple device, with a single small, free-moving propeller attached to the frontal, upper portion of each gear strut fairing. Added to induce a shocking psychological effect against the attacked target and anything around it, its installation was nevertheless a by-thought.[764] In flight, there was no manual way to turn this "siren" on, or more importantly off.[765] As such, on the way to the target the pilots would be accompanied by a constant wail that, while not as shrill and loud as in a dive, nevertheless caused constant annoyance. The improvised nature of the siren is also evident from the fact that during a pull out, these early models would occasionally sheer off, causing damage to the gear strut, or even the wing and tail.[766] Likewise, the associated drag of two small propellers caused a small but perceivable impact on the aircraft's performance.

With the D-type, an industry supplied model provided significant improvements. As can be read in the associated extract from the Ju 87 D manual printed in this book, the siren now featured an on-off switch, providing relief to the pilot's ears and nerves. Likewise, it appears that its more sophisticated manufacturing led to fewer structural failures. Notwithstanding, by this point the device had a firmly established negative reputation and doubts appeared regarding its psychological impact, which had appeared in earlier campaigns.[767] This led to numerous discussions within the higher command, which still considered it to be useful.

One account can be gleamed from the Generalluftzeugmeisterbesprechungen from 19th May 1942, with an account that the frontline units forgo their use due to an, given PoW statements, apparent lack of effect, while General von Richthofen[768] still valued them.[769] A later conversation from December 1942 reveals again that frontline troops were rejecting them due to their limited impact, leaving one commenter to suggest that this "children's toy"[770] had no

---

[764] Eddie J. Creek, *Junkers Ju 87 – From Dive-Bomber to Tank-Buster 1935-1945*, Classic: Ian Allen Publishing, Hersham, UK, 2012, p. 139.

[765] Peter C. Smith, *Stuka – Volume One – Luftwaffe Ju 87 Dive-Bomber Units 1939-1941*, Classic Colours, Manchester, UK, 2006, p. 40.

[766] Tinus Le Roux, in conversation with Ju 87 pilot Dr. Heinz Migeod, *Stuka pilot interview 45: Diving sirens of the Ju-87*, published on YouTube 10th July 2010, available at: https://www.youtube.com/watch?v=K-CQ5Sko3mk (last accessed: 05.10.2021).

[767] BArch, RL 3/17, *Stenographischer Bericht über die GL-Besprechung*, 1. December 1942.

[768] Generalfeldmarschall Wolfram Karl Ludwig Moritz Hermann Freiherr von Richthofen, in February 1943, cousin of Manfred and Lothar von Richthofen.

[769] BArch, RL 3/14, *Stenographischer Bericht über die GL-Besprechung*, 19. Mai 1942.

[770] Translation from "Kinderschreck", literally meaning "child's scare".

more effect. In contrast, Generals von Richthofen and Jeschonnek continued to demand their use.[771] Even at later dates when the siren remained by all accounts generally grounded, a "higher psychological effect"[772] was attributed to it, as can be glimpsed from a Luftwaffe academy instructional lecture from 1943.[773] Why exactly the higher command structures still championed their use might perhaps have to do with their effect on "fresh" recruits within the enemy's force that were unfamiliar with the noise. It is also possible that the psychological impact these sirens had on the friendly German forces was considered of importance. As German historian Roman Töppel recounts in quoting a soldier of the 7th Infantry Division at the Battle of Kursk: "The howling of the Stukas is music to our ears."[774] Here too the device was referred to as "noise propeller" and "wailing siren"[775]. It appears highly unlikely that by this point the sirens were still used in the same numbers as before.

The popular connection of the siren to the Ju 87 remains a narrative in the depiction of the Second World War, whether in documentaries, video games or movies, as does the ongoing erroneous labelling as "Jericho-trumpet". The audio-visual impact of this device on the observer was already realized during the Second World War. Given the frequent use of both Ju 87s and a looped siren sound in German propaganda footage, an open question remains of how much this continues to influence today's perception of this plane and the siren itself.[776]

While an integral part of the early operational history of the Ju 87, and a near unique attempt in psychological warfare, it should likewise be remembered that, for the most part the siren was disliked by Luftwaffe pilots, was only regularly mounted during the early campaigns, and that the origin of the designation "Jericho-trumpet" was most likely appropriated post-war from the little whistles attached to the actual bombs.

---

[771] BArch, RL 3/17, *Stenographischer Bericht über die GL-Besprechung*, 1. December 1942.
[772] Translation from "erhöhte moralische Wirkung". Emphasis original.
[773] TsAMO, F. 500 Op. 12452 D. 250, *Ausgegebene Umdrucke über Luftwaffenlehre – 7. Lehrgang, Vortrag Hauptmann von Schwenitz bei Offizier-Ausbildung, Zusammenarbeit von Nahkampf- und Aufklärungsverbänden der Luftwaffe mit der Erdtruppe*, 29. June 1943, p. 4.
[774] Roman Töppel, *Kursk 1943: The Greatest Battle of the Second World War*, Helion and Company, Warwick, UK, 2018, p. 158.
[775] Translation from "Lärmpropeller" and "Heulsirene" respectively. See TsAMO, F. 500 Op. 12452 D. 250, *Ausgegebene Umdrucke über Luftwaffenlehre – 7. Lehrgang, Vortrag Hauptmann von Schwenitz bei Offizier-Ausbildung, Zusammenarbeit von Nahkampf- und Aufklärungsverbänden der Luftwaffe mit der Erdtruppe*, 29. June 1943, p. 7.
[776] For more information, refer to *STUKA! – The Ju 87 in Picture, Sound and Memory*.

Photo 17: The Junkers Ju 87 was not the exclusive user of bombs with whistles. Another detailed look at the "Jericho-Gerät" can be seen in this photograph, as bombs are mounted on this Focke-Wulf Fw 189. Original caption: Soviet Union, Aircraft Focke Wulf Fw 189 onto an airfield, mounting of bombs. Early 1943. Credit: BArch, Bild 101I-331-3034-13A, Fotograf(in): Liedke.

Document: The Noise Device / Siren

This document is part of Archiv Hafner, D. (Luft) T.2087 D1 trop, *Ju 87 D-1 trop Flugzeug-Handbuch Teil 12D – Sondereinbauten - Heft 1: Lärmgerät*, from May 1942. It details the installation and technical use of the famous Ju 87 siren. Readers who find this technical information of interest, may also especially enjoy the opening Chapter *STUKA! – The Ju 87 in Picture, Sound and Memory*.

Preliminary Notes / Source Situation, Actuality and Formatting

Throughout this volume, we aimed to retain some of the original formatting, yet the editorial focus lay on legibility. One of the main editorial changes was that, in order to present a clearer layout, we did not follow the original page count as this would have resulted in empty or near empty pages throughout the book. Instead, the text has been reformatted to follow a more conventional structure, page by page.

Please be aware of the following formatting decisions and changes:

- We corrected formatting mistakes in the original version (for example missing spaces, paragraph breaks or others).
- The document has a header, which included the title and other data we omitted it since it would break with the general formatting of the book and does not provide any additional content.
- This chapter contains a lot of technical terms to refer to very specific parts of the Lärmgerät we did not explain most of them, since they are covered by the images.

D. (Luft) T.2087 D1 trop
Teil 12 D; Heft 1

For Service Use only!

Ju 87 D-1 trop

Aircraft handbook

Part 12D

Special Equipment

Booklet 1: Noise device

May 1942

290

Reich's Minister for Aviation
Commander-in-Chief of the Luftwaffe[777]

Berlin, 13. May 1942

Technical bureau[778]
GL/C-E 5 Nr. 20329/42 (VII C)

This regulation[779]: D. (Luft) T.2087 D-1 trop, Part 12D Booklet 1 – N.f.D.[780] – "Ju 87 D-1 trop, Aircraft handbook, Part 12D: Special equipment, Booklet 1 Siren, May 1942" is checked and is considered as a service instruction. It comes into force on the date of issue.

With the publication of this handbook, the publication Werkschrift 1035/12D, Booklet 1 – N.f.D. – December 1941 becomes invalid.

I.A.[781]

V o r w a l d

[Table of contents omitted.]

---

[777] See Reich's Minister for Aviation and Commander-in-Chief of the Luftwaffe (Reichsminister der Luftfahrt und Oberbefehlshaber der Luftwaffe).
[778] Technisches Amt.
[779] The literal translation of a "Druckvorschrift" would be "Print Regulation". Be aware that a "Druckvorschrift" is a printed "Dienstvorschrift", which means "Service Regulation". This term is still used nowadays in the Bundeswehr, whereas "Druckvorschrift" isn't.
[780] "N.f.D." is the abbreviation of "Nur für den Dienstgebrauch", indicating "For Service Use only".
[781] "I.A." is the abbreviation of "Im Auftrag", indicating "by proxy".

Noise Device / Siren

I. Short Description

To amplify the howling sound during a diving attack, a noise device is installed on the left and right gear fairings. Their propellers are driven by the airstream.

The noise device[782] are switched on and off by an electro-hydraulic system. Operation by the pilot is accomplished by setting the toggle switch (T 1) to the "on" or "off" position. The toggle switch (T 1) is located on the throttle quadrant[783] on the left-hand side of the cockpit.

The required pressurized oil is taken from the return flow line of the pressurized oil system of the switch for the dive brake.

Switching on the noise device must be done before the dive, before the dive brakes are extended.

Switching off the noise device must be done only after the dive, when the speed has dropped to 320 kph[784].

II. Arrangement and Working Method

Layout (Figure 1)

Pressure Oil System

Except for the two brakes (Hf 8 and Hf 9)[785], the pressurized oil system for the left and right noise device is installed in the left wing between ribs 1 b and 1 c behind spar II[786]. The devices attached to this bearing serve the following purposes:

---

[782] The German original word was "Lärmgerät", which can be literally translated as "noise device".

[783] See Glossary: Throttle quadrant (Drosselhabelkasten).

[784] 200 mph.

[785] These are the brakes that are applied on the siren, to stop them from moving in the airflow. The first iteration of sirens did not have these brakes and as such would be emitting a constant sound during cruise.

[786] The switch from Arabic to Roman numerals on the ribs and spar was most likely done to prevent confusion.

1) **The cross valve** (Hf 1) directs the incoming pressure oil to the second cross valve (Hf 2) via the check valve (Hf 3) and pressure accumulator (Hf 5).

2) **The cross valve** (Hf 2) directs the oil to the brake in the left and right siren.

3) **The pressure accumulator** (Hf 5) maintains the required oil pressure of at least 30 to 75 kg/cm^2.

4) **The hydraulic relay** (Hf 4) switches the cross valve (Hf 2) on or off depending on whether the pressure is above or below 30 kg/cm^2.

5) **The check valve** (Hf 3) installed in front of the pressure accumulator (Hf 5) prevents the oil from flowing back if the oil pressure drops due to the switching on of another system (dive brake).

6) **The orifice** (Hf 7), which is located in front of the cross valve (Hf 2), prevents a sudden drop in pressure when the cross valve (Hf 2) is opened, which would cause the system to shut down again.

The air filling connection port (Hf 12) for the pressure accumulator (Hf 5) as well as the pressure gauge (Hf 6) are also located on the mounting in the left wing.

[Explanation on the flow line layout of the pressurized oil system removed.]

Electrical System

The electrical system for operating the noise device is connected to the 24-volt on-board power supply via the two distributors (V 1 and V 2) and fused at the circuit-breaker (V 32) in the control panel.

The toggle switch (T 1) for switching the solenoid (T 5) on/off at the cross valve (Hf 1) is installed at the throttle quadrant. The distributor (T 2) is located on the mounting in the left wing. The two solenoid switches (T 4) and (T 5) belong to both cross valves and, like the switch (T 3) on the hydraulic relay, are installed in the bearing in the left wing.

The plug coupling (V 7/V 8) serves as the separation point when dismantling the left wing.

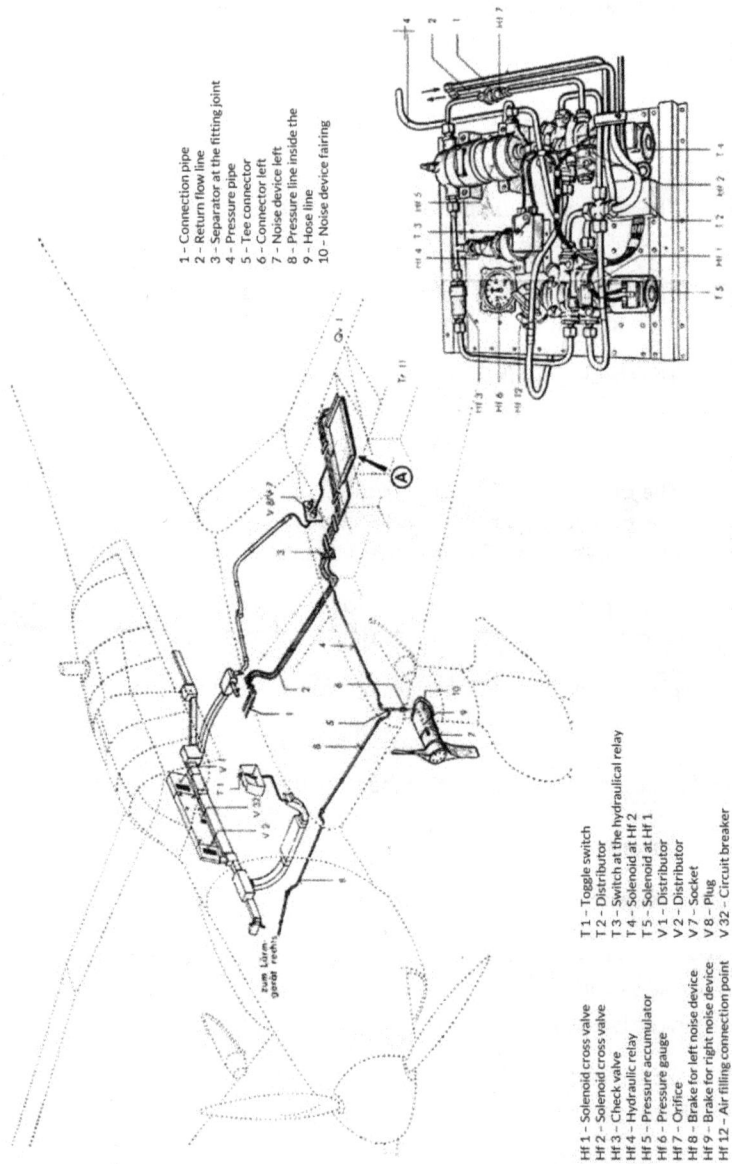

1 - Connection pipe
2 - Return flow line
3 - Separator at the fitting joint
4 - Pressure pipe
5 - Tee connector
6 - Connector left
7 - Noise device left
8 - Pressure line inside the
9 - Hose line
10 - Noise device fairing

Hf 1 - Solenoid cross valve
Hf 2 - Solenoid cross valve
Hf 3 - Check valve
Hf 4 - Hydraulic relay
Hf 5 - Pressure accumulator
Hf 6 - Pressure gauge
Hf 7 - Orifice
Hf 8 - Brake for left noise device
Hf 9 - Brake for right noise device
Hf 12 - Air filling connection point

T 1 - Toggle switch
T 2 - Distributor
T 3 - Switch at the hydraulical relay
T 4 - Solenoid at Hf 2
T 5 - Solenoid at Hf 1
V 1 - Distributor
V 2 - Distributor
V 7 - Socket
V 8 - Plug
V 32 - Circuit breaker

Figure 1 - Schematic of the electro-hydraulic actuation system of the noise devices.

Operation (Figure 2)

After switching on the circuit-breaker (V 32) and setting the toggle switch (T 1) to the "on" position, the solenoid switch (T 5) receives voltage and actuates the cross valve (Hf 1). This switches over and directs the pressure oil via the second cross valve (Hf 2) to the brake (Hf 8 or Hf 9). However, the second cross valve (Hf 2) is not switched on, and thus the brakes are not released, until the hydraulic relay (Hf 4) is overpressured, which switches on the solenoid switch (T 4) on the cross valve (Hf 2) via the switch (T 3). The overpressuring of the hydraulic relay (Hf 4) takes place after the oil pressure has risen to over 30 kg/cm^2.

A sudden drop in pressure when the cross valve (Hf 2) is switched on and the resulting drop in the hydraulic relay (Hf 4) is prevented by the orifice (Hf 7).

This oil pressure must be maintained on the brakes as long as these devices are to operate. When the oil pressure drops (when the dive brake is extended) in the pressurized oil system, the check valve (Hf 3) does not allow the oil to flow back, while the pressure accumulator (Hf 5) maintains the required oil pressure of 30 kg/cm^2.

As soon as the pressure drops below 30 kg/cm^2, the hydraulic relay (Hf 4) interrupts the circuit for the solenoid switch (T 4) of the cross valve (Hf 2) by opening the switch (T 3). This switches over and thereby connects the brake line, which is under 30 kg/cm^2 pressure, to the return line. By doing so, the insufficient pressure is completely removed from the brakes (Hf 8 and Hf 9) and the two noise devices are abruptly stopped by springs. This prevents the noise devices from overheating due to half-applied brakes.

To switch off the noise devices, the toggle switch (T 1) is set to the "off" position. This de-energizes the two solenoid switches (T 5) and (T 4) of the cross valves (Hf 1) and (Hf 2). The cross valves switch off, the pressure line to the brake (Hf 8 or Hf 9) is depressurized by its connection to the return line.

The line between the two cross valves (Hf 1) and (Hf 2) always remains pressurized by the accumulator (Hf 5).

Propeller of the noise device with
"brake disengaged"

Hf 9

Hf 1 – Solenoid cross valve
Hf 2 – Solenoid cross valve
Hf 3 – Check valve
Hf 4 – Hydraulic relay
Hf 5 – Pressure accumulator
Hf 6 – Pressure gauge
Hf 7 – Orifice
Hf 8 – Brake for left noise device
Hf 9 – Brake for right noise device
Hf 12 – Air filling connection point

T 1 – Toggle switch
T 2 – Distributor
T 3 – Switch at the hydraulical relay
T 4 – Solenoid at Hf 2
T 5 – Solenoid at Hf 1

V 1 – Distributor
V 2 – Distributor
V 7 – Socket
V 8 – Plug
V 32 – Circuit breaker

Electrical line
Compressed air line
Return flow line
Pressurized oil line
Pressurized oil inlet

Switchboard

V 2
V 32
V 1

T 1

V 8 V 7

T 2

Hf 7

T 4

Hf 5

Hf 2

30/75

Hf 4

T 3

Hf 3

Hf 6

Hf 12

T 5

Hf 8

Propeller of the noise device with
"brake engaged"

Schematic for the pressure oil system of
the noise devices

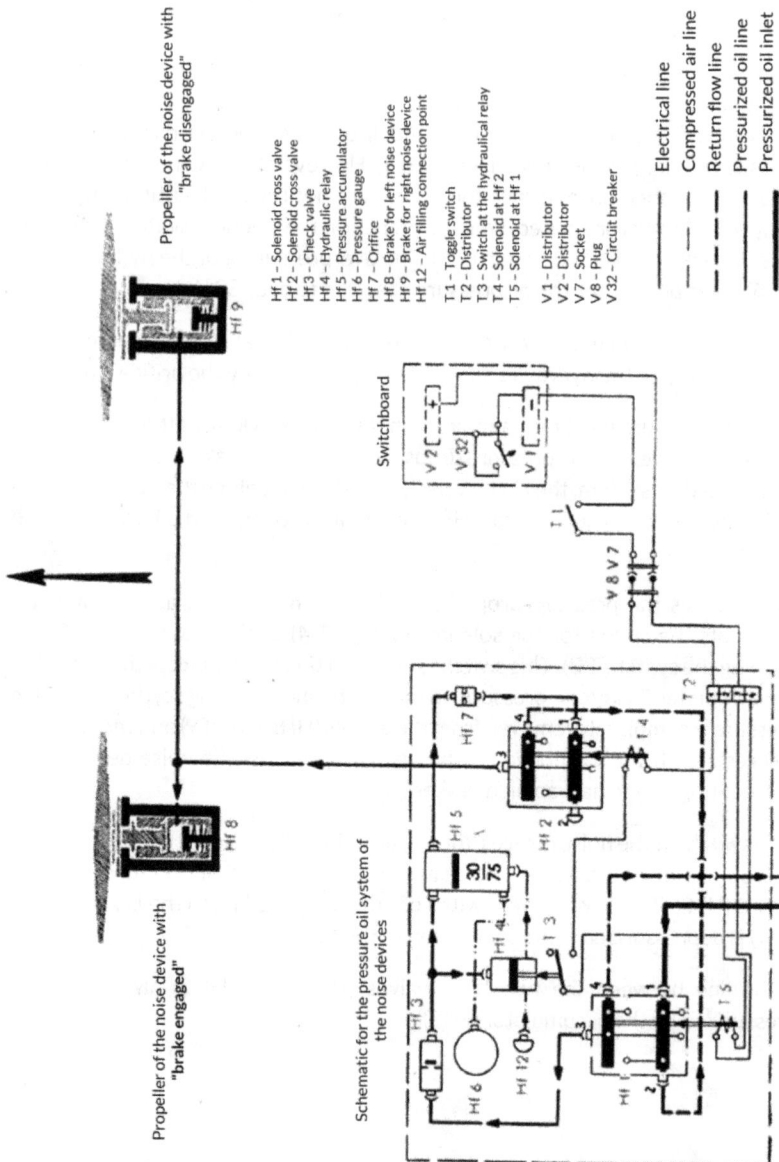

Figure 2 - Schematic of the electro-hydraulic actuation system of the noise devices.

Installation Instructions

Installation of the Noise Devices (Figure 3)

When mounting the noise device on the left or right driving position, proceed as follows.

Connect the line for the pressure oil-actuated brake in the noise device to the connection piece of the noise device (1). Place the noise device (1) with its base plate (2) on the mounting ring (3) of the support cylinder (4).

Fasten the siren with six galvanized hexagonal screws (5). These screws are secured with safety wire.

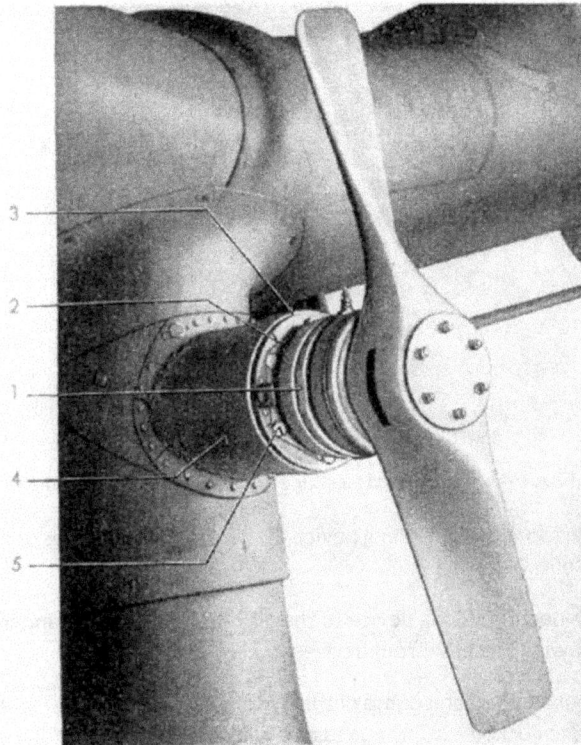

1 - Noise device 2 - Base plate 3 - Mounting ring
4 - Noise device fairing 5 - Fixing screw

Figure 3 - Mounting of the noise device on the left gear fairing.

Filling the Pressure Accumulator (Figure 4)

Before filling the pressure accumulator in the left wing between ribs 1 b and 1 c behind spar II, the toggle switch (T 1) in the operator's cabin must be set to the "on" position. Flaps and dive brake must be in the "0" position[787].

Figure 4 – Compressed air connection for pressure accumulator.

Filling is performed with a filling device FD 2 from supply bottles or compressor carts in the following way:

1)   Connect the filling device to the air filling port on the underside of the left wing (access through cover).

2)   Operate the hand pump of the hydraulic system on the right-hand side in the cockpit until the pressure gauge for the landing flap in the left-

---

[787] Neutral position.

hand cab indicates a pressure of 75 atü[788]. (Rotary control switch in "0" position.)

3)   Fill up with compressed air until the pressure gauge on the lower side of the left wing indicates 60 atü.

After filling, remove the filling device and close the cover on the underside of the wing.

III. Repair Instructions

Damaged noise device and built-in parts belonging to the electro-hydraulic actuation system are to be removed and sent back[789]. Minor damage and leaks are to be repaired according to the existing instructions for this purpose.

Damaged parts must be replaced with new ones of the same type. See also spare parts list Ju 87 D-1 trop.

For further information on maintenance, see also Aircraft Manual Ju 87 D-1 trop Teil 9 C "Druckölanlage".[790]

IV. Testing of the System

Checking the Installation

Check that all installation parts, devices and lines are properly fitted, fastened and secured.

Check further that the lines, hose connections and separation points of the pressurized oil system are sealed, and confirm that the line from the air filling connection point to the pressure gauge is also sealed.

Check that the connections of the electrical part of the pressure oil system are properly connected (see circuit diagram S 8700 - 7412, sheet 4[791]).

---

[788] See Glossary: atü.
[789] The German original word was "einzusenden", which can be literally translated as "sent in". It is likely that this means sending the parts back to the manufacturer or a dedicated workshop for repair.
[790] Referred to here is Werkschrift 1035/9C, *Ju 87 D-1 trop Flugzeug-Handbuch, Teil 9 C Druckölanlage*, June 1942.
[791] Not included in this volume.

Testing the System

Operate the hand pump of the pressurized oil system on the right side of the cockpit until the pressure gauge for flaps in the left cabin indicates a pressure of 75 kg/cm². Check if:

1) the pressure gauge for the pressure accumulator indicates at least 50 kg/cm²,

2) after setting the toggle switch (T 1) from the "on" position in the driver's cab, the propellers of the noise device can be turned, hence the brakes are released,

3) after setting the toggle switch to the "off" position, the propellers of the noise device are fixed, hence the brakes are applied.

Note: The inspection of the pressurized oil system as well as the filling, pressure testing, etc. is described in Part 9 C "Pressurized Oil System" of the Ju 87 D-1 trop manual[792].

---

[792] Referred to here is Werkschrift 1035/9C, *Ju 87 D-1 trop Flugzeug-Handbuch, Teil 9 C Druckölanlage*, June 1942.

Photo 18: This photograph of a Junkers Ju 87 D gives a good look at a siren and especially its size. Original caption: Frontline airfield, aircraft Junkers Ju 87 of Sturzkampfgeschwader 2 (II./Stg 2) with Gruppen emblem "Bamberger Reiter" and running engine before take-off / after landing. Approximately August 1942. Credit: BArch, Bild 101I-453-1042-33, Fotograf(in): Niermann.

Documents: 37mm AT-Gun Manuals

This Chapter consists of parts of two documents:

- Archiv Hafner, D. (Luft) T. 2087 G-2 Teil 12 A, *Ju 87 G-2 - Flugzeug-Handbuch Teil 12 A: Schußwaffenanlage mit zwei 3,7 cm BK*, October 1943.
- *Einbaumappe 3,7 cm BK – 43*, March 1944.

Both documents have been shortened to the relevant sections detailing the use of the 3.7cm anti-tank cannons, as well as relevant technical figures for the gun and ammunition.

Preliminary Notes / Source Situation, Actuality and Formatting

Throughout this volume, we aimed to retain some of the original formatting, yet the editorial focus lay on legibility. One of the main editorial changes was that, in order to present a clearer layout, we did not follow the original page count as this would have resulted in empty or near empty pages throughout the book. Instead, the text has been reformatted to follow a more conventional structure, page by page.

Please be aware of the following formatting decisions and changes:

- We corrected formatting mistakes in the original version (for example missing spaces, paragraph breaks or others).
- The document has a header, which included the title and other data we omitted it since it would break with the general formatting of the book and does not provide any additional content.

Ju 87 G-2, Aircraft Manual, Part 12 A: Armament with two 3.7 cm BK (October 1943)

[Section I. and II. removed.]

III. Firing In-Flight

[Sub-Section A. and B. removed.]

C. Flight

1. Take-Off

The aircraft starts with closed and synchronized breeches.

One cartridge is chambered.

The circuit-breakers[793] for the weapon system and heater on the main equipment panel are pressed in.

2. After Take-Off

a) Set the toggle switch for the heater to "on".

(The indicator lights respond and indicate that the electric priming is working.)

Note: The heaters may only be switched on during flight.

Approximately 5 minutes after being switched on, the display signs must disappear. The heaters continue to work by self-ignition.

If the white indicators do not disappear within 5 minutes, the system must be switched off immediately.

---

[793] See Glossary: Circuit-breaker (Selbstschalter).

3. Turning on the Reflector Sight

a) Turn on the reflector sight[794] by adjusting the contrast switch according to the current light conditions.

b) If required, flip up the colored glass[795] in front of the reflective screen.

4. Firing

a) Flip the safety switch on the SZKK-2[796] to "on".
(Indicators turn on.)

b) Flick trigger cover on the control stick to the front, over the A-button[797].

c) Press the B-trigger button.
(The weapons fire. The flickering indicators show that the weapon is working.)

5. Stoppages

The arrangement of the gunnery system does not allow the fixing of stoppages on the on-board guns during the flight. In case of failure of one BK[798] the second BK can most likely continue to deliver single fire, but the hit probabilities are questionable.

6. Prior to Landing

a) Set the toggle switch for the heater to "off".

Note: Operation must be done at the latest 5 minutes before landing.

b) Flip the safety switch on the SZKK-2 to "off".

c) Flick the trigger cover on the control stick back to the safety position over the B-button.

---

[794] See Glossary: Reflector sight (Reflexvisier [Revi]).

[795] This was a small glass panel, working similarly to sunglasses by increasing the contrast and reducing the change that the reflector sights reticule reflection is lost against a bright background.

[796] See Glossary: Master gun arm device (Schalt-, Zähl-, Kontrolkasten [SZKK]).

[797] The A-button is a small button on the control stick, usually activating the forward-facing fixed armament. It can be used by flipping the cover of the B-button, which acts as it's safety catch, forward. This uncovers the B-button which can now be used. The now flipped cover becomes the "trigger", and when pulled backwards, presses on the A-button, which activates the guns.

[798] See Glossary: Outboard cannon (Bordkanone [BK]).

If the ammunition supply is depleted, the indicator marks on the SZKK-2 are gone, as the breechblocks of the BK are locked to the rear.

7. After Landing

The aircraft must be positioned in such a way that neither persons nor material are in danger of being shot at.

Work on the aircraft may only be carried out after the armorer has checked that the barrels are clear.

8. Removing Ammunition and Empty Ammunition Frame

a) Open the center fairing.

b) Using a screwdriver or a round bar, press the pressure relief lever for the locking cam upwards.

c) Pull out a cartridge frame that still contains ammunition by means of a special hook through the extended loading frame.

d) Open slider on the empty cartridge frame box.

e) Take out the empty cartridge frame.

f) Close slider.

g) Operate the release lever.
(Since the breeches are still engaged, they will jolt forward. **Beware of hand injuries.**)
h) Disconnect the breech.

IV. Maintenance of the Weapon System

A. Removal and Cleaning of the Weapons

a) After each firing, clean and oil the tubes immediately.
Put on the safety caps.

b) Clean and grease the fasteners with "Fliegerfett blau"[799].

---

[799] "Fliegerfett blau", literally translating to "aviator fat blue", was often used to lubricate parts of AA or aircraft guns, as well as the respective ammunition. Sadly, we were so far unable to find additional information on this lubricant.

c) After about 150 rounds, dismantle the guns, disassemble them and clean thoroughly.

Removing the gun:

1) Take off the weapon's fairing.

2) Knock out the spring bolts at the rear suspension point.

3) Pull both spring bolts on the trunnion bearing outward.

4) Remove the bearing drum.

5) 3 to 4 men lift the weapon.

6) Check all parts for wear or damage.

For further maintenance see D. (Luft) 1.6018 Waffen-Handbuch 3,7 cm BK.

Reassembly is carried out in the reverse order as described above.

Photo 19. Original caption: Soviet Union, Ukraine.- Junkers Ju 87 G "Stuka" with 3.7-cm-FlaK 18 cannons ("Kanonenvogel") with painted tank on the engine cowling. Approximately 1943. Credit: BArch, Bild 101I-353-1645-04, Fotograf(in): Speck.

Photo 20: Original caption: Soviet Union - Don front, refueling a dive-bomber Junkers Ju 87 G "Stuka" with 3.7-cm Flak ("Kanonenvogel"). Approximately 1943./1944 Credit: BArch, Bild 101I-728-0322-23, Fotograf(in): Schneider.

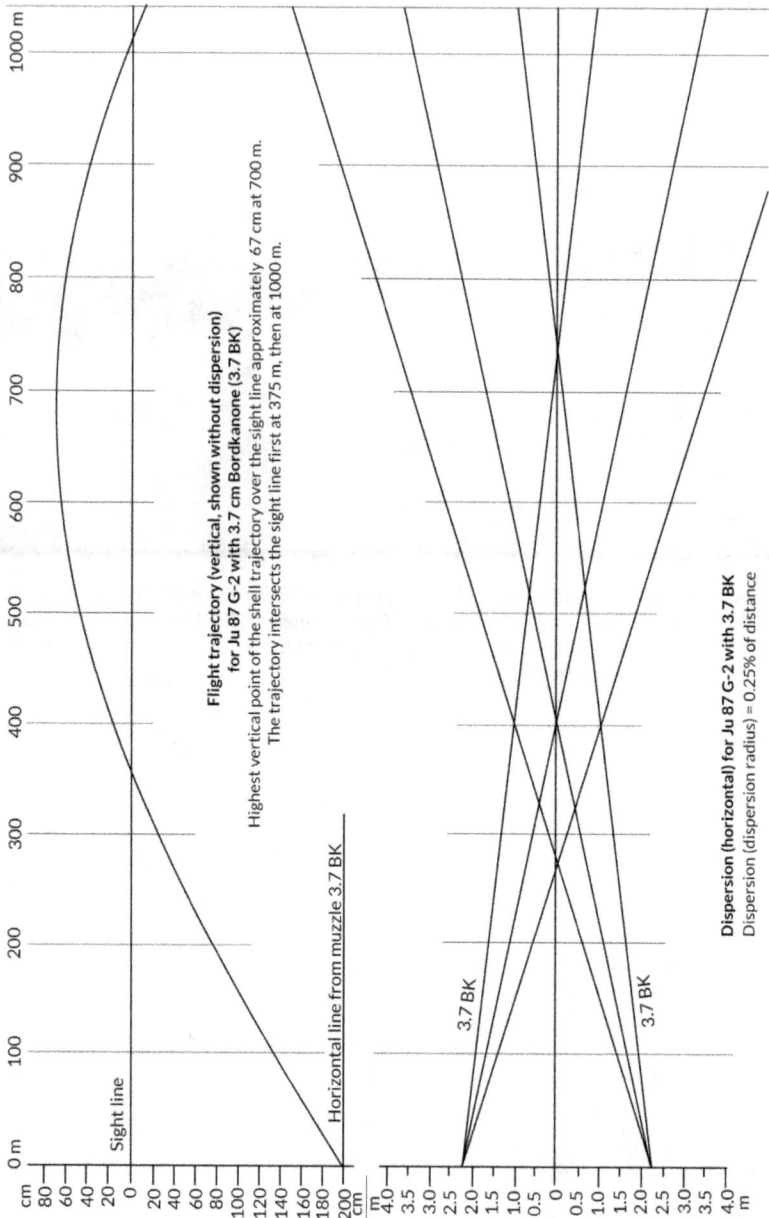

Flight trajectory (vertical, shown without dispersion) for Ju 87 G-2 with 3.7 cm Bordkanone (3.7 BK)
Highest vertical point of the shell trajectory over the sight line approximately 67 cm at 700 m.
The trajectory intersects the sight line first at 375 m, then at 1000 m.

Horizontal line from muzzle 3.7 BK

Sight line

Dispersion (horizontal) for Ju 87 G-2 with 3.7 BK
Dispersion (dispersion radius) = 0.25% of distance

3.7 BK

3.7 BK

Shell flight trajectory

Document: Installation Instruction 3.7 cm BK – 43 March 1944

Datasheet for 3.7 cm BK - 43

1. Caliber		37	mm
2. Muzzle velocity v_0	(HE)	840	m/s
	(Mine)	870	m/s
	(HVAP)	1150	m/s
3. Muzzle energy E_0	(HE)	22.48	mt
	(Mine)	22.18	mt
	(HVAP)	27.30	mt
4. Muzzle gas pressure		680	kg/cm
5. Rate of fire		235-250	/min
6. Recoil	normal	800	kg
	per single shot max.	1500	kg
7. Recoil absorption including buffer to rear, max.		120	mm
8. Length of weapon fairing from hard point			
	to the front	80	mm
	to the back	40	mm
9. Recoil absorption	back max.	10	mm
	front max.	15	mm
10. Recoil force in velocity approximately		1	m/s
11. Weight and balance of weapon		page 311	
12. Barrel weight		50	kg
13. Barrel length		2106	mm
14. Barrel removal		to the front	
15. Weapon length		3300	mm
16. Weapon height		530	mm
17. Weapon width (without loading frame)		300	mm
18. Priming with Zündschraube C/33		mechanical	
19. Trigger		electric pneumatic	
20. Compressed air cylinder, content		2	l
21. Number of shots (with 150 atü filling)		ca. 80	l
22. Charging the gun		by hand	

23. Weapon safety		mechanical	
24. Cartridge frame, weight of empty frame		3	kg
weight of filled frame (with 8 cartridges)		15	kg
measurements of the frame:			
maximum length approximately		450	mm
maximum width approximately		210	mm
maximum height approximately		48	mm

Construction Data of the 3.7 cm Flak 43

1. System: Gas-operated closed bolt with flapper locking

2. Maximum allowed gas pressure		3000	atü
3. Standard operating gas pressure (at 15° Pt[800])		2575	atü
4. Barrel length in caliber		57	
5. Length of rifling (barrel)		1838.4	mm
6. Rifling type		kub.par. 3° by 5°	
7. Number of rifling		20	
8. Depth of rifling		0.55	mm
9. Width of rifling		3.5 + 0.4	mm
10. Width of lands		2.01	mm
11. Bore diameter		37 + 0.2	mm
12. Rifling diameter		38.1 + 0.2	mm
13. Barrel throat		1 : 10	
14. Barrel construction material		Mn St V 70	
15. Bolt travel to bolt catch		629	mm
16. Bolt travel to buffer		642	mm
17. Maximum compression of bolt buffer		30	mm
18. Distance of locked recoil		45	mm
19. Lock and unlock distance		15	mm
20. Bolt travel to frame release of cartridge		230	mm

21. Shortest distance of weapon housing, that is required for a good stable firing platform from the bolt lock position

	to the front	45	mm
	to the back	10	mm
22. Recoil plate buffer	max.	10	mm
23. Bolt velocity	after unlocking	10	m/s
	before locking	5	m/s
24. Striker bolt face protrusion distance		1.7 ÷ 1.9	mm
25. Gas cylinder diameter		36.4 + 0.1	mm

---

[800] Pressure-temperature.

27. Gas plug diameter	34.9 ÷ 35.1	mm
28. Feed: Feed pawl overtravel	7.5 ± 2	mm
Feed pawl travel	54 ± 1	mm
Cartridge clip free travel	6.5 ± 2	mm

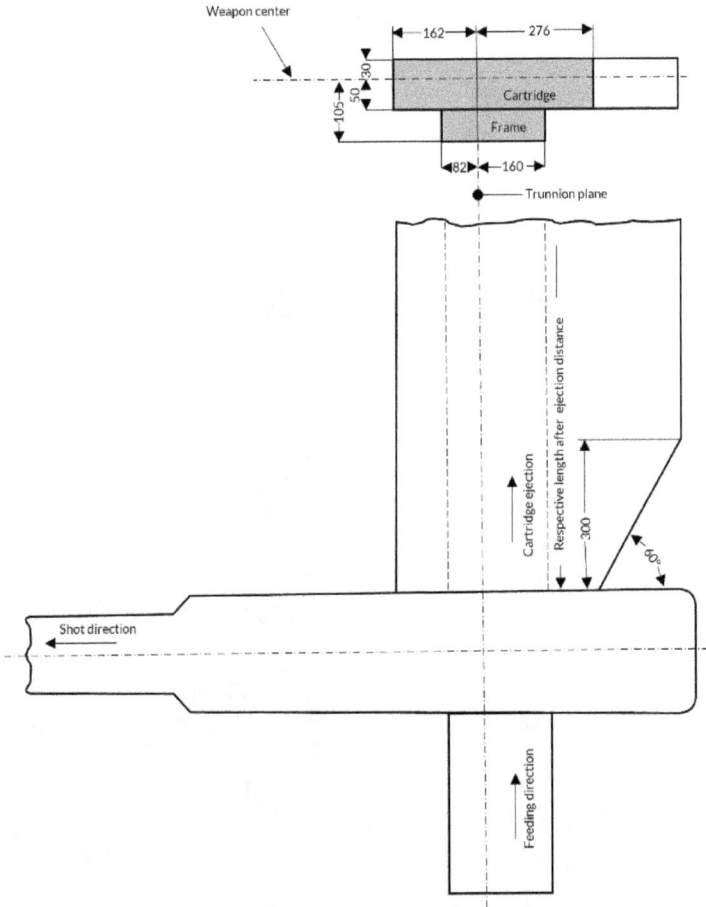

Space requirements for frame and cartridge ejection for 3.7cm BK – 43

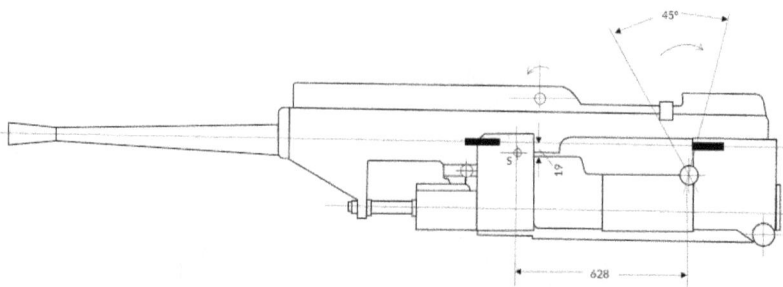

628 mm center of gravity with locked bolt and weapon body

558 mm center of gravity with open bolt and weapon body

Weight of Individual Components:

Barrel	50 kg
Breech	20 kg
Weapon body with bolt buffer	120 kg
Cover with feed pawl	27 kg
Trigger	7 kg
Feed	25 kg
Recuperator with muzzle brake	41 kg
Recuperator incl. housing	<u>65 kg</u>
	<u>355 kg</u> **Total weight of weapon**

Weights and balance of 3.7cm BK-43 weapon

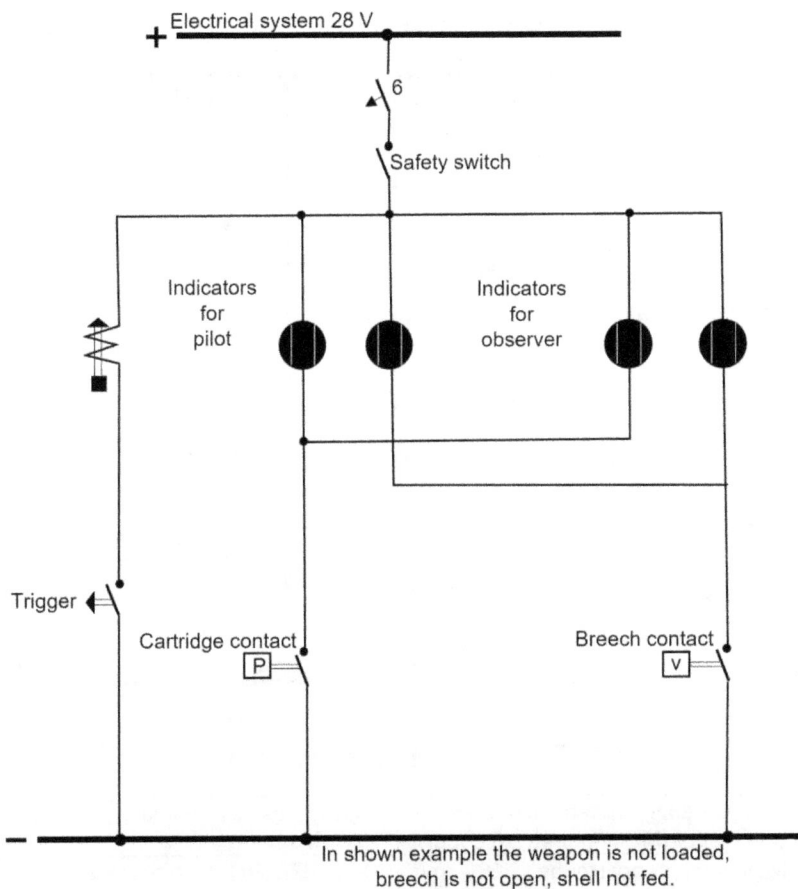

Electrical system 28 V

6

Safety switch

Indicators
for
pilot

Indicators
for
observer

Trigger

Cartridge contact
P

Breech contact
V

In shown example the weapon is not loaded,
breech is not open, shell not fed.

Electric circuit diagram of weapon system 3.7cm BK – 43

Ammunition Detail for 3.7cm BK – 43
Date: March 1944

	3.7cm Br.Sprgr. Patr.18 L'spur	3.7cm Mgr. Patr. 18 L'spur	3.7cm H-Pzgr. Patr. L'spur o. Zerl.	3.7cm Pzgr. Patr. 18 L'spur
Muzzle velocity. V_0 m/sec	820	870	1150	770
Projectile weight kg	0.644	0.575	0.405	0.685
Muzzle energy E_0 mt	22.1	22.2	27.3	20.7
Explosive filler g	46	86	Aluminum casing with special steel core[801]	13
Propellant charge g	202	222	244	202
Cartridge weight kg	1.5	1.46	1.31	1.55
Cartridge length mm	368	368	364	342
Cartridge case weight kg	0.660			
Cartridge case material	Steel brass plated			
Primer casing	C/33 St			

Translations of Cartridges

Brandsprenggranatenpatrone 18 mit Leuchtspur (Br.Sprgr. Patr.18 L'spur).	High-explosive incendiary (HEI) shell 18 with tracer.
Minengranatenpatreone 18 mit Leuchtspur (Mgr. Patr. 18 L'spur).	Mine (HEI) shell 18 with tracer.
Hartkernpanzergranatenpatrone[802] mit Leuchtspur ohne Zerleger (H-Pzgr. Patr. L'spur o. Zerl.).	High-velocity Armor penetrating (HVAP) shell 18 with tracer without self-destruct.
Panzergranatenpatrone 18 mit Leuchtspur.	Armor penetrating high-explosive (APHE) shell 18 with tracer.

---

[801] Although the steel penetrated was fashioned out of "Wolfram" (Tungsten), the original source referred to it as a steel core.
[802] Sometimes also known as "Hochgeschwindigkeitpanzergranatenpatrone".

Reference Figures for 3.7 cm Sprgr. Patr. 18

G_G	=	0.635 kg[803]
V_0	=	820 m/s
Volumetric displacement	=	1.2255 kg [sic!][804]

Distance m	Vertical lead /6400	Flight time S	Velocity m/s	Drop m
0	0	0	820	0
100	0.7	0.12	786	0.07
200	1.4	0.25	752	0.27
300	2.2	0.39	719	0.65
400	3.1	0.53	687	1.20
500	4.1	0.68	654	2.00
600	5.2	0.84	623	3.05
700	6.3	1.00	592	4.35
800	7.6	1.18	563	5.95
900	8.9	1.36	534	7.85
1000	10.3	1.55	506	10.10
1100	11.9	1.76	480	12.85
1200	13.5	1.97	454	15.90
1300	15.1	2.20	430	19.25
1400	16.8	2.44	408	23.05
1500	18.5	2.69	388	27.20

Based on LDV – 500/862

---

[803] Projectile weight.
[804] kg/m^3

Preliminary Reference Figures for the Special-P-Shell of the 3.7 cm B.K.

3.7 cm H.-Pzgr. Patr.

G_G	=	400 g
V_0	=	1170 m/s
Volumetric displacement	=	1.2255 kg/m³
Rated distance	=	937 m

X m	φ min	V m/s	T S	Y_s m	W mkg
0	0	1170	0	0	2800
100	1.3'	1122	0.087	0.01	2560
200	2.6'	1074	0.179	0.04	2360
300	4.0'	1028	0.274	0.09	2150
400	5.5'	982	0.374	0.17	1965
500	7.0'	937	0.478	0.28	1790
600	8.7'	893	0.587	0.42	1660
700	10.6'	849	0.702	0.61	1475
800	12.7'	810	0.815	0.82	1340
900	14.9'	766	0.950	1.11	1200
1000	17.2'	726	1.084	1.45	1080

Calculation based on Siacci III

3.7cm Br. Sprgr. Patr. 18 L'spur

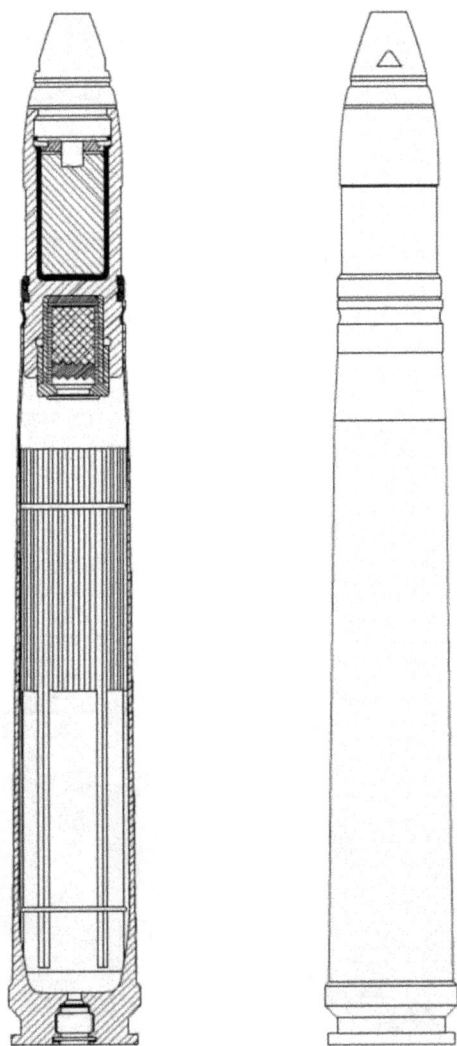

3.7cm Mgr. Patr. 18 L'spur

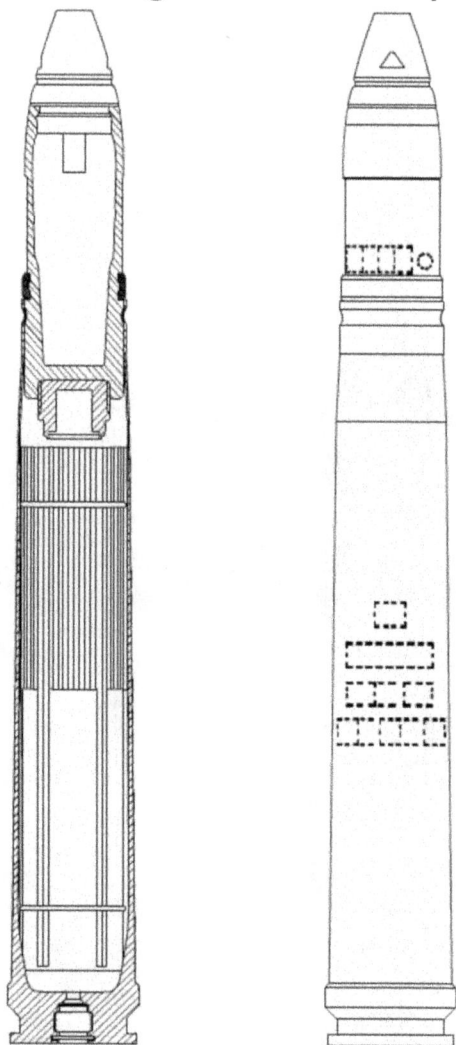

3.7cm H-Pzgr. Patr. L'spur o. Zerl.

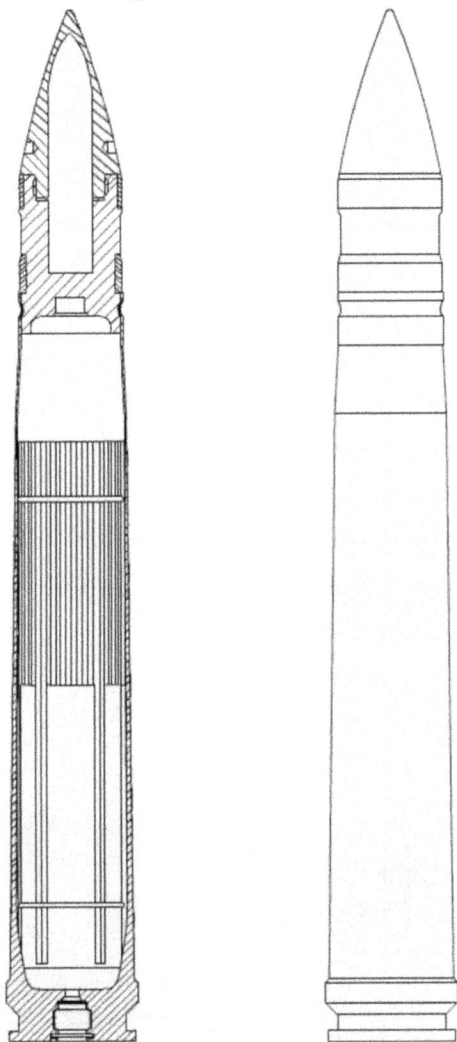

3.7cm Pzgr. Patr. 18 L'spur

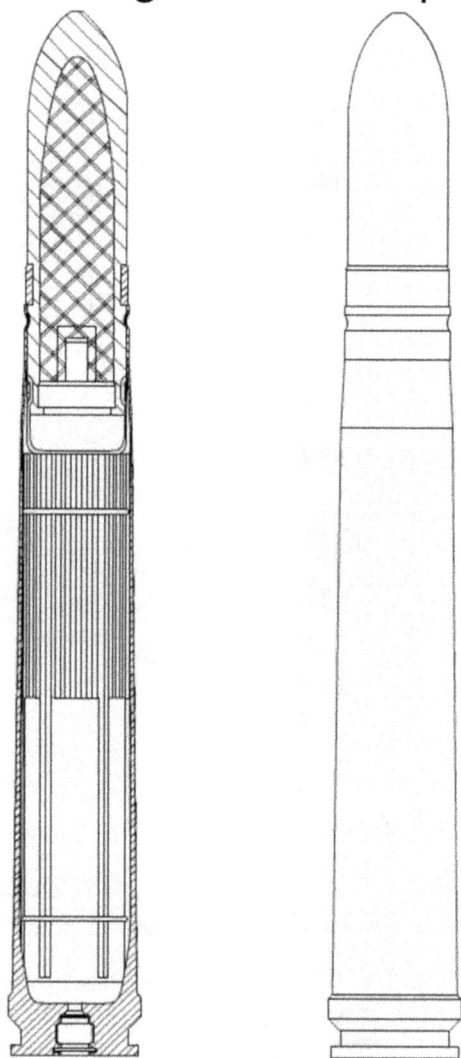

CHAPTER V
Glossary and Bibliography

Glossary

AA-defenses - light, medium and heavy (leichte, mittlere und schwere Flak): During the Second World War, anti-air (AA)-defenses were used to defend an area against air attack. These tended to be point defenses, only able to engage enemy aircraft within a limited range bubble. While different nations used different calibers and had their own definitions, nowadays these are commonly broken down into three categories of light (incl. light-machineguns around the 7.7 or 7.92mm and calibers of up to roughly 2 cm), medium (between 3-5 cm) and heavy defenses (7 cm upwards). Famous examples include:

- Light-AA: Soviet 7.62 mm Maxim, German 2cm Flak 38, Swiss 2 cm Oerlikon.
- Medium-AA: Soviet 3.7cm M1939 (61-K), Swedish 4 cm Bofors.
- Heavy-AA: German 8.8 cm Flak 18/36/37.

Interestingly, the following definitions from the German *Handbook of Contemporary Military Studies* from 1939, quoting the 1937 publication *Our AA-Defenses* by Pickert only identify two types: light and heavy. This is in-line with the designations of the German Army, which before the war also used mainly light and heavy, but not medium for the various weapons designations like machine guns, infantry support guns, etc. It should be remembered that this definition was not necessarily followed during the war, but it does find itself reflected in the Document: *Pamphlet on Attacking AA-Defenses with Bombers*.

Light-AA: "The task of the light-AA is to defend against low-altitude attacks and combatting enemy aircraft at close ranges. Light-AA are rapidly firing automatic weapons of smaller calibers, 2 - 4 cm. Light-AA is especially effective against low-flying aircraft and at close ranges, but can still be effective, at altitudes up to 1 500 – 2 000 m depending on the caliber."[805] Machine guns were included in a separate entry from light-AA.[806] Light AA- calibers also included guns from 2 cm up to 6 cm in a separate entry.[807]

Heavy-AA: "The task of the heavy-AA is to combat enemy aircraft at high altitudes and long range. Heavy-AA guns are weapons with a caliber of 7.5 cm or

---

[805] Hermann Franke (ed.), *Handbuch der neuzeitlichen Wehrwissenschaften – Dritter Band 2. Die Luftwaffe*, Walter de Gruyter & Co, Berlin, Germany, 1939, p. 56.

[806] Hermann Franke (ed.), *Handbuch der neuzeitlichen Wehrwissenschaften – Dritter Band 2. Die Luftwaffe*, Walter de Gruyter & Co, Berlin, Germany, 1939, p. 58.

[807] Hermann Franke (ed.), *Handbuch der neuzeitlichen Wehrwissenschaften – Dritter Band 2. Die Luftwaffe*, Walter de Gruyter & Co, Berlin, Germany, 1939, p. 58.

above. Usually collected in batteries of 4 guns, they work in conjunction with a ballistic director[808]. For ammunition they are equipped with shells that detonate after a set time due to a time-delay fuze."[809]

Another Luftwaffe instructional publication from 1940 mirrors this approach, equally classifying 2 cm and 3.7 cm AA-guns into the same light category, albeit with the concession of symbolizing these differently in visualizations.[810] Although this splits AA-guns into only two categories, this definition was not necessarily a given at the time or in Germany. For one in this book the term "medium" AA also appears in the *Mission Reports* and in *The Pamphlet on Night-Bombing with the Ju 87*, showing that it certainly was used at the time.

A 1923 definition from the German Army (Reichswehr[811]) in the important *H.Dv. 487: Command and Combat of Combined Arms (H.Dv. 487: Führung und Gefecht der verbundenen Waffen)* regulation also already includes three categories, light, medium and heavy. It is interesting to note that the mobility of medium AA-defenses and their ability to be rapidly moved from one place to another appears to factor into the classification: "From the AA-guns of medium caliber the horse-drawn variants is used due to its low stature in the frontal areas, and the motorized AA-guns due to their high mobility especially in a war of movement."[812] Another notice on the usage of medium AA-guns by the German Army from 1944 provides further information: "With light and medium weapons, the order to fire is given only after the target has flown into effective range (with 2 cm AA 1 200 m, with 3.7 cm AA 2 000m distance)."[813]

---

[808] See Glossary: Ballistic director (Kommandogerät).

[809] Hermann Franke (ed.), *Handbuch der neuzeitlichen Wehrwissenschaften – Dritter Band 2. Die Luftwaffe*, Walter de Gruyter & Co, Berlin, Germany, 1939, p. 56.

[810] Hauptmann Dierich, *Der Flieger – Dienstunterricht in der Fliegertruppe, Handbücher der Luftwaffe*, E.S. Mittler & Sohn, Berlin, Germany, 1940, p. 13.

[811] The Reichswehr (1919-1935) was the predecessor of the Wehrmacht (1935-1945). It was the unified armed forces of the Weimar Republic. The main difference was that the Reichswehr had only two branches the Army and the Navy, whereas as the Wehrmacht had also the Air Force as a branch.

[812] *H.Dv. 487: Führung und Gefecht der verbundenen Waffen (F. u. G.) Abschnitt XII-XVIII*, Verlag "Offene Worte", Berlin, Germany, 1923, p. 29.

[813] BArch, RH 12-2/162, *Entwicklung und Verwendung von Fliegerabwehr-Waffen der Infanterie*, Generalstab des Heeres, General Heeres-Flak, *Munitionseinsatz aller Flakgeschütze*, H.Qu., 29. December 1944, p. 57.

Aiming point / reference point (Haltepunkt): The aiming point is the spot (on the target) that aligns with the sight radius in the moment of the bomb drop. It can be influenced by the construction or the movement of the target.[814]

Air signal units (Luftnachrichtentruppe): This unit is responsible for "maintaining the many connections between the bases of the ground operations (command positions, airstrips and aerodromes) in both peace and war. It has a variety of special tasks like ground-air and air-air communications, air traffic control and flight reporting."[815]

Aircraft-class (Flugzeugklasse): During the Second World War, the Luftwaffe defined an aircraft's class typically by its carrying capacity. These classes are also reflected in the pilot licenses. The following is a listing of the original classes, as set out in 1940[816]:

Land-based aircraft (Examples for training aircraft in paratheses[817]):

- class A 1: Aircraft for one person with an all-up weight of up to 500 kg,
- class A 2: Aircraft with a crew of one to three with an all-up weight of up to 1 000 kg, provided they do not belong to class A 1,
- class B 1: Aircraft with a crew of one to four with an all-up weight of 1 000 to 2 500 kg,
- class B 2: Aircraft with a crew of one to eight with an all-up weight of 2 500 to 5 000 kg,
- class C: Aircraft with an all-up weight higher than 5 000 kg.

Seaplane:

- class A 1: Aircraft with an all-up weight up to 600 kg,
- class A 2: Aircraft with an all-up weight up to 2 200 kg,
- class B 1: Aircraft with an all-up weight up to 5 500 kg,
- class B 2: Aircraft with an all-up weight higher than 5 500 kg.

---

[814] See *L.Dv. 20/2: Luftwaffe Regulation 20/2 - Guidelines for Dive-Bombing Training.*
[815] Hermann Franke (ed.), *Handbuch der neuzeitlichen Wehrwissenschaften - Dritter Band 2. Die Luftwaffe*, Walter de Gruyter & Co, Berlin, Germany, 1939, p. 255.
[816] Hauptmann Dierich, *Der Flieger - Dienstunterricht in der Fliegertruppe, Handbücher der Luftwaffe*, E.S. Mittler & Sohn, Berlin, Germany, 1940, p. 63-64.
[817] All examples from Barry Ketley; Mark Rofle, *Luftwaffe Training Units & their Aircraft*, Hikoki Publications, Aldershot, UK, 1996, p. 11.

Airdrome operation company (Flughafenbetriebskompanien): A unit running the day-to-day activities of an airdrome. It provides administrative and maintenance assistance to aerial units based at the same airdrome.

Altitude – low, medium and high (niedrige, mittlere und große Höhe): Exact definitions can vary. One German handbook from 1939 defines "high altitude flights" as starting at 5 000 m, although "high altitude attacks" are defined as being between 4 000 – 7 000 m. Equally, no clear definition is given for low and medium altitudes, although "low altitude attacks" appear to be implied to start below 2 000 m.[818] The margin between low and high altitudes can by implication be considered medium altitudes.

ata: Stands for "absolute technische atmosphäre" and often translated as "absolute technical atmosphere". It is an outdated pressure unit used during the Second World War. It equals the absolute pressure starting at a vacuum, measured in kgf/cm^2. A measurement of 1.0 equals roughly 1 bar. This would indicate the standard atmospheric pressure. We have retained this unit as most readers of Second World War aviation history and German aircraft will be familiar with it, and because any conversion into another measurement unit would be both confusing and have the potential of producing an error.

atü: Stands for "technische atmosphäre überdruck" and it can be translated as "gauge pressure". It is an outdated pressure unit used during the Second World War. It equals the measurement of ata minus 1 to account for the standard atmospheric pressure of 1 kgf/cm^2. As such, if ata equals 3, atü equals 2 indicating that the pressure is 2 kgf/cm^2 above the standard atmospheric pressure of 1kgf/cm^2. We have retained this unit as most readers of Second World War aviation history and German aircraft will be familiar with it, and because any conversion into another measurement unit would be both confusing and have the potential of producing an error.

Ballistic director (Kommandogerät): The ballistic director directs the lead angle, elevation and fuze delay of AA-guns under its command based on the input of data from observers. [819] Note the literal translation of "Kommandogerät" would be "command device".

---

[818] Hermann Franke (ed.), *Handbuch der neuzeitlichen Wehrwissenschaften – Dritter Band 2. Die Luftwaffe,* Walter de Gruyter & Co, Berlin, Germany, 1939, p. 193-317.

[819] Hermann Franke (ed.), *Handbuch der neuzeitlichen Wehrwissenschaften – Dritter Band 2. Die Luftwaffe,* Walter de Gruyter & Co, Berlin, Germany, 1939, p. 59.

(Battlefield) Air interdiction: As described in *Aerial Tactics – The Dive-Bomber*, the main targets of the Ju 87s lay beyond the front lines. Overlapping with those of the bombers, the Ju 87s were also to be used against staging grounds, columns, stockpiles, infrastructure and transportation. Overall, the Luftwaffe made a distinction between operations on the "Gefechtsfeld" (battlefield – also Hauptgefechtsfeld, main battlefield) which ranged to about 30 km from the front lines, and the "Taktischer Raum" (tactical area) which extended to about 100 km[820]. It was within the latter that the main weight of effort of the Ju 87 was envisioned. This has some parallels to the contemporary concept of Battlefield Air Interdiction.

While commonly used as term to describe air attacks behind the front lines, air interdiction (AI) as a concept is ill-defined and continues to be described in fluid terms. For example, in the US Department of Defense *Dictionary of Military and Associated Terms* from August 2021, interdiction is generally defined as: "An action to divert, disrupt, delay, or destroy the enemy's military surface capability before it can be used effectively against friendly forces, or to achieve enemy objectives."[821] It further refers to *Joint Publication JP 3-09.3 Close Air Support* from November 2014[822] for air interdiction. The same referral to JP 3-03 is made in the entry for close air support (CAS).

In JP 3-09.3, the avid reader is then presented not with a straight definition but with a further referral to *Allied Joint Publication-3.3.2 Air Interdiction and Close Air Support*[823] and *Allied Tactical Publication-3.3.2.1(C) TTP for Close Air Support and Air Interdiction.*[824] The former includes the following definition: "Air Interdiction: Air operations conducted to destroy, neutralize, or delay the enemy's military potential before it can be brought to bear effectively against friendly forces at such distance from friendly forces that detailed integration of each air mission with the fire and movement of friendly forces is not required (AAP-6)."[825] In the latter, AI is not defined but generically described as: "a mission scheduled to

---

[820] See for example BArch, RL 2-II/157, Bd. 4 Bericht Wehrmachtsmanöver (Luftwaffe) 1937.

[821] DoD, *Dictionary of Military and Associated Terms*, August 2021, p. 109.

[822] *Joint Publication JP 3-09.3, Close Air Support*, November 2014.

[823] *Allied Joint Publication-3.3.2 Air Interdiction and Close Air Support.*

[824] NATO, *ATP-3.3.2.1, Tactics, Techniques and Procedures for Close Air Support and Air Interdiction*, Edition D, Version 1, April 2019, Unclassified, Chapter 6: Air Interdiction.

[825] NATO, *ATP-27(C) / AJP-3.3.2, Air Interdiction and Close Air Support*, June 1999, Unclassified.

strike particular targets in response to Joint force Commander or component target nominations."[826]

Furthermore, it includes a description of different mission sets: ground alert air interdiction (GAI), armed reconnaissance (XAI) and strike coordination and reconnaissance (SCAR), with targets falling into two classes: deliberate (e.g., known to exist) and dynamic (e.g., late identification or not previously included in target set, either anticipated or unanticipated).

Bomb release speed (Auslösegeschwindigkeit): The speed of the aircraft at the moment the bomb is released.[827]

Bomb score record (Wurfbuch): Used to record the bomb scores of trainee (dive-)bomber pilots during bombing exersises. It becomes property of the pilot and can be considered his official certificate. A copy of his bombing record is kept in the bomb score notebook, which is kept by the Staffel.

Bomber (Kampfflugzeug/ Kampfflieger): A German definition from 1939 described bombers in the following manner: "Bombers attack critical enemy installations, the supply and reinforcements of men and material, the industrial centers and strength reserves of the enemy, as well as the enemy's air force and navy. Their primary task is to shatter the targets psychological and material resistance. Their goal is the destruction of the attacked object."[828] In the same handbook, bombers are classed into three generic sub-categories: medium bombers (twin-engine), heavy bombers (four-engine) and dive-bombers. [829]

For "Kampfflieger", see Glossary: Unit type.

Bomber Geschwader (Kampfgeschwader): A bomber Geschwader is the largest organizational unit of bombers. The authorized strength of a bomber Geschwader was 117 aircraft including reserves and command flights, made up of three bomber Gruppen each with three bomber Staffeln (12 aircraft incl. reserves).[830]

---

[826] NATO ATP-3.3.2.1, *Tactics, Techniques and Procedures for Close Air Support and Air Interdiction*, Edition D, Version 1, April 2019, Unclassified, Chapter 6: Air Interdiction.

[827] See *L.Dv. 20/2: Luftwaffe Regulation 20/2 – Guidelines for Dive-Bombing Training.*

[828] Hermann Franke (ed.), *Handbuch der neuzeitlichen Wehrwissenschaften – Dritter Band 2. Die Luftwaffe*, Walter de Gruyter & Co, Berlin, Germany, 1939, p. 108.

[829] Hermann Franke (ed.), *Handbuch der neuzeitlichen Wehrwissenschaften – Dritter Band 2. Die Luftwaffe*, Walter de Gruyter & Co, Berlin, Germany, 1939, p. 108-109.

[830] See *Compendium for the Education at the Air-War Colleges – Aerial Tactics: The Dive-Bomber.*

Bomb score notebook (Wurfkladde): A notebook used to record the bomb scores of trainee pilots. This record is kept by the Staffel and thus differentiates itself with the bomb score record which becomes property of the pilot and acts as his bombing certificate.

Bomb setting device (Abwurfschaltkasten [ASK]): Allows the arming of bombers, as well as the setting of bomb drop sequences.

Bomb types (Bombenarten): During the Second World War, the Luftwaffe used various bomb types. Depending on bomb type, they were usually abbreviated with two letters, such as SD or PC. Alternative writing styles like S.D. or P.C. can be found. The number following the abbreviation, such as SD 50 indicate the weight of the bomb in kilograms, in this case 50 kg. This weight refers to the overall weight of the bomb, not the weight of the included explosive filler. The following is an overview of some of the bomb types found in the included documents.[831]

High explosive bombs:

- SC: High-explosive cylindrical general-purpose bomb (Sprengbombe cylindrisch): This bomb had an explosive filler that was roughly equivalent to 55% of the bombs total weight.[832] Sometimes referred to as mine bomb (Minenbombe) from 50 kg upwards.[833]
- SD: High-explosive thick-walled semi-armor piercing fragmentation bomb (Sprengbombe dickwandig): Due to increased thickness of the outer shell and a heavier nose, this bomb provides better fragmentation. Smaller bombs of 50 kg are considered primarily anti-personnel. A bomb was designed to have a greater shrapnel effect. Holds roughly 35% of its total weight as explosive filler.[834]

Armor piercing bombs:

---

[831] Hauptmann Dierich, *Der Flieger – Dienstunterricht in der Fliegertruppe, Handbücher der Luftwaffe,* E.S. Mittler & Sohn, Berlin, Germany, 1940, p. 119-130; and Wolfgang Thamm, *Fliegerbomben,* Bernard & Graefe Verlag, Bonn, Germany, 2003.

[832] OP 1966, *German Explosive Ordnance Vol. I: Bombs, Rockets, Grenades, Mines, Fuzes & Igniters,* Bureau of Ordnance, Washington D.C., USA, 11. June 1946 (Reprint 1966), p. 1.

[833] Hauptmann Dierich, *Der Flieger – Dienstunterricht in der Fliegertruppe, Handbücher der Luftwaffe,* E.S. Mittler & Sohn, Berlin: 1940, p. 119-130; and Wolfgang Thamm, *Fliegerbomben,* Bernard & Graefe Verlag, Bonn, Germany, 2003.

[834] OP 1966, *German Explosive Ordnance Vol. I: Bombs, Rockets, Grenades, Mines, Fuzes & Igniters,* Bureau of Ordnance, Washington D.C., 11. June 1946 (Reprint 1966), p. 1.

- PC: Armor-piercing cylindrical bomb (Panzersprengbombe cylindrisch): Germany's standard armor-piercing bomb, fuzed with a short delay. The explosive filler equals to roughly 20% of the overall weight.[835]

Note that while nowadays, the word cylindrical in German is written as "zylindrisch", the "C" in the abbreviations does in fact refer to the written style of "cylindrisch".

Circuit-breaker (Selbstschalter): A circuit-breaker is designed to "pop" to interrupt the flow of electrical power into a shorted circuit. In parallel, many circuit-breakers function as an on-off switch for the associated electrical system.

Circle (Lichtkreis): The outer circle as part of the sight picture shown on a reflector sight[836].

Close air support unit (Schlachtflieger): An ambiguous word typically used to describe close air support as a general unit type, but alternatively used for close air support aircraft, pilots or units. Defined as: "The Close Air Support unit is used directly in ground combat and supports friendly ground troops with MG-fire, bombs, napalm[837] and smoke. These low altitude attacks are especially effective due to their psychological nature on both enemy and friendly forces. The aim of the Close Air Support unit is to shake the enemy's resistance through repeated attacks, to distract him from his own combat tasks, and thus gain a decisive influence on the flow of the ground combat."[838] Note that the literal translation of "Schlachtflieger" is "battle aircraft/pilot".

For "Schlachtflieger", see also Glossary: Unit type.

Combat reconnaissance (Gefechtsaufklärer): A reconnaissance aircraft used to "recon the flight path and the target for the bombers". Also known as "Kampfaufklärer".[839] Doing so, it collects information on "weather conditions,

---

[835] OP 1966, *German Explosive Ordnance Vol. I: Bombs, Rockets, Grenades, Mines, Fuzes & Igniters*, Bureau of Ordnance, Washington D.C., 11. June 1946 (Reprint 1966), p. 2.

[836] See Glossary: Reflector sight (Reflexsvisier [Revi]).

[837] Note, meant here is a "Brandtank". The effect is similar to napalm.

[838] Hauptmann Dierich, *Der Flieger – Dienstunterricht in der Fliegertruppe, Handbücher der Luftwaffe*, E.S. Mittler & Sohn, Berlin, Germany, 1940, p. 8-9.

[839] Hermann Franke (ed.), *Handbuch der neuzeitlichen Wehrwissenschaften – Dritter Band 2. Die Luftwaffe*, Walter de Gruyter & Co, Berlin, Germany, 1939, p. 308.

enemy defenses and overwatch over mobile units already spotted by the tactical air reconnaissance".[840]

Command flight (Führungskette): The leading flight in a formation.

Company sergeant major (Hauptfeldwebel): In the Wehrmacht, the company sergeant major, often referred to as "Spieß" (literally "skewer") or "mother of the company", was not a rank but an appointment. The sergeant major's area of responsibility was the rear of the company. He mainly took care of the supply, such as work of the supply train, secretarial services a of all those tasks that were not directly related to combat.[841]

Concrete bombs (Zementbomben [Ze.-Bomben]): Practice bombs designed to simulate the weight (and feel) of real bombs for training purposes. Sometimes abbreviated ZC, these bombs were also extensively used by the German Reichswehr during their experiments at the Soviet training facility in Lipezk in the late 1920.[842] Note that a literal translation of "Zementbomben" would be "cement bombs".

Contact altimeter (Kontakthöhenmesser): The contact altimeter is a second altimeter carried in a Ju 87. It includes an additional indication dial, that can be manually set to a pre-determined altitude. Upon approaching this altitude, a horn will sound in the cockpit, alerting the pilot to the approaching drop altitude. The horn silences upon passing the set altitude, indicating that the bomb is to be dropped.[843]

Contact-fuze (Aufschlagzünder): A fuze designed to trigger on contact with another surface. When no delay is set, the bomb will explode on impact. A small delay can optionally be set, however the trigger mechanism still initiates the "countdown" on contact with a surface.[844] The contact-fuzes with delay were

---

[840] Hauptmann Dierich, *Der Flieger – Dienstunterricht in der Fliegertruppe, Handbücher der Luftwaffe*, E.S. Mittler & Sohn, Berlin, Germany, 1940, p. 11.

[841] Alex Buchner, *Das Handbuch der deutschen Infanterie 1939-1945*, Podzun-Pallas: Friedberg, 1987, p. 18-19.

[842] Wolfgang Thamm, *Fliegerbomben*, Bernard & Graefe Verlag, Bonn, Germany, 2003, p. 114-116, 150.

[843] Junkers, *Ju 87 B-2 Betriebsanleitung, Hauptabschnitt 90, Ausrüstung-Allgemeines*, June 1940, p. 12-13; and Junkers, Ju 87 B-2 Betriebsanleitung, Hauptabschnitt 10, Flugbetrieb, June 1940, p. 25.

[844] Hauptmann Dierich, *Der Flieger – Dienstunterricht in der Fliegertruppe, Handbücher der Luftwaffe*, E.S. Mittler & Sohn, Berlin, Germany, 1940, p. 124-130.

called "Aufschlagzünder mit Verzögerung / AZ m.V." and without delay "Aufschlagzünder ohne Verzögerung / AZ o.V.".

Courier aircraft (Reiseflugzeug): An aircraft used primarily for liaison or moving high-ranking personnel from one point to the other.

Direction-finding equipment (Peilgerät): Used in conjunction with a radio compass or similar instrument, directional-finding equipment used radio signals from a radio transmitter. A receiver in the plane allowed the pilot to navigate towards the transmitter. Such radio beacons are commonly used to allow pilots to find their way to an aerodrome.[845]

Dive-bomber squadron, group and wing (Sturzkampfstaffel, -gruppe, -geschwader): There is some difficulty in establishing a correct translation for the German unit designations of "Staffel", "Gruppe" and "Geschwader", as the corresponding units of the Allied Air Forces differ between them in both size and designation. For example, the U.S. Army Air Force (USAAF) used a slightly different naming system to the Royal Air Force (RAF) Bomber Command. At the same time, the official *U.S. Army German-English Military Dictionary TM 30-506*[846] from 1945 differs in its translations to the USAAF equivalents but corresponds with one exception to the naming hierarchy of the RAF.

The usual U.S. American styled translation, still used today, appears to be Flight for "Staffel", Squadron for "Gruppe", Group for "Geschwader" and with no German equivalent to Wing.[847] There continuous to be no standardization, even nowadays within NATO, with RAF or other Air Force designations, where these terms could correspond to completely different unit sizes both past and present.[848] Additionally, there is also the risk of linguistic confusion due to the German "Gruppe" and English "group".

In the Luftwaffe, a "Staffel" was the smallest organizational unit within a dive-bomber unit. As can be seen in *Aerial Tactics – The Dive-Bomber*[849], it has an authorized strength of 9 aircraft, or 12 including reserves. Three "Staffeln" would

---

[845] War Department, A.A.F Form No. 24, *Pilots' Information File 1944*, republished by Schiffer Military History Book, Atglen, PA, USA, 1995, PIF 2-14-5.

[846] *TM 30-506, German Military Dictionary: German-English, English-German*, War Department, May 1944, p. 75, 80, 95, 174.

[847] As appears on Wikipedia, *Wing (military unit)*, available at: https://en.wikipedia.org/wiki/Wing_(military_unit) (last accessed 07.11.2021).

[848] See for example: AFI 38-101, *Manpower and Organization*, United States Air Force e-publishing, 29. August 2019, p. 85; and RAF, *How We Are Organised*, available at: https://www.raf.mod.uk/our-organisation/overview/ (last accessed 12.02.2022).

[849] See *Aerial Tactics: The Dive-Bomber*.

form a Gruppe which, together with the command flight, had 30 aircraft, or 39 including reserves. Three "Gruppen" on the other hand made up a "Geschwader", the largest independent unit. Together with the command flight, the authorized strength was 93 aircraft.[850]

Taking the Luftwaffe and USAAF designations, we find a general overlap in corresponding unit size. Taking a Luftwaffe dive-bomber unit (Ju 87 incl. reserves) and USAAF Light Bombardment Group (A-20, or A-26, incl. reserves) as our main examples. Additionally, we have also added the RAF (Bomber Command) and the translation of TM 30-506 to illustrate the different nomenclatures.

Luftwaffe		TM-30 506	USAAF	
	a/c			a/c
Kette[851]	3	Flight	Element	3
Staffel	12	Squadron	Flight	2+ Elements
Gruppe	39	Group	Squadron	24
Geschwader	120	Wing	Group	96
			Wing	2+ Groups

Note that this breakdown uses the authorized strength **with reserves** of a German Sturzkampfgeschwader, as well as the authorized strength **with reserves** with the assumption of having four squadrons in a Light Bombardment Group.[852]

Luftwaffe		RAF (Bomber)	
	a/c		a/c
Kette[853]	3	Flight	3
Staffel	12	Squadron	16 – 24
Gruppe	39	Group	2+ Squadrons
Geschwader	120		
		Command	Made up by Groups

Note that this breakdown uses the authorized strength **with reserves** of a German Sturzkampfgeschwader, as well as the usual strength of a bomber unit within RAF Bomber Command (1942).[854]

---

[850] See Aerial Tactics: The Dive-Bomber.

[851] See Glossary: Flight (Kette).

[852] See Aerial Tactics: The Dive-Bomber, and Office of Statistical Control, Army Air Forces Statistical Digest: World War 2, December 1945, p. 1; and Maurer Maurer, Air Force Combat Units of World War 2, Office of Air force History, Washington D.C., USA, 1983; Army Air Forces Aid Society, The Official Guide to Army Air Forces, Bonanza Books, New York, 1988, p.260, 267-268; and William Wolf, The Douglas A-20 Havoc, Schiffer Publishing, Atglen, PA, USA, 2015, p. 220-233, 492-494.

[853] See Glossary: Flight (Kette).

[854] See Compendium for the Education at the Air-War Colleges – Aerial Tactics: The Dive-Bomber, and Organization circulars contained in TNA, AIR 14/1107, 1942.

332

Although perhaps not fully corresponding for the mission set, the light bombardment group and "Sturzkampfgeschwader" are perhaps the closest approximations of unit types considering their mission sets and payload. A fighter group, potentially deployed as a fighter-bomber unit, would be made up of 111-126 aircraft with reserves[855]. This would be another possible comparison.

This shows how difficult a translation for these terms is, as they carry an inherent expectation of unit size depending on purpose and origin, as well as a pre-set structural hierarchy. Consequently, this book uses the German designations to prevent confusion between different nations. The reader is invited to bookmark this page or the relevant pages in the Chapter *Aerial Tactics*, in the Introduction or in the Glossary, should repeated referencing be required.

Dive position (Sturzansatzposition): From our research, this appears to be simply a different term for the diving point (Abkipppunkt).[856] Literally translated "Sturzansatzposition" means "dive approach position".

Dive-recovery system (Abfangvorrichtung): "The purpose of the dive-recovery system is to neutralize the [starboard] elevator trim, which was set when the dive-brakes were deployed, after the bombs have been released, in order to initiate dive-recovery."[857]

While the dive-recovery system assists the pilot in pulling out of the dive, the aircraft does require manual control input to fully recover. During this pull-out, a control limiter prevents the pilot from over-pulling on the stick (maximum pull ~5°). This prevents the aircraft from exceeding the maximum load factor (n = 6). An emergency deflection of up to 13° is possible.[858]

In later iterations of the Ju 87, the control limiter was removed. The dive-recovery system was no longer coupled to the bomb release, activating instead on an additional control input, from the D-5 onwards.[859]

---

[855] Office of Statistical Control, *Army Air Forces Statistical Digest: World War 2*, December 1945, p. 1.
[856] See Glossary: Diving point (Abkipppunkt).
[857] Junkers, *Kurz-Betriebsanleitung Ju 87 B-2 Teil II Flugbetrieb*, June 1940, p. 12.
[858] Junkers, *Kurz-Betriebsanleitung Ju 87 B-2 Teil II Flugbetrieb*, June 1940, p. 12-13.
[859] Werkschrift 2087, *Ju 87 D-1 bis D-8, G-1, G-2, H-1 bis H-8, Bedienungsvorschrfit-Fl Teil II Flugbetrieb*, February 1944, p. 14-15.

Diving point (Abkipppunkt): The point at which a dive is initiated. In practical terms, this can be a landmark, easily identified from higher altitudes. [860] Literally translated "Abkipppunkt" means "tipping position".

Echelon (Reihe): An echelon is a formation by which aircraft are individually formed up in a diagonal line to the left or right of the lead aircraft. This could also include a vertical stagger and is thus not necessarily synonymous with a line abreast or line astern.[861]

Employment of the whole unit (Einsatz, geschlossen): The term "geschlossener Einsatz"[862] is often used in German regulations of the Second World War. To employ a unit as "geschlossen", means to employ its tactical elements together, see the following examples for infantry (1944) and tanks (1941 and 1943):

"As a rule, the SMG-platoon should be used as a whole. The use of the individual SMG-squads is the exception."[863]

"The medium tank company with its 14 vehicle-mounted guns (7.5 cm) forms the backbone of the tank battalion[864]. This strong firepower must be brought - in general by employing the unit as a whole - quickly to a decisive point and applied for destructive effect."[865]

"The employment as a whole company [in forests and mountains] is the exception. As a rule, half-platoons or individual vehicles will support the attacking riflemen."[866]

---

[860] See L.Dv. 20/2: Luftwaffe Regulation 20/2 – Guidelines for Dive-Bombing Training.

[861] Hermann Franke (ed.), Handbuch der neuzeitlichen Wehrwissenschaften – Dritter Band 2. Die Luftwaffe, Walter de Gruyter & Co, Berlin, Germany, 1939, p. 312.

[862] The literal translation of "geschlossener Einsatz" would be "closed employment".

[863] BArch, RH 11-I/83, Merkblatt 25a/16: Vorläufiges Merkblatt "Der M.P.-Zug der Grenadier-Kompanie", 1. February 1944, p. 15.

[864] In the German Army, units of some arms (like tanks, artillery, etc.) with the strength of a battalion, were called "Abteilung" (literally detachment/department) not "Bataillone" (battalions).

[865] H.Dv. 470/7: Ausbildungsvorschrift für die Panzertruppe. Heft 7: Die mittlere Panzerkompanie, Reichsdruckerei, Berlin, Germany, 1. Mai 1941, p. 5.

[866] H.Dv. 470/7: Die mittlere Panzerkompanie, p. 68.

"In the defense, keep the vehicles covered and together at minimum at a platoon strength, so that they, manned by the driver and gunner, can effectively take up the hasty counterattack[867]."[868]

But this term was also used in orders from the High Command of the Wehrmacht (OKW):

"The following guidelines apply for the employment:
a) The Luftwaffe-field brigades are to be employed as a whole. The units must not be torn apart."[869]

One problem is that we have not yet found a suitable English translation for "geschlossener Einsatz". In our translation of the *H.Dv. 470/7* we had decided after a long back and forth for "combined employment". We now think that this is wrong, because "combined" implies the combination of several different elements. We exchanged views with several people on the subject, for example Leo Niehorster suggested "massed employment".[870] This would also be in line with *Field Manual 17-32: The Tank Company, Light and Medium* of August 1942, which states with regard to the use in the jungle:

"In general, because of their sensitiveness to terrain, tanks are unsuited for mass employment in jungles."[871]

However, this created another problem because "massive employment" is also used - albeit less frequently - in German regulations, pointing to the concentrated employment of troops at a certain point.

In English "negative definitions" are common, for example:

---

[867] The Germans distinguished between a hasty counterattack ("Gegenstoß") and regular counterattack ("Gegenangriff"). The first was performed with local reserves and immediately, whereas was a planned attack with stronger support.

[868] TsAMO, F 500, Op. 12480, D 137: *Nachrichtenblatt der Panzertruppen. Nr. 1*, 15. Juli 1943, p. 10.

[869] Percy E. Schramm (ed.), *Kriegstagebuch des OKW. Eine Dokumentation: 1942. Band 4. Teilband 2*, Bechtermünz, Augsburg, Germany, 2005, p. 1299. Anlage 24: Führerbefehl vom 13. September 1942 betr. Ablösung abgekämpfter Divisionen aus dem Osten.

[870] Email Leo Niehorster from 28. July 2020.

[871] *FM 17-32: Armored Force Field Manual: The Tank Company, Light and Medium*, War Department, Washington, USA, August 1942, p. 77.

"They [larger units of the Armored Force] are to be employed on decisive missions. They must not be frittered away."[872]

"Tank attacks will be costly or will result in failure to reach their objective unless employed in decisive numbers."[873]

"The piecemeal employment of tank units is wrong; they must be used in large numbers in a coordinated effort. "[874]

Other alternatives that we have considered were:

- Unified employment: The problem here is that a unit is already "unified".
- Cohesive employment: Similar problem as with "unified employment".
- Closed employment: This could easily be confused with "close order" (geschlossene Ordnung) and is not very descriptive.
- Non-piecemeal employment: Is a "negative-definition".

Based on this, we have decided to translate "geschlossener Einsatz" with "employment of the whole unit" or "employing the unit as a whole", which is not without a certain irony.

Evaluation notebook (Auswertekladde): A notebook used to evaluate the scores of trainee pilots. After evaluation, the information is transcribed into the bomb score notebook and bomb score record.

Fighter unit (Jagdflieger): An ambiguous word typically used to describe single-engine fighters as a general unit type, but alternatively used for fighter aircraft, pilots or units. See also Glossary: Unit type.

As a unit type, it "maintains together with the AA-defenses the air defense. Its use is possible in

1. The operational area to combat the enemy fighter force, to establish air superiority over a limited area, for a limited time. Additionally, it protects the friendly ground and reconnaissance forces from enemy air attacks.

---

[872] *FM 17-10: Armored Force Field Manual: Tactics and Technique,* War Department, Washington, USA, March 1942, p. 3.

[873] *FM 17-10: Armored Force Field Manual: Tactics and Technique,* War Department, Washington, USA, March 1942, p. 90.

[874] *FM 17-10: Armored Force Field Manual: Tactics and Technique,* War Department, Washington, USA, March 1942, p. 131.

2. Over friendly [home] territory, where it is used against enemy reconnaissance and bomber units together with the AA defenses."[875]

Filter center (Flugwachkommando): A post that is part of the air defense network, used to collect, plot and track incoming and outgoing aircraft. Literally translated "Flugwachkommando" means "air guard command".

Flight (Kette): A formation of three aircraft, typically set in a Vic formation with one leading aircraft, and two aircraft, set individually to either side of the leader.[876]

Flight line astern (Kettenkolone): A formation in which two or more flights are arranged in a single or staggered line astern. Can also be known as Staffelkolonne or Gruppenkolonne or larger formations of a whole squadron or group.[877]

Freya device (Freya-Gerät): The ground-based Freya radar system was one of the most common radars used by the Germans next to Würzburg radar. Its role was providing early warning, while later one it also assisted the Luftwaffe in directing fighters towards incoming bombers. "At the beginning of the Second World War there were a total of eight Freya systems in operation, stationed on a handful of islands in the North Sea. [...] Having a range out to about 80km, due to a shortage of other types, these were also used for directing flak batteries and for fighter direction. These systems saw constant improvements to their range and accuracy.

In addition, variants of the FuMG 43 'Freya-Fahrstuhl' (Freya Elevator) saw operational service. "[878]

The Freya-Fahrstuhl had various advantages over the earlier types, as the antennas could be moved vertically. "The 'Freya-Fahrstuhl' consisted of the radar receiver antenna form a Freya radar, which could be raised and lowered at

---

[875] Hauptmann Dierich, *Der Flieger – Dienstunterricht in der Fliegertruppe, Handbücher der Luftwaffe*, E.S. Mittler & Sohn, Berlin, Germany, 1940, p. 6.

[876] Hauptmann Dierich, *Der Flieger – Dienstunterricht in der Fliegertruppe, Handbücher der Luftwaffe*, E.S. Mittler & Sohn, Berlin, Germany, 1940, p. 168.

[877] Hauptmann Dierich, *Der Flieger – Dienstunterricht in der Fliegertruppe, Handbücher der Luftwaffe*, E.S. Mittler & Sohn, Berlin, Germany, 1940, p. 170-171; and Hermann Franke (ed.), Handbuch der neuzeitlichen Wehrwissenschaften – Dritter Band 2. Die Luftwaffe, Walter de Gruyter & Co, Berlin, Germany, 1939, p. 312.

[878] Werner Müller, *Ground Radar Systems of the Luftwaffe*, Schiffer Publishing Ltd. Atglen, PA, USA, 1998, p. 3, 34, 35, 38.

will up and down its two masts. In doing so, it prevented the disappearance of approaching targets flying at high altitude "[879]

Additionally, some Freya radars also included an IFF antennas. It is noteworthy that Freya antennas were also installed in radar systems that carried a different name like "Wassermann" (literally translating into "water man") or "Mammut" (literally translating into "mammoth").[880]

The name Freya originates from the Norse goddess, translating into Old Norse as "lady".[881]

Fuze setting device (Zünderschaltkasten): Allows the setting of the fuze for horizontal or diving bomb drops, as well as the inclusion of a time delay.

German Armed Forces (Wehrmacht): The Wehrmacht was the German unified armed forces from 1935 to 1945, composed out of the three branches, namely the German Army (Heer), German Air Force (Luftwaffe) and German Navy (Kriegsmarine). Be aware that there were other armed organizations as well throughout the war like the Waffen-SS or the Reichs Labor Service (Reichsarbeitsdienst) that were not part of the Wehrmacht.

German Army (Heer): The German Army was, next to the Luftwaffe (German Air Force) and Kriegsmarine (German Navy), one of the three branches of the Wehrmacht. The German Army (Heer) is often confused with the Wehrmacht. The Wehrmacht however was the armed forces as a whole, composed out of the three branches, namely the German Army, German Air Force and German Navy.

German Navy (Kriegsmarine): The German Navy was, next to the Heer (German Army) and Luftwaffe (German Air Force), one of the three branches of the Wehrmacht. The literal translation of "Kriegsmarine" is "War Navy", in contrast to "Handelsmarine" which literally translates to "Trade Navy".

General-purpose aircraft (Mehrzweckflugzeug [Mz.-]): A navalized aircraft used for "the protection of friendly naval units against air attack, for reconnaissance over large areas of open sea and for independent combat

---

[879] Werner Müller, *Ground Radar Systems of the Luftwaffe*, Schiffer Publishing Ltd. Atglen, PA, USA, 1998, p. 38.

[880] Werner Müller, *Ground Radar Systems of the Luftwaffe*, Schiffer Publishing Ltd. Atglen, PA, USA, 1998, p. 40-41.

[881] The Editors of Encyclopedia Britannica, *Freyja - Norse mythology*, Encyclopedia Britannica, available at https://www.britannica.com/topic/Freyja (last accessed 14.11.2021).

duties."[882] Typically equipped with fixed forward weaponry, and the ability to carry a limited number of bombs or a torpedo. Also used for fire direction.[883]

Glide (Gleitflug): The glide is a controlled, oftentimes unpowered flight: "The glide is usually used to maneuver the aircraft from the gained into a lower altitude, or to land it. It is initiated by throttle back on the engine, and simultaneous movement of the elevator, by which the aircraft moves into the intended glide angle. Once it is reached, the control stick is moved into the neutral position and the glide continues while the predetermined glide speed, which is to be checked continuously on the airspeed indicator, is maintained."[884]

Harbor mole (Hafenmolen): "A long pier or breakwater forming part of the sea defenses of a port. It can be built either in the form of a detached mole constructed entirely in the sea or with one end of it connected to the shore."[885]

Heavy fighter (Zerstörer): Also known in German as "schwerer Jäger", literally translating to "heavy fighter". Originates from twin-seaters used to escort bombers during World War 1. During the inter-war period various countries experimented with the use of twin-engine aircraft, that due to their size and weight could carry more guns and fly longer ranges. Its tasks were "combating enemy bombers and reconnaissance, preferably over enemy territory both day and night, escorting friendly forces and night operations in reference to a specific object to be protected."[886] The literal translation of "Zerstörer" is "destroyer".

Hit result (Trefferergebnis): The accuracy results achieved during bombing.

Hs 123 (Henschel Hs 123): Single-engine biplane, designed for the Luftwaffe as a dive-bomber. Eventually used as a close air support aircraft.[887]

---

[882] Hermann Franke (ed.), *Handbuch der neuzeitlichen Wehrwissenschaften – Dritter Band 2. Die Luftwaffe,* Walter de Gruyter & Co, Berlin, Germany, 1939, p. 111, 113.

[883] Hermann Franke (ed.), *Handbuch der neuzeitlichen Wehrwissenschaften – Dritter Band 2. Die Luftwaffe,* Walter de Gruyter & Co, Berlin, Germany, 1939, p. 111, 113.

[884] Hermann Franke (ed.), *Handbuch der neuzeitlichen Wehrwissenschaften – Dritter Band 2. Die Luftwaffe,* Walter de Gruyter & Co, Berlin, Germany, 1939, p. 125.

[885] Oxford Reference, *Mole,* from *The Oxford Companion to Ships and the Sea (2),* available at: https://www.oxfordreference.com/view/10.1093/oi/authority.20110803100204386 (last accessed 07.11.2021).

[886] Hermann Franke (ed.), *Handbuch der neuzeitlichen Wehrwissenschaften – Dritter Band 2. Die Luftwaffe,* Walter de Gruyter & Co, Berlin, Germany, 1939, p. 308.

[887] Heinz J. Nowarra, *Die Deutsche Luftrüstung 1933-1945,* Band 3, Bernard & Graefe Verlag, Koblenz, Germany, 1993, p. 21-22.

Identification lights (Kennfeuer): Identification lights are often installed in the vicinity and directly at an aerodrome, guiding pilots towards the airstrip and marking the runway.[888]

Illumination guns (Lichtspucker): AA-guns firing illumination rounds, used to guide aircraft back to their airfield or towards a radio beacon.[889] The literal translation would be "light spitter".

"Illumination at night is meant to direct aircraft in the air towards their target and to ease their return flight. It is often required that air defense units assist and follow guidelines with a small number of obvious light sources (AA-guns, rockets, blind fire, search lights)."[890]

Instruction group II and I (Wurfklasse II und I): "In the first year of instruction, pilots follow the curriculum of the Instruction group II. If the pilot fulfills the drills of this class, he can move on to follow the curriculum of Instruction group I. In rare cases, a return into Instruction group II is possible."[891]

Interval bomb release (Reihenwurf): An interval bomb release automatically releases a pre-set number of bombs based on a set interval. The first bomb is released by the bombardier when aligned with the target, while the following bombs saturate the target area on the flight path based on the chosen interval.[892] Also known as train release.[893]

Leading flight (Führungskette): The flight leading a formation. Depending on availability, this could be the squadron, group or wing commander's flight.

Line of approach (Anfluglinie): Typically, the course flown towards a designated point (navigational reference, target, airfield etc.).

Master gun arm device (Schalt-, Zähl-, Kontrolkasten [SZKK]): A device installed in the cockpit which the pilot uses to arm the fixed weaponry. It includes

---

[888] L.Dv. 5/1, *Der Flugbetrieb der Luftwaffe, Anlage 4 Bodenorganisation*, Juni 1943, p. A 5 – A 9.

[889] Christian Möller , *Die Einsätze der Nachtschlachtgruppen 1, 2 und 20 an der Westfront von September 1944 bis Mai 1945*, Helios, Warwick, UK, 2008

[890] *H.Dv. 300: Truppenführung (T.F.) II. Teil. Abschnitt XIV-XXIII und Anhang*, Ernst Siegfried Mittler und Sohn, Berlin, Germany, 1934, p. 28.

[891] See *L.Dv. 20/2: Luftwaffe Regulation 20/2 - Guidelines for Dive-Bombing Training.*

[892] Hauptmann Dierich, *Der Flieger – Dienstunterricht in der Fliegertruppe, Handbücher der Luftwaffe*, E.S. Mittler & Sohn, Berlin, Germany, 1940, p. 134-139.

[893] *TM 30-506, German Military Dictionary: German-English, English- German*, War Department, May 1944, p. 146.

340

a counter showing the remaining ammo count, as well as a small dial which flashes during the operation of the gun, thus indicating the correct operation (no stoppages etc.).

Military penal code (Militär-Strafgesetzbuch [M.St.G.B.]): The German military penal code was originally from 1872. After the creation of the Wehrmacht in 1935, this code became stricter. The military justice system was gradually adjusted to the ideological legal development of national socialism, yet without major complications.[894]

"The M.St.G.B. applies to all soldiers from the lowest to the highest rank, in the field for the most part also to Wehrmacht civil servant. Its application begins on the day of entry into the Army and ends at the end of the day of discharge. However, military offenses committed before discharge are still judged based on the M.St.G.B. by military courts after discharge."[895]

Note literally translated "Militär-Strafgesetzbuch" means "military penal law book".

Mine effect (Minenwirkung): Usually used in reference to a high-explosive bomb with additional filling, e.g., a SC 50 bomb.[896] On explosion, it works "predominantly by blast effect, additionally a substantial shrapnel effect against living targets."[897]

Motorcycle (Krad): A "Krad" is an abbreviation of "Kraftrad" (literally "force/power bike"), which is an old German term for motorcycle.

Naval aircraft (Marine Flugzeug [M.-]): An aircraft, typically navalized (floatplane, seaplane etc.), generally used over the open sea by the Naval service branch.[898]

Navigation by dead reckoning (Koppelnavigation): Definition by *The American Practical Navigator*: "Dead reckoning (DR) allows a navigator to determine his

---

[894] Rolf-Dieter Müller, *Hitlers Wehrmacht 1935 bis 1945*, Oldenbourg, München, Germany, 2012, p. 34. For a in-depth look see Manfred Messerschmidt, *Die Wehrmachtjustiz, 1933-1945*, 2. durchgesehene Auflage, Ferdinand Schöningh, Paderborn, Germany, 2008.

[895] Hermann Franke (ed.), *Handbuch der neuzeitlichen Wehrwissenschaften - Erster Band. Wehrpolitik und Kriegführung*, Walter de Gruyter & Co, Berlin, Germany, 1936, p. 511.

[896] See Glossary: Bomb types (Bombenarten).

[897] Hauptmann Dierich, *Der Flieger - Dienstunterricht in der Fliegertruppe, Handbücher der Luftwaffe*, E.S. Mittler & Sohn, Berlin, Germany, 1940, p. 120.

[898] Hermann Franke (ed.), *Handbuch der neuzeitlichen Wehrwissenschaften - Dritter Band 2. Die Luftwaffe*, Walter de Gruyter & Co, Berlin, Germany, 1939, p. 113.

present position by projecting his past courses steered and speeds over ground from a known past position. He can also determine his future position by projecting an ordered course and speed of advance from a known present position. The DR position is only an approximate position because it does not allow for the effect of leeway, current, helmsman error, or gyro error."[899]

Nightfighter (Nachtjäger - dunkel / hell): Initially, German night fighters conducted the so called "helle Nachtjagd" and "dunkle Nachtjagd", this can be literally translated into "bright" and "dark night hunting". "Helle Nachtjagd" would be used during the brighter lunar phases, or in conjunction with searchlights illuminating clouds to provide a contrast on which approaching bombers could be spotted or, once directly catching a bomber in their beam, would attempt to keep it illuminated by slowly tracking its movement. This allowed night fighters, usually not yet equipped with air interception radar sets to locate and attack the bomber. The "dunkel Nachtjagd" would generally not make use of searchlights. Instead, ground based radar sets would locate a bomber and a ground controller would direct a fighter into visual contact. Once visual contact was established, the fighter would attack independently. Both methods were later combined and used in conjunction with Flak, but the overall effectiveness varied until airborne interception radars became more common.[900] By 1944, the Luftwaffe differentiated between four different types of night fighting.[901]

Non-commissioned officer with sword knot (Portepeeunteroffizier): In the Wehrmacht there were different classes of non-commissioned officers. Altrichter notes three classes, the most numerous were the "non-commissioned officers with sword knot" ("Unteroffiziere mit Portepee") and the "non-commissioned officers without sword knot" ("Unteroffiziere ohne Portepee"), whereas the first group included the ranks from Feldwebel to Stabsfeldwebel and the second from Unteroffizier to Unterfeldwebel.[902] Hence it was a way to distinguish between "regular" and senior non-commissioned officers. Note that

---

[899] U.S. Government Printing Office, *The American Practical Navigator – An Epitome of Navigation, Chapter 7 – Dead Reckoning*, Revised Edition, U.S. Government Printing Office, Washington D.C., USA, 2004, p. 99.
[900] David P. Williams, *Nachtjäger Volume 1– Luftwaffe Night Fighter Units 1939-1943*, Classic Publications, Hersham, UK, 2005, p. 6-9.
[901] BArch, RL 2-II/366, *Reichsluftverteidigung - Heft 2 – Die Jagdfliegerwaffe*, September 1944, p. 21.
[902] Friedrich Altrichter, *Der Reserveoffizier. Ein Handbuch für den Offizier und Offizieranwärter des Beurlaubtenstandes aller Waffen*, Vierzehnte, durchgesehene Auflage, Verlag E.S. Mittler & Sohn, Berlin, Germany, 1941, p. 159.

most ranks in the German Army and the Luftwaffe were equivalent in name, although in the early period of the Luftwaffe the prefix "airman-" ("Flieger-") was added before the Army rank, this was later discontinued.[903] Be aware that the German Armed Forces had a lot of specific ranks for each arm, e.g., "Brieftaubenunterfeldwebel" meaning "pigeon staff sergeant". In our list we limit ourselves to the generic ranks for the sake of brevity and sanity. See the following table for approximate rank equivalents.

Enlisted Men and Non-Commissioned Officers[904]

German Army	Luftwaffe	US Army
Stabsfeldwebel	Stabsfeldwebel	Master Sergeant[905]
Oberfeldwebel	Oberfeldwebel	Master/First Sergeant
Feldwebel	Feldwebel	Technical Sergeant
Unterfeldwebel	Unterfeldwebel	Staff Sergeant
Unteroffizier	Unteroffizier	Sergeant
-		Corporal
Hauptgefreiter	Hauptgefreiter	Private First Class
Obergefreiter	Obergefreiter	
Gefreiter	Gefreiter	
Obersoldat	Oberflieger	
Soldat	Flieger	Private

Officer candidate schools (Luft-Kriegsschulen): The officer candidate schools were tasked with training the officer cadets on military operations, tactics, administration, industrial and technical aspects, and more.[906] Note the literal translation of "Luft-Kriegsschulen" is "aerial war(fare) school".

---

[903] Adolf Schlicht; John R. Angolia, *Die deutsche Wehrmacht Uniformierung und Ausrüstung 1933 - 1945. Band 3: Die Luftwaffe*, 1. Auflage, Motorbuch Verlag, Stuttgart, Germany, 1999, p. 23-35, 56-79. See also contemporary rank tables by Gesterding Schwatlo; Hans-Joachim Feyerabend, *Unteroffizierthemen. Ein Handbuch für den Unteroffizierunterricht*, Fünfte, neubearbeitete Auflage, Verlag von E.S. Mittler & Sohn, Berlin, Germany, 1938, p. 36-37. See also the subsequent editions from 1940 at p. 38-39 and 1943 at p. 48-49.

[904] David Glantz et al., *Slaughterhouse: The Encyclopedia of the Eastern Front*, Military Book Club, Garden City, New York (State), USA, 2002, p. viii. See also: David Stahel, *Operation Barbarossa and Germany's Defeat in the East*, Cambridge University Press, Cambridge, UK, 2011 (2009), p. xv has in some cases different translations.

[905] Note that the Sergeant Major was not a rank in the US Army during the Second World War, see David Glantz et al., *Slaughterhouse: The Encyclopedia of the Eastern Front*, Military Book Club, Garden City, New York (State), USA, 2002, p. viii.

[906] Barry Ketley: Mark Rofle, *Luftwaffe Training Units & their Aircraft*, Hikoki Publications, Aldershot, UK, 1996; and Horst Boog, Die deutsche Luftwaffenführung 1935-1945 –

Open AA-positions (Flakstellung, offen): "An open, mobile heavy AA-battery is due to the requirements of all-round visibility, which often hinders an impeccable deployment within the terrain, as well as [hiding] the long barrels and gun carriage, easier to spot than a ground battery."[907]

This battery seemingly differentiates itself from other AA-defenses by being deployed temporarily and by circumstance. The "openness" most likely refers to the fact that it is not installed in a more permanent fashion which would allow the crews to use camouflage and protection.

Operational training schools (Ergänzungsstaffel): These units included pilots that had already checked out on trainer aircraft and were converting to their operational aircraft. The operational training schools were coupled to units in the field, thus providing opportunities for experience exchange and ad hoc training, as well as a steadily increasing use in operational missions on the front lines.[908]

Operations group (Führungsgruppe [Ia]): Within an air unit, the operations group would be running the air operations for all aircraft, as well as the air defense.[909] Narrowing the role of the Ia to purely tactical-operational military aspects was a cause of the "higher regard placed on tactical-operational command compared to other command elements such as replenishment and provisions, intelligence [Ic], technical matters, signals, training and logistics."[910] The makeup of the operations group office varied from its placement in the relevant command structure. For example, within the general staff the operations group could be composed out of several sub-groups known as "Referat" and abbreviated as "op". This can be translated as "department" or "unit". The "operations group (I) was composed out of the Ia op 1 for the processing of combat orders for the offensive air units, dealing with the organization and training requirements of the aerial units, as well as the cooperation with other elements of the Armed Forces." [911] The Ia op 2 would arrange and manage "the air defenses in cooperation with other elements of the

Führungsprobleme, Spitzengliederung, Generalstabsausbildung, DVA, Stuttgart, Germany, 1982, p. 644.

[907] See *Pamphlet on Attacking AA-Defenses with Bombers*.

[908] Barry Ketley; Mark Rofle, *Luftwaffe Training Units & their Aircraft*, Hikoki Publications, Aldershot, UK, 1996, p. 8

[909] Horst Boog, *Die deutsche Luftwaffenführung 1935-1945 – Führungsprobleme, Spitzengliederung, Generalstabsausbildung*, DVA, Stuttgart, Germany, 1982, p. 646.

[910] Horst Boog, *Die deutsche Luftwaffenführung 1935-1945 – Führungsprobleme, Spitzengliederung, Generalstabsausbildung*, DVA, Stuttgart, Germany, 1982, p. 499.

[911] Horst Boog, *Die deutsche Luftwaffenführung 1935-1945 – Führungsprobleme, Spitzengliederung, Generalstabsausbildung*, DVA, Stuttgart, Germany, 1982, p. 248.

armed forces, the use, organization and training of the aircraft warning service, the civil air defense." [912] Finally, the Ia op 3 would instruct and direct the signal units.[913] Additionally, the Ia op 4 and Ia op 5 were responsible for training and technical matters.[914]

Outboard cannon (Bordkanone [BK]): A cannon, usually of a higher caliber (for example 3 or 3.7 cm or larger), mounted in a special gun pod either under the wings, or in a centerline position under the fuselage.

Point of aim (Abkommpunkt): The point within the reflector sight, that is seen just before the bomb drop.[915]

Point target (Einzelziel, Punktziel): At first, we assumed that an "Einzelziel" is a single, or solitary moving target like a ship or tank, where as a "Punktziel" is a stationary point target. Intuitively, this made some sense given the German word. However, this does not align with various publications of the time. For example, in the section on dive-bombers in *Aerial Tactics*, both targets are mentioned as "Einzel- oder Punktziele".[916] This might imply a distinction, or that both words have the same meaning. Another educational publication, with a very similar text, refers only to "Punktziele", defining these as "small land or sea targets, that cannot be hit by bombers due to the bomb dispersion from horizontal flight".[917] Likewise, the text *Methods of Attacking Naval Targets with Dive-Bombers*[918], also refers to "Punktziele" as ships, while *The Pamphlet on Night-Bombing with the Ju 87* uses this term in reference to land targets.[919] There is only one reference to "Einzelziel" within our documents, and since "Punktziel" appears to be far more common, we assume that these terms are more or less synonymous within the context of the Luftwaffe.

For the German Army in the Second World War generally "Punktziel" was used for a single target, this seems to have continued into post-war German Army of

---

[912] Horst Boog, *Die deutsche Luftwaffenführung 1935-1945 - Führungsprobleme, Spitzengliederung, Generalstabsausbildung*, DVA, Stuttgart, Germany, 1982, p. 248-249.

[913] Horst Boog, *Die deutsche Luftwaffenführung 1935-1945 - Führungsprobleme, Spitzengliederung, Generalstabsausbildung*, DVA, Stuttgart, Germany, 1982, p. 249.

[914] Horst Boog, *Die deutsche Luftwaffenführung 1935-1945 - Führungsprobleme, Spitzengliederung, Generalstabsausbildung*, DVA, Stuttgart, Germany, 1982, p. 567.

[915] See *L.Dv. 20/2: Luftwaffe Regulation 20/2 - Guidelines for Dive-Bombing Training*.

[916] See *Compendium for the Education at the Air-War Colleges - Aerial Tactics: The Dive-Bomber*.

[917] Günter Elsner and Karl-Gustav Lerche, *Vom Pimpf zum Flieger*, Zentralverlag der NSDAP, München, Germany, 1940.

[918] See *Methods of Attacking Naval Targets with Dive-Bombers*.

[919] See *The Pamphlet on Night-Bombing with the Ju 87*.

the *Bundeswehr*. In a semi-official training booklet that was based on an official pamphlet for the M 41, M 47 and M 48 tanks there was an additional booklet added that contained a table with "alter Text" ("old text") and "neuer Text" ("new text"). One entry noted that "Punktziel" (literally "point target") was replaced by "Einzelziel" (literally "single target").[920] As such we can assume that for the German Army these two terms were equivalent.

In *TM 30-506*, "Einzelziel" is translated as point target for bombing, whereas "Punktziel" is a point target for gunnery.[921] Yet, as can be seen, both words were used somewhat interchangeably in the Luftwaffe.

Pull-out radius (Abfangradius): The pull-out radius refers to the radius of an aircraft flown when pulling out of a dive into level flight.

Radio navigation (Funknavigation): "Navigation with the aid of radio equipment, using direction-finding equipment[922]."[923] Depending on equipment and availability of one or more radio beacons, crews can use radio navigation to fly to a specific target or point, to determine their location and/or their distance to a beacon.[924]

Radio set (Funkgerät [FuG]): A radio set used primarily for communication. Includes a receiver and transmitter. Used, depending on type, in air-to-air and air-to-ground communication.

Reconnaissance aircraft F (F-Aufklärungsflugzeug) [F.-]): Within a reconnaissance unit or in relation to a reconnaissance aircraft, the suffix (F) stands for "fern", translating to "far". It is used to denote the use of a long-range aircraft with a larger crew. Its task is to "recon wide areas for the command [structures]"[925], and specifically provide "operational air reconnaissance for the

---

[920] Wilhelm Lechens, *Panzer-Schießfibel*, Verlag WEU / Offene Worte, Bonn, Germany, n.d.; with the booklet *Ergänzungen zur Panzer-Schießfibel*, Verlag Offene Wort, Bonn, Germany, n.d., p. 1.

[921] *TM 30-506, German Military Dictionary: German-English, English-German*, War Department, May 1944, p. 43, 142.

[922] See Glossary: Direction-finding equipment (Peilgerät).

[923] Hermann Franke (ed.), *Handbuch der neuzeitlichen Wehrwissenschaften – Dritter Band 2. Die Luftwaffe*, Walter de Gruyter & Co, Berlin, Germany, 1939, p. 270.

[924] Hermann Franke (ed.), *Handbuch der neuzeitlichen Wehrwissenschaften – Dritter Band 2. Die Luftwaffe*, Walter de Gruyter & Co, Berlin, Germany, 1939, p. 273.

[925] Hermann Franke (ed.), *Handbuch der neuzeitlichen Wehrwissenschaften – Dritter Band 2. Die Luftwaffe*, Walter de Gruyter & Co, Berlin, Germany, 1939, p. 308.

air war, tactical air reconnaissance for the air war", and "operational air reconnaissance for the Army."[926]

Reconnaissance aircraft K (K-Aufklärungsflugzeug): Within a reconnaissance unit or in relation to a reconnaissance aircraft, the suffix (K) stands for "Kurz", translating to "short". It is used to denote the use of a short-ranged light aircraft, which is typically flown by a crew of 2. Sometimes similar units would be attached to the Army, where the designation would change from (K) to (H).[927] This suffix stands for "Heer", or "Army".

Reflector sight (Reflexvisier [Revi]): Typically, this optical sight projects the virtual image of a reticle on to a canted glass element. This image will appear in front of the pilot, without obscuring the area "behind it". It provides the pilot with an aiming reference when using his weaponry.[928]

Reich's Minister for Aviation and and Commander-in-Chief of the Luftwaffe (Reichsminister der Luftfahrt und Oberbefehlshaber der Luftwaffe): These two positions where unified under the persona of Hermann Göring. The "Commander-in-Chief of the Luftwaffe commands the air war as the highest-ranking commander, on behalf and under the directives of the Führer and the Commander-in-Chief of the Armed Forces [Wehrmacht]."[929]

Reich's Ministry of Aviation (Reichsluftfahrtministerium): The ministry directing all German development and production of aircraft.

Shadow aircraft (Klebeflugzeug): "The shadow aircraft is used for reconnaissance. It attaches itself [or shadows] a spotted enemy [air] unit, in order to report its flight path and aerodrome."[930] Note that "Klebeflugzeug" literally translated means "sticky/glue aircraft".

---

[926] Hauptmann Dierich, *Der Flieger – Dienstunterricht in der Fliegertruppe, Handbücher der Luftwaffe*, E.S. Mittler & Sohn, Berlin, Germany, 1940, p. 11-12.

[927] Hauptmann Dierich, *Der Flieger – Dienstunterricht in der Fliegertruppe, Handbücher der Luftwaffe*, E.S. Mittler & Sohn, Berlin, Germany, 1940, p. 12.

[928] War Department, A.A.F Form No. 24, *Pilots' Information File 1944*, republished by Schiffer Military History Book, Atglen, PA, USA, 1995, PIF 7-4-2.

[929] Hauptmann Dierich, *Der Flieger – Dienstunterricht in der Fliegertruppe, Handbücher der Luftwaffe*, E.S. Mittler & Sohn, Berlin, Germany, 1940, p. 2.

[930] Hauptmann Dierich, *Der Flieger – Dienstunterricht in der Fliegertruppe, Handbücher der Luftwaffe*, E.S. Mittler & Sohn, Berlin, Germany, 1940, p. 230.

Shallow dive (Flachsturz): A dive made at 45-60°.[931] A more relaxed translation, a shallow dive would naturally also include the range between 1-44°.

Sperry: The Sperry Cooperation was a U.S. American company constructing aircraft and electronical equipment. For aircraft, Sperry is best known for complex instruments like artificial horizons and gyroscopic instruments, and later analogue computing systems, electrical devices and autopilots. The company's products were used in many inter-war and aircraft from the Second World War.

Spider-sight principle (Kreiskimmeprinzip): A spider-sight allows the operator to account for the lead required to hit a fast-moving target like an aircraft. It is usually attached in place of a conventional rear-sight, and sometimes used in conjunction with a conventional front-sight. By placing the target on the outer or inner rings of the sight, the operator can lead the gun based on a subjective estimate of range, speed, heading and projectile velocity.[932]

Staffel H.Q. (Staffeltrupp): The administrative, maintenance and logistical support unit of a squadron.[933]

Steep dive (Steilsturz): A dive made at 60-85°.[934] A more relaxed translation, a steep dive would naturally also include the range between 86-90°.

Table of organization and equipment (Kriegsstärkenachweisung): The literal translation of "Kriegsstärkenachweisung" is "war strength certificate", it is a table of organization and equipment.

Target (Zielpunkt): Generally, the target area. Can also be used in navigation as a point to navigate towards.

Target marker / pathfinder (Fühlungshalter): During the day, the target marker shadows and observes the designated target. At night, the target marker flies ahead of the formation and marks the targets with illumination flares.

---

[931] See *Compendium for the Education at the Air-War Colleges – Aerial Tactics: The Dive-Bomber*.

[932] Hans-Hermann Kritzinger; Friedrich Stuhlmann, *Artillerie und Ballistik in Stichworten*, Julius Springer Verlag, Berlin, Germany, 1939, p. 175.

[933] See, *Compendium for the Education at the Air-War Colleges – Aerial Tactics: The Dive-Bomber*.

[934] See *Compendium for the Education at the Air-War Colleges – Aerial Tactics: The Dive-Bomber*.

Similar to pathfinder missions flown by Allied air forces. Note the literal translation of "Fühlungshalter" is "feeler holder".

Thorough training (Durchbildung): For this term we need to refer to a German Army publication since we could not find a definition in Luftwaffe publications. The German Army defined four stages of training, namely introduction ("Einführung") which was defined as "general theoretical knowledge", instruction ("Unterweisung") defined as "knowledge and limited practical skill", training ("Ausbildung") as "full knowledge and practical skill" and finally thorough training ("Durchbildung") as "repetition and complete command/mastery".[935]

Throttle quadrant (Drosselhabelkasten): The throttle quadrant houses the throttle control of the aircraft's engine and, depending on aircraft, can include other controls such as the mixture and pitch control, as well as additional switches for radio communication, airbrakes and other systems.

Trail distance (Rücktriftstrecke): "The trail is the distance the bomb lags behind the aircraft at the moment of impact."[936]

Training year (Wurfjahr): The training year for dive-bomber units started on 1st October and ends the 30th September the following year. In official use, the training year appears to have been written with the relevant year. It is unclear whether this includes only the starting year, or both the start and engine years, e.g., Wurfjahr 1938 or Wurfjahr 1938-1939.[937]

Unit type (Kampflieger, Jagdflieger, Schlachtflieger, Sturzkampfflieger): An ambiguous word that can be used to describe either a bomber pilot or crews, unit or unit type. As a general rule, the term is used to describe a unit type, with a usage of "unsere Sturzkampfflieger", "der Sturzkampfflieger" or "ein Sturzkampfflieger" typically being synonymous to the English "our dive-bombers", "the dive-bomber" and "a dive-bomber". The general context is then provided within the sentences and accompanying text, giving clues as to whether the pilot or crew, or rather the unit type is meant. The latter is, especially in official documents, far more likely as can also be seen in *Chapter II: Doctrine, Training and Operational Thinking*.

This of course provides a challenge for an English translation. A literal translation of "Sturzkampfflieger" would be "dive-bomber flyer", or include the

---

[935] *H.Dv. 130/1: Ausbildungsvorschrift für die Infanterie. Heft 1. Leitsätze für Erziehung und Ausbildung, Reichsdruckerei*, Berlin, Germany, 1935, p. 19.

[936] F. Postlethwaite, *Notes on Enemy Bombsights*, Aircraft Engineering, Sept. 1942, p. 244.

[937] See *L.Dv. 20/2: Luftwaffe Regulation 20/2 - Guidelines for Dive-Bombing Training*.

349

alternatives of "pilot", "aviator" or "crew". This would only be correct if we were to consider it as a very general reference to these crews as making up a unit type, an interpretation that is not immediately clear, or intuitive. Likewise, a translation to simply "dive-bomber" is incorrect, as this refers more to the actual airframe, rather than the unit type. A translation to "dive-bomber unit" would also be misleading, as this is closer to the German "Sturzkampffliegerverband".[938] Within the German Army in the Second World War there was quite an inconsistent use of the terms "unit" ("Einheit") and "formation" ("Verband"). We generally opted to translate "Verband" with "unit" in this publication.

The solution to this issue could be to add additional information in paratheses such as "dive-bomber [unit]" and "dive-bomber [aircraft]", or a use of symbol like an asterisk (*) to differentiate the different meanings, with a consistent use of accompanying footnotes. Yet this might disturb the flow of the text, and potentially be more confusing than necessary.

As such, we have decided to translate "Sturzkampfflieger" to "dive-bomber", as the accompanying information typically provides the appropriate context. In cases of ambiguity even in the German text, a footnote has been added which provides some clarification as well as a reference to this section in the Glossary.

For definitions, see Glossary: Bomber (Kampfflugzeug/ Kampfflieger), fighter unit (Jagdflieger) and close air support unit (Schlachtflieger).

Weight of effort (Schwerpunkt): The term Schwerpunkt [which we translated as weight of effort] has stirred up quite a debate, especially in the English language literature and discussion.[939] A brief look at Clausewitz's *On War* shows that he used the term in (grand) strategic context, for example:

"From them [the prevailing relation of two states] a certain weight of effort, a center of force and motion, on which the whole depends, will be formed, and on

---

[938] In the *TM 30-506*, "Verband" is translated in aviation terms to "air force unit", "force" or "formation". See *TM 30-506, German Military Dictionary: German-English, English-German*, War Department, May 1944, p. 194.

[939] Milan Vego, *Clausewitz's Schwerpunkt. Mistranslated from German – Misunderstood in English*, in Military Review, January-February 2007, Fort Leavenworth, Kansas, USA, 2007, p. 101.

this weight of effort of the adversary the combined thrust of all forces must be directed."[940]

And also, in the further elaboration here:

"Alexander, Gustav Adolf, Charles XII, Frederick the Great had their weight of effort in their army; if this had been shattered, they would have played their role badly; in states torn apart by internal parties, it is usually in the capital; in small states supported by powerful ones, it is in the army of these allies; in alliances, it is in the unity of interest;"[941]

In *On War* the word "Schwerpunkt" and its variations occur a total of 49 times. However, Clausewitz uses the term long before he defines it. He writes, for example:

"How this idea of the weight of effort of enemy power becomes effective in the whole war plan, we shall consider in the last book, for that is where the object belongs in the first place, and so we have only borrowed it in order to leave no gap in the series of ideas."[942]

The historian Beatrice Heuser notes:

"Thus, in the writings of the realist Clausewitz, the weight of effort can have many manifestations – the enemy's army, his capital, public opinion."[943]

It is noticeable that the term does not always have the same meaning. The terms "Schwerpunkt" and "Schwerpunktbildung"[944] are mentioned repeatedly by the military historian Gerhard Groß in his book on the operational thinking of the German Army, rarely in a strategic, and primarily in an operational sense.[945]

---

[940] Ernesto Grassi (ed.); von Clausewitz, Carl, *Vom Kriege*, Rowohlt, Hamburg, Germany, 2005, p. 211.

[941] Oliver Corff (ed.); von Clausewitz, Carl, *Vom Kriege*, Erstausgabe von 1832-1834, A4 Version basierend auf Textdaten bibliotheca Augustana, Clausewitz-Gesellschaft e.V., Berlin, Germany, 2010, p. 459.

[942] Oliver Corff (ed.), von Clausewitz, Carl, *Vom Kriege*, Erstausgabe von 1832-1834, A4 Version basierend auf Textdaten bibliotheca Augustana, Clausewitz-Gesellschaft e.V., Berlin, Germany, 2010, p. 364.

[943] Beatrice Heuser, *Clausewitz lesen! Eine Einführung*, R. Oldenbourg Verlag, München, 2010, p. 94 (translation by the author).

[944] The term "Bildung" means "creation" in this context, but it can also mean "education".

[945] Gerhard P. Groß, *Mythos und Wirklichkeit: Die Geschichte des operativen Denkens im deutschen Heer von Moltke d. Ä. bis Heusinger*, Zeitalter der Weltkriege, Band 9, Ferdinand Schönigh, Paderborn, Germany, 2012, p. 67-68, 156, 166, 171, 173, 201.

In *Unit Command* the weight of effort is addressed and characterized:

"The weight of effort [in the attack] is characterized: in the commencement of the attack in narrow combat sectors, by measures for concentration fire of all weapons, also as adjacent combat sectors, and by the reinforcement of the fire by specially assigned heavy infantry weapons and artillery; during the execution of the attack by increasing the fire and using combat vehicles and reserves. The choice of the weight of effort is largely influenced by the artillery, sometimes also by the combat vehicles."[946]

This clearly no longer addresses the strategic, but the tactical-operational level. Likewise, Kühlwein in his book about the German squad:

"The weight of effort is put in the attack (at least at battalion-level) at the place where one wants to bring about the decisive outcome[947]. Here the main forces and the mass of ammunition are used. It is characterized by narrow combat sectors and by fire concentration of all weapons, also from adjacent combat sectors (flanking). The choice of the weight of effort is determined by the enemy's position (good advancement) and mainly by the favor of the terrain."[948]

A definition from 1944 also clearly orients itself on *Unit Command*:

"Weight of Effort: is formed by narrow combat sectors, increased use of heavy weapons and replenishment of reserves and ammunition at the point where the decisive outcome[949] is to be made."[950]

In *Unit Command*, the term weight of effort is used even more often:

---

[946] *H.Dv. 300/1: Truppenführung (T.F.) I. Teil. Abschnitt I – XIII*, Verlag Mittler & Sohn, Berlin, Germany, 1936, p. 123.

[947] Note the literal translation of "Entscheidung" would be "decision", but in this case it refers to the "Entscheidung" in the sense of decisive outcome, like it is used in "Entscheidungsschlacht" which is translated and well-known as "decisive battle".

[948] Fritz Kühlwein, *Die Gruppe im Gefecht. (Die neue Gruppe)*, E. S. Mittler & Sohn, Berlin, Germany, 1940, p. 14-15.

[949] Note the literal translation of "Entscheidung" would be "decision", but in this case it refers to the "Entscheidung" in the sense of decisive outcome, like it is used in "Entscheidungsschlacht" which is translated and well-known as "decisive battle".

[950] BArch, RH 17/809, Schule VII: *Taktische Grundbegriffe*, August 1944, p. 4.

"If the artillery working directly with the infantry is not sufficient for support, the artillery commander must help out with the rest of the artillery, preferably by supporting the infantry attacking at the weight of effort."[951]

The historians Condell and Zabecki commented on this in their translation:

"In the original, the term Schwerpunkt is used. What was really meant, however, was decisive point [entscheidende Stelle], not center of gravity as Clausewitz defined the term."[952]

This, of course, assumes that someone kept to the rather vague use of weight of effort by Clausewitz and at the same time applied it from the (grand) strategic level to the tactical-operational level.

Looking through official and semi-official[953] publications of the time give the impression that emphasis was a very practical term, used primarily at the tactical level. This pragmatic approach is also evident when Altrichter writes in *Reserve Officer* from 1941 about "Schwerpunktbildung"[954]:

"Choice of the weight of effort where, according to enemy position and terrain, the best conditions for success are available. If the decisive point cannot be recognized from the outset, the weight of effort must be formed in the unknown and, if necessary, moved later."[955]

And this is followed by specific instructions for action:

"Formation of the weight of effort is achieved by:

allocation of narrow combat sectors,

fire concentration of all weapons, also from neighboring combat sectors,

---

[951] *H.Dv. 300/1: Truppenführung (T.F.) I. Teil. Abschnitt I – XIII*, Verlag Mittler & Sohn, Berlin, Germany, 1936, p. 144.

[952] Bruce Condell (ed.), David T. Zabecki (ed.), *On the German Art of War. Truppenführung.* Stackpole Books, Mechanicsburg, PA, USA, 2009 (2001), p. 102.

[953] In many cases, entire text passages, graphics and miscellaneous are 1:1 or almost 1:1 identical, but without detailed research it is difficult to determine who "copied" from whom or whether in some cases it was not one and the same author.

[954] The term "Bildung" means "creation" in this context, but it can also mean "education".

[955] Friedrich Altrichter, *Der Reserveoffizer. Ein Handbuch für den Offizier und Offizieranwärter des Beurlaubtenstandes aller Waffen*, Vierzehnte, durchgesehene Auflage, Verlag von E. S. Mittler & Sohn, Berlin, Germany, 1941, p. 259.

reinforcement of fire with specially assigned artillery and heavy infantry weapons,

intensification of the fire,

employment of tank units and reserves,

employment of air forces."[956]

The historian Roman Töppel, who has spent decades in his research dealing with operation orders, war diaries, mission reports and other sources and who has also interviewed veterans on the subject of weight of effort, when asked about a definition for weight of effort for the German armed forces in the Second World War provided the following definition:

"Weight of effort is the point at which the mass of forces is used to achieve the main operational objective."[957]

This definition and the other definitions cited from contemporary sources have little or nothing to do with Clausewitz' use, as neither the level nor the practical approach is consistent.

Finally, it should be noted that "Schwerpunkt" is often used in the German language in a more general manner. The following quotations originating from the *Preliminary Pamphlet: The SMG-Platoon of the Grenadier-Company* also printed in this book makes this clear: "The focus [Schwerpunkt] of the training is on the handling of the weapon and in basic live fire combat exercise."[958] Thus, this word is used on a tactical, operational and strategic level, while at the same time being a word of daily relevance, as it can simple describe a certain "focus".

Wind correction angle (Luvwinkel): The wind correction angle (WCA) is also known as crab angle. It is "the angle between the course and the heading that is required for the aircraft to track that course when there is wind."[959] The WCA is

---

[956] Friedrich Altrichter, *Der Reserveoffizer. Ein Handbuch für den Offizier und Offizieranwärter des Beurlaubtenstandes aller Waffen*, Vierzehnte, durchgesehene Auflage, Verlag von E. S. Mittler & Sohn, Berlin, Germany, 1941, p. 259.

[957] Email from Roman Töppel, 8. November 2020.

[958] BArch, RH 11-I/83, *Merkblatt 25a/16: Vorläufiges Merkblatt "Der M.P.-Zug der Grenadier-Kompanie"*, 1.2.1944, p. 10.

[959] Luiz Roberto Monoteiro de Oliveria, *Calculating the Wind Correction Angle*, 2010, available   at http://www.luizmonteiro.com/Article_Estimating_Wind_Correction_Angle_Printable.htm, (last accessed 07.11.2021).

determined by "the wind's speed, the angle between the wind direction and the airplane's longitudinal axis, and the airspeed of the airplane."[960]

Wind shear (Windsprung): Wind shear is "a change in wind velocity (speed and/or direction) with height."[961]

Windward (Luv): The side of the aircraft or ship facing the wind. The opposite side would be referred to as "lee" in German, or "leeward" in English.[962]

---

[960] U.S. Department of Transportation, FAA-H-8083-3C, *Airplane Flying Handbook Chapter 7: Ground Reference Maneuvers*, Federal Aviation Administration, Oklahoma City, USA, p. 7-2, available at https://www.faa.gov/regulations_policies/handbooks_manuals/aviation/airplane_handbook/ (last accessed 07.11.2021).

[961] The University of Rhode Island, Hurricanes: Science and Society – Glossary, available at http://www.hurricanescience.org/glossary/ (last accessed 07.11.2021).

[962] Merriam Webster Dictionary, *weather* side, available at https://www.merriam-webster.com/dictionary/weather%20side (last accessed 07.11.2021).

Bibliography

Primary Sources

AFI 38-101, *Manpower and Organization*, United States Air Force e-publishing, 29. August 2019.

Air Force Historical Research Agency, Numbered USAF studies 151-200, available at https://www.afhra.af.mil/Information/Studies/Numbered-USAF-Historical-Studies-151-200/ (last accessed 27.10.2021).

Allied Joint Publication, *AJP-3.3.2 Air Interdiction and Close Air Support*.

Archiv Hafner, D. (Luft) T.2087 D1 trop, *Ju 87 D-1 trop Flugzeug-Handbuch Teil 12D – Sondereinbauten - Heft 1: Lärmgerät*, May 1942.

Archiv Hafner, D. (Luft) T. 2087 G-2 Teil 12 A, *Ju 87 G-2 - Flugzeug-Handbuch Teil 12 A: Schußwaffenanlage mit zwei 3,7 cm BK*, October 1943.

Archiv Hafner, L. Dv. T 2087 R-2/Fl, *Ju 87 R-2 Bedienungsvorschrift-Fl, Teil II, Flugbetrieb*, May 1941.

Archiv Hafner, Junkers Flugzeug- und -Motorenwerke, *Junkers Flugmotor JUMO 211 B u. D – Baureihe 1 – Betriebsanweisung und Wartungsvorschrift*, 2. Ausgabe, March 1940.

Archiv Hafner, Junkers Flugzeug- und -Motorenwerke, *Junkers Flugmotor JUMO 211 B und D – Baureihe 1 u. 2, Kurz-Betriebs- und Wartungs- Anweisung*, 3. Ausgabe, February 1940.

Archiv Hafner, Junkers Flugzeug- und -Motorenwerke, *Junkers Flugmotor JUMO 211 F u. J – Baureihe 1, Auszug*, 2. Ausgabe, September 1941.

Archiv Hafner, Junkers Flugzeug- und -Motorenwerke, *Junkers Flugmotor JUMO 211 F u. J – Baureihe 1 – Motoren-Handbuch*, August 1941.

Archiv Hafner, *Werkschrift 2087 D-1 bis D-8, G-1, G-2, H-1 bis H-8/Fl, Ju 87 D-1 bis D-8, G-1, G-2, H-1 bis H-8 Bedienungsvorschrift-Fl, Teil II – Flugbetrieb*, Februar 1944.

Army Air Forces Aid Society, *The Official Guide to Army Air Forces*, Bonanza Books, New York, USA, 1988.

BArch, RH 11-I/83, *Merkblatt 25a/16: Vorläufiges Merkblatt "Der M.P.-Zug der Grenadier-Kompanie"*, 1. February 1944.

BArch, RH 12-2/162, *Entwicklung und Verwendung von Fliegerabwehr-Waffen der Infanterie*, 29. December 1944.

BArch, RH 17/809, *Schule VII: Taktische Grundbegriffe*, August 1944.

BArch, RH 19-XVI/3, *Merkblatt für den Einsatz von Kampf- und Sturzkampfverbänden gegen schnell bewegliche Erdtruppen*, RLM, Berlin, Germany, 1938.

BArch, RL 1/641, *L.Dv. 8/1 (Entwurf), Der Bombenwurf, Teil 1, Grundbegriffe des Bombenwurfes*, April 1941.

BArch, RL 1/642, *L.Dv. 8/5 zugleich L.Dv. 20/3 Der Bombenwurf Teil 5 der L.Dv. 8 bzw. Teil 3 der L.Dv. 20*, January 1940.

BArch, RL 1/658, *L.Dv. 16 Luftkriegführung und Luftkriegführung als Nachdruck*, RLM, Berlin, Germany, 1935.

BArch, RL 1/660 *L.Dv. 20/2 Die Ausbildung im Bombenwurf aus dem Sturzflug*, Reich's Printing Office, Berlin, Germany, 1940.

BArch, RL 1/1096, *L.Dv. 366: Luftwaffe Regulation 366 – Special Guidelines for Diving with the Hs 123 and Ju 87*, Reich's Printing Office, Berlin, Germany, 1937.

BArch, RL 2-II/142, *Merkblatt: Die Nachtschlachtflieger-Verbände*, March 1943.

BArch, RL 2-II/157, *Bd. 4 Bericht Wehrmachtsmanöver (Luftwaffe)*, 1937.

BArch, RL 2-II/366, *Reichsluftverteidigung - Heft 2 – Die Jagdfliegerwaffe*, September 1944.

BArch, RL 2-II/1029, *Pamphlet on Attacking AA-Defenses with Bombers*, RLM, Berlin, Germany, 1938.

BArch, RL 2-III/561, *Kriegsstärkennachweisung (Luftw.) Nr. 1185 – 1188 (L)*, November 1939.

BArch, RL 3/13, *Stenographischer Bericht über die GL-Besprechung*, 5. May 1942.

BArch, RL 3/14, *Stenographischer Bericht über die GL-Besprechung*, 19. May 1942.

BArch, RL 3/15, *Stenographischer Bericht über die GL-Besprechung*, 19. June 1942.

BArch, RL 3/16, *Stenographischer Bericht über die GL-Besprechung*, 27. October 1942.

BArch, RL 3/17, *Stenographischer Bericht über die GL-Besprechung*, 1. December 1942.

BArch, RL 3/8233, *Lehrblätter für die technische Ausbildung in der Luftwaffe, mathematische und mechanische Grundbegriffe*, Berlin, Germany, 1938.

BArch, RL 3/8400, *Flugzeugproduktion*, n.d.

BArch, RL 7-1/12, *Erfahrungsberichte der Führungsstellen und unterstellten Verbänden über den Einsatz in Polen*, 1939.

BArch, RL 7-6/14, *Luftwaffenkommando Ost / Luftwaffenkommando 6, Abteilung Ia, Anlagen zum Kriegstagebuch, Band 7*, February 1945.

BArch, RL 10/348, *Polenkrieg Kriegstagebuch I./Stuka 77*, 1939.

BArch, RL 10/350, *Kriegstagebuch Polenkrieg I. /Stuka 77 Anlagen*, 1939.

BArch, RL 10/473a, *Erfolgsmeldungen des IV. Fliegerkorps*, 1942.

BArch, RL 10/512, *Einsatz England und Mittelmeerraum 1940/41*, n.d.

BArch, RL 16-2/6, *Merkblatt für den Nachteinsatz mit Junkers Ju 87*, 1942.

BArch, RM 7/2383, *Entwicklungsstand des Materials der Seeluftstreitkräfte*, 1938.

BArch, ZA 1/993, Dinort, Oskar; Hitschhold, Hubertus: *See-Luft-Schlacht um Kreta am 22.5.1941: Sonderbericht des Sturzkampfgeschwaders 2 "Immelmann"*, 1947.

BArch, ZA 3/282, *Jagdbomber, Sturzkampf- und Panzerbekämpfungsflugzeuge, Transporter, Sonderflugzeuge*.

B.R. 1736 (2) Naval Staff History, *Naval Operations in the Battle of Crete 20th May-1st June 1941 (Battle Summary No. 4)*, Admiralty, 1960.

Curt Strohmeyer, *Stukas! – Erlebnis eines Fliegerkorps*, Die Heimbücherei, Berlin, Germany, 1940.

DoD, *Dictionary of Military and Associated Terms*, August 2021.

Einbaumappe 3,7 cm BK – 43, March 1944.

F. Postlethwaite, *Notes on Enemy Bombsights*, Aircraft Engineering, September 1942.

FM 17-10: Armored Force Field Manual: Tactics and Technique, War Department, Washington, USA, March 1942.

FM 17-32: Armored Force Field Manual: The Tank Company, Light and Medium, War Department, Washington, USA, August 1942.

Friedrich Altrichter, *Der Reserveoffizer. Ein Handbuch für den Offizier und Offizieranwärter des Beurlaubtenstandes aller Waffen*, Vierzehnte, durchgesehene Auflage, Verlag von E. S. Mittler & Sohn, Berlin, Germany, 1941.

Fritz Kühlwein, *Die Gruppe im Gefecht. (Die neue Gruppe)*, E. S. Mittler & Sohn, Berlin, Germany, 1940.

Gesterding Schwatlo; Hans-Joachim Feyerabend, *Unteroffizierthemen. Ein Handbuch für den Unteroffizierunterricht*, Fünfte, neubearbeitete Auflage, Verlag von E.S. Mittler & Sohn, Berlin, Germany, 1938.

Gesterding Schwatlo; Hans-Joachim Feyerabend, *Unteroffizierthemen. Ein Handbuch für den Unteroffizierunterricht*, Sechste, neubearbeitete Auflage, Verlag von E.S. Mittler & Sohn, Berlin, Germany, 1940.

Gesterding Schwatlo; Hans-Joachim Feyerabend, *Unteroffizierthemen. Ein Handbuch für den Unteroffizierunterricht*, Siebente, neubearbeitete Auflage, Verlag von E.S. Mittler & Sohn, Berlin, Germany, 1943.

Günter Elsner; Karl-Gustav Lerche, *Vom Pimpf zum Flieger*, Zentralverlag der NSDAP, München, Germany, 1940.

Hans-Hermann Kritzinger; Friedrich Stuhlmann, *Artillerie und Ballistik in Stichworten*, Julius Springer Verlag, Berlin, Germany, 1939.

Hauptmann Dierich, *Der Flieger – Dienstunterricht in der Fliegertruppe*, Handbücher der Luftwaffe, E.S. Mittler & Sohn, Berlin, Germany, 1940.

H.Dv. 130/1: Ausbildungsvorschrift für die Infanterie. Heft 1. Leitsätze für Erziehung und Ausbildung, Reichsdruckerei, Berlin, Germany, 1935.

H.Dv. 300: Truppenführung (T.F.) II. Teil. Abschnitt XIV-XXIII und Anhang, Ernst Siegfried Mittler und Sohn, Berlin, Germany, 1934.

H.Dv. 300/1: Truppenführung (T.F.) I. Teil. Abschnitt I – XIII, Verlag Mittler & Sohn, Berlin, Germany, 1936.

H.Dv. 487: *Führung und Gefecht der verbundenen Waffen (F. u. G.) Abschnitt XII-XVIII*, Verlag "Offene Worte", Berlin, Germany, 1923.

Hermann Franke, *Handbuch der neuzeitlichen Wehrwissenschaften – Erster Band. Wehrpolitik und Kriegführung*, Walter de Gruyter & Co, Berlin, Germany 1936.

Hermann Franke, *Handbuch der neuzeitlichen Wehrwissenschaften – Zweiter Band. Das Heer*, Walter de Gruyter & Co, Berlin, Germany 1937.

Hermann Franke, *Handbuch der neuzeitlichen Wehrwissenschaften – Dritter Band 1. Teil: Die Kriegsmarine*, Walter de Gruyter & Co, Berlin, Germany, 1938.

Hermann Franke, *Handbuch der neuzeitlichen Wehrwissenschaften – Dritter Band 2. Teil: Die Luftwaffe*, Walter de Gruyter & Co, Berlin, Germany, 1939.

Joint Publication, *JP 3-09.3, Close Air Support*, November 2014.

Junkers, *Ju 87 A-1 Betriebsanleitung, III.Entwurf*, July 1937.

Junkers, *Ju 87 B-2 Betriebsanleitung, Hauptabschnitt 10, Flugbetrieb*, June 1940.

Junkers, *Ju 87 B-2 Betriebsanleitung, Hauptabschnitt 90, Ausrüstung-Allgemeines*, Juni 1940.

Junkers, *Ju 87 B-2 Kurz-Betriebsanleitung, Teil II, Flugbetrieb*, June 1940.

Karl Ritter, *Stukas*, UFA, 1941, available at: https://archive.org/details/1941-Stukas (last accessed 02.01.2022).

L.Dv. 5/1, *Der Flugbetrieb der Luftwaffe, Anlage 4 Bodenorganisation*, Juni 1943.

Maurer Maurer, *Air Force Combat Units of World War 2*, Office of Air force History, Washington D.C., USA, 1983.

Ministry of Home Security, Civil Defence Training Pamphlet No. 2 (3rd ed.), *Objects dropped from the air*, His Majesty's Stationery Office, London, UK, 1944.

NARA 226-750140-32-2-225, Office of Strategic Services, *Summary of Strategic Information: European Axis Economy – The German Civilian Labour Force*, November 1943.

NARA, *M1035 Fiche 0614, B-640, 2nd Stuka Wing in the Crete Operation*. By Generalmajor Oscar Dinort and Generalmajor Hubertus Hitschhold, 1947.

NATO, *ATP-3.3.2.1, Tactics, Techniques and Procedures for Close Air Support and Air Interdiction*, Edition D, Version 1, April 2019, Unclassified, Chapter 6: Air Interdiction.

NATO, *ATP-27(C) / AJP-3.3.2, Air Interdiction and Close Air Support*, June 1999, Unclassified.

Office of Statistical Control, *Army Air Forces Statistical Digest: World War 2*, December 1945.

OP 1966, *German Explosive Ordnance Vol. I: Bombs, Rockets, Grenades, Mines, Fuzes & Igniters*, Bureau of Ordnance, Washington D.C., USA, 11 June 1946 (Reprint 1966).

TM 30-506, German Military Dictionary: German-English, English- German, War Department, May 1944.

TNA, *ADM 199/39, M022061/40 Report of HMS Vanity*, 4.11.40.

TNA, *ADM 199/39, M022639/40 Report of HMS Vimiera*, 12.11.40.

TNA, *ADM 199/32, TD(C) 1296/40 FN 29*, 18.11.40.

TNA, *ADM 199/32, TD(C) 66/41 FN 32*, 21.11.40.

TNA, *AIR 14/1107*, 1942.

TsAMO, F 500, Op. 12480, D. 137: *Nachrichtenblatt der Panzertruppen. Nr. 1*, 15. July 1943.

TsAMO, F. 500 Op. 12452 D. 239, *Leitfaden für den Unterricht auf den Luft-Kriegsschulen – Lufttaktik*, n.d.

TsAMO, F. 500 Op. 12452 D. 250, *Ausgegebene Umdrucke über Luftwaffenlehre – 7. Lehrgang, Vortrag Hauptmann von Schwenitz bei Offizier-Ausbildung, Zusammenarbeit von Nahkampf- und Aufklärungsverbänden der Luftwaffe mit der Erdtruppe*, 29.6.1943.

Wilhelm Lechens, *Panzer-Schießfibel*, Verlag WEU / Offene Worte, Bonn, Germany, n.d.

Secondary Sources

Adam Tooze, *The Wages of Destruction, The Making & Breaking of the Nazi Economy*, Penguin Books, London, UK, 2007.

Adolf Schlicht; John R. Angolia, *Die deutsche Wehrmacht Uniformierung und Ausrüstung 1933 - 1945. Band 3: Die Luftwaffe*, 1. Auflage, Motorbuch Verlag, Stuttgart, Germany, 1999.

Alex Buchner, *Das Handbuch der deutschen Infanterie 1939-1945*, Podzun-Pallas, Friedberg, Germany, 1987.

Arnold Hague Convoy Database, *FS Convoy Series*, available at: http://www.convoyweb.org.uk/fs/index.html (last accessed 18.11.2021).

Arnold Hague Convoy Database, *FS Convoy Series*, available at: http://www.convoyweb.org.uk/fn/index.html (last accessed 18.11.2021).

Barry C. Rosch, *Luftwaffe Codes, Markings & Units 1939-1945*, Schiffer Publishing Ltd, Atglen, PA, USA, 1995.

Barry Ketley; Mark Rofle, *Luftwaffe Training Units & their Aircraft*, Hikoki Publications, Aldershot, UK, 1996.

Beatrice Heuser, *Clausewitz lesen! Eine Einführung*, R. Oldenbourg Verlag, München, Germany, 2010.

Bernhard Kast; Christoph Bergs, *H.Dv. 470/7: Die Mittlere Panzerkompanie - The Medium Tank Company 1941*, Bernhard Kast, Linz, Austria, 2019.

Bremische Bürgerschaft Landtag 11. Wahlperiode, *Einsatz von Zwangsarbeitern während der nationalsozialistischen Herrschaft in Bremen*, Drucksache 11/804: 16. December 1986.

Bruce Condell (ed.); David T. Zabecki (ed.), *On the German Art of War. Truppenführung*. Stackpole Books, Mechanicsburg, PA, USA, 2009.

Christian Kehrt, *Moderne Krieger - Die Technikerfahrungen deutscher Militärpiloten 1910-1945*, Ferdinand Schöningh, Paderborn, Germany, 2010.

Christian Möller, *Die Einsätze der Nachtschlachtgruppen 1, 2 und 20 an der Westfront von September 1944 bis Mai 1945*, Helios, Aachen, Germany, 2008.

Daniel Uziel, *Arming the Luftwaffe - The German Aviation Industry in World War II*, McFarland & Company, Jefferson, NC, USA, 1967.

David Glantz et al., *Slaughterhouse: The Encyclopedia of the Eastern Front*, Military Book Club, Garden City, New York (State), USA, 2002.

David P. Williams, *Nachtjäger Volume 1– Luftwaffe Night Fighter Units 1939-1943*, Classic Publications, Hersham, UK, 2005.

David Stahel, *Operation Barbarossa and Germany's Defeat in the East*, Cambridge University Press, Cambridge, UK, 2011 (2009).

Daniel Uziel, *Propaganda, Kriegsberichterstattung und die Wehrmacht – Stellenwert und Funktion der Propagandatruppen im NS-Staat*, in Rainer Rother (ed.); Judith Prokasky (ed.), *Die Kamera als Waffe – Propagandabilder des Zweiten Weltkrieges*, Richard Boorberg Verlag GmBH & Co KG, München, Germany, 2010.

Dieter Krüger, *Neue deutsche Biographie*, Band: 24, Stader, Berlin, 2010, p. 648-649, available at: https://daten.digitale-sammlungen.de/0008/bsb00085893/images/index.html?seite=672 (last accessed 27.10.2021).

Eddie J. Creek, *Junkers Ju 87 – From Dive-Bomber to Tank-Buster 1935-1945*, Classic: Ian Allen Publishing, Hersham, UK, 2012.

Edgar Lersch, *Gegen das Diktat der Bilder? Die Fernseh Serie Das Dritte Reich 1960/61*, in Rainer Rother (ed.); Judith Prokasky (ed.), *Die Kamera als Waffe – Propagandabilder des Zweiten Weltkrieges*, Richard Boorberg Verlag GmBH & Co KG, München, Germany, 2010.

Edward Homze, *Arming the Luftwaffe – The Reichs Air Minsistry and the German Aircraft Industry, 1919-39*, University of Nebraska Press, Lincoln, Nebraska, USA, 1976.

Erich Gröner; Peter Mickel; Franz Mrva, *Die deutschen Kriegsschiffe 1815-1945. Band 1: Panzerschiffe, Linienschiffe, Schlachtschiffe, Flugzeugträger, Kreuzer, Kanonenboote*, Bernard & Graefe Verlag, Koblenz, Germany, 1982.

Ernesto Grassi (ed.); von Clausewitz, Carl, *Vom Kriege*, Rowohlt, Hamburg, Germany, 2005.

Encyclopedia Britannica, available at https://www.britannica.com/ (last accessed 14.11.2021).

Falko Bell, *Britische Feindaufklärung im Zweiten Weltkrieg - Stellenwert und Wirkung der "Human Intelligence" in der britischen Kriegführung 1939–1945*, Ferdinand & Schönigh, Paderborn, Germany, 2016.

Friedrich Lauck, *Der Lufttorpedo – Entwicklung und Technik in Deutschland 1915-1945*, Wehrtechnische Handbücher, Bernard & Graefe Verlag, München, Germany, 1981.

F.-Herbert Wenz, *Flughafen Tempelhof – Chronik des Berliner Werkes der "Weser" Flugzeugbau GmbH – Bremen*, Stedinger Verlag, Lemwerder, Germany, 2000.

Gerhard P. Groß, *Mythos und Wirklichkeit: Die Geschichte des operativen Denkens im deutschen Heer von Moltke d. Ä. bis Heusinger, Zeitalter der Weltkriege, Band 9*, Ferdinand Schönigh, Paderborn, Germany, 2012.

Georg Hentschel, *Die Geheimen Konferenzen des Generalluftzeugmeisters, Ausgewählte und Kommentierte Dokumente zur Geschichte der Deutschen Luftrüstung und des Luftkrieges 1942-1944*, Bernard & Graefe Verlag, Koblenz, Germany, 1989.

Hans Umbreit, *Die Auswirkungen des "totalen Krieges" auf die deutsche Besatzungsherrschaft*, in *Das Deutsche Reich und der Zweite Weltkrieg, Band 5/2 - Organisation und Mobilisierung des deutschen Machtbereichs: Kriegsverwaltung, Wirtschaft und personelle Ressourcen 1942-1945*, DVA, Stuttgart, Germany, 1999.

Hans-Erich Volkmann, *Wolfram von Richthofen, die Zerstörung Wieluńs und das Kriegsvölkerrecht*, in *Militärgeschichtliche Zeitschrift 70*, Potsdam, Germany, 2011, p. 287–328.

Hans H. Hildebrand; Albert Röhr; Hans-Otto Steinmetz, *Die Deutschen Kriegsschiffe. Biographien - ein Spiegel der Marinegeschichte von 1815 bis zur Gegenwart. Band 8: Geschichtlicher Überblick Schiffsbiographien von Udine bis Zieten*. Koehlers Verlagsgesellschaft mbH, Hamburg, Germany, n.d.

Hans Ulrich Rudel, *Mein Kriegstagebuch – Aufzeichnungen eines Stukafliegers*, 2nd ed., Limes Verlag Niedermayer und Schlüter GmbH, München, Germany, 1987.

Hartmut Pophanken, *Gründung und Ausbau der "Weser"-Flugzeugbau GmbH 1933 bis 1939*, H. M. Hauschild GmbH, Bremen, Germany, 2000.

Heinz J. Nowarra, *Die Deutsche Luftrüstung 1933-1945, Band 1 bis 4*, Bernard & Graefe Verlag, Koblenz, Germany, 1993.

Helmut Mahlke, *Memoirs of a Stuka Pilot*, Frontline Books, Barnsley, UK, 2013.

Horst Boog, *Die deutsche Luftwaffenführung 1935-1945 – Führungsprobleme, Spitzengliederung, Generalstabsausbildung*, DVA, Stuttgart, Germany, 1982.

James S. Corum, *The Luftwaffe – Creating the Operational Air War, 1918-1940*, University Press of Kansas, Lawrence, USA, 1997.

J.J. Colledge; Ben Warlow, *Ships of the Royal Navy*, 3rd Ed. Chatham Publishing, London, UK, 2006.

Johow-Foerster, *Hilfsbuch für den Schiffbau, Erster Band*, Fünfte Auflage, Springer-Verlag, Berlin, Germany, 1928.

Judith Keilbach, *Krieg recyceln - Zum Einsatz von PK-Aufnahmen in bundesdeutschen Fernsehdokumentationen*, in Rainer Rother (ed.); Judith Prokasky (ed.), *Die Kamera als Waffe - Propagandabilder des Zweiten Weltkrieges*, Richard Boorberg Verlag GmBH & Co KG, München, Germany, 2010.

Jürgen Rohwer; Gerhard Hümmelchen, *Chronik des Seekrieges 1939-1945*, Bibliothek für Zeitgeschichte, Württembergische Landesbibliothek, Online-Ausgabe 2007, available via: https://www.wlb-stuttgart.de/index.php?id=250 (last accessed 15.03.2022).

Karl-Heinz Völker, *Die Deutsche Luftwaffe 1933-1939 - Aufbau, Führung und Rüstung der Luftwaffe sowie die Entwicklung der deutschen Luftkriegstheorie*, DVA, Stuttgart, Germany, 1967.

Karl Prümm, *Klangbilder des Krieges - Zu den Propagandastrategien des Kompilationsfilmes*, in Rainer Rother (ed.); Judith Prokasky (ed.), *Die Kamera als Waffe - Propagandabilder des Zweiten Weltkrieges*, Richard Boorberg Verlag GmBH & Co KG, München, Germany, 2010.

Klaus Kreimeier, *Sensomotorik - Das unbegriffene Erbe der Propagandakompanien*, in Rainer Rother (ed.); Judith Prokasky (ed.), *Die Kamera als Waffe - Propagandabilder des Zweiten Weltkrieges*, Richard Boorberg Verlag GmBH & Co KG, München, Germany, 2010.

Luiz Roberto Monoteiro de Oliveria, *Calculating the Wind Correction Angle*, 2010, available at http://www.luizmonteiro.com/Article_Estimating_Wind_Correction_Angle_Prin table.htm, (last accessed 07.11.2021).

Manfred Griehl, *Junkers Ju 87 Stuka, Teil 1 - Die frühen Varianten A, B, C und R des Sturzkampfbombers der Luftwaffe*, AirDoc, Erlangen, Germany, 2006.

Manfred Messerschmidt, *Die Wehrmachtjustiz, 1933-1945*, 2. durchgesehene Auflage, Ferdinand Schöningh, Paderborn, Germany, 2008.

Mark Spoerer, *Die soziale Differenzierung der ausländischen Zivilarbeiter, Kriegsgefangenen und Häftlinge im Deutschen Reich*, in *Das Deutsche Reich und der Zweite Weltkrieg, Band 9/2 - Die deutsche Kriegsgesellschaft 1939 bis 1945, Ausbeutung, Deutungen, Ausgrenzung*, DVA, Stuttgart, Germany, 2005.

Martin Middlebrook; Chris Everitt, *The Bomber Command War Diaries - An Operational Reference Book, 1939-1945*, Penguin Books, Harmondsworth, UK, 1985.

Merriam Webster Dictionary, available at https://www.merriam-webster.com/dictionary/ (last accessed 07.11.2021).

Michel Forget, *Die Zusammenarbeit zwischen Luftwaffe und Heer bvei den französischen und deutschen Luftstreitkräften im Zweiten Weltkrieg*, in Horst Boog (ed.), *Luftkriegsführung im Zweiten Weltkrieg. Ein internationaler Vergleich*, E.S. Mittler & Sohn GmbH, Bonn, Germany, 1993.

Milan Vego, *Clausewitz's Schwerpunkt. Mistranslated from German - Misunderstood in English*, in *Military Review*, January-February 2007, Fort Leavenworth, Kansas, USA, 2007, p. 101-109.

NavWeapos.com, *German Krupp "Wotan" Steels*, http://www.navweaps.com/index_nathan/metalprpsept2009.php#%22Wotan_H%C3%A4rte%22_%28Wh%29 (last accessed 31.12.2021).

Nick Beale, *Ghost Bombers - The Moonlight War of NSG 9: Luftwaffe Night Attack Operations from Anzio to the Alps*, Classic Publications, Manchester, UK, 2001.

Oliver Corff (ed.); *Carl von Clausewitz, Vom Kriege, Erstausgabe von 1832-1834*, A4 Version basierend auf Textdaten bibliotheca Augustana, Clausewitz-Gesellschaft e.V., Berlin, Germany, 2010.

Oxford Reference, by Oxford University Press available at: https://www.oxfordreference.com/view/10.1093/oi/authority.20110803100204386 (last accessed 07.11.2021).

Percy E. Schramm (ed.), *Kriegstagebuch des OKW. Eine Dokumentation: 1942. Band 4. Teilband 2*, Bechtermünz, Augsburg, Germany, 2005.

Peter C. Smith, *Stuka - Volume One - Luftwaffe Ju 87 Dive-Bomber Units 1939-1941*, Classic Colours, Manchester, UK, 2006.

RAF, *How We Are Organised*, available at: https://www.raf.mod.uk/our-organisation/overview/ (last accessed 12.02.2022).

Rainer Rother, *Die Kriegswochenschau - Entstehung einer Form*, in Rainer Rother (ed.); Judith Prokasky (ed.), *Die Kamera als Waffe - Propagandabilder des Zweiten Weltkrieges*, Richard Boorberg Verlag GmBH & Co KG, München, Germany, 2010.

Richard Overy, *The Bombing War, Europe 1939-1945*, Penguin Books, London, UK, 1994.

Richard Overy, *The Battle of Britain*, Carlton, London, UK, 2014 (EBook edition).

Roger Moorhouse, *First to Fight: The Polish War 1939*, Vintage, London, UK, 2020.

Rolf-Dieter Müller, *Hitlers Wehrmacht 1935 bis 1945*, Oldenbourg, München, Germany, 2012.

Roman Töppel, *Kursk 1943: The Greatest Battle of the Second World War*, Helion and Company, Warwick, UK, 2018.

Siegfried Breyer, *The German Aircraft Carrier: Graf Zeppelin*, Schiffer Publishing, West Chester, UK, 1989.

Technikmuseum Hugo Junkers Dessau, *Lebenslauf – Hugo Junkers*, 04.02.2019, available at: https://technikmuseum-dessau.org/lebenslauf/#page-content (last accessed 06.08.2021).

Tempelhofer Unfreiheit, *Zwangsarbeit bei Unternehmen auf dem Gelände des Flughafen Tempelhof: Weser Flugzeugbau*, available at https://www.tempelhofer-unfreiheit.de/de/zwangsarbeit-bei-unternehmen-auf-dem-gelaende-des-flughafen-tempelhof, (last accessed 06.09.2021).

The University of Rhode Island, *Hurricanes: Science and Society – Glossary*, available at http://www.hurricanescience.org/glossary/ (last accessed 07.11.2021).

Thomas Houlihan, *Kriegsprache – Glossary of World War II German Military- and Period-Specific Words, Phrases and Abbreviations for Historians, Researchers and Hobbyists*, Maps At War, Lake Orion, Michigan, USA, 2009.

Tinus Le Roux, in conversation with Ju 87 pilot Dr. Heinz Migeod, *Stuka pilot interview 45: Diving sirens of the Ju-87*, published on YouTube 10th July 2010, available at: https://www.youtube.com/watch?v=K-CQ5Sko3mk (last accessed: 05.10.2021).

uboat.net, *HMS Terror (I 03)*, available at https://uboat.net/allies/warships/ship/5460.html (last accessed 27.10.2021).

U.S. Department of Transportation, *FAA-H-8083-3C, Airplane Flying Handbook Chapter 7: Ground Reference Maneuvers*, Federal Aviation Administration, Oklahoma City, available at https://www.faa.gov/regulations_policies/handbooks_manuals/aviation/airplan e_handbook/ (last accessed 07.11.2021).

U.S. Government Printing Office, *The American Practical Navigator – An Epitome of Navigation, Chapter 7 – Dead Reckoning*, Revised Edition, U.S. Government Printing Office, Washington D.C., USA, 2004.

War Department, *A.A.F Form No. 24, Pilots' Information File 1944*, republished by Schiffer Military History Book, Atglen, PA, USA, 1995.

Werner Müller, *Ground Radar Systems of the Luftwaffe*, Schiffer Publishing Ltd. Atglen, PA, USA, 1998.

Wilhelm Lechens, *Panzer-Schießfibel*, Verlag WEU / Offene Worte, Bonn, Germany, n.d.; with the booklet *Ergänzungen zur Panzer-Schießfibel*, Verlag Offene Wort, Bonn, Germany, n.d.

William Wolf, *The Douglas A-20 Havoc*, Schiffer Publishing, Atglen, PA, USA, 2015.

Wolfgang Thamm, *Fliegerbomben*, Bernard & Graefe Verlag, Bonn, Germany, 2003.

W.S. Nye, *Guide to Foreign Military Studies 1945-54*, Headquarters United States Army, Europe, 1954, available at: https://www.ibiblio.org/hyperwar/Germany/FMS/index.html (last accessed 27.10.2021).

Wrecksite, *HMS Fiona*, available at https://www.wrecksite.eu/wreck.aspx?140064 (last accessed 27.10.2021).

Wrecksite, *HMS Terror (I-03)*, available at https://www.wrecksite.eu/wreck.aspx?98977 (last accessed 27.10.2021).

Wrecksite, *SS Scotia*, available at: https://www.wrecksite.eu/wreck.aspx?42 (last accessed 02.01.2021).

www.ingramcontent.com/pod-product-compliance
Lightning Source LLC
Chambersburg PA
CBHW060309100426
42812CB00003B/718